THE JEWS OF ARGENTINA

ROBERT WEISBROT

With the research assistance of Robert Murciano

THE
JEWS
OF
ARGENTINA
FROM THE INQUISITION TO PERÓN

The Jewish Publication Society of America
Philadelphia 5739 / 1979

Copyright © 1979
by The Jewish Publication Society of America
All rights reserved
First edition
ISBN 0-8276-0114-X
Library of Congress catalog card number 78-62060
Manufactured in the United States of America
Designed by Warren Infield

Acknowledgment is gratefully extended to Jacobo Kovadloff for many of the photographs not bearing credit lines.

To My Father and Mother

CONTENTS

Preface   xi
Abbreviations   2
Introduction   3

Part One: THE SETTLERS

1 Origins   15
New Christians in Spanish America/Jews in the New
Nation/The East European Jewish Legacy/Russian
Jewish Settlement/The Progress of the Colonies

2 Community   57
Political Evolution/Social Organization/The German
Jewish Community

Part Two: THE CULTURE

3 Secular Jewish Culture   87
Zionism/Judaic Literature

4 Religion   115
Observance of Tradition/Synagogues and Congrega-
tions/The Rabbinate/Bet Din/Religion in the Inte-
rior/The Liberal Movements/Denominational Trends

5 Education   137
Roots of the Problem/Ideological Upheaval/Levels of
Instruction/The Interior Communities/The Worsen-
ing Condition

6 Sephardim   155
The Sephardic Communities/Sephardic Culture/Inte-
rior Sephardic Communities/Change

CONTENTS

Part Three: THE COUNTRY

7 Acculturation   175
   Economic Activity/Literature and Other Cultural
   Media/Politics

8 The Roots of Anti-Semitism   209

9 Perón and the Jews   227

10 Anti-Semitism During and After the Perónist Exile   241
   The Nazi Threat/The Seizure of Eichmann and the
   Rise of Tacuara/The Arab League and the Rise of
   Anti-Semitism/President Onganía and the Military
   Repression/The Return of Perón/The Continuing
   Danger

Epilogue: A GENERATION OF THE DESERT   277

Sources   293

Bibliography   299

Notes   309

Index   335

Illustrations follow pages 56, 80, 130, 240

TABLES

Table 1. Population of Buenos Aires, 1936   71
         2. National Status of AMIA Affiliates, 1970   76
         3. Age Distribution of AMIA Affiliates, 1970   77
         4. The AMIA Election of 1969   93
         5. Annual *Aliyah* Rates for the United States and
            Selected Latin American Nations, 1973   97
         6. *Aliyah* Statistics for Latin America from 1947 to
            March 1972   98
         7. Categories of Argentine Immigrants to Israel,
            1963   99
         8. Extent of Jewish Education in Argentina, 1963   146
         9. Lineal Depiction of Extent of Jewish Education
            in Argentina, 1963   147
        10. Class Groups in Argentine Society, 1961   178
        11. Occupational Distribution Among Members of
            the Jewish Community of Buenos Aires,
            1961–67   180
        12. Distribution of Professionals, 1963   181
        13. Argentine Acceptance of Jews in Different So-
            cial Roles, 1964   211
        14. Qualities Argentines Attributed to Jews, 1964   211
        15. Anti-Semitism Among Different Social Sectors,
            1962   212
        16. Anti-Semitism Among Different Social Sectors,
            1967   213
        17. Proportion of Argentines Who Would Bar Im-
            migrant Groups: Opinion Among Three Sub-
            groups, 1964   215
        18. Jewish Youth in Buenos Aires, 1971   282

PREFACE

This book originated with a special friendship. As undergraduates at Brandeis University, Robert Murciano and I sought to give our interests in Judaism and history a common focus. We therefore designed a research project, sponsored by the history and Judaica departments at Brandeis, to study the Jewish community in Argentina. Our intent was to trace the major social and cultural developments of this community, emphasizing its current character and challenges. Aided by a grant from the Saval-Sachar Scholarship Fund, we traveled to Argentina in 1972 and worked as a team to conduct interviews and research archival records of the Jewish institutions in Buenos Aires and the interior. An abundance of source material and the limited time available led us to focus on selected aspects of the community: organizational patterns; religious, Zionist, and educational activities; and Sephardic culture. The resulting joint senior honors thesis provided the basis for much of the research and analysis that followed over the next six years.

Despite the demands of graduate work in other fields, this project continued to absorb my attention. I was motivated, first of all, by the hope that a study of the Jews in Argentina would add to our knowledge of Diaspora life and culture and perhaps lead to further investigations of the subject. On a more personal level, I found that, through immersion in the history of this community, I was able to understand more fully my own Jewish heritage and identity. My efforts on this study have benefited from much generous aid, which I am happy to acknowledge here:

Milton Vanger guided the project at Brandeis, gave my work

kind encouragement, and remained ever on hand to share his expertise in Latin American history. Several outstanding scholars of Argentine Jewish history— Bernard Ansel, Victor Mirelman, Haim Avni, and Morton Winsberg—facilitated my introduction to the field with helpful counsel and the example of their own pathbreaking work. The task of translating documents from several languages was lightened by the energetic assistance of Anna Polsky, Steven Simons, Linda Sher, and Raphael Tarrago. Eric Goldman, who earlier inspired me to study history as a profession, warmly offered numerous wise suggestions during my attempts to publish on this subject. David Geller and John Womack examined drafts of the manuscript and imparted valuable advice for revision. I also profited from working with Yosef Yerushalmi, whose penetrating criticisms served to strengthen the sections treating the community's early history. The editorial skills of Maier Deshell and Frances Noyes helped measurably to refine the manuscript during its latter stages. I am especially grateful to Jacobo Kovadloff for taking the time, amid difficult circumstances, to aid my study in various important ways. My primary debt remains to Robert Murciano, who contributed valuably to the development of many ideas presented in this volume. None of these individuals is responsible for whatever flaws may remain; but their efforts have made this a better book.

Some of the material in this book has previously appeared, in slightly different form, in various journals.

I wish to thank the editors of *Present Tense, Judaism,* and *Midstream* for permission to reprint passages from the following articles: "A Generation of the Desert," *Present Tense,* 1, no. 4 (Summer 1974): 9–11; "Jews in Argentina Today," *Judaism,* 25, no. 4 (Fall 1976): 390–401; and "Anti-Semitism in Argentina," *Midstream,* 24, no. 5 (May 1978): 12–23.

The officials of the Argentine Jewish community were, on the whole, remarkably open and cooperative. There is not space to list them all by name, but the citations of interviews and archives at the end of this volume may suggest the generosity with which the community's leaders facilitated and enriched my study.

Finally, I would like to express a personal word of appreciation to Nathan Glazer, Arthur Hertzberg, and Murray Polner, for their active encouragement and support of my work; to Steven Georgiou, for brightening the routine of research and writing; and to my parents, for their deeply valued help in many ways, throughout.

Cambridge, Massachusetts
August 1978

THE JEWS OF ARGENTINA

ABBREVIATIONS

AMIA	Asociación Mutual Israelita Argentina
DAIA	Delegación de Asociaciones Israelitas Argentinas
ICA	Jewish Colonization Association
JAPGW	Jewish Association for the Protection of Girls and Women
OIA	Organización Israelita Argentina
OSA	Organización Sionista Argentina

INTRODUCTION

Argentina has long been far more notorious as a haven for Nazi fugitives from justice than famed for its Jewish population. Yet there are presently close to half a million Jews in Argentina, forming the fifth largest Jewish community in the world. Only the United States, Russia, Israel, and France surpass Argentina in this regard; and no Western city outside the United States can match the Jewish population of Buenos Aires, some 350,000 persons.

The historical importance of Argentina's Jewish community lies in its unique development of East European Jewish traditions and in its adjustment to a society alternately inviting and virulent toward Jews. Both these processes reflect the peculiar chemistry of interaction between the heritage of Russian and Polish Jewry and the patterns of Hispanic-American society.

The legacy of the Old World Jewish communities is immediately visible even to the casual observer. There are neighborhoods in Buenos Aires, such as the business district Once (pronounced own-say), where Jewish residents have preserved much of the flavor and appearance of the East European *shtetl.* Yiddish mingles easily with Spanish in many conversations heard along such primary streets as Corrientes and Tucumán. Judaic books in numerous languages and greeting cards for the Jewish New Year are sold in several stores. Occasionally, one still finds Hasidim in traditional long sideburns and Old World garb. They will greet you in Yiddish and Hebrew, but Spanish often comes with more difficulty. For many, it is as if Lodz and Vilna were simply moved across the oceans into Argentina.

3

Argentine Jewry departs from the dominant East European Jewish tradition, however, by rejecting religion as the center of Jewish culture. In Vilna or Minsk, rabbinic figures were the source of Jewish leadership and legend; in Buenos Aires, such roles in the Jewish community have been filled by Socialists and Zionists.

The shift from a religious to a secular ethic traces to developments in Eastern Europe during the nineteenth century. The Enlightenment seeping in from the West, the rise of Marxism, and the formation of Zionist societies in reaction to anti-Semitic violence, all undermined the insulated religious character of the Russian and Polish Jewish communities.

Argentine life accelerated the process of secularization. The organized Jewish community, or *kehillah,* proved unable to compete with the wealthier and more numerous American Jewish centers in attracting rabbinic talent from Europe. The resulting scarcity of religious leadership, together with the existence of acute anti-Semitism and widespread economic inequality, led Jews in Argentina to magnify the importance of social activism as an alternative expression of Judaic commitment.

It is the genius of the Argentine Jew to have isolated one element of East European Jewish culture—a newly crystallizing ideological militance for the rights of Jews and all other oppressed people and to have created from it a new basis for Jewish identity. Argentine Judaism thus became a highly politicized culture, invested with the forms of East European Judaism but lacking its central commitment to religious tradition.

The distinctive qualities of Argentine Judaism are evident in comparison with American Judaism. Though both communities descend largely from East European immigrants, the Americans have many more synagogues and Jewish schools in relation to their demographic strength than do the Argentines. Yet the much smaller Argentine community sent more settlers to Israel from its creation in 1948 until 1967, when the Six-Day War catalyzed a new American Zionist fervor. The Socialist leadership of most Argentine Jewish institutions is of course altogether unparalleled by American Jewry. The very thought of a Socialist B'nai B'rith, for instance, would be simply anathema to most American Jews.

Argentine Judaism may therefore be considered a vital and yet creative inheritor of the East European Jewish heritage. The secular

4

utopian ethos nurtured for over three-quarters of a century in Argentina represents both a major and a distinctive contribution to the development of Jewish culture in the Diaspora.

Argentine Jewish history is distinguished also by the turbulent relations between Jews and the larger society. Far more than most other Diaspora communities, Argentine Jews have found adjustment to their new land a difficult, often traumatic experience. The uncertainty posed by a nation alternately democratic and authoritarian, pluralistic and xenophobic, calm and violent marks Argentina even among Latin American nations as a dangerous, if often generous, host to its Jewish inhabitants.

Jews entered Argentina while it was still a frontier land just beginning to tap its industrial potential and in need of new labor. They quickly obtained employment, first as workers in farm colonies and flourishing factories, later as skilled artisans, businessmen and professionals.

Jewish cultural as well as economic contributions found an attentive national audience. Folksingers such as the currently popular Dina Rot have added Judaic melodies to the older Argentine standards. Jewish writers have sharpened Argentine appreciation of the country's varied origins through works like Alberto Gerchunoff's *Los gauchos judíos.* This classic novel about Argentine Jewish immigration is regularly assigned in schools throughout the nation.

Adjustment to Argentine life-styles has also been rapid, as a look at a Jewish family in Once may illustrate. Raúl Mayer works as a salesman in a novelty shop in Buenos Aires, earning a living that would be considered lower middle class by American standards but somewhat above average for Argentines. The Mayer family lives in a fourth-story apartment with hot running water (gas-heated and manually lit for the shower), good lighting, and refrigeration. Even the apartment elevator travels as rapidly as all but the most modern American models. Air conditioners, dishwashers, television, and the like remain beyond the family's means.

Raúl's six-day work week includes the Jewish Sabbath, a fact that he probably does not realize. Neither he nor his wife, who works part time as a typist to help make ends meet, is particularly concerned with religion, though both recall their Jewish background with deep emotion. "I feel Jewish," the father told me

5

when I asked if he had an interest in maintaining his heritage.

The two elder children, Roberto and Daniel, have had no Jewish education. They are interested in their university studies, politics, and social life and find no reason to recover their Jewish past. Although their social circle includes both Jews and Gentiles, the children frequent a Jewish center, the Sociedad Hebraica Argentina, because of its social and cultural facilities. The family's youngest child is an attractive eighteen-year-old girl just beginning her studies in the School of Philosophy and Letters at the University of Buenos Aires. Less interested in politics than are her brothers, she is determined instead to be a "hippie" like the American youths she and many other Argentines picture. With heavy make-up and a treasured American-made perfume called Patchouli, she appears more eager to assimilate as an American than as an Argentine. Like her brothers, though, she takes her schoolwork seriously and consistently earns high grades, to the immense pride of her parents.

Although the Mayer children are all of college age, the entire family still dines together. Raúl invariably returns from his work in time for the Argentine supper hour of nine o'clock. Dinner reveals the family as still close and affectionate despite the difference of generations. In particular, the children show their father a respect not always seen in the United States. In the conservative Argentine society, Jews have readily preserved the traditional kinship ties and love of family that characterized the Jewish communities in Poland and Russia.

Among families more attached to their Jewish heritage than are the Mayers, there still is generally a strong desire to acculturate as fully as possible without altogether assimilating. Frequent and self-conscious assertions of loyalty to Argentina reflect both genuine affection for a pride in their nation and often acute insecurities over their acceptance by non-Jewish countrymen. Jaime Goldenov, a Jew in Santa Fe, succinctly expressed this prevalent attitude "We are Jewish Argentines rather than Argentine Jews, because we are citizens fully tied to this country."

Despite this eminently successful acculturation, Jews never have achieved full acceptance or security in their adopted land. Ultra-nationalist rabble-rousers depict them, in leaflets and journals, as unassimilable aliens. Guerrilla bands have inflicted more acts of violence on Argentine Jews than on almost any other Diaspora community since the Holocaust.

The paradox of openness and hostility toward Jews is more than simply a function of intermittent anti-Semitism. Argentines are quick to note that Jews are by no means the sole targets of the political terrorism that has plagued Argentina for decades. Although Jews are prominent among the businessmen and intellectuals who form two major groups besieged by either left- or right-wing guerrilla movements, all Argentines, including Roman Catholic priests, are vulnerable to assault. As one Argentine told me, "You could make a case that this country is anti-Argentine, if you look at all the victims of the terrorists."

Argentines show an ambivalence toward foreigners generally that extends beyond their attitudes toward Jewish settlers. Jews, in fact, formed only a small part of the flood of immigrants that between 1880 and 1930 transformed the nation into a largely foreign-born population. The change strained Argentina's already fragile sense of pluralism and social stability.

Like the Jews, other immigrant groups discovered Argentine hospitality to be a sharply mixed blessing, as the Italian experience exemplifies. The Italians contributed about 40 percent of all settlers to Argentina after 1880, and they left a strong cultural imprint in Buenos Aires and other cities. Spanish speech in the capital, for example, is markedly Italianized. The crisp, rapid Spanish common to the interior and most of the rest of Latin America has given way to a slower, drawled dialect, with double *ll*s pronounced like *j*s and syllables lazily omitted from many participles. This peculiar Argentine-urban brand of Spanish is well regarded in neighboring countries, which admire *castellano* (pronounced cas-ta-ja-no) as aesthetic and even sophisticated.

Dietary patterns in Buenos Aires also suggest more of Rome than of Latin America. Common luncheon dishes include pizza, ravioli, and other pasta. With the rising cost of beef-steak, such specialties as prosciutto and *milanesa de lomo* (breaded veal cutlet) have become more popular than ever.

Italians contributed vitally to the urban labor force in the fast-growing industrial sector and increasingly entered their own entrepreneurial ventures. Torcuato Di Tella from Abruzzi in central Italy, the outstanding example of such initiative, guided his appliance firm to become the dominant conglomerate in Argentina over the past quarter-century.

The Italians nevertheless failed for many years to gain the full trust of the native-born Argentines, or *criollos*. Many of the *criollos* feared that immigrants were fast becoming too numerous to assimilate smoothly into the established order. Some native Argentines openly ridiculed the Italians and other immigrants in speeches and journals. Buenos Aires also featured popular farces called *sainetes* whose main object during the early twentieth century often appeared to be the mockery of Italian settlers.

Argentina's erratic responses toward foreigners are exacerbated by a dual identity as a European and a Third World nation. White European racism and a clear regional superiority in economic progress have led to a celebrated, or perhaps notorious, chauvinism that abrades neighboring Latin American republics. Yet Argentines throughout their history have been acutely aware and resentful of their inferior economic status compared with the major industrial powers whose ranks Argentina has long sought to join.

Argentine sentiments toward Americans classically illustrate these mixed feelings toward foreign nationals. Argentines are unusually vocal about their anti-Americanism, even for a Third World nation. They freely denounce "Yankee imperialism" and "Anglo-American exploitation." The late President Juan Perón won a memorable election in 1946 against a favored coalition of opponents, in large part by convincing enough Argentines that the United States firmly opposed his candidacy. At the same time, though, few Third World nations have shown such blatant, if unspoken admiration for American goods, technology, and culture, as if the United States were providing the archetype for what Argentina could and should become.

"Yankee" influences permeate the nation. American films compose the bulk of the average citizen's cinematic fare. American cars, generally not the newest models, line the capital's streets as if a period film were in mid-scene. During a visit to a large cinema on Corrientes Street, the audience viewed a pre-film commercial for an American car. An automobile rose slowly, majestically to the sound of drum rolls and music, through a special hollow in the stage in front of the screen. As the car surfaced, an off-screen voice intoned in Spanish, "Realize all your dreams! Buy a Chevy, a

8

Chevy, yes, the car of all your fantasies!" After this unlikely hymn to America, the audience settled back to enjoy a Hollywood-made epic that drew crowds in the hundreds, while, nearby, Argentine-made films gathered only straggling customers.

Menus in Argentine cafés and restaurants make ample room for the people's choice of soft-drinks—Coke, Pepsi, and Seven-Up. The sight of several youths heatedly condemning American imperialism to me while passing around a huge bottle of Coca-Cola reflects a confusion of feelings toward Americans—and foreigners generally—that applies to many, if not most, Argentines.

Jews have experienced elements of the above-mentioned reactions both to immigrants such as the Italians and to Americans and other foreign nationals. Both Jewish and Italian immigrants enjoyed the economic bounty and cultural malleability of a nation in the early stages of industrialization and urbanization. They also suffered the xenophobic backlash of a people who felt themselves suddenly overwhelmed by millions of foreigners changing the nature of the country.

Argentine sentiments toward Jews and Americans also reveal strong parallels. Because Jews rapidly became the most educated and one of the wealthier groups in Argentine society, they have played a highly conspicuous role in the nation's cultural and economic life. Yet this very success has subjected them to the special resentment reserved for Americans and other "advanced" peoples. They are frequently depicted as "exploiters" who allegedly control and drain the country. Jews are, in this sense, the hapless surrogates for Argentine antipathy toward the great powers.

The numerous similarities between the fortunes of Jews and other ethnic and national groups nevertheless cannot obscure the existence of powerful anti-Semitic forces in Argentina. In a society suspicious of foreigners, Jews are most suspect; in a land of vulnerable citizens, Jews are by far the most vulnerable.

A look at Argentine history indicates that anti-Semitic sentiment has long existed independently of the nation's vague and far-reaching xenophobia. As a Spanish colony for several hundred years, the region presently called Argentina actively aided the Inquisition in America. After achieving independence from Spain in the early nineteenth century, Argentina began to concede basic Jewish civil and religious rights, though slowly and tenuously. As

9

late as 1943, for example, a conservative military regime stopped Yiddish presses and restricted the processing of kosher meat, until cooler heads reversed the decision in response to high-level pressure from the American government.

Nazis and other openly anti-Semitic groups flourish in the chaos that in recent decades has substituted for Argentine politics. These elements became especially brazen after the military ousted Isabel Perón's weak civilian government, in March 1976, to suppress left-wing guerrilla activity. The ensuing cooperation between government forces and right-wing extremists opened an era of unprecedented danger to the Jewish community.

The current atmosphere of terror has touched the most respected Jewish institutions and leaders. The president of the American Jewish Committee stunned the *kehillah* by announcing, in June 1977, that the organization "has been forced to close" its office in Buenos Aires. He cited the "repeated acts of intimidation and threats to the lives of its representatives" and added this ominous note: "It is apparent to us that the Argentine government has not cleansed itself of subversive and anti-democratic forces within its own structure."

No resolution appears imminent to either the guerilla violence or the military repression, both rooted in Argentina's economic and political instability. Amid this turmoil, the nation's Jews will likely remain the most gravely endangered civilian group for years to come.

Precarious as individual Jews find life in Argentina, the collective fate of Judaism there is even less assured. A new generation of native-born Jews is rapidly jettisoning its East European traditions and, in the process, Judaism itself. This crisis of cultural continuity dwarfs the problems that have evoked similar warnings among leaders of American Jewry. Intermarriage in some interior centers of Argentina reaches 100 percent, while in the cities even those who marry within the faith tend to have little knowledge of it. Fewer than one in six Jewish children attend a Jewish school for even one year, and the number of rabbis in the country is now less than one for every 20,000 Jews.

The secular bulwarks of Jewish identity are also eroding for lack of a broader cultural awareness. Progressive ideological movements affiliated with the *kehillah* no longer appeal to a university-educated generation that seeks social change largely through campus-based left-wing groups. Many young Jews would agree with the Jewish student at the University of Buenos Aires who told me, "Judaism can never be a force for social justice because the Jewish bourgeoisie is aloof from the suffering masses." This judgment is painfully discordant with the facts of Argentine Jewish history, but it typifies the view of a rapidly growing number of Jewish youth.

Zionism, too, is weakening under a barrage of propaganda by right-wing journals and anti-Semitic groups like the powerful Arab League. Argentina, in common with many other Third World nations, has experienced increasingly widespread and strident rhetoric against Israel in the past decade. Many Jews who already are alienated from their cultural roots now shun Zionism for fear of being thought unpatriotic Argentines.

The picture of cultural change in the *kehillah* contains a cautiously optimistic side. New forms of Jewish observance have taken root in the sixties and seventies, including Conservative and Reform religious movements, the use of Spanish instead of Yiddish in many communal ceremonies, and the ordainment of more indigenously trained rabbis. The question of Jewish survival in Argentina reduces to one of time—can Judaism adapt rapidly enough to retain the loyalty of its youth while preserving enough Old World traditions to satisfy the elders who still control the community's institutions?

Judaism in Argentina today thus involves two critical challenges. The community must confront the external dangers of a nation in which nearly half the world's recorded incidents of anti-Semitic violence annually occur. It must also fashion a new cultural balance to insure the continuance of Jewish tradition while contributing fully to Argentine society. In an era of upheaval for all Argentines, these people are writing both a unique and integral chapter of modern Jewish history.

11

PART ONE

THE
SETTLERS

1 ORIGINS

New Christians in Spanish America

The torture of Diego Núñez de Silva, the eminent physician, was entirely routine. At the time of his ordeal, July 1605, the Inquisition was at its height in Spanish America, and de Silva was a suspected "Judaizer," or hidden Jew. The tribunal in Lima had accumulated its usual evidence against such potential miscreants; informers noted that de Silva was always speaking of the Old Testament, that he washed his hands with suspicious frequency, and that on occasion he had declined to eat pork.

Whether Jew or Christian, Diego Núñez was a practical man and permitted the Inquisitorial tribunal to correct him with all speed. Terribly shaken, aching for many months afterward from the pain of the rack, he was, once again, a free man.

For the son of Diego Núñez, however, the episode of the Inquisition's barbarism left him no peace of mind. As a boy of thirteen, Francisco Maldonado de Silva had bravely stood in the great hall of the tribunal as his father faced his interrogators. Francisco could see little reason for these grim proceedings. Since his birth in Tucumán, he had been raised as a devout Roman Catholic. But at Callao, the provincial town to which his father had been banished, the memory of those terrible days in Lima continued to burn in Francisco's brain. He began reading an anti-Jewish polemic, *Scrutinium Scripturarum,* written by the apostate Pablo de Santa María (formerly Solomon Halevi). He questioned his father intently about the merits of this scorned religion and was rewarded

15

for his insatiable curiosity with a momentous revelation. In the decade before his death in 1616, Diego Núñez acknowledged his secret love for Judaism to his son and led Francisco Maldonado to a study of his ancient heritage.

When his father died, Francisco settled in what is now Chile. There he married and obtained an appointment in the hospital in Santiago, continuing his family's medical tradition. He also promptly outraged the ecclesiastical authorities of Spanish America. Other people coming to and from the New World were also secret Jews, but it was usually quite difficult to identify them. With Francisco, this was not so. Despite all he had seen as a child, and without the restraining influence of his father, not only did de Silva observe Jewish ritual in the most complete form, but he also endeavored to convince his two sisters to follow in his path. Both women were incredulous and then angered. On July 8, 1626, the chronicle of the Inquisition relates, the thirty-four-year-old physician Francisco Maldonado de Silva, having been denounced by his two sisters as a Judaizer, was apprehended and brought to trial.

Francisco's first interrogation shocked the pious men of the Holy Tribunal, several of whom recalled his presence in the same hall twenty-two years ago. De Silva began by refusing to swear in conformity with the Catholic ritual. "If I must swear," he said with unique candor, "I will swear by the living God, that He made the heavens and the earth and that He is the God of Israel." For the first time in its history, the words of the Hebrew prophets resounded before an audience of the Santo Oficio, the holy office of the Inquisition. The Inquisitors, accustomed to facing a trembling criminal begging forgiveness, were severely disturbed.

The Inquisitors and de Silva locked wills over his stubborn retention of Judaic faith. During his twelve years spent in the Inquisition's dungeons, de Silva endured fourteen attempts by theologians to better him in religious debate and one year of terrible physical pain. Still he would not recant.

The Inquisition's records describe diverse and astonishing details of de Silva's resistance. Instead of renouncing Judaism, he circumcised himself with a pocketknife. He also frequently resorted to long and agonizing fasts, as if the tortures of the Inquisition's devising were not sufficient challenge. De Silva signed his testimony after each hearing, "Eli Ha-Nazir, unworthy servant of the God of Israel, alias Silva."

For eighty days, the Inquisition chronicles note, de Silva survived on green ears of maize. With the husks he created a rope, which he used to lower himself into other cells, strengthening other Jews in their faith and even converting Catholics to Judaism. He apparently also devised a plan for escape, but his attempt failed.

De Silva's Jewish activities actually intensified in prison. Using scraps of paper and a pen made from a chicken bone, he wrote several tracts in support of his religious beliefs. One must remember his circumstances to realize the full magnitude of his deeds— the dungeons of the Spanish American Inquisition were hardly fertile ground for the exposition of Jewish philosophy.

On January 23, 1639, Lima held the greatest *auto-da-fé* in its history. The fires burned for hours, as one convicted Judaizer after another was led to his execution. Last to walk from the dungeons that day was the weakened, tortured physician, Francisco Maldonado de Silva. Perhaps now, the members of the Grand Tribunal may have thought, this champion of Judaism would finally recant. Looking at the sky before his death, de Silva said simply, "This has been ordained by the God of Israel, to see me face to face from the heavens."[1]

De Silva's martyrdom, spectacular with courage, was only a small part of a wider tragedy. From the early sixteenth century through much of the seventeenth, scores of prisoners of the Spanish American Inquisition answered with their lives for their alleged Jewish faith. Many more were imprisoned, tortured, and robbed of all possessions, also on charges of being secret Jews.

Beyond the astonishing and quixotic exception of de Silva, there were in fact no openly professing Jews in all Spanish America. The martyrs and other suspected Judaizers were known as New Christians, the descendants of Jews who had been baptized in Spain and Portugal in the fourteenth and fifteenth centuries.

The Spanish treated the New Christians with uniform suspicion and indeed periodically prohibited by law their entry into the Americas. They tended to believe, with varying degrees of zeal, in the proverb, "In three cases water has flowed in vain: the water of the river into the sea, the water in wine, and the water at a Jew's baptism."[2]

17

The suspicion that a large proportion of New Christians may have been Marranos, or secret Jews, was not ill founded. Many New Christians held no incentive for allegiance to Christianity other than the desire to survive in a society that would not tolerate their Judaizing. Moreover, though not every New Christian was a Marrano, "even before he began to Judaize, every New Christian was a potential Marrano, whom a variety of circumstances could transform into an active Marrano."[3] The New Christians remained a separate and conspicuous element in Spanish and Portuguese society into the seventeenth century, "and in the popular mind the line between 'New Christian' and 'Jew' was often blurred."[4]

The Americas offered New Christians relative safety, compared with their situation in Spain and Portugal. Accordingly, a steady stream made their way to the New World, especially after Portugal permitted its harassed New Christian population to emigrate, in 1507. For the next fifty years, Portugal continued to allow New Christians to enter its Brazilian territory. In 1568, the Portuguese prohibited further settlement of Brazil by these immigrants, but the passage of nine years and the payment of 1.7 million cruzados by the New Christians of Lisbon mellowed Portuguese policy, and the ban was rescinded.

From Brazil, some New Christians moved, often covertly, into Spanish domains, including the region of modern Argentina. This territory included coastal settlements in the basin of the Río de la Plata as well as interior towns like Córdoba, Tucumán, and Mendoza, which developed as sources of supply for Peruvian mining centers. These scattered settlements remained subordinate to the viceroy of Peru until 1776, when the Spanish crown merged them into the new viceroyalty of the Río de la Plata.

The region of colonial Argentina shared with other Spanish possessions in the Americas an active antipathy toward possible Judaizers. The nearest tribunal of the Inquisition, in Lima, tried its first martyr, Diego Padilla de Córdoba, from this territory in 1579. The de Silvas were among subsequent victims from this area. Not till the early nineteenth century, when revolutionaries carved an independent United Provinces of the Río de la Plata from the Spanish domains, did the Inquisition there end its formal reign.

The backward state of this colonial territory kept its New Christian population fairly small compared with neighboring areas.

During the sixteenth and early seventeenth centuries, fewer New Christians lived in the whole Río de la Plata region than in either Lima or the rich mining center of Potosí. Yet the very backwardness of the region proved a blessing to the New Christians who did settle there. José Monin, an Argentine historian, writes that "the vastness of these territories and their economic poverty saved the Judaizers from the dangers of the establishment of the Tribunal of the Holy Office of the Inquisition." The potential confiscated wealth of New Christian defendants was deemed too small to justify the operations of a tribunal in the region.[5] Consequently, the Inquisition established tribunals in Lima, Mexico City, and Cartagena, but never in the area of the Río de la Plata. This, of course, was no guarantee that a suspected Judaizer would not be summarily apprehended by officials in the area and transported, like the de Silvas, to the closest tribunal in Lima. Nevertheless, the difficulty of patrolling the vast and sparsely populated region of the Río de la Plata worked to shield the New Christian inhabitants.

Which persons in the settlements of the Río de la Plata region were New Christians? The problem of identifying them reliably here, as in all Spanish American lands, is very great. Other than the Inquisition's records, there is scant information concerning these individuals, who of course had no desire to publicize their backgrounds.

Many New Christians settling in the territory appeared to have occupied an important place in the nascent economic system. Entrepreneurs of various types seem to have formed a disproportionate number of the New Christian population; so, too, did physicians. In this undeveloped land, apothecaries without medical diplomas would nevertheless "practice medicine," generally to the detriment of all but the morticians of the region. Skilled and licensed doctors were in demand, and a New Christian physician, if prudent about his personal conduct, might enjoy considerable patronage from his Old Christian neighbors.

Numerous Portuguese who settled in Buenos Aires, Córdoba, Tucumán, and elsewhere in the Argentine territory were thought by Spanish officials to be New Christians or, worse, Marranos. Yet these suspicions may have reflected more on the Spanish tendency to fear all Portuguese as possible Judaizers than on the actual state of events in the New World. Although the Portuguese clearly constituted a conspicuous minority group in this region, it is impossible to ascertain how many of these were New Christians.[6]

The difficulties of determining who was Judaizing, although taxing to modern scholarship, apparently took a greater toll on the Spanish officials of the period. Reports during the seventeenth century despairingly accused Jews, Portuguese, and merchants— terms synonymous to Spaniards—of appearing everywhere to take the wealth from the land.[7] New Christian merchants did participate in the trade, both legal and illegal, that occurred along all routes from Buenos Aires to Potosí and Lima. Perplexed officials recorded that Buenos Aires served as a key port for these Portuguese New Christians and Judaizers.[8]

From both royal and ecclesiastical reports it appears that economic motives played almost as great a role as religious devotion in stimulating Judeophobia. The motives were reciprocally reinforcing, a phenomenon that would recur repeatedly, in somewhat differing forms, in later Argentine history. The difference is that in modern Argentina, economic diatribes against the Jews have inflamed a latent religious prejudice; whereas, in the colonial period, the formal condemnations of Judaizers were cast almost exclusively in religious terms.

The case of Juan Acuña de Noroña, a Portuguese-born merchant, illustrates this combination of religious and economic motives behind the Inquisition's conduct. Noroña conducted his business affairs with great success in Santiago del Estero, in the Río de la Plata region, despite his known Jewish descent. It is likely that a number of citizens owed him money and that none would have grieved long if some mischance had separated this New Christian from his business credits. Noroña eventually succumbed to just such poor fortune, through his incautious temperament and the efforts of his fellow townsmen.

Apparently Noroña had the dangerous inclination to confront his "friends" and neighbors with theological problems and critical questions about the Bible. As a result, he arrived as a prisoner in Lima on June 27, 1622. The charges against him form a compendium of the Inquisition's most frequent accusations against heretics, Jews, and other contemporary insufferables. They included Noroña's frequent allusions to the Old Testament; refusal to consult the New Testament for spiritual guidance; failure to call upon

Jesus or Mary for help; declaring "Praised be God, blessed be the Master of the Heavens: great is the God of Israel, Abraham, Isaac, and Jacob"; failure to take rosary, hear Mass, confess, or receive sacrament; criticizing the celibate state of monks; living in scandal with concubines; and, perhaps more to the heart of the matter, practicing usury.

Some thirty persons rushed to testify against Noroña. One neighbor related how the prisoner had once told him that God is the great Lord, so powerful that there was nowhere to hold Him, for no place was worthy or able to do this. Therefore, the bread and wine in the holiest sacrament of the altar do not hold God, but God is with all things and with His servants on earth.

In 1625, the Inquisition officials ordered Noroña tortured. He denied the charges against him and begged for death as a release from his agony. At length he agreed to confess anything if only they would take him away from the minister of torture, for to see him caused "the sweat of death." The holy men of the tribunal freed him long enough to obtain his confession to all charges, even the most absurd, that he publicly told his neighbors that all Christians were his enemies. He was then returned to prison and sometime later executed.[9]

The Spanish abhorrence of the New Christians both as an economic and a religious threat finds further confirmation in the fate of Captain Alvaro Rodríguez de Acevedo. This merchant of Portuguese origin lived in Córdoba during the mid-seventeenth century. The Inquisition charged him with Judaizing and, on these grounds, confiscated his vast real estate and liquidated his business affairs. At Lima, Acevedo denied all charges but could not clear his racial origin. Affected by the situation and by old age, Acevedo grew gravely sick in prison. By 1675, two years after the Inquisition condemned him first for sacrilege and then for graver offenses, his case remained unresolved. In the unlikely event of his release, Acevedo would have emerged ruined in health and stripped of all his property and money. Yet he probably never left prison except to meet an executioner.[10]

Despite the constant risks facing New Christians, the Río de la Plata region offered them hope as well. Without ever producing paeans to the ideal of tolerance, many Spanish American officials tacitly recognized the value of educated and enterprising settlers from any background. Irrational fears that New Christians threatened established interests coexisted, to a much greater degree than in Iberia, with the knowledge that the New Christians contributed to the commercial development of the region. Therefore, exceptional New Christians managed to overcome the handicap of their racial background and prospered in the Spanish lands.

The career of Francisco de Vitoria is a striking example of a New Christian penetrating Spanish American society at its highest levels. Vitoria's father was burned at the stake in Granada. A brother, Diego Pérez de Acosta, was among the first victims of the Inquisition of Lima. Vitoria of necessity early mastered the art of survival, professing his faith in Jesus so convincingly—and by all known evidence, sincerely—that other Catholics looked to him for guidance. Vitoria eventually received appointment as Bishop of Tucumán, a city valued for its production of grain, cotton, and domestic animals, all needed by the mining areas of Peru. Vitoria simultaneously pursued a successful entrepreneurial career. From Brazil he introduced the first machinery for sugar-refining and established a network of commercial relations in the area of the Río de la Plata. In 1592, Vitoria was named Archbishop of Mexico, a height which proved unsafe for any New Christian to ascend. The Inquisition in the Americas believed it inopportune to condemn Vitoria himself, but arranged to have him recalled to Spain for investigation. Vitoria died shortly thereafter, the investigation remaining uncompleted.[11]

The León family from Lisbon was the most distinguished one of Jewish background to prosper in the colonial society. Diego López de León was appointed alderman of Córdoba in 1608. His official responsibilities were limited to participating in community burials and preparing letters for the City Council, a task well suited to his talents in calligraphy.

López de León soon found that composing eulogies and drafting mundane documents constituted an inadequate outlet for his abilities, and he redirected his energies to the challenge of replanning the entire city. He directed the repair of bridges crossing the main aqueduct, expanded the streets, and supervised the construction of new houses. His accomplishments led one writer to observe, "In such manner, under the direction and vigilance of the celebrated New Christian, the design of Córdoba . . . was assured for the future."[12]

Diego de León Pinelo, scion of the tireless alderman of Córdoba, exceeded the achievements of his father. Born in 1608 in the Río de la Plata region, this New Christian became the first celebrated writer in Argentine history. He was also the first student born in the Americas to obtain a degree in *canones y leyes* (ecclesiastical and secular law) from the University of Salamanca, in Spain. Upon earning his degree at the age of twenty-four, he returned to the New World to settle in Lima, where his father had become a clergyman and superintendent to the Archbishop Fernando Arias de Ugarte. The younger León obtained his doctorate at the University of Lima and became both a professor and a counselor to the viceroy. Inevitably, his Jewish origins became a subject of scandal when the Inquisition discovered that his professorship was in Roman Catholic theology. León tactfully avoided the tribunal's wrath by resigning the professorship and by assuring the Inquisitors that his last wish was to incur the desecration of "such a holy tribunal." The former theologian turned to the more innocuous field of literature with great success. His foremost work, *Alegato apologético en defensa de la Universidad limense* (Apologetic Exposition in Defense of the University of Lima), is actually a long encomium to the New World, written in rhapsodic language.

Diego de León Pinelo died March 17, 1671, his memory preserved by the inhabitants of his native Córdoba. At the beginning of the twentieth century, they christened with his name one of the streets planned by his own father. Sadly, their orthography was not to the standard of his father's architecture, and his name appeared *Pinedo.* Surely, though, this descendant of Marranos, so attached to the land of the Río de la Plata, would have been proud.[13]

Diego's elder brother, Antonio de León Pinelo, was popularly known as the Justinian of Buenos Aires. The Argentine historian Ricardo Levene calls him "perhaps the greatest American scholar and bibliophile: his thought and action contributed in the highest degree bring to a head codification of the laws of the Indies."[14] His juridical achievements are especially noteworthy because Spanish society, at least theoretically, was intensely legalistic. Unlike the English approach to colonial administration during this period,

Spanish rule of a vast empire featured a gigantic bureaucracy, centralized decisionmaking, and an unparalleled concern for adherence to the letter of the most minute laws. Antonio de León Pinelo streamlined the cumbersome governing system of Spanish America through such works as *Discurso acerca de la importancia, forma y disposición de la recopilación de las leyes de Indias* (Treatise on the Importance, Form, and Arrangement of the Compilation of Laws of the Indies) and *Tratado de las confirmaciones reales* (A Treatise on Royal Ratifications).

Antonio Pinelo attempted to change Spanish policy toward trade with the Americas, which policy he believed injurious to the inhabitants of the Río de la Plata territory. Pinelo even traveled to Spain to plead his case personally. Although persons of Jewish extraction usually would have been barred from making such a voyage, Pinelo's importance as a legal adviser afforded him extra privileges. Pinelo's powers of persuasion also included 500 ducats to the governor of the region. He was therefore able to sail from Buenos Aires without strict interrogation.

In Spain, Antonio Pinelo argued cogently, though futilely, against the royal policies toward Buenos Aires. Possibly his mission had no chance to succeed, for with the exception of its missionizing zeal, the Spanish government thought of the colonies in the New World almost wholly in terms of plundering their resources rather than developing their potential for industry and varied trade. Although all European nations attempted to profit from their colonies, Spain took this policy to counterproductive extremes by imposing exacting and rigid trade laws, most of which were inefficiently administered. Pinelo could do no more than reveal this system's sad consequences for the American colonies and, in the long run, for Spain as well. His writings on the subject remain the most important documents extant on commerce in the Río de la Plata area. These writings also enhanced his popular reputation both as a thinker of rare ability and as a defender of the region's welfare.[15]

Balancing the Vitorias and Pinelos against the wider experience of New Christians in the territory of the Río de la Plata, one is compelled to conclude that the former individuals did not redeem or notably improve the lot of the common New Christian; they merely transcended it. One is still left with a basic pattern of

24

hostility toward any apparent vestige of Judaic identity. The most successful New Christians carried with them a haunting awareness of the Inquisition's vigilance. Of greater significance culturally is the fact that even while some New Christians prospered in the Spanish colonies, Judaism itself never took root. There are only sporadic accounts of Judaizing after the major *auto-da-fé* in Lima occurred in 1639. Indeed, the New Christian deliberately cast off his cultural heritage. Ever conscious of his danger and concerned with improving his security and status, he soon learned to hide, then eliminate, all actions that might indicate Jewish descent. At most, he lit candles on Friday night, abstained when feasible from pork, and perhaps said an annual prayer. Even these disappeared with the passing of a few generations. By the eve of colonial independence in 1810, all New Christians—so far as contemporaries could judge—had long since vanished into the larger Catholic population.

The elements of religious and racial prejudice that characterized Spanish American society did not perish together with the remnants of Judaic identity, however. Indeed the survival of this prejudice, rather than the heritage of the New Christians themselves, exerted the greater influence on later Jewish life in the region. Time may have blurred popular memories of these New Christians once so feared by Spanish officials. Time would even erode the power of the Catholic church, to the point where government leaders in the late nineteenth century would actively court Jewish as well as non-Jewish colonization of the developing land. Various immigrant groups in modern times would bring their own inherited attitudes toward Jews, which were largely unrelated to the values of colonial Argentine society. Yet for all these changes, there remained the centuries-old spirit of Hispanic religious animosity, interlaid with economic resentments and a generalized xenophobia. The spirit would often be latent, but always potent. In colonial years, the focal point of these dark sentiments was the New Christian; in modern Argentina, it would be the Jew.

25

Jews in the new nation

Few Jews lived in Argentina during its first half-century of nation-hood, nor did there exist any organized Jewish community in this period. The scarcity of Jewish (and other) immigration traces in large part to the ambivalence of the Argentine government over the extent to which foreigners should be recruited and, once in Argentina, accommodated. In the abstract, the government was quick to extend a warm welcome to potential immigrants. Even while their land still verged on independence, leaders in Buenos Aires were expressing concern with the territory's sparse popula-tion, sluggish trade, and the numerical predominance of backward Indian tribes compared with Spanish inhabitants.[16] The white Euro-pean elite of the region perceived a simple solution to all these problems: bring in more white Europeans. Accordingly, they enacted new laws to stimulate such immigration, promising to new settlers all the benefits of citizenship without the obligations.[17]

Despite this general encouragement of immigration, the gov-ernment at first failed to offer more tangible inducements to settle the new land. It declined to provide transportation, parcels of land to till, or short-term capital for would-be colonists. This indiffer-ence by the government was a critical stumbling block to immigra-tion, for the difficult voyage from Europe to Argentina tended to discourage all but the most enthusiastic adventurers.

Historian James Scobie writes of the problems dissuading pro-spective settlers:

To reach this remote portion of the southern hemisphere, Europeans had to travel twice as far as to the United States, with a consequent increase in expense, inconvenience, and risk. They ventured into an unknown area, for Rio de Janeiro, Montevideo, and Buenos Aires blurred together in Europe's ignorance about these ports so recently liberated from colonial status.[18]

Argentina's uncertain attitudes toward religious toleration also militated against Jewish immigration during its early national pe-riod. Notwithstanding the liberal overtures to foreigners, Argen-tina was steeped in a legacy of the Inquisition's zeal that could scarcely be expected to abate suddenly. The annals of the State Court list the names of criminals whose sole guilt lay in disregarding the state religion, a violation of the nation's fundamental law.[19] In 1821, for example, an adventist named Ramos Mejía was accused of committing "Jewish observances." The charge was considered serious enough for the head of the Triumvirate governing Argentina, Bernadino Rivadavia, to demand "that one Don Francisco Ramos Mejía stop promoting practices contrary to the state religion and cease creating scandals against the public order."[20]

The full frenzy of religious piety exploded in 1825, after Argentina and Great Britain entered into a Pact of Friendship, Trade, and Navigation. One provision in the treaty granted the British then living in Argentina full religious freedom, including rights to build churches, maintain a cemetery, and worship in public. The representatives of the provinces were aghast. The written constitutions in all but one province specifically sanctioned a state religion and opposed religious toleration. In San Juan, the sole exception, a mob burned the new constitution that permitted each citizen to practice his own religion in public. Anti-Protestant sentiment played a major role in the decision by all the provinces to reject the treaty with Great Britain. Soon after, the Province of Santa Fe took the growing religious hysteria to its height by outlawing all other religious practices and beliefs, even in private. The desire for British capital goods and the fear of attack by British capital ships eventually led Argentina to extend a measure of religious toleration, but this was confined to the Buenos Aires Province and was applied to Protestants alone.

Understandably, Jews who sailed to Argentina in this era did so for reasons of individual opportunity rather than in hope of founding a secure, culturally active Jewish community. Thus, before 1825 there is record of only one Jew, an English cargo merchant known as "Señor Jacob." Ten years later, the first Argentine Jewish family from France settled and carried on an import and export trade. All the members of this family, the Lehmans, assimilated, emigrated, or died by 1880. The brothers married Gentiles and from the first had little to do with Judaism.

Other Jews in Argentina during the early nineteenth century displayed no more than the most minimal retention of their heritage. They were frequently already successful in Europe before

27

coming to Argentina, a condition largely dictated by the expense of the voyage. The most eminent of these early immigrants was an English Jew, Henry Naftali Hart, who arrived in Buenos Aires on a commercial venture sometime before 1844. Hart belonged to the exclusive British merchants' society, the Club for Foreign Residents, to which only three other Jews were admitted before 1889. There was a formidable entrance fee of 300 pesos and monthly dues of 30 pesos.

For a British gentleman of wealth and standing, Hart knew a share of Jewish adversity. For during the 1850s, his business partner had him falsely accused of illegal speculation. He was pardoned in 1855 only to be jailed three months later in a new lawsuit. Three English friends soon extended the 4,000 pesos required to secure his release, but two more years passed before his acquittal. Despite these setbacks, Hart regained his stature in the Anglo-Argentine community and was also among the first settlers in this period to acknowledge freely his Jewish background. He later became an important patron of the early Argentine Jewish community.[21]

Jewish immigration increased somewhat during the third quarter of the nineteenth century. Justo José de Urquiza, president of Argentina from 1854 to 1860, deserves much credit for attracting English and other foreign settlers.

Urquiza was among the *caudillos,* or military leaders, who controlled the Argentine provinces. His domain was in Entre Ríos, just north of Buenos Aires Province but far less settled and economically advanced. Like an increasing number of *caudillos* and diverse other elements of the population, Urquiza gradually became disillusioned with the leadership of the dominant *caudillo,* Juan Manuel de Rosas, who had ruled for some two decades from his native province of Buenos Aires. While Rosas's stern and increasing authoritarianism disturbed many, others were most alienated by his apparent lack of long-range plans to develop the whole region. In 1851, Urquiza led a full-scale revolt in alliance with armies from neighboring Brazil and Uruguay. The conflict ended in the decisive rout of Rosas at the battle of Caseros, on February 3, 1852. Urquiza assumed the leadership of the new Argentine Confederation, while Rosas found asylum in England.

Unlike other generals who proclaimed popular sovereignty and enforced their wills with guns and horses, Urquiza remained

faithful to his own rhetoric. His administration also created a climate of democratic accommodation of minority groups. This policy, among its many significant effects, fostered the gradual formation of a Jewish community with civil and religious rights.

The new liberal trends could be seen in the formation of a
national constitution by provincial delegates at Santa Fe in 1853.
Modeled largely on the American Constitution, the new document
included passages on toleration especially relevant to Jews. Two
clauses established complete religious freedom for all citizens and
foreign residents. Of course, the conservative forces of the nation
were not without influence, despite the dominance of liberals in the
legislative assembly. The Constitution did not separate church and
state. Article 2 decreed that the government would support the
Roman Catholic church, and Article 76 stipulated that the president
and vice president of the government must be a Roman Catholic,
a provision nominally in force to this day. Still, the Constitution—
which needed seven more years of vehement dispute to secure
ratification—represented a decisive advance toward religious toleration.

The new government indirectly aided Jews in another important respect, by promoting immigration through a variety of incen-
tives. Unlike the Argentina of Rosas, Urquiza's confederation
lacked the all-important city of Buenos Aires, whose leaders feared
the loss of its supremacy to the combined influence of the interior
provinces. The aloof position of Buenos Aires deprived Urquiza of
a prime source of new immigrants and spurred him to compensate
by actively courting potential settlers. The Constitution reflected
this outlook. Article 25, inspired by Juan Bautista Alberdi's maxim
that "to govern is to populate," committed the government to
encourage immigration and to refrain from restricting foreign settlement and from imposing taxes on foreign entry.

Urquiza also appears to have been sincerely committed to
tolerating diversity in religion and national origin. An example of
his enlightened attitude regards his dispatch of a clergyman to Italy
to recruit colonists for his native Entre Ríos. Despite clear instructions to select all who were fit to work new farmland, the cleric
chose only Catholics. When Urquiza discovered this, he angrily
wrote that this violated his instructions, and he recalled the cleric
at once.[22]

29

Jews under Urquiza's rule found that their opportunities for public service and social advancement were greater than they had ever been in the Río de la Plata region. An outstanding case in point is the career of Louis Hartwig Brie, who came to South America from Germany at the age of thirteen.

Brie was born in 1834 to a merchant family in Hamburg. As a youth he participated in an abortive uprising in his native city and then fled the country, arriving in Brazil in 1847. He found living conditions oppressive and hastened to join a military unit composed of German adventurers. Brie was admitted as a cadet and then served in the Fourth Artillery Battery. This outfit and several other Brazilian units were recruited to fight in the revolution raging in Argentina, where General Urquiza was rallying troops against the dictator Rosas.

Brie's unit joined the other Brazilian forces at Caseros, in which he fought with distinction.[23] For thirty years thereafter, Brie alternated modest civilian ventures with exploits in the Argentine army. He fought in the war against Paraguay (1865–70) in which Argentina, aided by Brazil and Uruguay, won a costly but decisive victory. The Paraguayan armed forces were obliterated and the country's population plunged disastrously, from half a million to little more than 200,000.

Brie later helped suppress a revolution within Argentina, led by a former friend, Leandro Alem, in 1890. The revolutionaries had considerable justification for their actions, for the government was corrupt, bankrupt, and demonstrably unable to manage national resources. Yet Brie accorded more weight to the fact that the nation's rulers were, in constitutional terms, fully legitimate. His defense of the existing government marked Brie's last major action as a soldier.

Brie's Jewish consciousness was marginal during his early years in Brazil and Argentina. He accepted his medals for valor at Caseros and married a Roman Catholic in a church ceremony in Buenos Aires. Toward the latter part of his life, however, Brie felt the need to serve in a new cause, that of his own heritage as a Jew. The process may have been precipitated to some degree by the death of his Catholic wife in 1892, but Brie had always maintained some contact with members of the young Jewish community. He served as a leading official in several Jewish institutions in Buenos Aires until his remarriage in 1900, again to a Catholic, drew him from his active interest in Jewish affairs.

The successful revolt against Rosas also brought other Jewish talent to light, such as the Alsatian immigrant, Joseph Alexander Bernheim, a printer. He had spent some years as aide to Domingo Faustino Sarmiento, the fiercely liberal opponent of the *caudillo* Rosas and in later years, president of the nation (1868–74). During the campaign against Rosas, Sarmiento served as *boletinero,* or press attaché, to Urquiza. Sarmiento resigned this position when Urquiza became president and Bernheim succeeded him, even receiving a printing press from the new Argentine leader. Bernheim also founded in Buenos Aires the city's first French daily, *Le Courrier de la Plata.*[24]

The Navarro family, of Jewish ancestry, included several innovative and ambitious members.[25] Octaviano Navarro (1826–84) governed Catamarca Province in the late 1850s and again in the early 1870s. Navarro introduced printing to Catamarca and founded its first journal. He also installed lighting and fostered mining and other industry.

Both Ramón Gil Navarro (1828–83) and Angel Aurelio Navarro (1810–75) were lawyers, writers, and politicians who came to prominence in the democratic atmosphere of Urquiza's Argentina. Both had fled the country during the authoritarian Rosas era, returning shortly after Urquiza's victory at Caseros. Ramón Gil was elected several times as a national deputy to the Argentine Parliament. He also enjoyed the support of President Bartolomé Mitre (1862–68) in establishing a liberal periodical, *El Progreso,* in 1867. Angel Aurelio spent many years in Brazil, where he was appointed by Emperor Dom Pedro the Second as national librarian. Later, in Argentina he became active in politics, representing Catamarca in the National Senate (1862–68) and eventually becoming vice president of that body.

Even in religion, the Navarros made their mark on Argentine society. Luis Gabriel Segura, bishop of Entre Ríos, was descended from the Jewish Navarro family. He was thus among the highest clerical officials in Argentina of known Jewish ancestry since Francisco de Vitoria served as bishop of Tucumán in the late sixteenth century.

The most distinguished member of this remarkable family was

31

Mordecai Navarro, a trusted aide to Urquiza both during and after his presidency. Navarro's one known gesture to his Jewish origins was modest. Although he hispanicized his first name, he periodically reverted to transliterating his given Hebrew name of Mordecai when signing letters and documents.

Mordecai Navarro was twenty-five years old when he began working for Urquiza in 1859, organizing the bookkeeping for his estates and business transactions. Navarro was also valuable to Urquiza for the ring of contacts he held in intellectual circles, confirmed by the voluminous correspondence that survives from Navarro's friendships.

After three years, Navarro and Urquiza parted company. Navarro himself appears to have caused the breach with the Argentine leader. According to the historian Pablo Schvartzman, Navarro was a passionate federalist, a native of Entre Ríos who distrusted the townsmen, or *porteños,* of Buenos Aires and was jealous for the liberties of his own province. He was among many inhabitants of the interior provinces who came to view Urquiza, with his ideas about national unity and attempts to lure or force Buenos Aires into the confederation, as a traitor to federalist ideals. Urquiza in fact met death in 1870 at the hands of a crazed gaucho thinking to strike a blow for the freedom of the interior provinces. Navarro tried to do much the same thing with his pen during the 1860s, publishing a bitter attack on Urquiza, which included the charge that he had failed to pay his business debts. It is unclear whether Navarro's accusations were accurate or, as is equally likely, he simply resorted to distortion and slander to undermine Urquiza's prestige.[26]

Urquiza was easily more farsighted than Navarro. His policies aimed to conciliate heterogeneous elements in Argentine society, giving substance to his motto after the battle of Caseros, *ni vencedores ni vencidos* (neither victors nor vanquished). The antagonism between *gaucho* and *porteño,* between the outer provinces and the great port city, proved insoluble for Urquiza and his successors for two decades. Not till 1880, following a brief civil war, was Buenos Aires finally federalized as the national capital and the unification of the Argentine Republic completed. Yet what Urquiza achieved during his reign as president was equally impressive and enduring: a set of laws and policies upon which to base a democratic nation open to all who wished to settle and develop it.

A culturally active Jewish community coalesced in Buenos Aires in the decades immediately following Urquiza's rule. The community gained most basic civil rights during these years, though only after persistent initiatives and legal challenges by Jewish representatives. Recalling that this society had accorded legal force to the Inquisition only half a century earlier, one may fairly conclude that progress toward religious liberty was encouragingly rapid.

The first Jewish wedding in Argentina, in 1860, also occasioned a larger celebration: it marked the first governmental recognition of public Jewish observance. Solomon Levy, a French immigrant residing in Buenos Aires, began a complicated legal process with his attempt, ultimately successful, to marry according to Jewish rite. The real hero of this controversy, however, was a deeply pious Catholic lawyer named Miguel Navarro-Viola, who argued Levy's case before the highest court of Buenos Aires.

Navarro-Viola faced a formidable array of obstacles. Argentine social traditions clearly militated against his efforts and two recent legal decrees further discouraged his case. One decree, enacted by the Municipality of Buenos Aires in 1857, required "Catholic priests and the chaplains and ministers of the 'reformed' religions" to handle records of marriage.[27] This legislation essentially dictated that marriage ceremonies were valid only if they were religious in nature; yet nowhere were Jews legally entitled to act as religious officials. The words *reformed religions* referred only to Protestant sects.[28]

A second decree, issued by the Superior Tribunal of Justice in Buenos Aires during this same period, was still more explicit on the subject of Jewish ritual in marriage. The chief justice of the court prohibited such a ceremony because, in his opinion, religious tolerance "referred exclusively to Christians and not to a sect 'that still awaits the coming of the Messiah.' "[29]

Navarro-Viola offered an eloquent and cogent brief to meet these legal problems. He based his case in part on the Constitution of Buenos Aires, a province then separated from the other Argentine provinces although not a fully independent nation. He referred particularly to Article 4, which declared "the inalienable right of every man in the territory of the State to worship God Almighty according to his conscience." In addition, he argued that a national decree in 1833 "speaks generally of matrimonial privileges of faiths other than the Catholic religion, among which the Mosaic one should be included."[30]

The court reacted favorably to Navarro-Viola's skillful presentation—yet still another problem faced his client Solomon Levy. A decree, passed in Buenos Aires Province in 1833, required "all ministers of beliefs other than the Roman Catholic religion" to verify their titles.[31] Even if the court recognized a rabbi as simply another chaplain of a "reformed religion," there was not a rabbi to be found for hundreds of miles, nor seminaries for training them, nor hopes for obtaining any from abroad. It is doubtful if there were any in the whole of South America at that time.[32]

Despite these discouragements, Navarro-Viola obtained a magnanimous "compromise between the letter of the law of 1857 and reality."[33] A *minyan,* the Jewish religious quorum of ten men, was permitted to substitute for a rabbi, and the marriage ceremony took place in the presence of two additional witnesses, a notary public, and the attorney Navarro-Viola.

The wedding ceremony resembled those in contemporary Jewish communities of Western Europe. The presentation of the ring, the drinking of the wine and its benediction, and the breaking of the glass cup (a traditional practice to commemorate the destruction of the temple in Jerusalem) were followed by a banquet, with many toasts in French and German. Navarro-Viola noted, with the bewilderment of the well-meaning outsider, that despite the veneer of the West European, the Jews still used "that guttural language [Yiddish] which seems like a fusion of German and Greek."[34]

Henry Naftali Hart, the English Jew whose wealth had earlier been restored, paid for the entire wedding celebration. Hart praised Navarro-Viola as the personification of Argentine liberalism. The toast by Hart was fully merited, for Navarro-Viola had helped to fashion a landmark decision protecting Jewish rights, despite his own fervent Catholicism and his conviction that the church should play a major role in Argentine society.

The court decision set a major precedent for Jewish religious freedom in Argentina, though it resulted as much from practical politics as from idealism. For to have ruled against Levy's request would have meant deliberately excluding a specific group from the benefits of Argentina's new-found and growing commitment to

34

individual liberties. It might have unsettled at least some of the other foreign-born residents and potential immigrants concerned with the possibility of a more widespread surge of religious intolerance. Given the small number of Jews then living in all Argentina, the court ruling was symbolically satisfying to liberal mentalities without threatening in any concrete way the powers of the church.

Two years after Levy's marriage, the earliest congregation of Argentine Jews held its first public meeting. The multitude of contributing nationalities included natives of Germany, France, England, Holland, Belgium, and Italy. The diversity was all too impressive, resulting in a conglomeration of factions rather than in a united congregation. Within a few years, the congregation formally disbanded. A more successful attempt to bind the Jews of Buenos Aires into a cohesive religious unit occurred in 1868 with the creation of a second Jewish congregation. The construction of a permanent temple in 1875 and the membership of distinguished Argentines, like Joseph Alexander Bernheim and Henry Naftali Hart, helped the Jewish Congregation of the Argentine Republic to remain united.

The community still lacked a rabbi. The need for such an official was especially great in a society basing its organization on religious units, as was prescribed by Argentine law until the 1880s. The cleric for each parish was the sole legal officer for social registers as well as for other, purely religious ceremonies, including marriages.

The Jewish community's formal request for legal recognition drew an ambivalent response from Argentine Minister of Culture José Gutierrez. The minister agreed to let the Jews keep a separate registry but denied them the right to institute their own religious officials. He explained, in a message to the president of the Jewish Congregation in 1877, that such a grant of authority to the Jewish community would usurp the powers of the individual provinces. He added that since the president of the congregation, Segismundo Auerbach, lacked the titles accrediting him as a religious leader, there was no way he could validate any Jewish ceremonies officials.[35]

Providence parted the sea of bureaucracy for the Jews. The Municipality of Buenos Aires, pressed by the need to keep strict civil registers and aware that Jews could not be listed with the

Catholic or Protestant parishes, decided in 1878 to cut its own bureaucratic Gordian knot. Therefore, it permitted the Jews the privileges that Gutierrez had withheld a year earlier.

The first rabbi in Argentine history, Henry Joseph, began his service to the Jewish community in 1882, amid more controversy than rejoicing. Even today, scholars of early Argentine Jewry continue to debate the role of Joseph, a character rare in the annals of religious Judaism.

Henry Joseph was born in England in 1838 and came to Argentina in his early twenties, where he became prosperous as a merchant in Buenos Aires. Though a Jew by birth, he had little formal Jewish education. He married a Roman Catholic and participated in the rituals of that faith. Joseph showed scarcely any interest in the religion of his ancestors prior to assuming the position of chief rabbi, the most important religious office a Jewish community can bestow.

Joseph volunteered for the office of chief rabbi, in part, it seems, because of a strong sense of social responsibility. He knew the community to be in great need of a rabbi and felt it incumbent upon him to offer his services in this crisis. As to why the community should have chosen Joseph, a man largely unfamiliar with Jewish ritual and increasingly affiliated with Catholicism, there are no certain answers. Indeed, his selection as chief rabbi came to be regarded by a growing number of Jews as an unmitigated disgrace to the community.

One point in Joseph's favor was his prominence in secular activities. Despite sharp vicissitudes in his business ventures, Joseph had once enjoyed a wide prestige as an entrepreneur. His efforts at philanthropy conferred further stature upon him in the eyes of many in the Jewish community.

It is more of a mystery why the General Consistory of France, representing French Jewry, agreed to ordain Joseph in 1882 for rabbinical service in Argentina. Lazare Isidor, the man who commissioned Joseph, had been Grand Rabbi of Paris for twenty-four years before being appointed head of the French rabbinate in 1867. That a man of his experience and qualifications should have approved Joseph is inexplicable in terms of any theological or personal kinship. Perhaps Isidor and the French Consistory, detached from the problems of Argentine Jewry and eager to extend their nominal authority into the Americas, would have approved almost any candidate suggested to them except an outright Christian—and there were some who sneered that the Consistory had violated even this distinction in the case of Joseph.

The new Grand Rabbi did not take his responsibilities lightly. Indeed, he appeared infused with a new sense of mission. Joseph persuaded his wife to convert to Judaism and had his sons listed in the Jewish register. He encouraged his congregants to participate in the religious festival services and organized several new institutions, including a women's charity organization, a mutual aid and burial society, and the Jewish hospital Ezra.

Joseph never developed into a religious figure of impressive Judaic learning. Yet, at least initially, his rabbinical leadership was not wholly unrepresentative of the temper of this community. Joseph embodied in exaggerated form the ambivalent attitudes of a people severed from their Jewish heritage by West European and Hispanic-American influences.

It may at first appear incongruous that a community which formed a congregation, built a temple, and organized institutions for the social welfare of its members was losing its cultural identity. But the members of the community at heart made only concessions rather than a full commitment to their Jewish heritage. The Sabbath and the dietary laws of *kashrut* were largely forgotten. Only the most rudimentary efforts were made to educate the children in Jewish law or even Jewish lore. The community preferred to compromise with the past rather than build for the future.

The Enlightenment in Europe had done much to dilute the Jewish loyalties of these people. Most of the immigrants had come from France, Germany, and England, where secularist thought was fashionable. For the Jews, the Enlightenment carried the added hope of emancipation from the ghettos, perhaps even of full social equality. Many Jews welcomed the assurances by various European leaders that they might at last join the general flow of human progress, unshackled either by bigotry or by their own "superstitious" past.

By the time many Jewish immigrants reached Argentina, they had already discarded all commitment to their heritage but for a nebulous nostalgia that was seldom transmitted to their children. Moreover, intermarriage was the rule in a community that, typical of immigrant societies, contained far more males than females.

Economic as well as cultural factors contributed to the gradual disintegration of ethnic identity, as sociologist Irving Louis Horowitz describes:

Other than setting up a house of religious worship, they [the Argentine Jews] tended to improve their occupational roles by consolidating their social prestige within the larger gentile society. The process of absorption was enhanced by the relatively excellent opportunities for early Jewish settlers, their rapid linguistic adaptation from one Romance language to another, and by a highly "Protestantized" self-vision of fulfilling providential will through commercial and business enterprise.[36]

The community's Judaic identity probably would have disappeared within a few generations had its members been left to themselves. As it happened, these Westernized Jews, fast assimilating into the Hispanic-American society around them, were destined for a clash of cultures far greater than they had known upon coming to Argentina. The first organized settlements of Slavic Jews arrived in Buenos Aires in 1889, and others followed in greater numbers over the next four decades. These immigrants came from another world in time as well as in geography. They proved the ruin of Henry Joseph and in the process dramatically altered the character of Argentine Jewry. The present community still bears the stamp of these bold settlers.

The East European Jewish legacy

To understand the present Argentine Jewish community, one must begin not in Argentina but in the Jewish centers of Eastern Europe. There the Jew developed a culture and way of life that deeply affected the Jewish settlers in the New World. Even today, the legacy of those East European communities is a major shaping force on Argentine Jewish culture.

The religious orientation of East European Jewry remained central even when, in the early nineteenth century, powerful assimilationist forces were at work among Jews in the West. During the latter part of the nineteenth century, however, the insulated attitudes of these Jewish communities experienced new tremors of change.

38

During the reign of Alexander II of Russia, trends of the Enlightenment within Jewry were stimulated from without. The Russian government, seeking to resolve its "Jewish problem" in a more enlightened way, encouraged Jews to integrate into the larger society. The new czar permitted those Jews with special skills, wealth, and education to move from the rural Pale of Settlement (to which most Jews had been legally restricted) and into the cities. Alexander also allowed them to compete for admission to the nation's schools and ended the discrimination against Jews in the Russian army's conscription policies.

Jews responded with inflated optimism to these overtures. The historian Louis Greenberg writes about this largely unrealistic surge of hope:

In their pathetic eagerness to bridge the gulf which separated them from their Christian neighbors, Jews interpreted a friendly gesture on the part of non-Jews as evidence of a complete change of heart. Every minor concession granted by the government was hailed as an assurance of coming civil emancipation.[37]

Assimilation suddenly became fashionable in certain centers of East European Jewry. It was a minority sentiment, but one of growing strength and concentrated among the intelligentsia. In the major cities of Russia and Russian Poland, some Jews organized clubs to foster assimilation among their brethren.

The latter part of Alexander's reign, however, was characterized by an erosion of tolerance and an increase in repression. Discrimination in the army and other areas of Russian society increased, while anti-Semitic rumors sped across Russia on the wings of government approval.

These developments intensified with the assassination of Alexander by revolutionary terrorists in 1881. That year a wave of pogroms broke across the nation, a tribute to the one bond of common sentiment linking the abject peasants and their despotic rulers.

In this savage manner, the hopes of the Jewish assimilationists were dashed. But if they could no longer espouse the old liberal optimism about Russian society, neither could they return to the Judaism of the *yeshivah,* a passive people in an imprisoned culture. They sought a wholly new answer.

Nationalism attracted many Jews by providing the most direct response to the failure of attempts at assimilation. Leon Pinsker, a prominent Russian physician, became one of its foremost early apostles. He had formerly been a member in the assimilationist Society for the Dissemination of Enlightenment among Jews in Russia. Pinsker nevertheless had the intellectual honesty to perceive that in 1881 the Russian peasant had shattered the assimilationists' optimistic philosophy with rocks and sticks. Pinsker declared following these outbreaks:

If we are ill-treated, robbed, plundered, outraged, we do not dare defend ourselves, and, worse still, we look upon it almost as a matter of course. . . . If no notice is taken of our descent and we are treated like others born in the country, we are thankful to the point of actually turning renegades. . . . we persuade ourselves, and others, that we are not Jews any longer, but full-blooded sons of the fatherland. Idle delusion! You may prove yourselves patriots ever so true, you will still be reminded at every opportunity of your Semitic descent. This fateful *memento mori* will not prevent you, however, from enjoying the hospitality extended, until some fine morning you are cast out of the country, until the sceptical mob reminds you that you are, after all, nothing but nomads and parasites, protected by no law.[38]

Three years later, Pinsker joined Hovevei Zion (Lovers of Zion), one of the numerous nascent Zionist societies in Russia, rising from the ashes of the discredited assimilationist clubs.

Socialism appeared a more inviting alternative to Jews who despaired over the structure of Russian society but not over Russia itself. Radical labor organizations like the Jewish Social Democratic Group, of Vilna, took root in Russia during the late nineteenth century. In 1897, the Socialist group known as the Bund began its activities, quickly becoming the leading Jewish workers' movement and also holding the support of many in the Jewish intelligentsia.

As the ranks of Jewish activists swelled, Zionist and Socialist ideologies collided. The latter groups increasingly opposed Jewish national aspirations, other than demanding greater cultural autonomy within Russia. They theorized that whatever detracted from the class struggle did more harm than good. Typical of such attitudes was the pronouncement by the Fourth Congress of the Bund, in 1901, that branded Zionism as merely a bourgeois reaction to

40

anti-Semitism.[39] By 1904, the Bund's representatives were describing Zionism as "the most evil enemy of the organized Jewish proletariat fighting under the Social Democratic flag of the Bund."[40]

Zionists during the early twentieth century replied with equal vigor to the Bundists' tart appraisals of their movement. After the terrible pogrom in Kishinev in 1903, a Zionist leader in Odessa suggested that the Bund "and its pernicious activities bear the blame if so much blood is needlessly spilled in Russia and if the government has worked its suspicion of the Jews up to the point of persecution." He added, in a final twist of his polemical knife, that the Bund showed a strange faith in its alleged class allies, the Russian workers from whose ranks the pogromists were drawn.[41]

Another major wedge between the two Jewish ideological movements was that in an almost literal sense they did not speak the same language. Bundists wanted to maintain Yiddish as the language of the Jew, while the Zionists disdained Yiddish as the language only of dispersion and bondage. To the Bundists, the attempts to promote Hebrew as the true Jewish language were the work of arrogant elitists, cut off from the masses. Jews, the Bundists noted, used Hebrew only in prayer and religious study but otherwise spoke Yiddish, as they had for hundreds of years in every community from France to Russia.

The result was to fragment the Jewish movements into an ever-changing kaleidoscope of utopian parties. Eventually, however, a form of Zionist socialism arose, such as that represented by the group Po'alei Zion. Its leader was Ber Borochov, a fervent Zionist and a staunch Marxist. Soon after Borochov created his synthesis, rival organizations like the more pragmatic and nationalistic and less class-conscious Hapoel Hatza'ir (Young Workers), began to enrich the spectrum of Socialist-Zionist theory.

Throughout these ideological developments in the East European Jewish communities, the *yeshivah* culture survived, and the number of these schools even increased during the twentieth century. However, the insularity of its culture clearly had been punctured by powerful new forces. Assimilationism, Zionism, and socialism had effected a truly radical cultural upheaval within the Judaism of Eastern Europe: an attempt to replace religious Judaism with insurgent secular ideologies. The clash of these vigorous cul-

41

tural forces was still much unresolved when the first Russian emigrants reached the shore of Argentina to begin a new life.

Russian Jewish settlement

The year 1889 opened a new era for Argentine Jewry, with the arrival of the first organized Russian Jewish immigration. There had been sporadic Russian Jewish settlement before then but of no permanent nature and on a very small scale. By the late 1880s, however, the combined effect of Russian persecution, Jewish philanthropy, and Argentine encouragement led to a more substantial and well-planned exodus from Russia. Aboard the vessel SS *Weser,* which reached Buenos Aires on August 14, 1889, were 824 passengers from 136 families. These Jews came with the intent to purchase farmland and to establish new roots in Argentina. While other Russian Jews eagerly awaited news of their fate, two Hebrew-language journals in Russia obtained a report on the established Jewish community in Buenos Aires and the prospects for new settlers:

The Jewish community of Buenos Ayres does not appear to be in a flourishing condition. There is no regular synagogue and no minister [a sharp cut at Rabbi Joseph]. . . . There is a strong demand for labour in all departments, and the chances of success are very favourable . . . and single men, or even married couples who know some trade and are prepared to be thrifty and saving can get on, providing they can get over the initial difficulty of the language. . . . Assisted or free passages could be arranged for with the Argentine Government authorities. My informant adds some remarks concerning the religious difficulties. He says that Saturday is not recognized as a Jewish Sabbath and there are no Jewish employers of labour. He considers that in case Jewish emigrants are sent out an official agent should be dispatched in advance, empowered to pay all their expenses and to provide for their maintenance until they are able to understand the language and gain their own living. The congregation are too poor to *support* them, but they would be willing to assist them to the utmost of their power.[42]

The cautious encouragement of the above report was supplemented liberally by the appeals of agents for the Argentine government. Three decades after Urquiza had first promoted immigrant settlements, Argentina was still far from realizing the full economic potential of immigration. President Julio Roca (1880–86) offered inducements to a variety of national groups to settle the Argentine frontier areas, only recently extended by ruthless campaigns against the native Indian tribes. On August 6, 1881, he issued a decree that encouraged the Russian Jews in particular to establish themselves in Argentina. He even appointed a chief agent, José María Bustos, to recruit Jews from the Old World as colonists for new villages and farms.

Jews were merely a small part of a rising tide of European settlement in Argentina, but they drew the sharpest criticisms from *criollos* who looked with horror at the influx of foreigners. Leading Argentine dailies vigorously condemned Jewish immigration, and even the journal for the presumably enlightened French-speaking population printed an editorial unlikely to serve the cause of racial tolerance:

We do not know what people would ever have the idea of sending an agent outside to gather noxious insects, powerful parasites; we do not fully understand a physician who having to treat a growing body which is in need of daily renewed blood, does not know better than to inject leeches instead.[43]

The article, entitled "The Jewish Immigration," appeared August 22, 1881, even before the organized immigration began. On this occasion, the Jews enjoyed a measure of satisfaction. Segismundo Auerbach, the president of the Jewish community, submitted a formal complaint to the municipal court against the editor of the offending journal, while two other Jews by the names of Schnabel and Simmel sought more direct redress by challenging the editor to a duel. Confronted by these assorted legal and mortal threats, the French editor publicly rethought his position within four days of the slandering article. He meant absolutely no harm, according to a clarifying column in his journal, *L'Unión Française,* but respected the honor of the Jewish community of Buenos Aires and surrounding areas. The community, Schnabel and Simmel included, was mollified by this change of sentiment and withdrew its challenges to the editor.[44]

Little could be done, however, when prominent Argentines echoed the sentiments of *L'Unión Française.* Bartolomé Mitre, a former president of the nation, an editor of the widely sold news-

43

paper *La Nación,* also warned against the influx of Jewish farmers and vehemently protested the efforts of Baron Maurice de Hirsch, the major sponsor of the Jewish colonization. Domingo Sarmiento, another former president (1868–74) and long a crusader for "liberal" ideals, developed a strong hostility toward the Jews. Once an advocate of immigration, he gradually became xenophobic, and by the time of the first Russian Jewish settlements, he issued a number of anti-Semitic polemics. For example, on July 9, 1890, he ridiculed the Jewish dietary rituals, and the next day he entitled an article, "Jewish Tariffs," referring not to Jews at all but to excessive tariff rates charged by an Argentine railroad company.

Notwithstanding these conspicuous exceptions, the official Argentine policy toward the Jews was cordial and sufficed to draw increasing numbers away from their oppressors in Russia. The efforts of these government leaders were complemented by Jewish organizations and wealthy individuals who sought to facilitate the transition from *shtetl* to pampa. The Bavarian-born baron Maurice de Hirsch was easily the most important of these people. He believed that his coreligionists in Russia could achieve freedom and security only by emigrating to a nation whose leaders were neither autocratic nor anti-Semitic. After long study of the possibilities, Hirsch concluded that Argentina was a highly promising site for new colonization. There Jews could develop the sparsely settled interior, returning to the soil for the first time since biblical days.

Hirsch's ideas were immensely ambitious, but he had an asset not often given to dreamers. The baron was one of the world's richest men, a banker whose wealth invited respectful comparisons with the Rothschilds. In 1891, Hirsch created the Jewish Colonization Association (ICA) to carry out his plans. He personally invested it with 2 million pounds sterling and later added three times that amount to insure its continued activity.[45]

Hirsch stated his aims in an essay written in 1891, the year in which he helped establish the first Jewish frontier colony in Argentina:

What I desire to accomplish, what, after many failures has come to be the object of my life, and that for which I am ready to stake my wealth and my intellectual powers is to give a portion of my companions in faith the possibility of finding a new existence, primarily as farmers and also as handicraftsmen, in those lands where the laws and religious tolerance permit them to carry on the struggle for existence as noble and responsible subjects of a human government.[46]

Hirsch created his first colony with Jewish settlers who had already come to Argentina independently of his aid or plans. The passengers on the *Weser* divided into two groups upon disembarking at Buenos Aires in 1889. Many travelers changed their initial plan of colonizing new farmland and instead settled in the capital city. Others persisted in their original goal and journeyed to Santa Fe, where the wealthy rancher Pedro Palacios had offered, through an intermediary, to sell them land. The Jews arrived there only to discover that the capricious Palacios refused to sell any of his property after all. Stranded in the interior without money, knowing only Yiddish, and completely helpless in a country that was totally unfamiliar to them, these Russian Jews lived along a railroad embankment outside the Palacios ranch, subsisting on whatever charity the local populace and the passengers on the trains would extend to them.[47]

Hirsch heard of the vagrant Jews in 1890, after many had already succumbed from starvation, illness, and exposure during the unusually harsh winter months. Hirsch's agents persuaded Palacios to sell some of his property, and with it Hirsch founded the first Jewish colony in Argentina, which became known as Moisésville.

From the year of this first Jewish settlement, in 1891, a steady stream of Russian Jews poured into Argentina. Some came to work on land purchased by the ICA or lesser independent contractors. Others preferred to settle in the cities, chiefly Buenos Aires. Within a short time, these Jews far outnumbered the original Jewish community from Western Europe.

Henry Joseph directed the efforts of the established Jews to care for their Russian brethren, giving generously of their lodging space, provisions, and time to help the immigrants adjust to their new life. However, the older, comparatively assimilated Jewish community could not understand the parochial attitudes of many immigrants nor the utopian ideologies of others. The Russian Jews were equally critical of the indigenous Jewish pop-

45

ulation, as may be seen in the testimony of one of the first settlers:

When the Russian Jews came to Buenos Aires, they couldn't find kosher meat, nor a *mikvah* [ritual bath], and they didn't even have a place to hold *minyan*. . . . Buenos Aires is probably the only big Jewish community that doesn't have its own big synagogue. This shows us that even the oldest and strongest bond that united Jews from all over the world is for us weaker than for all other Jews. . . .

In Buenos Aires it was impossible to tell apart the grave of a Jew from the grave of a Christian. On both graves was a cross in the width and in the height. There were no organized Jewish religious funeral parlors. There was no separate place to mourn a dead person and there was no place for Jewish bones to rest, so they had to be put to rest in a Catholic cemetery. . . .

Buenos Aires had a "Grand Rabbi" who married a Christian woman and led his daughter in marriage in a Church.[48]

This immigrant's caustic allusion to Rabbi Joseph captured the strong contempt in which he was held by many Russian Jews. Joseph's role had never been easy, for the apathy of the West European community had earlier driven him to many private expressions of despair. He had even convoked an extraordinary assembly of the congregation, in June 1886, to warn that he was on the brink of resigning. When he became rabbi to the community four years before, Joseph told his listeners, it was with the expressed stipulation that all members of the congregation lend him their cooperation for the proper execution of the duties of his holy office and help to establish firmly the Jewish religion in Argentina. His congregants had treated their promises as a "dead letter," and if they did not aid him more wholeheartedly, he would terminate his service in the rabbinate. With the coming of the Russian Jews, Joseph faced a very different kind of grief and one that appears to have scarred him still more severely. The Argentine historian, Boleslao Lewin, claims that Joseph was the victim of the most vicious prejudices by these new settlers, who were suspicious of anyone who did not come from the most rigidly Orthodox background. Accordingly, his image in history is tarnished, Lewin writes, despite his efforts to help the very Russian immigrants who despised him.[49]

For all Joseph's integrity and devotion, his rabbinical credentials still were sadly vulnerable. His bare knowledge of the most rudimentary Jewish customs, his complete ignorance of Talmud, and his less than inspiring religious past for a Grand Rabbi all strained to the limit the quality of mercy. Joseph's total lack of comprehension of the East European Jewish mentality soon left him incapable of representing the increasingly Russianized congregation, except in the capacity of a philanthropist.

A sample of the abuse Joseph endured from his own community is contained in this polemic by the dour journalist, Abraham Vermont:

We call Joseph an imposter. . . . He is a modest merchant, almost unlettered, with little natural intelligence, who a long time ago had a serious bankruptcy in his business. . . . He has no right to call himself Grand Rabbi for in his theological and Hebrew knowledge, he is far behind any ignorant Russian immigrant . . . and doctor [!] only [universities] can offer that title. . . . Let him produce it . . . until then he is unmasked as an imposter Rabbi and false as a doctor. . . . He could not even inculcate his own children with a love for our religion.[50]

Joseph continued as Grand Rabbi until 1894, but the mutual misunderstanding and distrust between him and his congregation was never effectively resolved. They viewed Judaism from two different worlds. Joseph represented the secular humanist side of Judaism characteristic of many West European Jews. To the Jewish centers of Eastern Europe, there was an inseparable bond between the humanitarian and religious traditions of Judaism. Beyond this fatal dichotomy of views, Joseph presided over a community fast assimilating, while the Russian Jews were intent on establishing an insular community in Argentina much as they had known in Russia. To these immigrants, Judaism in Argentina was leading intolerably and inevitably to cultural oblivion.

On October 13, 1894, Joseph wrote to the president of the congregation, "Permit me to resign. I cannot continue on, the abuse is too much."[51] He was succeeded by a Russian Jew, Solomon Liebeschutz, who became interim religious head of the congregation. Joseph continued to be a faithful member of the community. On his deathbed, he called the rabbi and the president of the congregation before him and made them promise, in front of his heirs, to bury him in accord with Jewish ritual. He died May 23,

1913, and was interred in the main Jewish cemetery, in adherence to his request, by a community that had never fully accepted him during his lifetime.

The West European Jews continued to exercise a strong influence within the congregation even after the virtual ouster of Henry Joseph. They were the more affluent of the two Jewish groups, and being more acculturated as well as longer established, they were better received by the non-Jewish *criollos*.

The West European Jews gained added purpose and influence when in the 1890s, the celebrated patriot Louis Brie brought his great prestige and abilities to the leadership of the congregation. The death of Brie's Catholic wife in 1892 was simultaneously a blow to him and a spur toward activity in the Jewish community. No longer bound to adhere to the Catholic faith in deference to his wife, Brie moved openly to declare his ties with his coreligionists. He was a natural choice to assume a position of leadership. He was not only the community's most renowned affiliate, but as the historian Bernard Ansel writes, based on an interview with Brie's daughter-in-law, "During his long disassociation from Judaism, he had continued his friendship with leading personalities of the Jewish community. . . . Rarely had these gentlemen missed a Saturday night reunion together for poker in each other's homes for over twenty-five years. Now Brie was to join them in their deliberations and in the management of community affairs."[52]

Brie became the first president of the Hevra Kaddisha Ashkenazi (Jewish Mutual Aid and Burial Society), created in 1894. Within a year, he was elected president of the congregation as well. Brie thus presided simultaneously over the two most important organizations in the Jewish community.

The first building exclusively dedicated to Jewish religious activities was completed in 1897. Significantly, while the most observant Jews came from Eastern Europe, the architectural principles were those used for the temples of Central Europe.[53] Representatives of the national government attended the ceremony of placing the cornerstone. This was the first time such an honor was ever paid to the community. It also proved to be the highwater mark in the role of the Western Ashkenazim in establishing Judaism in Argentina. The temple and concommitant government homage constituted the third decisive advance for the community after the Levy court case of 1860 and the ruling of 1878, permitting a rabbinate in the country. After this time, however, Brie's involvement in the life of the community sharply declined because of his limited financial means, his second marriage in 1900—again to a Gentile—and the frictions created by the massive immigration from Eastern Europe.

Brie never suffered the disrepute which befell Henry Joseph, because his position in the community was not so directly linked to the rabbinical aspects of Jewish communal life. Nonetheless, Brie's rigid manner, perhaps a legacy of his days in the military, and his Westernized mentality precluded rapport with the Russian and Polish settlers.

By 1900, just a decade after the first Russian arrivals, more than 90 percent of the 17,795 Jews living in Argentina were from Eastern Europe.[54] German and English Jews still formed the aristocracy of the community through their superior economic attainments and cultural adaptation; but the ascendant influence in matters of social ideology, religious orientation, and Jewish ethnic preservation clearly had passed to their brethren from Eastern Europe.

The progress of the colonies

The efforts of the agricultural colonists to create a new Zion in Argentina dominates the early history of the modern Jewish community. As late as the 1920s, when nearly four out of five Jews lived in an urban center, the resources of the ICA and the extensive organizational networks of the colonies gave the rural centers importance beyond their numbers.

The Zion these settlers desired to build stressed the cultivation of wheat rather than of Judaism. This was partly the consequence of encountering harsh frontier conditions that preoccupied the early colonists. Yet these early priorities soon congealed into a fixed pattern of development that characterized the colonies for decades after.

The colonists adjusted rapidly and with great success to Argentine ways, especially considering the immense difficulties that early beset them. Their two most urgent tasks were to establish good working relations with the native *gauchos* nearby and to overcome their generally scant knowledge of farming and of Argentine agriculture in particular.

The ICA bears responsibility for some of the most unfortunate errors in farming. It showed poor judgment in hiring agricultural "technicians" who lacked the slightest familiarity with Argentine soil and climactic limitations. The Argentine historian Gregorio Vertibsky notes that the ICA's chief agricultural adviser in Argentina was a French Jew whose expertise had been limited to viticulture, even though the Jews in the colonies were attempting to raise wheat, the basic crop in the interior.[55]

The scarcity of land added a further grueling dimension to the settlers' hard lives and reached extreme levels as immigration surged. Lázaro Liacho, a famed Jewish writer and the child of colonists, recalled how the need for space compelled his future parents to marry each other solely for reasons of living room:

My father was a bachelor not yet eighteen. He was obliged to find a fiancée immediately, to marry her without loss of time, in order to conserve the property of the field and clear the way by this means for the families of a new emigration. My mother was the only woman of marriageable age who lived in the colony. The choice was imperative. The elders gave their consent, the fiancés courted for several weeks and the wedding took place without any ostentation.[56]

These early stringencies took their toll in low crop yields, poor health, and depressed morale. Between 1889 and 1914, of the 158,167 mostly Jewish immigrants from Russia, 64,020, or over 40 percent, left their new Argentine homes, some of whom returned to their native countries.[57]

A pleasant and somewhat surprising development lightened some of the burden during these early trials. Jewish interaction with the hardened *gauchos* was generally cordial from the outset. Memoirs by colonists generally describe the neighboring *gauchos* as willing to deal with Jewish settlers as fully and fairly as with others in the provinces. A man in Buenos Aires told me:

I recall from my mother, who was then in Clara [one of the first colonies] that the *gauchos* around there would often come to her house to sample her baked bread—very good bread, as I know—and would often bring our family all sorts of things, good leather saddles, *maté* [an Argentine tea], and once even helped round up some cows that had drifted away. . . . No, from what my parents admitted, I can't say that the Jews were quite the horsemen as the native *gauchos*, but you know, my parents came from Minsk, where they had a bakery and did not go about riding horses at all till they came to Argentina, and my parents said that the *gauchos* were impressed with us at Clara. We learned quickly.

Not all was honeyed camaraderie between Jews and Christians in the interior. Alberto Gerchunoff, the celebrated Jewish colonist and author of classic paeans to Argentina as a Jewish refuge, lost his father when a *gaucho* murdered him over some trifle. Gerchunoff himself would likely have explained this barbarism as a phenomenon of frontier life, totally divorced from anti-Semitism or ethnic prejudice of any kind.

The Jews absorbed much of the distinctive Argentine flavor of this rugged frontier existence, as their folklore illustrates. Morton Winsberg writes in his history of the Jewish colonies:

Today, just as some Americans venerate many of the more infamous figures of the Far West of the United States, so Baron Hirsch has its folk hero, Shmilekl the Gaucho. Though little more than a gunman and common thief, Shmilekl added a peculiar twist to the gunman's motivations. Imbued with the revolutionary ideas of nineteenth-century Russia, he was also an anarchist, fighting for his distorted idea of social justice. Eventually, Shmilekl met his end the way he had chosen to live, shot down on the main street of the infant town of Rivera.[58]

Within the lifetimes of the original settlers, the Jewish frontier lands began to prosper. Organizational genius was decisive in overcoming the early adversities and inchoate nature of the settlements. Despite the ICA's conspicuous errors, it achieved a remarkable record for planning and innovation with the colonies. It should be noted that before the Jewish immigration, the Argentine government aided colonization in a somewhat haphazard fashion, giving virgin soil, tools, and work animals to new settlers in the interior, but providing little guidance for developing the region. The ICA immediately introduced rationalized administration of colonization based on prior planning. Its techniques proved so successful that after World War II, the Argentine government created an Institute for Colonization of the Provinces and an Agrarian National Council to reorganize its colonization system. The new institutions adopted most of the ideas that the ICA pioneered a half-century earlier.[59]

The ICA formed the new colonies based upon findings of careful studies of life in such rural outposts. The colonies were shaped longitudinally and were traversed by broad roads between two groups of modest homes, or *chacras*. Houses stood in nuclei of four, at a distance of no more than a thousand meters to the next such center of homes. The ICA system facilitated access to railroad stations and to other colonies. At the same time, the grouping in units of four reduced the isolation that had proved a terrible burden to previous settlers in the interior.

The ICA also began the practice of preparing for the new farmer a *chacra* already equipped for home life, with drinkable water, utilities, tools for work, and credit for meeting the first expenses until the colonist had the chance to reap the first harvests.

Cooperative institutions operated in some of the first Jewish colonies and were possibly the prime contribution made by these settlers to Argentine social and economic patterns. The cooperatives marked the culmination both of Jewish social ideals and organizational talent that have characterized the community throughout its history. They involved pooling community resources, sharing benefits from the produce, and aiding less fortunate colonists against the effects of natural disasters such as premature rainfall, which could ruin an entire harvest.

The first Jewish cooperative in Argentina was founded in the colony of Lucienville at Basavilbaso, Entre Ríos, in 1900. Its aims were to provide members with tools and goods, to market products jointly, and to procure credit to facilitate production.

Jewish colonists formed two of the next three Argentine cooperatives: one in Clara in 1904 and the other, four years later, in the famous colony of Moisésville. Soon, Jewish cooperatives appeared throughout the agricultural communities and even in Buenos Aires, where manufacturers and peddlers found them an excellent means of obtaining credit for business operations.

The cooperatives formed the backbone of the Jewish colonies. They enabled bulk purchases of seeds and equipment at wholesale rates and insured against bad years for individual colonists. In the early years, the security afforded by cooperatives staved off disintegration in the wake of many setbacks.

After a decade of settlement, the Jewish farmers overcame much of their earlier inexperience in agriculture and began to increase their productivity by great strides. A half-century later, by the late 1940s, the Jewish colonies were producing 12 million pesos worth of goods annually (2.8 million dollars), 5 million of which were in grain products alone. Twelve cooperatives, united in a central agency called the Fraternidad Agraria, handled market transactions and distributed both equipment and earnings. Ten credit centers advanced money and tools to needy colonists. Other cooperatives in the settlement included six creameries, two cheesemaking plants, five butcher shops, and one bakery.[60]

The initial inexperience with Argentine soil and climate became an asset by fostering imaginative experimentation. The Jews introduced crop diversification into Argentine farming. At Moisésville an administrator named Kohn alternated alfalfa cultivation, milk production, livestock breeding, and cereal-grain planting, setting a trend away from monocultivation. The new methods were highly successful, and other colonies soon copied them, with variations. In Entre Ríos, where most Jewish farmers lived, colonists ceased to specialize in cereals and turned their efforts as well to livestock, milk, sorghum for forage, and the harvesting of seeds. In Médanos, the colonists added a new and popular product, garlic; and in the small colony of the Río Negro, south of Buenos Aires (independent of the ICA), farmers grew such seed-fruits as apples, pears, and grapes. Farmers in Buenos Aires Province produced cereals like wheat and rye, but also sold milk products such as cheese, and forage grains like alfalfa.

The Jews also introduced major agricultural commodities into Argentina. The most notable is the sunflower seed, first grown in the colony Mauricio (named after Baron Maurice de Hirsch), in the province of Carlos Casares. In 1934, that colony held 33,000 of the 35,000 hectares in the entire republic used for cultivation of this product. Since then, the sunflower seed has become the principal source of edible oil in the nation and has also become a major export item, helping maintain Argentina's balance of trade. By 1960, some two million hectares of Argentine farmland were devoted to cultivating sunflower seeds.[61]

The paradox of the Jewish colonies is that their struggle for survival succeeded beyond expectations, measured in agricultural

productivity and elevated living standards, but this was accompanied by accelerated population declines and the disappearance of the Judaic characteristics. The colonies' efforts at adaptation have blurred with the process of full assimilation and participation in a wider national trend toward urbanization.

Living standards are presently higher than ever for the colonists. Mechanization has imparted an easier life-style, and standards of food, clothing, and shelter are above average. The colonists now purchase most of their food, except for milk, eggs, fowl, and some vegetables. Abundant servings of meat characterize both lunch and dinner meals. Clothing varies for work and social life and is of good quality. Like the *criollos* of the interior, many have colorful long shawls and belts and other leather apparel.

The *chacras* are reasonably spacious, and with the exodus of so many farmers to the cities, there is no longer the once-severe problem of adequate farmland for individual families. The *chacras* are fairly uniform, though they vary to some degree with family size and economic means. Most contain at least three rooms, with basic comforts and pure drinking water obtained from deep springs.

Despite the collective economic success of the colonies, the postwar decades have also realized a very different trend, an exodus of colonists to the cities. In this, the Jews are merely part, though a disproportionately large part, of a national shift away from the rural interior and into the urban centers.

This urbanizing trend during the 1940s and 1950s was spurred by then President Juan Perón, who gave protective tariffs to manufacturers while artificially lowering agricultural prices in order to propel industrialization. Farmers, desperate, began deserting their lands to find work as city laborers in recognition of changing market conditions. In the Jewish colonies, young men were especially quick to leave, so that the remaining population was increasingly upper-middle-aged adults and children too young to break away from their rural setting.

The mode of life even for those who remain on the farms has become detached from a fully rural existence. The typical Jewish farmer is one who works in the *chacra* but no longer lives there. Rather, he dwells in a nearby village, which has more of the modern comforts of both culture and technology. The increased availability of cars and trucks makes such commuting possible. There are

also many Jews who no longer take an active interest in their farms but who merely rent them to field laborers and are in all other ways divorced from rural life.

Jewish ranching enterprises highlight the trend toward vicarious farming. Livestock has much more importance for the colonies now than in the past, affording landowners over half their income. However, some of the most prosperous ranchers actually live in the cities, never see their herds even from a distance, and lack the knowledge of raising cattle on their own. According to Juan Tenembaum, a distinguished engineer for colonial planning, these Jewish ranchers seldom enter this field for commercial reasons. They are in most cases already highly successful in other businesses and do this mainly for the satisfaction of some indirect contact with rural life.[62]

Fewer than a thousand Jewish families now live in all the settlements combined. Many of those who have abandoned the land have been replaced by Christians, increasing the already tolerant atmosphere between religious groups in the interior. Historian Morton Winsberg writes that in colony Barón Hirsch, one of the earliest Jewish settlements, membership of the Centro Cultural Israelita, the town's leading club, was 15 percent Christian in 1960. The colony itself had about the same proportion of Jewish and Christian families.[63] In the majority of cases, though, when a Jewish family abandons a colony, the land is simply unused or else taken over by a nearby family. In colony Dora, for example, a settlement established in 1912 in Chaco Province (in which Moisésville is located), the total number of Jewish landowning colonists in 1960 was twelve.[64]

The isolation of rural life, the excitement of the cities, and the fact that Jews and Jewish organizations are preponderantly located in the major urban centers have contributed to the increasing movement of farmers from the interior. I spoke with an articulate young man in Córdoba who had only recently left the colony of Santa Isabel in Entre Ríos because he "became bored with the life there." I asked if he had felt any pride in working the land, adding that this seemed to have been a great motivation for many of the earlier colonists. "I have not forgotten that; don't believe that we don't remember who we are, even those with little education." His tone was not as militant as his words; after a reflective pause, he added:

My grandparents, whom I did not know personally, I'm told were idealists in everything—working the land, Socialism, they were religious, too. This is all good and my parents have these sentiments, too. I myself am a Socialist and I believe in the God of Israel, I consider myself religious. But I have not inherited their love for working the land. I am training to be a doctor here and why leave? It's a pleasant city. . . . For my parents, for their parents, there was something of Judaism in working the land, but not for me.

"So," he concluded wryly but earnestly, "I will find something of Judaism in the city." A great majority of Jews from the colonies have done just that. The colonies today prosper and remind the visitor of the roots of Argentine Jewry; but the city holds the future of the community.

Jewish Gaucho

Settlers and Carts

An Agricultural Cooperative

Group of Colonists

2 COMMUNITY

The proverb that predicts, "where there are two Jews there will soon be three synagogues," might be taken to apply to almost any aspect of Jewish organizational life in most parts of the globe. American Jewry, for example, classically illustrates the tendency among Jewish communities toward fragmentation. *Time* magazine stated in 1975 that "there are more than 300 national Jewish organizations and countless local federations and societies" in this country.[1] Abraham Duker, surveying "the problems of coordination and unity" facing American Jewry, concludes that "overall unity has thus far proved unattainable. This objective remains on the agenda of American Jewry as an item of high priority."[2]

This widespread pattern of decentralized Jewish community life admits a striking exception—the Argentine Jews. At the highest levels of group leadership, they have united to a degree unmatched by any other substantial Jewish community in the Diaspora. The nature and origin of this phenomenon are basically twofold. Federation of all important Jewish organizations resulted from the threat of anti-Semitism in forms more virulent than any encountered by American Jews. At the same time, the intensive concentration of Jewish citizens in Buenos Aires enabled an unprecedented centralization of social services and cultural activity.

57

Political evolution

The Argentine historian Jacob Shatzky writes of the first Jewish settlers, "Those immigrants had already formed a *kehillah* while still in the ship, en route to Argentina. . . . They brought with them rabbis, ritual slaughterers, and other religious functionaries; in other words all that was necessary for Jewish community life." Yet this "community" divided many times on the basis of national origin—Russian, Polish, Lithuanian, Romanian, and so forth. As waves of settlers from various European cities arrived in different neighborhoods in Buenos Aires, even local origins became the basis for new community divisions. Each successive Argentine Jewish neighborhood thus became a self-contained *kehillah* in miniature, with its own clubs, schools, synagogues, youth groups, and so on, as in Villa Crespo, Flores, Mataderos, Barracas, and other districts in the capital and provinces.[3]

The proliferation of political and cultural groups with strongly differing ideals split the Argentine Jewish community still further, thus reproducing the factionalization that characterized the Jews in Russia.

Unity appealed to the diverse Jewish groups in the abstract, and there were several attempts between 1889 and 1930 to establish a central Jewish body. In the absence of an overriding motive to invest such a roof organization with real power, these movements inevitably failed.

A general assembly of Argentine Jewish leaders in 1908 approved the formation of a central organization called the Federación Israelita Argentina. Its component bodies included the mutual aid and burial society Hevra Kaddisha, the school Talmud Torah, a welfare society and its hospital, Ezra, and delegates from Zionist and labor groups. The life of this federation proved very brief—two years. But its symbolic significance was greater, for its statutes affirmed the concept of a distinct and coordinated Jewish community.[4]

Jewish leaders made a second attempt to merge their major institutions in February 1916. Once more they were obliged to accept symbolic rather than tangible progress, for internal divisions prevented effective federation. Still, the roster of organizations in attendance was impressive and indicated at least a general willingness to explore possibilities for unification. In addition to the four groups of the disbanded Federación Israelita Argentina, participating institutions included the Jewish Congregation of Buenos Aires, the Zionist Federation, the Jewish Youth Association, and diverse synagogues, schools, and library representatives. Also present were delegates from the small but growing Sephardic communities of Jewish immigrants from North Africa, the Middle East, and the Balkans. Throughout this and the succeeding decade, however, these organizations failed to coordinate their aims or fundraising efforts, preferring autonomy to strength.

The early settlers also faced the divisive menace of the Zevi Migdal, or Jewish "white slavers." These criminals entered the prostitution rackets thriving in Argentina and quickly expanded into a wealthy and powerful syndicate. Their determined efforts to join and control the respectable Argentine Jewish community were for several decades a source of conflict and shame to the *kehillah.*

Argentina during the late nineteenth century was an inviting place for the white slavers to operate. Argentine law permitted licensed brothels, and the predominance of males in all the immigrant groups ensured a dependable and growing market for the dealers' human merchandise. The lax atmosphere in which this trade flourished was most visible in the theaters, where hundreds of prostitutes nightly patrolled the balconies in search of customers. An investigator for the League of Nations reported on this practice:

These women are permitted by the management to ply their trade, and may enter without paying any admission fee. The majority of these women are of foreign birth. . . . Rarely, if ever, except in redlight prostitution districts, has the investigator—in a somewhat wide experience—seen such a varied supply of women as existed in this international market-place.[5]

Jews were latecomers to prostitution in Argentina, the French having all but monopolized this carnal trade by the late nineteenth century. The extensive network of French brothels boasted women who were commonly judged the elite of their trade by those in a position to comment. Accordingly, they drew higher prices than their native and foreign competition in Buenos Aires. Yet the bosses of the Zevi Migdal, coming from Warsaw, established themselves firmly in the New World, aided by connections in Europe and by superior business organization.

The Jewish slavers pooled their financial resources in a guild that centralized their business decisions and operations. The guild leaders conducted their enterprise in the manner of corporation executives, seeking to maximize profits in complex international transactions and responsible only to the "shareholders," who formed the membership.

The families who established the white-slaver guild in Argentina at the turn of the century also set the pattern for its continued success and expansion. The family heads were masters of finance and planning who set up a hierarchy of housekeepers, agents, commissionaires, and notaries. Under their careful supervision, capital expenditures went into acquisitions of property and also for loans enabling agents to obtain women from Europe. They also reinvested much of the guild's profits in bribes to police chiefs and other officials, to insure that operations remained free from government interference. Over the decades, the guild continued to enjoy the most capable leadership, especially in deflecting opposition to its activities. An investigator of the guild in 1927 acknowledged that its leader was a formidable adversary and added, "In devising ways and means to evade the regulations and outwit the officials, he shows flashes of genius."[6]

The Jewish slavers profited to such an extent that by 1909, of 199 licensed brothels in Buenos Aires, 102 (51 percent) were run by Jewish madams, often wives of the slavers. The percentage of Jewish prostitutes was probably much higher, considering the great number who were underage for licensing or who were simply kidnapped and exploited secretively.[7]

The slavers used many ways to obtain their attractive prisoners. Their agents would often write to young women in Russia, Poland, and Romania, telling them that either husbands or "employment" awaited them in Argentina. The agents would even pay their passage across the Atlantic to Buenos Aires. These unsuspecting women would make the trip only to be met by thugs who abducted them to houses of prostitution.

The slavers preferred to induce their women to participate voluntarily in the brothels and some did. In many of these cases, they had already been seduced by agents while in Europe and were persuaded afterwards to join the brothels. Some agents would even marry their intended victims in order to gain their confidence and provide a cover of legitimacy for their business. The slavers had no scruples about resorting to force, however. If a woman refused to work in a brothel, the slavers and their agents would most likely rape her. Aside from the physical intimidation and the trauma, the loss of virginity would often suffice to end the woman's will to offer further resistance against her captors. The woman generally felt ruined after such an experience and would numbly adjust to life imprisoned in the slavers' brothels.

Surprisingly, and to the infinite dismay of other Argentine Jews, the slavers from Warsaw also identified themselves as Jews and wanted to be so recognized by the main *kehillah*. As early as the 1890s, even before the formation of a separate slavers' guild, these criminals pressured the central Jewish community for membership in the Hevra Kaddisha and the right to be buried in the Jewish cemetery. In return, the slavers offered protection and aid to the common Jewish citizen.

It was no simple matter for the *kehillah*'s leaders to brush aside these demands as immoral. The slavers' control of many police and government officials and their economic influence in the Jewish community gave them considerable leverage in pressing their case. The slavers made donations to the community to ingratiate themselves with leaders and ordinary citizens. They also controlled a large interest in the Yiddish theater, subsidizing many of its productions while using women to "win over" individuals in the audience during intermission.

Some leaders in the *kehillah*'s debates over the status of the slavers argued that they might be made unofficial members who could still be buried in a Jewish cemetery. The small contingent of Jews from Morocco, taking a more lenient view of burial than the more numerous Jewish groups from Eastern and Western Europe, actually sided with the slavers' demands. This is particularly curious because the Moroccan Jews were in no way involved in the slave trade and considered it a disgrace; the slavers were exclusively Polish and Russian. Yet the practical Moroccans held to the maxim, "Of the dead, say nothing but good," and argued also that without the contributions of the affluent slavers there might not be *any* burial field to dispute.[8]

61

Despite these pleas for moderation, the community emphatically rejected the slavers' demands. Rabbi Reuben Hacohen Sinai helped to sway the course of these debates with a forceful sermon against the slavers. He declared that "in case the *temeyim* [unclean elements] were accepted into the sacred field, he would write in his testament that after his death he should be interred in the municipal cemetery. 'I prefer to lie among honorable gentiles than among our *temeyim.*' "9

The *kehillah*'s formal ostracism of the slavers led them to form a separate society that not only handled all business arrangements but attempted to maintain a full Jewish identity. In a grim parody of Jewish concern for social welfare and communal responsibility, the new guild paralleled the institutions of the legitimate Jewish community by establishing a burial society and a synagogue. As a final travesty, the slavers called themselves the Warsaw Society for Mutual Assistance and Burial Rights.

The Warsaw Society's public identification as a Jewish group spurred some elements in the *kehillah* to attempt to uproot the *temeyim* altogether. Most such efforts centered around the Jewish Association for the Protection of Girls and Women (JAPGW). This London-based organization set up a branch in Argentina in 1901 with the cooperation of Henry Joseph and a new rabbi, Samuel Halphon. The group worked to undermine the slavers' operations by intercepting agents at the harbors and by rescuing girls already transported to the brothels.

The efforts of the JAPGW had some positive effects. Often their members were able to prevent harm by exposing traffickers escorting women just arrived in Buenos Aires from Europe. In one typical year (1922), such intervention saved 120 women from a life of forced prostitution. A report by the JAPGW on activities in that year notes, for example, the case of a sixteen-year-old girl, coming from Eastern Europe to Buenos Aires where she had just disembarked:

[She] was met by an aunt, who seemed suspicious to the dock officer. He therefore prevented the woman from taking the girl away until enquiries had been made. These enquiries led to the fact that the aunt was a brothel keeper and that her sister was keeping another brothel. The aunt was therefore arrested, and she confessed that she had brought the girl to

Buenos Aires by means of false documents, she being still under age. The young girl was removed from her aunt and has been placed with respectable relatives in the town.[10]

The JAPGW also saved those fortunate enough to smuggle out of the brothels a sign of their place of captivity. One such case involved a woman, who after two months in Argentina entered a brothel at her husband's insistence in order to avoid being beaten by him. She succeeded in sending a letter to her parents in Europe which said in part, "I have heard that somewhere there is a Jewish society which seeks to save unhappy women like me . . ." An extensive search by the JAPGW eventually traced her to a provincial brothel, and soon after she was rescued by police.[11]

The JAPGW activities, despite numerous individual successes, failed to break up the vice rings themselves. The maze of corruption was so extensive and complex as to defy penetration. Prostitutes, whether or not they willingly entered their work, showed extreme reluctance to testify against their keepers, fearing reprisals by the agents of the guild. On the occasions when some spoke out against a slaver, the courts—often under the influence of the slavers' guild—seldom enforced the law to its full extent. Records of JAPGW reports abound in phrases like, "through influence, the case was transferred to another judge, and the man liberated."[12]

The obstacles faced by the JAPGW are most evident in the results of their denunciation of the Warsaw Society to the Inspector of Legally Recognized Societies in Avelleneda, the suburb of Buenos Aires where the slavers owned their cemetery. The inspector, doubtless deriving his legal opinion from the pesos he received from the slavers, solemnly declared that "all the members of the society were respectable people," and concluded that no action could be taken. The JAPGW had to accept an empty victory when, in conjunction with pressure from the Polish Ministry, they persuaded officials to require that the slavers stop calling themselves the Warsaw Society. The slavers thereupon renamed their guild Zevi Migdal, after its founder, and went on happily collecting huge profits, undisturbed by government officials.[13]

Vigilante actions proved to be the most effective Jewish response to the slavers' operations. These raids on brothels in the

Jewish quarter of Buenos Aires parallel the mass actions in England and America in earlier centuries, where outraged citizens acted in lieu of negligent authorities to cleanse their neighborhoods of a detested element. The Yiddish writer Leib Malick described this unofficial but powerful protest:

The time soon came when war was literally waged. Blood ran in the streets. Jewish workmen armed themselves with clubs and iron pipes, and invaded the brothel quarters, determined to drive their debased brethren by force from the city or at least from the Jewish community. The war was carried on in the streets, in the cafes, in the theatres, until finally the Jewish section at least could be said to be cleansed, made fit for honest Jews to come build, to work, to live in a Jewish manner.[14]

Even these mob actions gained only a local victory. The Zevi Migdal was invulnerable while large elements of the police and judiciary favored the slavers, a relationship between law enforcers and criminals by no means peculiar to Argentine society. Moreover, the slavers adjusted their tactics so as to defuse pressure against the guild. An investigator wrote in 1925 that the JAPGW's work resulted in new subtleties by the dealers:

They know the danger of introducing innocent girls of minor age into a country for immoral purposes, and so they begin their nefarious work of seduction in Europe and generally in the girl's native country. The progress towards becoming a prostitute does not take very long. Once this has occurred, it is very easy to "trade" with her for oversea [sic] countries.[15]

The year 1930 marked a turning point in the fortunes of the Zevi Migdal with the case of Rachel Lieberman. Lieberman had worked in a brothel against her will since arriving in Argentina from her native Poland in 1924. She managed to leave after four years and, like most other women in her position, preferred to maintain silence about her past treatment. Lieberman invested her modest savings in an art shop and began a new and successful life. Her business netted an accumulated profit of some 90,000 pesos, and during this time she married a seemingly sympathetic man, Solomón Jose Korn, in a religious ceremony in Buenos Aires. Korn then suddenly revealed himself to be one of the leading slavers in the Zevi Migdal, robbed her of all her belongings, and threatened her with violence if she did not return to work in the brothels. This time, though, Rachel Lieberman decided to fight back, and she managed to inform the police of Korn's threats.

Lieberman's testimony against the Zevi Migdal was an invaluable aid to the federal police officer, Julio Alsogaray, who had long tried to break the vice rings in Buenos Aires without success. His investigation of Lieberman's charges reached all the key figures in the slavers' operations, with some help by the JAPGW in tracing the location of certain criminals. Alsogaray's staff issued 424 warrants against members of the Zevi Migdal and followed this with a series of raids and arrests.[16]

The judge, Manuel Rodríguez Ocampo, processed these cases as zealously as Alsogaray pursued his investigations. Sentencing the slavers severely, Judge Ocampo also made a point of explicitly exonerating the Jewish community of any blame for the actions of the Zevi Migdal's few hundred members. He added that the roots of the white slave trade traced to the leniency of Argentine laws on brothels, the corruption of many police officers, and careless immigration screenings.[17]

The Zevi Migdal had a brief last laugh at Judge Ocampo's expense. The traffickers still possessed enough influence to escape legal punishment. Shortly after Ocampo's judgment, the Appeals Court overruled him, claiming that the evidence did not show that the Zevi Migdal society per se acted against the morality of the state. It ordered all prisoners immediately released.

For Alsogaray, who had long seen his efforts as "the struggle of a Lilliputian against Hercules," the news of this travesty of justice brought the most bitter pain. The slavers hastened to alert Alsogaray of their escape in order to demoralize him. They hoped, as Alsogaray later recalled, that

I would abandon my persistent initiative because, in the last analysis, it would do them no harm. But in spite of such circumstances, I used all means to defeat them in their own fortress, defended by money from pandering and by the collaboration of servile and unworthy officials. Against all the painful setbacks, I continued to believe in the sanctity of the laws and in the good character of a few men![18]

This unshakable will to continue the campaign against the slave trade brought Alsogaray his long awaited—and lasting—success. The slavers' operations were already in a shambles after the efficient raids Alsogaray and his special staff had conducted. His relentless efforts, even after the release of the slavers, insured that their operations would not safely revive as they had done so often in the past.

The coup d'etat in 1930 by General José Felix Uriburu also brought vital conservative support to the campaign to obliterate the white slave trade. Although many government officials in the early 1930s continued to appall Alsogaray by their venality, the more puritanical atmosphere of the nation under Uriburu's moralistic rule helped to curtail the trade in women. In addition, the heavy restrictions on immigration imposed by the new government had the important side effect of drastically restricting the slavers' operations between Europe and America. By the early 1930s, the last slave dealers left the country and the Jewish community was rid of its worst internal menace.

Lesser divisive influences still existed among Argentine Jews but a new threat, from outside the community, provided a dominant unifying force. If the new wave of conservatism deserves some credit for eliminating the slavers, the remedy soon proved far more pernicious than the disease, so far as the Jews were concerned. Fascism, having already poisoned much of European society, swept across Argentina during the thirties, in reaction to the vacillating, corrupt, and discredited liberal governments of the previous decades. Many sectors, but Jews above all, suffered from the consequent atmosphere of repression and intimidation. From necessity, the Jews finally transcended the pattern of tentative institutional alignment and subsequent breakup, and coalesced during the dark era of the 1930s into a single federated community.

The anti-Semitism in this period was largely an exacerbation of a general anti-immigrant sentiment among controlling groups in the government. Uriburu held the support of the most conservative elements in the society, and he was intent to purge not only the civilian president elected in 1928, the aging Hipólito Yrigoyen, but also to curb Yrigoyen's modest efforts to help integrate all immigrants into the society. During periods of prosperity this liberal sentiment enjoyed wide favor, but the depression gave new force to the resentments of established *criollos*. Uriburu expressed the new conservatism by reducing immigration and creating stricter barriers against naturalization of foreigners already living in Argentina. Under Uriburu and his successors, the Special Section of elite police officers, designed to combat internal threats, turned so anti-Semitic that the German population in Argentina, in sympathy with the Nazi movement in their native land, contributed funds to the organization. The German embassy also directly aided the Special Section.

Because outbreaks against Jews were common and unpunished during the thirties, Jews created their own defense operations. The Jewish Communists were the first to act, forming the People's Organization Against Anti-Semitism in 1933. That same year the Committee Against the Persecution of the Jews in Germany was formed to oppose Nazi influence abroad, and the following year, the Committee Against Anti-Semitism and Racism combated fascism in Argentina.

The Delegación de Asociaciones Israelitas Argentinas (DAIA) evolved from the Committee Against Anti-Semitism and Racism to become the prime organ for Jewish self-defense in Argentina. Twenty-eight organizations joined the DAIA in 1936 when it was founded, counting every major Jewish group except those with Communist and Anarchist affiliation. DAIA's propaganda efforts countered Nazi charges and attempted to tie anti-Semitism to elements undermining Argentine democracy, the church, and society in general. The DAIA met with government officials and also organized self-defense programs similar to those of the Jewish Defense League in the United States.[19]

The DAIA experienced sharp vicissitudes in its anti-Nazi campaigns. During the 1930s its lobbying efforts bore limited results because the government was sympathetic to Nazi groups. Only when the Argentine government discovered evidence of Nazi subversion in 1939 did it retaliate by passing a law against all German nationals. The DAIA's influence in the passage of this legislation could not have been significant, because the law comprehended even Jewish refugees from Germany, some of whom were officials in Jewish institutions.[20]

The DAIA's direct battles with anti-Semitic groups did rather more for the organization's prestige than its lobbying activities. Jewish defense volunteers won individual skirmishes against Nazi thugs who assaulted Jewish buildings and assemblies. The DAIA's direction of these salutary demonstrations of Jewish will was perhaps its most useful service toward securing Jewish rights in this decade.

The unifying influences of the 1930s left an enduring legacy. Ever since that time, the DAIA has been the single major spokesman for all organized Jewry. Its role was challenged during the presidency of Juan Perón (1946–55) when the Argentine leader formed a rival, puppet organization of Jewish officials, Organización Israelita Argentina (OIA). This group, however, achieved neither widespread support from the community nor a way to perpetuate itself after Perón was deposed. The DAIA, on the other hand, always retained the loyalty of the vast majority of Jewish organizations. Today, most important religious, social, and political Jewish groups from Buenos Aires and from the communities of the interior attend the DAIA's councils.

How effectively has the modern DAIA defended Jewish rights? Observers disagree, and the verdict appears checkered according to different areas of activity. Certainly it has been aggressive on behalf of Jews in foreign lands, and especially the people of Israel. The DAIA organizes frequent demonstrations in support of the Jewish State, with marchers participating in all areas of Argentina. The DAIA also has taken strong stands against anti-Semitism elsewhere, most notably during the vicious Prague trials in 1952. In these courts of injustice, Soviet leaders ordered many Czechoslovakian officials branded as traitors, and Jews figured in extremely high proportion among those executed by Stalin's henchmen. Despite strong dissent within the DAIA against denunciation of Communist actions, the DAIA's leadership vigorously condemned the Soviet government. Eight leftist organizations seceded from the DAIA rather than join in the censure, but the DAIA held firm even at the cost of this schism.

The DAIA's record in checking internal anti-Semitism is more controversial. The leadership tends toward extreme caution in responding to provocations, beyond petitioning and circulating leaflets among the Argentine people. The strongest actions by the DAIA to draw attention to anti-Semitic campaigns have been boycotts, but these are tried only on the rarest occasions and in the most limited way. Generally, these have come as requests to close shops an hour early. The DAIA shuns any real confrontation with the

Argentine government, but rather acts—with some justification—as if disturbing the powerful elements in Argentine society might create unknown consequences more harmful than beneficial.

The DAIA's concern with institutional self-preservation partially offsets its potential economic and political leverage. Although it encompasses every major Jewish group in Argentina and is therefore, at least on paper, an influential organization, its conservatism precludes development of a serious impact upon government officials.[21]

For all its limitations, the DAIA commands wide respect among Argentine Jews for its dedicated and even energetic leadership within the sphere of activity it pursues. The Israeli scholar Haim Avni agrees with the high popular opinion of the DAIA in his evaluation of its long history:

The DAIA has been in existence for thirty-six years, and is by now able to claim some considerable achievements, of which the first and most important is indeed its very existence. This fact is all the more striking if it is remembered that its principal function has been and still remains its political activity with the Argentine generally and amongst the Jews, during a stormy and unstable period.[22]

Ultimately, anti-Semitism in Argentina can be eradicated only by a truly national commitment. The DAIA can be one important element in the struggle against prejudice, but it needs firmer allies if it is to succeed. That the DAIA has unified all Argentine Jewry behind this effort is an impressive accomplishment, but whether it has used that unity to fullest advantage in the face of continual anti-Semitic outrages is less clear. This may be the central task of the *kehillah*'s political activity in the coming years—to build upon the unity forged by the DAIA and to assume a more aggressive orientation in defense of Jewish rights.

Social organization

Argentine Jewry's centralized communal structure reflects the change from a largely rural and dispersed community in the interior to an urbanized and densely concentrated population.[23] For the first few decades of settlement, there were two main centers of Jewry in Argentina: one in the capital city and the other in the loose network of colonies formed by the ICA and other groups. Because of the administrative and financial power of the ICA, the colonies remained the primary locus of Jewish activity even into the 1920s, despite the fact that most Jews then lived in the capital. During the 1930s, however, this balance began to yield. The proportion of Jews in the agricultural villages declined from 22 percent in 1920 to only 11 percent by 1935.[24]

Even in absolute figures, the colonies were losing their importance in Jewish life. The colonization efforts peaked in 1927, when the combined Jewish population of the colonies totaled 33,084. During this time, Argentina enjoyed agricultural prosperity, and immigration from Eastern Europe was at its height. After 1927, Jewish immigration shrank, as the Argentine government imposed stricter limitations. Within Argentina itself, Jews formed part of a wider migration from the rural areas to the city. As a result, except for the years 1934 to 1940 when German Jewish refugees settled in several interior colonies, the population of the colonies declined continuously from the middle twenties.[25]

The consolidation of Jewish life in the urban centers accelerated with the withdrawal of the ICA from Jewish communal affairs. The ICA had been the dominant institution of Argentine Jewry for some forty years. The desperate problems of the Jews in Europe and Palestine, however, led the ICA to concentrate its funds in those areas and to relinquish its administrative functions in Argentine Jewish life. Leadership passed almost by default to the Jewish urban organizations and especially to those in Buenos Aires.

By 1936, of approximately 120,000 Jews in Buenos Aires, over 60 percent were foreign born. These immigrants came from many countries, but the Slavic elements from Russia and Poland overwhelmingly predominated. (See Table 1.)

No new demographic trends have affected Argentine Jewry since the 1930s. The tightening of Argentine immigration laws and the Holocaust in Eastern Europe virtually eliminated further Jewish settlement in Argentina. There has actually been a heightened shift away from the colonies and into the urban centers. A corresponding trend in economic life has resulted in the growth of a strong Jewish business and professional class. Many of the members of this skilled and affluent middle class have their roots in the rural centers

Table 1: Population of Buenos Aires, 1936

Foreign Born Country of Origin	Jews
Russia	31,172
Poland	23,171
Romania	5,175
Syria-Lebanon	3,408
Turkey	2,978
Germany	1,376
Austria	1,092
Lithuania	1,056
Hungary	499
Italy	330
Other Europe	1,662
Other Asia	491
Other Africa	419
Other Remainder	739
TOTAL	73,588

SOURCE: Adapted from *Municipalidad de la ciudad de Buenos Aires: cuarto censo general, poblacíon,* October 22, 1936.

that flourished earlier. These rapid changes have led Argentine Jews to refer to their experience of "sowing wheat and reaping doctors."

Today, greater Buenos Aires, including the Federal Capital and its suburbs, contains 70 percent of the Argentine Jewish population (compared with only 40 percent of the general population), about 350,000 Jews. Rosario, the second largest Argentine city, also has the second greatest Jewish settlement (15,000), followed by Córdoba (10,000), and Santa Fe and La Plata (6,000 each).[26]

The above distribution of Jews has led to an organic relationship among the 140 Argentine Jewish communities, united by the common locus of leadership, funding, and manpower in the *kehillah* of the Federal Capital and its environs. The hegemony of this Jewish community in Buenos Aires rather than the process of urbanization per se has been responsible for the centralization of Argentine Jewish institutions.

A comparison with the American Jewish community may reveal the distinctive Argentine situation more vividly. A recent study showed that over 96 percent of American Jews live in cities, compared with less than two-thirds of the larger American population.[27] Yet the American Jewish community is far less centralized than the Argentine *kehillah,* with many more autonomous and varied groups and a much wider geographic distribution of institutional activity.

The above differences between the two communities relate at least in part to their dissimilar demographic distributions. New York City, for example, contains more than five times the number of Jews in all Argentina, but still accounts for only about 40 percent of the American Jewish community. The entire Middle Atlantic region holds little more than half of all the Jews in the United States.[28] There is, in short, nothing to compare with the clustering of Argentine Jews in the Buenos Aires metropolitan area and the location of almost every major roof organization on a single block in Plaza Once.

The primary implication of centralization within the *kehillah* is an added emphasis on unified action along lines conceived by more traditional leaders, at the expense of a greater diversity in Jewish activism. Greater organizational stability has been achieved at some cost in vitality along a periphery, both geographic and intellectual.

This sense of organizational stability emerges most clearly in the remarkable tradition of leadership in the *kehillah.* At the same time that geographic and institutional realignments have greatly altered the structure of the Jewish community, the character of its directing bodies has remained largely unchanged for many decades. Almost all officials of the divers institutions are strongly Zionist. Leftist politics, including socialism, also distinguishes the leadership, though the main Jewish organizations exclude Communists, in part to appease the Argentine government. Another common denominator is language; almost every leader of consequence among Jews from Eastern Europe speaks and writes some Yiddish.

The directors of the *kehillah* tend to combine community service with a successful career in business or some profession. It is, of course, natural that community officials are chosen from among more successful members. A more practical consideration, though, is the long tradition by which leaders in the *kehillah* serve without salary. A combination of noblesse oblige and a powerful ethic of communal solidarity underlies this practice and necessitates that these persons simultaneously earn a livelihood in some field outside their Judaic work.

The Argentine Jewish ideal of community leadership is perhaps best represented by a physician named Noé Yarcho, who lived among the earliest colonists of Entre Ríos and who still thrives in Jewish and non-Jewish legends.[29]

Yarcho displayed during his younger years in Russia those qualities of philanthropic concern and professional achievement that later brought him praise in Argentina. He was graduated from the University of the Ukraine at age twenty-three, receiving a gold medal for the finest thesis among more than a thousand submitted. Characteristically, Yarcho sold his prize in order to aid poor companions at the university. During the height of a cholera epidemic, accompanied by rumors that Jews had somehow caused this affliction, Yarcho ministered to stricken Ukrainian peasants, who were unaware of his Jewish identity.

Yarcho's most fortunate ministry was as tutor to the children of the wealthy Jewish family, the Sajaroffs, who employed Yarcho's father as their accountant. As so often in his life, Noé exceeded the call of his responsibilities, but this time by befriending the Sajaroff's son, Miguel, and marrying their attractive daughter, María. All three later embarked for Entre Ríos, joining the first settlers of the colony Clara.

Yarcho's activism spanned a broad range of commitments. He was a fervent Zionist and belonged to several of the Jewish organizations in Entre Ríos. His concern for the welfare of the colonists led him to embrace another area of Jewish enterprise as well. With his brother-in-law Miguel and with Isaac Kaplan, he founded one of the first Jewish cooperative societies in Argentina, at the colony Clara.

Yarcho's richly deserved hagiographies were more concerned with quite another facet of his life—his devotion to medicine. Upon arriving in colony Clara, Yarcho was horrified at the severe overcrowding in the region's primitive hospitals, resulting in unhygienic conditions and the rejection of many seriously ill patients who had to be returned to their farms. Yarcho became a peripatetic healer in Entre Ríos to compensate for the shortage of physicians, and the inhabitants soon came to look upon him as a savior. The writer Alberto Gerchunoff immortalized Yarcho's memory in an affectionate short story entitled, "The Miraculous Doctor," whom Jewish and non-Jewish settlers alike revered for "his remarkable ability, his benevolent skill, his stories, and his smile."[30]

The leadership of the *kehillah* still reflects the values of Zionism, social concern, and professional achievement that Yarcho exemplified. Mario Steingart, for example, was a leader in this tradition until his death in 1970 at the age of seventy-seven. He was president of the Argentine B'nai B'rith and later headed the Argentine Jewish Institute of Culture and Information during the 1960s. He also participated on the board of governors of the Hebrew University in Jerusalem. At the same time, Steingart was known as one of the foremost endocrinologists in the nation. He founded and directed the Center of Diagnostic Endocrinology, in which he also conducted research. One of his medical treatises won a national science prize.

Another outstanding spokesman for the *kehillah*, Dr. Moisés Goldman, was long active in the major community organizations. He recalls with great nostalgia his early life in Moisésville, where his parents were among the original colonists. Goldman left the colony to study chemistry in Córdoba and worked as a physician throughout his years of community service. Now in his seventies, Goldman still maintains his medical practice in a modest office on the Calle Larea in Buenos Aires.

Businessmen also play important roles in community life, as is exemplified by the Mirelman family. During the early twentieth century, the Mirelmans developed a single silk-weaving factory into a large and successful textile firm. Since then, they have aided almost every kind of Jewish philanthropy, while several of the Mirelman brothers have been active in a number of Argentine Jewish organizations.

The Mirelmans' commitment to Jewish causes typifies the generally greater cohesion of the Jewish community compared with many other immigrant groups in Argentina, including the large Italian population. This is clearly seen, for example, in the life of the Italian immigrant, Torcuato Di Tella, who by the 1940s had

74

become the nation's leading entrepreneur and whose company, Sociedad Industrial Americana de Maquinarias, still spearheads Argentine industrial progress.[31] Di Tella, a farsighted and compassionate man, devised many social welfare plans for his employees. He also placed many members of his family in positions of corporate responsibility. Yet despite Di Tella's keen awareness of his immigrant roots and his philanthropic nature, he gave little time or money to the Italian community as such. This may be because the Italians in Argentina were more numerous, more geographically diffuse, and better accepted socially than the Jews. Di Tella's behavior also reflects a tendency among Italian immigrants in Argentina to emphasize family responsibilities but not such intense community ties as characterize the Jewish population.

The primary social organization of the Argentine Jews is called the Asociación Mutual Israelita Argentina (AMIA). It operates in Buenos Aires and is the hub around which revolve most of the Jewish communal activities in the capital, its suburbs, and the interior communities.

The AMIA evolved from the original Hevra Kaddisha, or burial society, founded in 1894 through the initiative of Henry Joseph. The exceptional concern for social welfare among the immigrants from Eastern Europe led the Hevra Kaddisha steadily to expand its services during the early twentieth century. It gradually became the central institution for coordinating or subsidizing a great variety of philanthropic, educational, and other programs. In 1940, the Hevra Kaddisha officially assumed the name AMIA, in recognition of its broadening involvement in the activities of the *kehillah*. Nevertheless, the cemeteries remained of central importance in the AMIA, providing through funeral fees a critical percentage of the organization's operating funds.

Who are among the AMIA's 50,000 members? The most striking feature of this group is the high percentage of foreign-born and first-generation Argentines. Less than 6 percent of the affiliates in 1970 were Argentines of the second generation, that is, whose parents were native-born Argentine. Of those born in Europe, six of seven are of Slavic origin. Table 2 shows the composition of the AMIA by national origins.

The Jews in the AMIA have been uncertain to what extent their community should strive to include Jews who are not of East

Table 2: National Status of AMIA Affiliates, 1970

Category	Percent Representation
Argentines (second generation)	5.3
Argentines (first generation)	44.4
Europeans of Slavic origins	43.4
Europeans of German, Austrian, and Hungarian origins	6.9
	100.0

SOURCE: "The Organized Jewish Community of Buenos Aires—A.M.I.A.," preliminary report by Teresa Kaplanski de Caryevschi of a research project undertaken by the AMIA Institute for Social Research in May 1970, *Dispersion and Unity,* no. 11 (1970), p. 153.

European background. Perhaps more than 20 percent of Argentina's Jewish population is of Central European, Sephardic (Spanish), or Oriental origin. Many German-speaking Jews came during the 1930s and created their own cultural institutions. The Sephardic and Oriental Jews have created a number of distinct organizational structures based on their specific national origins. The AMIA's leaders have made some overtures to these minority groups within Argentine Jewry but thus far have been to little effect. Often, these attempts to broaden the AMIA's appeal have been essentially symbolic gestures. In 1949, for example, the AMIA took the name The Ashkenazic Community of Buenos Aires to suggest a unity of all Ashkenazim, or Jews whose ancestry traces to Central and Eastern Europe. Yet this induced few Jews of Germanic descent to join the AMIA, while the title Ashkenazic added one more barrier between the East European and the Sephardic and Oriental Jewish communities. During the 1960s, in recognition of these facts, the AMIA quietly removed the word *Ashkenazic* from its official title.

The limited moves toward expanding the AMIA's constituency reflect a painful dilemma. On the one hand, the leaders of the AMIA want to include as many Jews as possible in their organization in order to raise additional funds, coordinate activities more fully, and establish a unified and efficient structure of Jewish communal groups. Yet the same leaders have retained Yiddish as the AMIA's official language, although Sephardic Jews do not understand it. In many other respects as well, the AMIA preserves its Ashkenazic—and especially East European—customs and orientation. In short, the desire to nourish a specifically Yiddish–East European culture runs even deeper than the urge to unify. This has effectively precluded a merger of the Ashkenazic and Sephardic institutions and, to a lesser extent, of the East and West European Ashkenazic groups.

The AMIA membership tends to be nearly as homogeneous in its social and economic character as it is in its national origins. Those who join are generally of the modest middle class, with a lower proportion of university graduates and professionals than is the case for the larger Jewish population. Some 23 percent are unemployed, and if housewives are included in the calculation, the figure goes up to one-third of the total membership.[32] This reflects in part the advanced age of the AMIA affiliates. More than 70 percent are over fifty years old, while nearly half the members are at least sixty, as shown in Table 3.

The fact that only heads of families may join the AMIA accounts in part for the advanced age of its membership. A more important reason, though, is that those of the older generation, with their roots embedded in the heritage of Eastern Europe, are more likely to be affiliated with the AMIA than the younger, Argentine-born Jews.

Aside from the devotion to Yiddish, a major legacy of the East European heritage may be seen in the AMIA's dedication to extensive community welfare programs. There are eighteen Jewish social

Table 3: Age Distribution of AMIA Affiliates, 1970

Members' Ages	Proportion of Total Membership (in percent)
70 or older	17
60 to 70	29
50 to 60	25
36 to 49	20
35 or younger	9
	100

SOURCE: "The Organized Jewish Community of Buenos Aires—A.M.I.A.," *Dispersion and Unity*, no. 11 (1970), p. 155.

welfare organizations in Buenos Aires alone, twelve of them founded by East European Jews and subsidized by AMIA funds. The AMIA also maintains a Department of Social Aid, which in one recent year, according to a community study, aided 1,248 petitioners, spending 50 million pesos (more than 140,000 dollars) for the unemployed, the ill, the aged, the handicapped, and other needy cases. The AMIA has a related Department of Loans without Interest, for special hardship cases. The Department awards such loans and some grants mostly to families where the father has died.[33]

Jewish centers for care of the ill and disadvantaged, supported by the AMIA, are among the finest in Argentina. The Jewish Hospital Ezra, founded by a welfare society in 1900, has long been the most advanced medical institution in the nation, and the hospital is continually expanding its facilities. In 1966, for example, the Mirelman family and several other donors gave 50,000 dollars for the installation of modern X-ray equipment. In 1969, the hospital added a Department of Prevention and Detection of Cancer, equipped with the most modern laboratories.[34]

Jewish communal care for orphaned and aged persons has set an enviable model for Argentine society. Outstanding among numerous examples is the Hogar Huérfanas Israelitas, or Jewish Orphanage for Girls, which cares for sixty persons. Kosher food and observance of Jewish holidays give the orphanage a distinctively Jewish atmosphere. The children also receive a sound Hebrew education. "We do not want the children to all go to one school, though," explained director Deborah Manassen de Lang, a woman of both refinement and obvious enthusiasm for her philanthropic work. "They go a few each to different schools so that they mingle with other children and learn to become part of the outside community." Half of the sixty girls live in homes of relatives or foster parents and receive monthly subsidies from the orphanage. The girls who live in the orphanage, a pleasant and uncrowded building set in a beautiful neighborhood of Buenos Aires called Belgrano, appear not only well adjusted but with a surer sense of their own Jewish identity than the average Jewish citizen has.

The excellent results of the Jewish-orphanage approach mirror the capabilities of its planners, in particular Señora de Lang. A descendant of the prominent Dutch Jew, Menashe Ben Ephraim, she emigrated from Holland to Argentina during the 1950s and has long been a leader in the Society of Argentine Jewish Women, a federation of ten social aid organizations. She has been especially active in working for the Orphanage, having chosen its present site and helping to plan and supervise its activities. She commented on the operation of this center, "Our most thoughtful task has always been in the choosing of personnel. We want people who not only will be competent workers and cooks, but who also love the children. All our staff is extremely dedicated to the children."[35]

Despite this very great commitment to social aid, or perhaps because of it, community-sponsored studies have subjected Jewish welfare programs to exacting standards and found many with serious deficiencies. A report to the AMIA in 1961 assailed the Jewish social aid institutions for the absence of a "professional" approach to their tasks. The report added that, just as in Eastern Europe, the concern of Jewry for aiding its less fortunate members is fragmentary. Dispensations of money, clothes, food, and other material benefits were given in piecemeal fashion, without any deeper attempts to rehabilitate individuals vocationally, educationally, or psychologically.[36]

It is true that much Jewish social aid in Argentina involves traditional *tzedakah,* or charity, rather than rehabilitation. But the community's considerable expenditures of funds for the disadvantaged have provided generously for people beyond what they would have received from other Argentine institutions, including government assistance. The harsh critique contained in the AMIA report should perhaps be viewed as one more expression of the community's desire to improve its social services, a refusal to become complacent, rather than as a sign that the community is uncaring about the plight of the needy among them. In all, the community has been remarkably faithful to the social idealism proclaimed by so many of its early settlers.

A more tenable indictment against the community involves its financial structure, linked to its funeral services and, until recently, to a wide network of cooperatives. The former method of fund-raising is arbitrary and haphazard, the latter method seriously inequitable.

The fees from burials in the past provided close to 90 percent of the community's funds. As a result, officials in the *kehillah* often try desperately to compensate for the paucity of other sources of aid

79

by charging absurdly inflated prices for funerals. It is, at best, a risky system of finance. Even when successful, the methods themselves appear somewhat dubious. For example, Grand Rabbi Guillermo Schlesinger explained to writer J.X. Cohen during the late 1930s "that occasionally there is delay in the holding of the funeral services while the Hevra Kadisha and the family work out the 'tax' problem." Cohen relates, "In one case, the interment 'donation' was 100,000 pesos, which is a lot of money for a grave even in American dollars—about $25,000 U.S.A."[37]

The method of finance through Jewish cooperatives is even more questionable. The cooperatives began as altruistic institutions, lending funds at nominal interest rates to needy members and contributing heavily to educational, social, and other Jewish organizations. With time, the cooperatives became more profit-oriented, like most other businesses. Their interest rates rose, while their subscribers remained largely those with insufficient collateral to obtain loans from regular banks. The cooperatives never forgot their sense of responsibility to the community as a whole and continued to be a financial bulwark to dozens of Jewish institutions across the nation, supplementing the contributions of the AMIA and other sources of aid. The result, however, was to make the Jewish organizations disproportionately dependent on funds "contributed" by its poorer members.

The process of inverting the relation between a member's wealth and his support for the community was gradual and of course unplanned. The community leaders themselves were upright and deeply committed to aiding the community's neediest members. But the dependence upon contributions from the cooperatives partially offset the admirable dedication of the *kehillah* to social aid. As one community official told me, "The result was to make our structure of funding unsound and unjust."

The financial panic that extended throughout the 1960s and after finally bankrupted the Jewish cooperatives. The government ordered them closed in 1972, at a time when the community was already borrowing heavily from Israel and elsewhere to sustain its basic institutions. The one cautious hope for the *kehillah* is that the collapse of the cooperatives may lead to a new system, at once more equitable and more logical, to provide communal activities with a solid and independent financial base.

Jewish Explorer Julio Popper, ca. 1880

Louis Brie, First President of the Hevra Kaddisha Ashkenazi, 1894

Isaac Kaplan, Pioneer of Cooperativism in Argentina

Noé Yarco, Famed Physician in Agricultural Colonies

Colman Saslavsky (center), Composer and Choirmaster

Berta Singerman, Actress on the Yiddish and Spanish Stages

Alberto Gerchunoff, Novelist of Jewish Immigrant Life

Jacobo Timerman, Leading Publisher and Recent Political Prisoner of the of the Argentine Junta

(Panorama, *Oct. 14, 1974*)

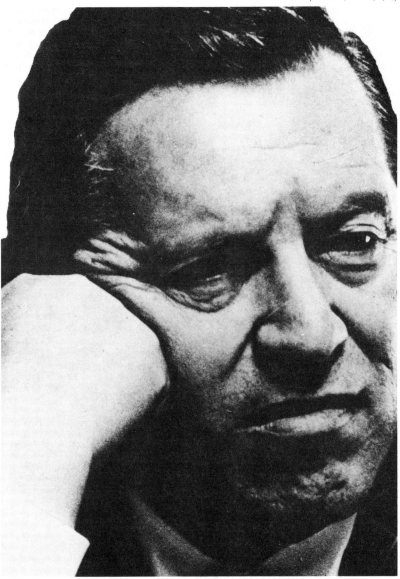

José Ber Gelbard, Finance Minister under the Late President Juan Perón

*Jacobo Kovadloff, Director of the American Jewish Committee's
South American Office*

The German Jewish community

Some 45,000 Jews of German and Austrian origin live in Argentina at the present time. They are an affluent, cultured, and elite group even within the Ashkenazic Jewish community. In Europe, the cosmopolitan and frequently secularized German Jews tended to look down upon their religious brethren in Russia and Poland. They preserved this traditional disdain intact upon coming to Argentina, and formed their own *Gemeinschaften,* or communal centers. These perform much the same functions of social welfare and cultural activity as do the AMIA-related organizations, but have the perceived advantage of being exclusively German and Austrian in membership. The two leading institutions in the community are known as the Asociación Filantrópica Israelita, formed in 1933, and the Juedische Kulturgemeinschaft, begun in 1937.[38]

Most German Jews in Argentina are descended from refugees who fled in the 1930s from the madness of Europe. Others, despite the severe obstacles of tightened immigration quotas, came immediately after the war, often without certification by immigration officers. Many suffered harrassment in Argentina because of their inability to demonstrate full visa credentials, an obvious impossibility for those who narrowly escaped the concentration camps.

The German immigrants came with professional and craft skills that could not be immediately absorbed by the Argentine economy. Therefore, many doctors and lawyers worked in factories or served as waiters and washers, often for just three or four pesos a day. They did this despite an ingrained distaste for such positions, yet curiously, hardly any German Jews became peddlers as did many of the Russian Jewish immigrants of an earlier generation. It was already a difficult blow for them to leave Germany and forsake their professional status, without the final indignity of becoming itinerant tradesmen.[39]

Within just a few decades, the economic position of the German Jews changed sharply for the better. Their education, discipline, and intensive effort to master the language of the land were rewarded with rapid ascent in social standing. Today, professionals and businessmen distinguish the German Jewish niche in the Argentine economy. Importers and exporters do an especially thriving business, in part because of contacts with Germany and other European nations. German Jewish establishments also specialize in clothes and finery for women, metal and leather products, sewing machines, electrical equipment, chemical and pharmaceutical products, and chocolates; they have also established printing plants and some fifty restaurants. The German Jewish porcelain company Emporio de la Loza has branches throughout the nation.[40]

Politics in the German Jewish community is rather conservative compared with the large proportion of radicals and Socialists among the Russian-Polish Jews. German Jews have not been as active politically as a group, despite their high level of education, and they are noted for their accommodating, law-abiding mentality. Much of their commitment to social aid is absorbed by organizations like the Hilfsverein Deutschsprechender Juden (Welfare Society for German-Speaking Jews) founded in 1933 to provide homes, schools, centers for occupational reorientation, and so forth for the refugees whose lives were shattered by the Nazi catastrophe.

The Judaic commitment of the German Jews is impressive though uneven. Surprisingly, this highly literate community has had only a small output of German-language newspapers. A Jewish weekly, *Juedische Wochenschau,* appeared for some years under the energetic direction of Hardi Swarsensky, who arrived in Argentina in 1940 as a fugitive from the German Gestapo. Swarsensky became a leading journalist as well as an important figure in the World Jewish Congress in Argentina and the DAIA. But following his death in 1968, at the age of sixty, German Jewish papers ceased for a time to publish regularly. During the mid-seventies, the one consistently appearing journal was the German-Spanish weekly *Juedisches Wochenblatt.*

The German Jews have emphasized religious identification in addition to secular cohesiveness. They have been in the vanguard of the liberal religious movements that have only recently taken root in Argentina. In this, they recall the German Jewish leaders of the nineteenth century, including Abraham Geiger and Zacharias Frankel, who promulgated Reform and Conservative philosophies of religious Judaism long before such thoughts made any impact in Eastern Europe.

The exclusiveness of the German Jews in Argentina has been

rather more acute than a similar phenomenon in the United States. A gradual intermingling of the ethnic subgroups, however, is dissolving this intra-Jewish elitism at its roots. As marriages between German and Russian Jews continue to increase over the next few decades, institutional realignment and increased unity will be the inevitable result.

PART TWO

THE
CULTURE

3 SECULAR JEWISH CULTURE

The essential elements of Jewish culture in Argentina—Zionist activity and a varied literary tradition in Yiddish and Spanish—are both distinguished by their largely secular outlook. These elements explore and develop ethnic values based less on religious devotion than on a sense of shared historical experience among Jews in Argentina and other lands.

Zionism

The Zionist commitment to a Jewish national homeland provides the ideological, emotional, and spiritual core of Judaism in Argentina. For in this secularized *kehillah,* stirring with Socialist and other utopian currents, Zionism is the one major movement dedicated above all else to the common destiny of the Jewish people.

European Zionist thought quickly penetrated Argentina, reaching even to the fast-assimilating Jews from Central and Western Europe. Among these early Zionist spokesmen, German-born Simon Ostwald merits special mention.

Ostwald first gained renown in Argentina as a pioneer in the graphics industry and as a prolific publisher. He also tried his hand at writing, producing five volumes of Argentine history. These works, written in the early 1880s, touched only marginally upon Judaic concerns. Yet Ostwald retained an interest in his Jewish heritage. His home became a center for eminent writers to discuss Jewish cultural questions. Toward the end of the century, Ostwald became increasingly involved with the plight of the Jewish people around the world and turned for answers to the father of modern Zionist thought, Austrian-born Theodore Herzl. Upon Herzl's death in 1894, Ostwald eulogized him in Buenos Aires, revealing in this speech his own evolution toward Zionist ideals:

At least outwardly, the Jew wants to amalgamate with his fellow citizens. But in general he does not achieve that aim. It is not enough to say that I am not a Jew in order for it to be so in reality. . . . And he who completely devotes himself to saturating himself with foreign feelings and thoughts condemns himself to a comic game and to playing a false role all his life.

When for the first time I heard discussion of Zionism I thought that it dealt with a utopia. Now I am taken with the idea and not because I believe that its realization will be easy; on the contrary, I think that it requires the commitment of entire generations. . . . Zionism is indispensable, because civilization and progress of humankind are advancing in giant steps and cannot permit seven million Jews to continue their existence as pariahs among the nations, without a political ideal and without their own refuge on the face of the earth.[1]

The Russian Jewish immigrants to Argentina gave Ostwald's ideals organizational vitality if not harmony. As early as 1897 the first Zionist fund-raising efforts coalesced in a group named after the Hovevei Zion of Eastern Europe. Launched by the brilliant and compulsive organizer, Jacob Simon Liachovitzky, the new branch of Hovevei Zion counted only fifty members at its inception, but it sparked a proliferation of Zionist groups.

The early decades of Zionist activity in Argentina resolved two major questions: the possibility of a Socialist-Zionist alliance and the potential for creating a Jewish nation in Argentina itself. That the former rapidly developed and the latter even more quickly dissolved surprised more than a few Zionist leaders.

The early European Zionists were actually ready to consider Argentina as a possible location for the ingathering of Diaspora Jews. These exponents of a political Zionism wished to create a Jewish nation by gathering refugees in a small and sparsely populated land, whether in Palestine, Uganda, or an undeveloped and unsettled area in Argentina.

The bulk of Russian Zionists rejected the purely political approach favored by Herzl, preferring instead a more historical-cultural variety of nationalism centered on Palestine. Nevertheless, the recurrent talk of Zion in Argentina, as a central refuge even apart from political considerations, had its determined supporters. Baron de Hirsch was already attempting to realize such aims through his ambitious program to transfer groups of Russian Jews to backward Argentine lands, with the cooperation of the Argentine government.

Developments of potentially greater significance for those who favored Argentina for Jewish resettlement were unfolding even before Hirsch's projects in Entre Ríos. During the 1880s, the Jewish adventurer Julius Popper was carving for himself both a legend and a minor principality in the hitherto undeveloped isle of Tierra del Fuego in the south of Argentina. Though Popper's Jewish consciousness was peripheral, his achievements sparked some Jewish colonization of southern Argentina. Had his reign over Tierra del Fuego endured longer than its brief few years, it seems possible that Zionist attention might have focused increasingly on the sparse lands of Popper's southern domains.

Popper's short life offers a study in charisma, daring, versatility, and braggadocio as would have delighted a Theodore Roosevelt. Born in Bucharest in 1857, the son of a prominent Hebrew teacher and bookseller, Popper left Romania while still a youth to seek adventure. He apparently found it in the Orient, the United States, Mexico, and Cuba. In the last three countries, Popper applied his early training as an engineer to invent more efficient mining techniques, and in Cuba he also designed the first sewer system for Havana. When he arrived next in Argentina in 1885, he was not yet twenty-nine years old, but already he held a wide reputation as a natural leader and innovator.

Popper's range of abilities comprises a small dictionary of occupations. One biographer described him as "an engineer of rare attainments—a civil, mechanical, and mining engineer—good in all three branches; an astronomer; a linguist who spoke and wrote a dozen languages fluently. He could with equal grace and precision conduct a lady to dinner or knock all the fight out of a claim-jumper."[2] He was also a preeminent navigator, a military commander, a cartographer, a distinguished lecturer and author, and an unusually capable administrator.

During the 1880s, Popper led several expeditions into southern Argentina to establish mining enterprises. He was the first prospector to explore this region, drafting detailed maps and preparing notes on the natural life of the area. In March 1887, he spoke before an audience of the Instituto Geográfico Argentina, the most respected naturalist society in the nation, on his discoveries in Tierra del Fuego.

Popper turned the island into a virtual personal satrapy. He guarded it with a motley band of followers whom he molded into a small army. Popper the military strategist was quite as remarkable as Popper the explorer and Popper the engineer. He insisted on rigid discipline, though his only authority over his followers was inherent charisma rather than any binding obligation. Popper outfitted them with uniforms similar to those used by the Austro-Hungarian army, including the fur-covered cylindrical caps. He also provided his men with Winchester carbines for maximum fire power. His precautions were justified by continual rival claims on his mines and frequent armed attacks, from Chile as well as Argentina.

The general fought his most imaginative campaign against invaders in the Battle of Arroyo Beta. The enemy band had entrenched itself against horseback charges by Popper's small group of followers. Popper swiftly changed tactics, keeping five defenders to divert fire while he and two others rushed upon the enemy rearguard, capturing their horses, and routing them completely. The Argentine Armando Braun Menéndez writes of this victory: "And the five soldiers of the reserve? . . . They were not such at all." Popper had improvised several 'bodies' from "some hats and uniforms filled with straw and some sticks to simulate carbines, transformed at a distance into fearsome soldiers."[3]

Popper showed equal resourcefulness in administering his island, which thrived under his careful supervision. He designed new machines for extracting gold from the area, minted his own coins, and printed stamps for postal service. The Argentine government gave him free reign, perhaps because it was content for the while to have Popper lay the groundwork for the island's prosperity.

Popper's exploits encouraged other Jews to immigrate from Europe. Iaacov Rubel, a scholar of Argentine Jewish immigration, writes that articles about Popper, giving optimistic accounts of life in Argentina, began to appear in the Russian Jewish journals.[4] Moreover, although Popper himself was not an observant Jew, his brother and close aide, Máximo, openly affirmed his Jewish heri-

90

tage and was officially a member of the Jewish Congregation in Buenos Aires since 1887. Máximo served as lieutenant governor of Tierra del Fuego, a remarkable position of power for a professed Jew to hold in Latin America.

Zionist interest in Tierra del Fuego conceivably might have blossomed had the Poppers maintained control of the region. Within a short time, however, these possibilities unraveled as a result of their untimely deaths. Máximo died at the tragically young age of twenty-three, a victim of the harsh Patagonian climate. Soon after, Julius died suddenly of unknown causes while working on his island. Until the last he had shown exceptional vigor and had been preparing ambitious new expeditions as far south as Antarctica. Scholars suspect that some of Popper's numerous enemies, whether rival enterprisers or unpaid creditors, had a hand in his death.[5]

Popper's memory was accorded warmer care by Catholic Argentines than by the Jewish community. Despite his Jewish descent and the affiliation of his brother with the Jewish Congregation, Popper received burial in the sepulchre of the family Ayerza, the most traditional and aristocratic burial place in Buenos Aires. At his funeral, the prominent writer, Lucio López, praised Popper as a national hero, another Livingstone, whose achievements foreshadowed in generations to come "the victories of civilization over barbarism and of society against the desert."[6]

With Popper's death, the sepulchre of Ayerza also received the stillborn potential to make southern Argentina a major focus of Jewish resettlement plans. Neither could Zionists maintain great hopes for the ICA colonies to the north, however impressive their progress, for these did not approach the population levels Hirsch and others had envisioned for them. Argentine Zionism thus remained from its early years centered on Palestine, the historically logical site for Jewish nationality, and almost not at all upon Argentina. The continued small proportion of Jews in the provinces and cities, coupled with their rapid political identification as fully loyal Argentines, insured that their Zionist goals would hew totally clear of Argentine territory.

During this early period of Argentine Zionism, the possibilities for an alliance of Socialists and Zionists came to unexpectedly rapid fruition. Initially, the two ideologies made strange, even ven-

91

omous bedfellows, but the new conditions of Argentine life facilitated a détente. One helpful factor was that the battle between
Yiddishists and Hebraists quickly lost even its irrational significance, for the low level of Jewish education precluded a widespread
knowledge of Hebrew among the settlers or their children. Therefore Yiddish dominated Zionist meetings almost as thoroughly as
it did the Socialist gatherings. Indeed the Yiddish language became
so integral a part of Jewish identity to both groups as to overwhelm
the linguistic conflict in its infancy.

Zionists and Socialists also came together of necessity. In this
strange land, Socialist institutions like the credit cooperative proved
an invaluable blessing to Jews of all ideological persuasions. Similarly, the occurrence of widespread anti-Semitic violence, directed
above all against Jewish Marxists, led even many ardent Socialists
to perceive the value of the Zionists' call to Jewish solidarity.

Of course the combination of Zionist and Socialist elements
was often volatile; mergers and schisms of the various organizations
have continued into the present. The clear trend, though, has been
toward a continuing hegemony by Socialist-leaning Zionist groups
over other factions in community politics.

The strength of left-Zionist groups—and Zionists of all political affiliations—has become especially visible since 1956. In that
year, the *kehillah* received government permission to revise its
internal statutes, and it incorporated a political structure based
explicitly on the Israeli model. The elections for officers of the
dominant group, the AMIA, have since featured proportional representation of delegates corresponding to the percentage of each
party's vote, leadership by coalition government as in Israel, and
even counterparts to Israeli parties. The result has been, in the
words of Israeli scholar Moshe Davis, the "quasi parliament of the
Jews of Argentina."[7]

Since 1957, the AMIA's triennial elections have revealed a
marked loyalty to the left-leaning Zionist parties. In the election of
1969, for example, the six Zionist parties captured 81 of the 90
delegate positions contested. The four leftist Zionist parties alone
took a clear majority of the seats, winning 48 of 90. (See Table 4.)

The most notable feature in Table 4, apart from the collective
domination of Socialist-Zionist parties, is the individual power of

Table 4: The AMIA Election of 1969

Party	Number of Votes	Number of Delegates	Delegates (in percent)
Zionist Right			
Zionist Federation	2,521	17	19
Mizrachi-Ha-poel Hamizrachi	838	6	7
Agudat Israel	543	4	4
Zionist Left			
Mapai	5,865	40	44
Ha-Shomer ha-Za'ir (Mapam)	1,112	8	9
Left			
Bundist	697	5	6
Independent			
Central Europe	647	4	4
Independent Zionists	919	6	7
Nonvalid votes	41	– –	– –
TOTAL	13,183	90	100

SOURCE: Adapted from Haim Avni, *Yahadut Be-Argentina* (Argentine Jewry) (Jerusalem: Hebrew University, 1972), p. 60.

Mapai. This is the counterpart to the Israeli namesake party, which ruled Israel from its creation in 1948 until 1976. The Argentine Mapai has exercised similar authority in the *kehillah,* after evolving from a rapidly shifting series of constellations of the leftist-Zionist factions. Ha-Shomer ha-Za'ir (Mapam—United Workers Party) is the second largest Zionist party of Socialist inclination. It refused to be amalgamated by the more doctrinaire Mifleget Po'alei Erez Israel (Mapai—Labor Party) but has never approached the latter's strength in communal politics.

Among the Zionist Right in Argentina, the so-called Zionist Federation reflects the merger of various non-Socialist groups. It has yet to offer a serious challenge to the Socialist-Zionist coalitions. Religious Zionists have made even less headway than the Zionist Federation in garnering community support. The Mizrachi party established in Argentina in 1940 appears consigned to the role of a permanent dissenter role in the AMIA. It has, however, overshadowed the Agudat Israel, a party even more scrupulously Orthodox. The history of the Agudat Israel (Union of Israel) is a strange one and, like other Argentine parties, has its roots in European Zionist politics. Its European founders initially opposed establishing a Jewish State, justifying their position on the grounds that God had not decreed an end to the exile, but motivated mainly by fear that the end of the Diaspora would also mean the end of religious Judaism. After the Holocaust, however, leaders of Agudat Israel moved toward the Zionist cause, extracted certain compromises from the new Israeli government on the relation between state and biblical laws, and accepted representation in the Israeli cabinet. The Agudat Israel in Argentina is composed of a core of observant Jews pressing for a return to Orthodoxy both in Israel and in the Argentine *kehillah.* Unsurprisingly, in the secularized Argentine community, their influence is sharply limited.[8]

Looking beyond the factions and disputes over Zionist terms and tactics, one is impressed by the deeper solidarity of Zionist sentiment in the *kehillah.* This intimate tie between Zionism and Judaism in Argentina since 1890 is especially striking, compared with the strong divisions between American Jewish Zionists and non-Zionists during the same period. The contrast has blurred considerably in recent decades. However, during the fifty years prior to World War II, the American Jewish community included numerous and important foes of Zionist thought. Not until the Holocaust and the creation of the State of Israel did American Jewry shed its deep ambivalence over the propriety of Jewish nationalism. Not for another two decades, when the Six-Day War heightened Zionist passions, did American Jewry approach the near unanimity of Zionist fervor long enjoyed by their Argentine brethren.

The existence of anti-Semitism in Argentina, beyond all parallel in the United States, helps account for the earlier Zionist consensus in the former community. While American Jews suffered economic quotas and various forms of social discrimination, they never experienced the massive waves of violence and terror that periodically gripped the Jewish community in Argentina. As a result, the Jews in the United States felt less urgent cause to seek a Palestinian or other refuge for Jewry. Conversely, they had more incentive to secure their status as Americans by avoiding the smallest suspicion of dual loyalties, such as Zionism might have incurred.

The earlier acceptance of Jewish nationalism in the Argentine *kehillah* traces as well to the absence of strong religious sentiments that could have undermined a secular approach to Jewish culture and identity. In the United States, many Orthodox Jews thought it sacrilege to create a Jewish State before the Messiah chose to bring about this miracle. Numerous Reform Jews joined their more observant coreligionists on somewhat different grounds. They condemned Zionism as a secular, particularistic movement that controverted the ideal of Judaism as a universal and purely religious force.

Several important American Reform groups during the early twentieth century issued strong statements against Zionist activity. The Central Conference of American Rabbis opposed Zionism altogether until 1920 and thereafter would cooperate with Zionists only on an unofficial basis and solely in philanthropic efforts. The powerful American Jewish Committee staunchly opposed Zionism until after the Balfour Declaration in 1917 promised British support for a Jewish national home. Even into the forties, it remained ambivalent, opposing the Biltmore Program of 1942, which proposed to establish a Jewish Commonwealth in Palestine.

The American Reform rabbis and lay leaders of the American Council for Judaism, begun in 1942, made a determined last stand against Jewish nationalism in America. The council at one point claimed some 20,000 members, certainly a minority within American Jewry but a reflection of the still vigorous doubts about the Zionist philosophy.

The stronger commitment to Zionism by Argentine Jews as compared with American Jews is seen in figures for *aliyah,* or settlement in Palestine (later Israel). *Aliyah* is the heart of Zionist philosophy and there are some who claim—though not without encountering heated debate—that it is identical with true Zionism. The figures for *aliyah* among Argentine Jews compare favorably with those for the much larger Jewish community in the United States. Although the latter community is now a dozen times larger than the former, its total number of settlers in Israel is only one and a half times as great. Even more surprising are the figures before the Arab-Israeli War of 1967, which marked a turning point for American Jewish awareness of their ties with Israel. *Aliyah* figures between 1950 and 1966 indicate that Argentina sent 13,940 Jews to Israel compared with only 8,502 from the United States.[9]

The Argentine Jewish movement for *aliyah* antedated the establishment of the State of Israel. During World War I, the Volunteer Movement of the Jewish Legion sent thirty-five Argentine Jews to Palestine to serve the Allied cause. A second group formed just as the armistice was signed. Most volunteers from the original group remained in Palestine after the war.

During the 1940s, the prospect of a reborn Jewish State inspired a youthful idealism in Jewish communities in many nations. In Argentina, six of seven Zionist youth organizations in this period were oriented toward pioneer settlement in Palestine. Many members of these groups were born in Europe and an even greater proportion were working-class youth. A census in 1942 reveals that of the 3,410 youths involved in these centers, 1,520, or 44 percent, were between the ages of six and fourteen.[10]

Two years before Israel came into existence, training centers formed in rural Jewish communities in Argentina for future *aliyah.* By the end of 1951, these camps provided the core of the 1,134 Jewish pioneers who left Argentina for new lives in Israel. This figure is well over half the number of American Jewish immigrants during this same period (1,909 settlers from May 1948 to December 1951).[11]

The youthful pioneer movements of the 1940s gave way to a more heterogeneous stage of Argentine Zionism during the 1950s. The Israeli scholar of Latin American *aliyah,* Moshe Kitron, writes that parents who once bitterly opposed their children's decision to make *aliyah* now wanted to be closer to their families and so also began moving to Israel. Others who wished to escape the economic and social crises in Argentina during the successor governments to Juan Perón joined the flow of *aliyah.* Finally, the professionals— doctors, engineers, chemists—who desired to contribute their skills to a still-fluid society, added another dimension to this Argentine emigration.[12]

Aliyah gained momentum from events in the 1960s both in Argentina and Israel. When anti-Semitic terrorism flared during the early part of the decade, it sparked a sharply increased interest in Israel. Over 4,000 Argentines moved there in 1963 alone. Young people were especially affected, including many who had previously considered themselves fully assimilated Argentines.

After the peak year of 1963, *aliyah* figures fell sharply, but a

Table 5: Annual Aliyah *Rates for the United States and Selected Latin American Nations, 1973*

Year	Argentina	United States	Mexico	Brazil	Uruguay	Total for Americas and Oceania
1950	435	761	37	197	131	1,954
1951	325	568	47	109	61	1,286
1952	291	292	10	134	50	950
1953	427	202	41	98	57	930
1954	398	294	18	123	42	1,091
1955	363	321	50	144	40	1,155
1956	505	187	16	137	64	1,067
1957	665	277	21	115	111	1,410
1958	515	378	28	105	112	1,320
1959	420	330	16	117	58	1,147
1960	337	413	23	96	73	1,158
1961	495	313	35	108	147	1,969
1962	693	619	70	213	179	2,187
1963	4,255	868	38	283	518	6,497
1964	1,998	1,006	31	404	289	4,188
1965	1,154	924	44	290	278	3,096
1966	664	749	31	201	163	2,132
1967	547	665	37	145	104	1,771
1968	559	932	43	199	148	2,275
1969	1,274	5,739	193	604	278	9,601
1970	1,457	6,424	174	752	295	11,405
1971	2,107	7,364	196	594	422	12,885
1972	2,598	5,515	145	451	544	10,814
TOTAL	22,482	35,141	1,344	5,619	4,164	82,288

SOURCE: *Immigration to Israel, 1948–1972, Part I, Annual Data* (Jerusalem: Central Bureau of Statistics, Special Series, no. 416), 1973, pp. 20–24, Table 4, "Immigrants and Tourists Settling (in Israel) by Country of Residence."

new catalyst, the stunning Israeli victory over Egypt, Syria, and Jordan in 1967, once again accelerated Argentine *aliyah.* Israel became more strongly than ever before the source of Argentine Jewish pride and ethnic identity. In 1969, the annual *aliyah* rate exceeded 1,000. This doubled the figures from the previous two years combined and started an upward climb that by 1973 reached almost 3,000 settlers in Israel a year. *Aliyah* dipped briefly in 1974 and 1975—two full years of elected civilian rule in Argentina— only to rise dramatically again after the military coup in 1976.[13] (See Tables 5 and 6.)

Almost all Argentines coming to Israel find permanent roots there. Their adjustment is often facilitated by their willingness to work the land, an attitude perhaps inherited from family memories of Jewish colonial life in the Argentine interior. The high percentage of professionals and craftsmen among the immigrants also speeds integration into Israeli society. The youth of these immigrants—Kitron finds that three-quarters are no more than thirty-five years old—also helps to explain their remarkable adaptability to Israeli life despite the initial strains of adjustment.[14]

More than one-third of all Argentines making *aliyah* have settled in kibbutzim, the voluntary agricultural communes in Israel. Kitron points out that the Latin American Jew tends to regard settlement on a kibbutz as socially prestigious, despite the constant toil, although he would not consider taking a job involving manual labor outside a collective settlement.[15] (See Table 7.)

The remaining immigrants from Argentina are divided equally

Table 6: Aliyah *Statistics for Latin America from 1947 to March 1972*

Nation	Aliyah
Argentina	22,814
Brazil	6,418
Uruguay	3,223
Chile	2,882
Mexico	1,124
Colombia	519
Venezuela	456
Peru	196
Bolivia	151
Cuba	139
Panama	50
Others	5,137
TOTAL	43,109

SOURCE: World Zionist Congress, Department of Information, letter to branch executives of every country, June 18, 1972.

among Zones of Development (the new population centers of immigrants, ranging from Eilat on the Red Sea to Kiriat Shmona in Upper Galilee) and the older urban centers, especially Tel Aviv, Haifa, and Jerusalem. There is also an important Latin American settlement in Beersheba, the historic town on the edge of the Negev desert.

For all its activity, Argentine Zionism has sharp critics in the *kehillah*. Some charge that the numbers making *aliyah* are far too low for a community united mainly by support for Israel. Lázaro Rubinson of the main Zionist group called Organización Sionista Argentina (OSA) candidly acknowledged the incongruity of a Diaspora-oriented Zionism:

Ninety per cent or more of Argentine Jewry claims to be Zionist, yet only 22,000 souls have made *aliya* since the State of Israel was created. That is only one quarter of one per cent of the population! It is a tragic paradox for the Zionist movement here.[16]

One possible cause of the low *aliyah* figures, according to Rubinson, is that "Jews here identify with Judaism only through nationalism and not through religion. Many support Israel as a social cause, a refuge for the Jews, for human freedom—but they themselves do not want to live a fully Jewish life in Israel. They do not see Zionism from a fully Jewish perspective."[17]

Table 7: Categories of Argentine Immigrants to Israel, 1963

Category	Percent
Pioneer *aliyah*	3.4
Kibbutz	39.6
Urban	33.7
Development areas	4.6
Temporary housing	7.5
Working farmers	5.0
Adolescents	2.0
Youth *aliyah*	3.0
Undefined	1.2
TOTAL	100.0

SOURCE: Adapted from Moshe Kitron, "Yahadut America Ha-Dromit Ubayoteha" (Latin American Jewry and Its Problems), *Bi-Tfutzot Hagola*, 30/31, (Winter 1964), p. 165.

The editor of a militantly Zionist magazine named *Raíces* despaired that the Argentine Jews who go to Israel are not generally well established in the society or knowledgeable about Judaism. Rather, the emigrants tend to leave Argentina less out of idealism than from confusion about their own lives and goals. The editor added that the *kehillah* needs to attract to the movement for *aliyah* those who are already committed to Judaism, the potential leaders of the Jewish community.[18]

Other critics of Argentine Zionism stress its organizational troubles. Despite the power of the AMIA and the Zionist sympathies of most Jewish officials, the OSA has never held the power to control or even fully coordinate the policies of the diverse Zionist factions. Natan Lerner, the DAIA official and son of a noted Yiddish writer, Falik Lerner, writes that the OSA "does not presently have a satisfactory life of its own. It is rather a sort of political federation with autonomous components, whose own work seems insufficient."[19]

The critical comments on Zionism, particularly those on *aliyah,* must be balanced against a number of encouraging facts. *Aliyah* from Argentina per capita of the Jewish population compares favorably with that of many nations, as seen clearly in the case of the United States. Then, too, Argentine Jews find numerous outlets for their Zionist sentiments besides *aliyah.* These include the large-scale fund-raising campaign for Israel parallel to so much of American Zionist activity.

A multitude of Jewish organizations like Keren Hayesod and the Jewish National Fund appeal regularly for aid to the Jewish State. Donation boxes on behalf of Israel appear on many Jewish shop counters. The mass support for such activities may be gauged by the growth of the Women's International Zionist Organization (WIZO) in Argentina. This London-based group began work in Argentina over fifty years ago during a fund-raising campaign by Keren Hayesod. Its Argentine operations have since evolved into a network of 337 branches and 35,000 members.[20]

Remarkably, these and other Jewish activities continue to function even in the present atmosphere of political repression and anti-Semitic terrorism. One marvels, for example, at the many festive gatherings on Israel Independence Day, on May 5, 1977, including large public demonstrations to register support for the Jewish State.

The above activities clearly suggest that the Argentine Jew intends to be a "Zionist in the Diaspora." The impression is confirmed by a survey of newly married Jewish couples in 1965. Ninety percent of the respondents expressed their belief that one could lead a fully Jewish life outside Israel.[21] Such Jews scarcely regard *aliyah* as the acid test either of their Jewishness or their Zionist loyalties, whatever some Zionists allege on historical or philosophical grounds.

The long-range value of Argentine Zionism to Israel may well prove less significant than the value it holds for the *kehillah* itself. Zionism has reinforced Argentine Jewish life with a sense of purpose and cohesion unmatched by any other aspect of communal activity. Nor have the militant critics of Argentine Zionism thus far discovered a clearly superior solution to the problem of cultural continuity. In the absence of a strong religious tradition, Zionism has been—and will likely continue to be—the indispensable bulwark of Argentine Jewish identity and idealism.

Judaic literature

Jewish cultural activity in Argentina is richly varied in style and language. Spanish, Yiddish, and to a lesser degree Hebrew have served as vehicles for literary, theatrical, and journalistic expressions of Judaic thought. Themes range from religious to secular, from socialist polemic to animal fable, and from nostalgia to bitter revolt against the past. Always, however, the influence of the East European way of life, whether as inspiration, setting, or target, colors these writings.

Argentina has been one of the two great centers of Yiddish language and culture since the Holocaust. A versatile and durable conglomerate of German, Hebrew, and elements of assorted Romance and other languages, Yiddish was enjoying a period of great literary creativity in the late nineteenth century, when the first East European Jews came to Argentina.

The new Argentines inherited a wide range of styles and moods from the great contemporary Yiddish writers in Europe. Yet the authors who influenced them most strongly often did so less for

101

reasons of style than of ideological content. Argentine Yiddish writers fastened upon the radical qualities in many of the works by Isaac Leib Peretz and certain other Russian Jewish authors. Social themes quickly became even more prominent a part of Yiddish literature in Argentina than in Europe. Indeed, an early emphasis on stylistic excellence in Argentine Yiddish writing was largely eclipsed, during the early twentieth century, by the ascendance of ideological considerations.[22]

The treatments of social issues varied widely. Jacobo Streicher wrote poignant and realistic poems of the workers' hard fate of poverty and oppression. Abraham Moscovich went to the other extreme, writing idealized accounts of the laborers in the agricultural colonies but still flashing vague revolutionary impulses. Noé Vital's vigorous and emotional style aroused indignation against the victimization of factory workers in Buenos Aires and the miserable conditions they endured. Jacobo Aisenstein urged "world liberation" in his novels, while the early leader of the Bund in Argentina, Pinhas Wald, devoted two volumes of memoirs to his efforts to further the cause of the working class.

The trend toward ideologically motivated literature swept up many who at first had little interest in social issues. The works of poet Jaime Wolf and poet-novelist Moisés Granitstein reveal a definite emergence of social concern among authors once committed only to literary achievement. Other writers, like Arón Faierman, while not propounding a specific ideology, wrote of the difficult lot of the laboring masses. Faierman concentrated his stories on the hard and lonely life of the immigrant workers.

Amid the ideological swirl, a number of other currents may be discerned. Israel Helfman probed the darker recesses of human psychology in his book of tales, *Fun mayn gemit* (From My Thoughts). Although it is his sole published work, it is memorable for its portrayal of characters filled with ambition and lust. Benito Bendarsky channeled his love of the new land and of animals into emotional stories about the Jewish colonies. Zalman Wassertzug, still active in Yiddish letters, began his career as a writer of children's stories, such as *Far di kinders vegn* (For the Children's Sake).

The number of authors and contributions in nonideological subjects can be multiplied. Yet it is the high proportion of ideologically colored works that gives Argentine Yiddish literature its most distinctive trait. For this literature, despite the variety of themes and styles, is above all a reflection of the secularized and politicized culture characteristic of the Russian Jewish immigrants and their descendants.

The Yiddish theater in Argentina has attracted some of the most talented Jewish artists as well as some of the most impassioned polemicists. Perhaps its single best-known figure was an actress rather than a playwright, by the name of Berta Singerman. She was born in Minsk in 1897 and came to Argentina while still a child. She soon became the most lauded player since Bernard Waisman brought the first Yiddish troupe to Buenos Aires in 1901. Curiously, though, she found that gaining a spotlight in the national Argentine theater was a trifling matter compared with her early attempts to gain recognition within the Jewish community. She began her performing efforts as a member of the liturgical choir organized by the Jewish prodigy, Colman Saslavsky, but the more traditional congregants were scandalized by the inclusion of women in the choir and banned it from the synagogue. The determined young woman countered this action by donning men's clothing and continuing to sing, this time in an "all-male" choir. She also joined Argentine theater troupes and, while still in her twenties, gained preeminence as a Spanish-language performer with recitals of poetry and prose. Roles in plays by Henrik Ibsen and others enhanced her stature. At the same time, Singerman contributed to Yiddish theater, receiving a vastly more enthusiastic reception than she had ever enjoyed in her days with the choir. The Singerman family became something of a dynasty in theater: Berta's younger sister, Argentine-born Paulina, starred in her own company, while a granddaughter, Nora, also entered an acting career.

Ideology followed Jews right into the theater. Provocative productions by angry playwrights more than once turned audiences into vehement and even violent players in unplanned scenes of off-stage dialogue, saltier than any in the plays themselves.

Leib Malick's play *Ibergus* (Transfusion), written in 1926, was so controversial that all the established theater troupes refused to perform it. Its theme was the influence of the white-slave trade in which Jewish criminals played a major part. Previously Malick had confined himself to innocuous writings, such as his impressions of his travels to Palestine, Spain, and other nations, and he had en-

103

joyed great popularity since his arrival in Argentina in 1921. With *Ibergus,* though, he became the center of an ideological and emotional storm. *Ibergus* reached the stage only after a Yiddish critic and writer named Jacobo Botoschanski organized a new troupe, which performed the play in the largest theater, Politeama, before more than 2,000 people. The production created virtual civil war between the two regular theaters in Buenos Aires. This led eventually to the failure of the lesser theater group, led by actor and director Rudolf Zazslavsky. Malick himself did not long survive the controversy; he died in Paris at the age of forty-two.

After the factionalism over the white-slave trade abated, the Yiddish theater became a more respectable and widely patronized institution. It expanded during the 1930s to four establishments: the Excelsior, the Olympia, the Ombi, and the Argentino. The actors organized a guild, which by 1950 still claimed 120 members of various theater groups. Since the peak years of the 1930s, however, the rise of a native-born Spanish-speaking generation of Jews has left the sponsors and players of the Yiddish theater in a condition resembling that of the proverbial fiddler on the roof. Recently, visiting artists from North America have supported the Yiddish theater in Argentina, as financial difficulties forced the reduction of theaters to a single establishment. Despite this tenuous position, performances continue into the 1970s.[23]

Yiddish has found its most prolific and popular Argentine outlet in journalism. Such activities began almost with the disembarkation from the vessel, the *Weser,* in 1889. As may be expected, the early journals were fiercely polemical, communicating the multiplicity of Socialist, Zionist, and other ideological tenets of their publishers and writers.[24]

Nearly a decade passed before the community made the transition from handwritten to printed periodicals. The journal *Der Viderkol* (Echo) initiated the succession of mass-produced Yiddish papers in March 1898. Its Germanized Yiddish was atrocious, but its downfall after only three issues resulted primarily from lack of a printing press. This key deficiency made even the production of a four-page publication a monumental struggle requiring the services of an expert calligrapher. His stone engravings were aesthetic but so slow as to suggest some printing technique employed in Chelm, the mythical village of Jewish foolishness. The collaborators on this ill-fated journal included Jacob Simon Liachovitzky and Abraham Vermont. In the future these men would each make a profound impression on Jewish journalism in Argentina.

Viderkol did not die in vain. The community was so taken with the idea of a Jewish press that in the same year it acquired a printing machine with the Hebrew characters used in printing Yiddish words. The first fruit of this new wave of enthusiasm was *Der Yidisher Fonograf.* Jacob Joselevich edited the paper, which focused on the thoughts and deeds of leading Zionists. Like *Viderkol,* its life-span was short—this one lasted only six months.

A better fate awaited the Yiddish daily, *Di Yidishe Folkshtime* (People's Voice), also begun in 1898. The editor, Abraham Vermont, was a colorful personality who used his paper as a weapon to guard the interests, as he perceived them, of the Russian immigrants. His editorials, unrestrained by the smallest considerations of tact, denounced the Barón Hirsch project, the Germans and other West Europeans who ran it, and anyone else who chanced to disagree with his views. Victims of his blistering attacks suggested that Vermont saw every well-meaning critic as a conspirator, a traitor to his people. Yet Vermont's sure instinct for journalism turned this controversy and most others to advantage. He guided his paper through sixteen years of issues, for that time an extremely ripe, old age.

Vermont cowed many in the community, but his excitable and self-righteous nature made him a perfect target for the numerous humor magazines springing up as early as 1899. The pungent, often devastating Yiddish wit that arrived vigorous and restless from Eastern Europe found in Vermont's pretension and arrogance merely a standing invitation to parody. Of the two earliest humor magazines, *Der Poyk* (Drum) discovered mirth in a variety of subjects, but *Di Blum* (Flower) fired all its satirical volleys at the irrascible Vermont.

The years 1904 to 1914 witnessed a great expansion in the activities of the Yiddish press. *Der Tsionist,* begun in 1904, represented the Liga Theodore Herzl and was the first publication of purely Zionist character. Jacob Simon Liachovitzky edited this journal and headed the league sponsoring it. Liachovitzky was already a veteran of the Zionist movement in Argentina, having formed the Hovevei Zion society a number of years before. *Der Tsionist* would

105

prove only one of innumerable projects to dance off his imagination and into print.

Other Zionist papers in this period include the first Yiddish newspaper, *Dos Yidishe Lebn* (Jewish Life). It appeared in 1906 and introduced a Zionist-Socialist ideology into the daily news format. The inexperience of its very youthful founders, inclined more to polemic than printing, led to its collapse after seventeen days.

Jacob Joselevich, one of those people who awake each morning with a new plan to implement, published several short-lived journals before beginning publication of a monthly organ called *Di Yidishe Hofnung* (Jewish Hope). Begun in 1908, it flourished and in 1917 became the official paper of the Federación Sionista Argentina, with the new title *Di Yidishe Velt* (Jewish World).

The Socialists were also active during this time, sparked by the leader of the Bund, Pinhas Wald. He collaborated with Solomon Kaplansky to found the Bundist monthly, *Der Avangard,* in 1908. It spread the ideology of the Social Democratic Party, which originated in 1897 with many followers in Russia, Poland, and Lithuania. Editors of *Der Avangard* appeared in Argentina until 1920. Wald also published *Unzer Vort* (Our Word), which according to the scholar Lázaro Schallman, "was Bundist first and Russian Social Democratic second," in its commitment to Jewish identity.[25] *Unzer Vort* had the best Argentine writers of the day in Israel Helfman, Moshe Pinchevsky, Aarón Brodsky, Noé Vital, and Abraham Kliguer.

Socialism in the colonies spread its ideals in *Yidisher Kolonist in Argentine,* founded in the colony Clara in 1909. The journal included works on Argentine history, news of the Old World, and cultural and social events, while explaining and defending the ideals of cooperativism and agricultural life. Isaac Kaplan, the humanist utopian thinker, was one of many distinguished intellectuals who contributed to the journal. Financial pressures forced it to close in 1912, but it resumed five years later under the name *Kolonist Kooperator.*

An important gap remained in Yiddish journalism, despite the waves of Zionist and Socialist literature in that language; there still was no daily newspaper. The ambitious Liachovitzky remedied this in 1914 with a morning journal called *Der Tog* (Day). It proved tremendously popular from the first, though the mercurial Liachovitzky soon left the paper in search of new literary schemes. *Di Yidishe Tsaytung,* another of his projects, appeared daily sometime later in 1914 and until 1972, when financial pressures forced its closure, was the most successful Yiddish publication in Argentine history. Another journal, *Di Prese,* printed its first issues in 1918 and still serves a daily Yiddish readership.

As Yiddish has declined in recent decades relative to the use of Spanish among Argentine Jews, its exponents have gradually turned more to introspective and scholarly examinations of Jewish history and, in particular, Yiddish culture. *Davke,* a scholarly publication founded in 1949, presents philosophical essays on Jewish themes, including articles on Philo, Maimonides, Spinoza, and others. Among Yiddish journals throughout the world, *Davke's* format is unique. Another Yiddish publication, *Shriften,* was founded in 1942 and contains writings on Judaism from ancient times to the present.

The relationship between Yiddish journalism, literature, and historiography has always been very close. Marcos Alperson, who had a pen in nearly all the Jewish publications in the first years of the twentieth century and who wrote plays, satires, and novels, produced his magnum opus with a historical investigation of a single Jewish colony, Mauricio. The two Yiddish dailies published commemorative studies of early Argentine Jewish development, in 1938 *(Yoyvel Bukh* of *Di Prese)* and 1940 *(Yoyvel Bukh* of *Di Yidishe Tsaytung).* A third commemorative anthology, in Spanish, appeared in 1939 under the direction of José Mendelson, a renowned Yiddish novelist and journalist. The Ukrainian-born Mendelson rounded out his prolific career with a succession of translations of numerous novels from Russian, Spanish, French, and English into Yiddish. From 1943 to his death in 1969, he directed the Hebrew Yiddish Teachers Seminary in Buenos Aires.

The Yidisher Visenshaftlikher Institut (YIVO), an international organization dedicated to preserving Yiddish culture, has operated in Argentina since 1928. It sponsors local writers, provides lectures for Yiddish-speaking members of the community, and compiles Yiddish records of Argentine Jewish history. Many officials in the *kehillah* have cooperated with and supplemented these efforts to maintain an awareness of the Yiddish-speaking world in which the immigrants originated.

107

Among community leaders today, Marc Turkow is especially renowned for efforts to memorialize the centers of Jewry in Eastern Europe, through a series of volumes on pre-Holocaust culture. Turkow was born in 1904 into a Polish family that has produced several talented exponents of Yiddish culture. His brothers Zygmunt (1896–1970) and Jonas (1898–) were both prominent in the Yiddish theater in Poland. Another brother, Itzhak (1906–70), also acted in the Yiddish theater but gained even greater fame as a writer and journalist, both in Poland and after moving to Israel in 1957.

Turkow began his career as a journalist, coediting the Warsaw *Moment,* a Yiddish daily, before coming to Buenos Aires in 1930. He took an active interest in the Argentine *kehillah,* directing the Hebrew Immigrant Aid Society from 1946 and representing Latin America in the World Jewish Congress from 1954 to the present.

Turkow's obvious position of eminence at community meetings is softened by his own good humor and perhaps just a faint air of tolerant bemusement at the inevitable minor nonsense that accompanies the *kehillah*'s constructive discussions. At one council featuring Jewish leaders from all Latin America, an Argentine speaker droned endlessly before the helpless audience. After some time, Turkow quietly excused himself for a few moments and then just as modestly returned—but it was to no avail. No sooner had he reseated himself than the speaker suddenly stopped for the first time and, anxious to hold the attention of the prestigious Turkow, whirled toward him with an enthusiastic, "Ah, Turkow, TURKOW! I was saying . . ." and completely repeated himself. Turkow accepted the verbal onslaught with resigned dignity.

Turkow's greatest personal satisfaction in his long career of communal service is his activity as president of the Central Unión Israelita Polaca from 1941 to 1945. While the Germans thoroughly devastated the centers of East European Jewry, Turkow worked to save the civilization these Jews had created. He initiated a library of some 175 volumes on Jewish history and culture, including many works on the Holocaust written especially for the Central Unión Israelita Polaca. Later, he also began supervising a project to establish a Jewish Popular Library of booklets thirty-two to forty pages long, in both Yiddish and Spanish, to bring to a mass readership great Jewish personalities and events from Abraham to the creation of the new Jewish State. Turkow said of this effort, "It is dedicated to the youth of today, for the Jews and also for the non-Jews, and we have given these volumes to the public and university libraries, as well as to Jewish schools."[26]

Turkow's own work, *Los postreros de una magna generación* (Remnants of a Great Generation), narrates the development and destruction of Polish Jewry. The historian José Liebermann called this book and the other volumes of the Central Unión Israelita Polaca important, "not merely as an expression of culture but as a spiritual affirmation of a lost world whose traditional feelings endure in the present day."[27]

Argentine Jewish culture has increasingly drawn upon the riches of the Spanish language. In a land sensitive to the immigrant experience, Jewish writers in Spanish frequently have commanded a national readership for books with Judaic themes and settings, as well as for more general works. Among the many nationally known authors whose works stress Jewish and immigrant life are Alberto Gerchunoff, Israel Zeitlin, Carlos Grünberg, Samuel Glusberg, José Rabinovich (an anomaly whose Yiddish writings were published in Spanish editions), Antonio Portnoy, and Aarón Spivak. These authors tended to retain the ethnic concerns shown by their colleagues who wrote in Yiddish, while emphasizing to a greater degree their new Argentine roots.

Lázaro Liacho, the Argentine-born son of Jacob Liachovitzky, typified this generational continuity of interests with his Spanish tales of Jewish immigrant conditions. Liacho's short story "La Tierra" (The Land) observed the metamorphosis of Jewish life in the harsh agricultural routine of the interior settlements. A character named Aunt Esther recites poetry alone every morning, wistfully realizing that times have changed: "No one is concerned with poetry in this pampa." The wind blows the leaves of paper containing the poems across the field, where they circle aimlessly. Liacho's tale still exudes optimism, as if the colonies were the chrysalis of a new culture, "the prophetic seed of Israel in the green fields of the New World."[28]

Younger Jewish writers have dealt with new questions of generational change. Samuel Pecar has led the way as one of the few eminent writers of the third generation, devoting his talents largely to Judaic themes. Introspection and anguished wrestling with Judaism mark his works, which began receiving attention in the 1950s with *Cuentos de Kleinville* (Tales of Kleinville, 1954), *La generación olvidada* (Forgotten Generation, 1958), and *Los rebeldes y los perplejos* (The Rebels and the Bewildered, 1959). Pecar confronts problems of cultural identity, the task of imparting to one's children a Jewish education, and patterns of Jewish life in Argentina. The emphasis common to first-generation authors on adapting to Argentine culture recedes in Pecar's work before a new emphasis on maintaining a Judaic heritage and even on the merits of settling in Israel.

Jewish journalism in Argentina has always featured some Spanish publications, even at the height of Yiddish writings.[29] The two foremost journalists of the early community included Spanish supplements for their Yiddish papers. Abraham Vermont added a Spanish section to his *Di Yidishe Folkshtime,* while Jacob Liachovitzky simultaneously edited the Yiddish *Der Tsionist* and the Spanish *El Sionista,* the latter spanning forty-seven issues between 1904 and 1906.

Since those early years, a series of Spanish journals such as *Juventud* (Youth) and *Vida Nuestra* (Our Life) have explored Jewish history and traditions and the problems within the *kehillah.*

A Sephardic family of Turkish descent established in 1931 one of the great intellectual magazines in the Argentine Jewish community. David Elnecavé and, since his death in 1956, his son Nissim have guided the bimonthly *La Luz* (Light) to its present stature as a leading Spanish journal in the *kehillah.*

David Elnecavé was born in Haskery, Turkey, in 1882 and studied for the rabbinate in Constantinople. His polemical bent led him to seek a wider forum, and he dedicated his life to journalism, publishing magazines in Turkey and, later, in Bulgaria (1921–31), where there was a sizable Sephardic community. In 1931, he moved to Argentina and founded *La Luz* in that same year. As in his previous writings, Zionist themes pervade this journal. Elnecavé's great prestige in all three countries in which he fought for the Zionist cause earned him a place at the Twelfth Zionist Congress in Karlsbad. He also served as envoy from the Hebrew University in Jerusalem to several Latin American nations. Elnecavé's writings include several incisive commentaries on biblical themes, but his best-known work is the Zionist volume, *Eretz Israel, La patria de los hebreos* (Land of Israel, Country of the Hebrews), published in 1946.

The present editor of *La Luz,* Nissim Elnecavé, is a man of profound religious and secular erudition who has written essays in both Hebrew and Spanish on a range of subjects. His articles in *La Luz* belligerently challenge the parochial instincts of the *kehillah,* the complacence of the Argentine government toward anti-Semitism, and other conditions and issues involving Jewry in Argentina and other countries. Elnecavé urges a course of Jewish integration into the mainstream of Argentine life, cautioning that "the Diaspora Jew cannot live in a ghetto in the modern world."[30]

A brief but glorious life was the fate of the journal *Judaica,* which Alberto Gerchunoff praised for letting the reader explore deeply the bonds linking Judaic literature in all the republics on the continent.[31] It printed poems, essays, and cultural studies, including several articles on Yiddish literature. Among the contributors were Gerchunoff himself, the journalist and historian José Mendelson, novelists Antonio Portnoy, Aarón Spivak, and Marcos Weinstein, and poet José Isaacson. *Judaica* appeared from 1933 to 1946, under the editorial leadership of the versatile Solomon Resnick, who formerly worked as a translator and as an associate editor with the first Spanish Jewish weekly magazine, *Mundo Israelita* (Jewish World).

The outstanding Zionist leader, Abraham Mibashan, began *Eretz Israel* (Land of Israel), an illustrated magazine that published articles on Israeli life from Argentina and abroad. At present the journal is edited by Mibashan's son, Asher. The Mibashan family is of Romanian Ashkenazic descent and has established itself as one of the two great Jewish publishing concerns in Argentina, under the imprimatur Editorial Candelabro.

The firm grasp Yiddish has had in community affairs accounts for the fact that twenty-five years elapsed between the founding of the first Jewish weekly in Spanish, *Mundo Israelita*, in 1923, and the appearance of the first Jewish daily in that language. *Amanecer* (To Dawn) printed its first issue in March 1957, edited by the prolific scholar, Lázaro Schallman. Schallman has written numerous works on Judaism in Argentina and is also a noted linguist in both Hebrew and Spanish. In 1952, the Royal Spanish Academy included his name in its list of authorities of the Spanish language. Schallman

111

also taught literature to Argentine university students and wrote works on how to improve and humanize the educational process. Under his leadership, *Amanecer* earned the highest critical acclaim for its intelligent format and probing columns. In fact, *Amanecer* achieved everything except financial success. With few readers among the commercial and working classes and a host of financial troubles, the journal ceased publication after fourteen months, once again leaving a void in Spanish-language Jewish dailies that still is to be filled.

Although Yiddish remains the basic language for Argentine Jewish historical records, Jewish writers are increasingly turning to Spanish, led by the dean of the *kehillah*'s historians, Boleslao Lewin. Lewin came to Latin America in 1931 from his native town of Lodz, Poland. He had little religious training as a child and in fact broke relations with his Orthodox family over conflicts in the observance of Jewish ritual. However, while in Uruguay, Lewin became dismayed by the rise of Nazism in Europe and realized that his friends no longer saw him as the "Pole" but as the "Jew." "Then I realized the fact of my own Jewishness," Lewin said, "so I decided to identify myself with it and come to know it."[32]

Lewin's publications on Argentine Jewish history are vast. His many writings in Yiddish include articles for the YIVO *Bleter* of New York and other journals. At the same time, Lewin's proficiency in Spanish and his reputation as a historian led to an appointment as professor of South American history at the universities of the Litoral (Rosario) and La Plata (Buenos Aires) in 1955. Lewin continues to conduct research into the origins of Argentine Jewry and other Jewish communities in Latin America.

The institutional center of Spanish Jewish culture in Argentina is a social and cultural organization called the Sociedad Hebraica Argentina. A jurist named Marcos Satanowski established the society in 1926, uniting the three major Jewish youth groups, including the sponsor of the magazine *Juventud* (Youth). Satanowski, a native Argentine, taught commercial law at the University of Buenos Aires until Perón purged the universities of liberals in the late 1940s. When Perón fell from power in 1955, Satanowski reassumed his former position. In addition to teaching, he wrote legal and other scholarly works.

The distinguished philosopher Leon Dujovne guided the SHA

with continued success after Satanowski was tragically murdered, by a lone criminal, in his office in 1957. Dujovne was a perfect symbol for the society's humanistic and Judaic values. He edited the Spanish supplement in *Di Yidishe Tsaytung* and the journal *Mundo Israelita,* but was equally well known for general writings. He analyzed Spinoza's works in four volumes and wrote books on Martin Buber, Thomas Mann, and others. His own ideas on philosophy appear in several volumes.

The Sociedad Hebraica Argentina attracts outstanding artists and intellectuals and maintains youth groups, sporting facilities, a collection of murals and paintings by Jewish artists, and a superb Judaica library of some 40,000 volumes (one of the nation's ten largest libraries). Lecturers at the society have included the Argentine writer Jorge Luis Borges, violinist Mischa Elman, and piano virtuoso Arthur Rubinstein, among others. Albert Einstein and social critic Waldo Frank both visited the society from the United States, becoming its only two honorary members.[33]

The Sociedad Hebraica publishes a bimonthly magazine, *Davar* (Word). Since 1945, it has gathered contributions from leading Jewish writers for over a hundred issues, more than any Argentine literary magazine but *Sur.*[34]

Another society promoting Spanish Judaic culture is the Instituto Judío de Cultura y Información, which received a large measure of support from the American Jewish Committee. Until recently it published a respected trimonthly magazine, *Comentario.* Its first issue appeared in 1953, with the intent of offering readers of the Spanish-speaking world "a forum for contemporary thought and problems, among which Jewish themes figure prominently."[35] Like the journal *Davar,* it featured provocative essays by some of the most distinguished Jewish writers in Argentina, and strengthened the *kehillah*'s already impressive tradition of Spanish Judaic thought.

The weak third sister among languages in the *kehillah* is Hebrew. *Ha-Bima Ha-Ivrit* (Hebrew Platform), the first Hebrew periodical in Argentina, had a sporadic existence from 1921 till its demise in 1930, from lack of a readership. Six years later, the Hebrew Association, which published it, regrouped and in 1938 printed the periodical *Darom* (South) on a regular basis. However,

113

the Hebrew Association was unable to attract mass support for its meetings or publications, and Hebrew remained a minor language for Argentine Jews. Much of the most widely circulated literature in Hebrew written by Argentines appeared only in European publications such as *Ha-Tzefirah* (The Dawn) and *Ha-Melitz* (The Advocate).

The establishment of the Jewish State in 1948 sparked a minor renaissance in Hebrew study. The secondary school called the Hebrew Midrasha, founded in 1949, is the most notable of several similar centers created around this time. Sales of Hebrew books also rose sharply. Today, one of the five professorships at the Jewish Institute for Advanced Studies, a secondary school sponsored by the Sociedad Hebraica, is in the field of Hebrew language and literature. The increase in *aliyah,* a new emphasis in Jewish schools on Hebrew instruction, and the AMIA's sponsorship of youth trips to Israel have all lifted community interest in Hebrew in recent years.

The number and diversity of publications in Yiddish, Spanish, and Hebrew attest to a core of intellectual vitality in the *kehillah.* Yet the future of this Judaic cultural activity is uncertain at best. The problem, as David Ben-Gurion once commented about Israel's fear for its survival despite its military quality, is that "numbers count, too." In Argentina today, the exponents of Jewish culture are few indeed, despite the generally high level of education in the community.

The scarcity of intellectuals concerned with Judaic themes appears to have become more acute in recent decades. The accelerating pace of acculturation has seen, as a by-product, a general drift away from cultural interests widely viewed as "parochial." As a result of this trend, writers like Samuel Pecar have become scattered guardians of a fading literary and intellectual heritage. The great challenge to the *kehillah,* therefore, is to attract Jews to the rich outlets already available for the creative exploration and renewal of their culture. There is at present little sign that the community, hard pressed by all manner of other concerns, is successfully meeting that challenge.

4 RELIGION

The Jew of Eastern Europe adhered to the Mosaic Law completely. It would have been unthinkable to him to violate the Sabbath by working on the seventh day or to disregard the dietary laws by eating pork. Yet in Argentina, journalist Jacob Beller records attending a luncheon at the Sociedad Hebraica honoring the Yiddish poet J. J. Schwartz, in which the poet was chagrined at being served ham upon completion of his recital.[1]

It is commonly said in the *kehillah* that Jews arriving in Argentina often "left their phylacteries on the boat" in their desire for a life free of all Old World restrictions. Although the religious impulse still moved many settlers, later waves of East European Jews were influenced far more by the Enlightenment and secular currents of Zionism and socialism than by the *yeshivah*.

Most Argentine Jews cannot understand the attitudes of their American brethren who tend to perceive commitment to Judaism in terms of religious observance. Nor, until recently, have Argentine Jews had any experience with religious denominations to parallel the American Jewish penchant for self-classification as Orthodox, Conservative, Reform, or Reconstructionist. In Argentina, any degree of Jewish religious observance has generally sufficed to be called Orthodox, however puzzling or disconcerting it appears to many who keep the Mosaic Law more completely.

The United States immigration quotas during the 1920s, diverting to Argentina a large number of Jews already impressed by secular ideologies, contributed to the divergent mentalities of the two communities. By this time, the Russian Revolution had led to the creation of the Soviet Socialist regime; whereas, the British Balfour Declaration in 1917 offered to Jews renewed hope of establishing a national homeland. For many Jews living during this period, the religious tradition simply became irrelevant.

Observance of tradition

Today, religious ritual is largely absent from Jewish communal life in Argentina. The secular trends are highlighted by a member survey in 1966, involving 150 young married couples in the Socie-dad Hebraica. Most of the males interviewed (71 percent) and nearly half of their wives (43 percent) have had some form of Jewish education that, together with their membership in the Socie-dad Hebraica, indicates a more positive identification with Judaism than is shown by the majority of Jewish Argentines. Of those sur-veyed, however, only 6 percent belong to Jewish religious institu-tions of any kind.[2]

No more than 8 percent of all Jews in Buenos Aires consume kosher meat, based on an estimate made in 1969.[3] The severe shortage of *shohetim* (ritual slaughterers) outside Buenos Aires dic-tates a still lower percentage of dietary observance in the communi-ties of the interior.

Observance appears to be faltering even from this low level. In the summer of 1971, for example, only three kosher restaurants operated in the whole city of Buenos Aires, all of them in the very heavily Jewish district, Once. By the summer of 1972, two of the restaurants were forced to go out of business.

In one peripheral respect, dietary tradition still flourishes in the *kehillah*. A Hungarian immigrant in 1952 began a kosher wine plant in the heart of the Argentine vineyards in Mendoza. Today there are three such kosher wine centers, producing 100,000 liters annually of the sweet red wines also popular among American Jews.

Overall, though, the central prescriptions of the dietary laws —the ritual slaughter of animals sanctioned for food by the Bible and the strict separation of meat and milk products—are in a gen-eral state of neglect among Argentine Jews.

Sabbath observers are even more the exception. The Jewish day of rest was an early victim of the journey from Eastern Europe to Argentina. The writer-politician Enrique Dickmann recalled in his *Memoirs of a Militant Socialist* his rebellion "against the classic biblical rest of the Sabbath, which had been converted into an absurd day of antisocial fanaticism." Aware that his own father was still strictly observant, Enrique nevertheless made a point of rising early the first Sabbath after the arrival of his parents in the colony, making a fire in the kitchen, and boiling water for *maté,* or tea. This violated the biblical stricture against kindling a fire on the Sabbath. To make certain no one misunderstood his antireligious intentions, he also saddled his horse and did chores in the *chacra.* "Papa," Enrique Dickmann relates, "began to pray, mama to cry. But my brothers obeyed my orders, because they agreed with me. My violent procedure was effective and produced the desired result— to have done with this ancestral fanaticism, a product of religious persecution and racial servitude of the old countries of the Old World, and to begin a new and free life in the New World, in a free Argentina."[4]

Social and economic considerations also influence Jewish attitudes toward the holy days. Sabbath observance is impeded because few Argentine businesses and institutions, with the exception of banks, accept Saturday as a day of rest. Therefore a Jewish Sabbath observer may encounter great difficulty finding work in Argentina.

Many people who otherwise have no contact with the religious aspects of Judaism do close their shops on Yom Kippur, the most solemn and important of Jewish holy days. Remarkably, pressure to do so has come not only from the organized Jewish community and individual religious impulse, but from the nominally religious climate of Catholic Argentina. One Jewish businessman who does not work on Yom Kippur explained, "I am not religious, but my customers know that I am Jewish and, just as a good Catholic keeps his festivals, so they expect a Jew to respect his own holy days. They would be offended were I to violate them."

Birth and death are probably the only times Jewish rite is strictly observed by a sizable proportion of the community. Of the members, nearly 100 percent of the couples interviewed in the Sociedad Hebraica indicated that they have had their male children circumcised or planned to do so when they have children.[5] In the interior, qualified *mohalim,* or ritual circumcisers, are scarcer than in the capital, but even there, traveling *mohalim* make periodic stops at different villages to circumcise many babies at once.

117

Perhaps the most striking feature of Argentine Jewish observance is the central place held by the dead. The AMIA's involvement
in funeral services transcends the traditional Jewish concern to give
the community members a religious burial and common final rest-
ing ground. To the community at large, funerals represent the
major occasion for display of religious fervor. The Argentine Jewish historian Jacob Shatzky, searching for an optimistic note in the
dark picture of Argentine Jewish indifference to tradition, called
the burials the highpoint of the *kehillah*'s religious activity and
added that the funeral services "are strictly observed in accordance
with established rite."[6]

Nearly all the large Jewish communities of the interior, including the agricultural colonies, have their own cemeteries. Many of
the latter have been abandoned as the Jews progressively migrate
to the cities. Yet some of the larger towns of the interior, like
Córdoba and Mendoza, have two Jewish cemeteries in use, for
separate Ashkenazic and Sephardic burials.

The community of Mendoza provides a classic example of the
Argentine Jewish emphasis on cemeteries to a degree difficult for
outsiders—and for an increasing number of Argentine Jews as well
—to comprehend. The Mendozan community has long been without the services of a single rabbi or *shohet*. Although it has made
some progress in education with the construction of basic and inter-
mediate-level Jewish schools, Mendoza will not soon be mistaken
for Vilna in this respect. By contrast, the main cemetery has long
been a wonder of the Argentine Jewish world. The cemetery not
only possesses a *geniza,* or funeral chamber for the burial of deteri-
orated sacred texts, but is even paved completely with cement,
replacing the more old-fashioned grass between the tombstones.
Photographs have been attached to many of the grave sites. The
nearby chapel is also unlike that of any other cemetery in Argentina, and perhaps outside the country as well, boasting an ultramod-
ern architectural design. As one of the community's leaders noted
with considerable satisfaction, "It is the most modern cemetery in
Argentina."

The AMIA recently calculated that, thanks to the purchase of
new cemetery reserve plots, there would be enough burial space for
the next two hundred years.[7] There is a certain grim irony in the
fact that, with critical problems in Jewish education, the rabbinate,

and mere cultural survival, the AMIA appears more prepared to bury the community than to save it.

Synagogues and congregations

The synagogue has been a major center for Argentine Jewish activities. Unlike its East European and American counterparts, it is not primarily a religious institution but a social one. The evolution of the Argentine synagogue, from a traditional prayer center and old-style Hebrew school into a meeting place for largely secular convocations, mirrors the transformation of the Argentine Jewish mentality from Orthodox to irreligious.

Today there are close to fifty synagogues in greater Buenos Aires.[8] This far exceeds the number that gather a *minyan,* or religious quorum of ten men, for Friday night or Saturday morning services. Nearly all the congregations are nominally "Orthodox," with separate seating for men and women and use of the traditional liturgy for services. At the synagogues I visited, sermons were mercifully brief and delivered in Spanish, but Yiddish was also used in many synagogues.

Other similarities to Orthodox congregations are, in most cases, purely superficial. Violations of Jewish Law occur repeatedly in both religious and social ceremonies, including acts prohibited on the Sabbath and the serving of unkosher food at bar mitzvah and wedding celebrations.[9]

The rabbinate

The rabbi has always been a key figure in Judaism, as spiritual leader, community spokesman and, above all, as teacher. Argentine Jewry's acute problem of religious and cultural continuity is most glaring in its dearth of rabbis, since the earliest settlements till the present. As late as 1970, scarcely twenty rabbis were to be found in the entire country, an astounding ratio of one rabbi for every 25,000 Jews.[10]

Henry Joseph, the well-meaning and devoted Grand Rabbi with a manifest ignorance of Jewish Law and culture, did much to weaken the authority of the rabbinate in Argentine Jewish life. Indeed, when even the religious in the community despised the

119

rabbi, it became all but impossible to salvage the once-great prestige of rabbinical authority in this secularized community.

Twelve years passed after the resignation of Joseph in 1894 before the Buenos Aires congregation was able to obtain another rabbi. Samuel Halphon's legitimate rabbinical credentials marked a quantum leap forward in the development of the Argentine rabbinate. Under his leadership, the community added a regular choir with organ and other music. Sermons became a permanent feature of temple services as did a benediction for the Argentine homeland.[11] Yet Halphon still could not overcome the inherent weaknesses of Argentine Jewish culture, chiefly the inadequate educational system and the lack of indigenously trained (or even foreign-educated) leaders. The number of rabbis over the next several decades remained minimal, and the influence they exercised generally did not extend far beyond the synagogues in which they practiced.

Refugees from Central Europe during the 1930s contributed to a renovation of community religious life and the enhancement of the rabbinate. The neo-Orthodox rabbis created religious Zionist organizations and centers for religious youth. Swiss-born Guillermo Schlesinger was the most successful of these new rabbis. He entered Argentina in 1937 on a mission for the Jewish Colonization Association (ICA) and expanded the kehillah's social and philanthropic activities to compensate for the withdrawal of ICA funds and administration. Schlesinger helped to organize the B'nai B'rith, the Argentine Zionist Federation, the Argentine Jewish Institute of Culture and Information, the Higher Council of Synagogues, and the Daughters of Israel.[12]

Schlesinger's greatest asset was a rare flexibility in working among a community of strong ideological passions. Much later, he would demonstrate this same quality by joining the Conservative Jewish movement and by reaching out to Christian leaders in interfaith dialogue. During the 1930s he used his talents for mediation and moderation to consolidate the links between Jewish groups across the country.

Although Schlesinger's organizational feats were impressive, the rabbinate during this period had little luster. In 1944, the only Argentine Jew deemed knowledgeable and prestigious enough to head a new central rabbinate was a Rabbi Rubinstein, who declined on grounds of uncertain health. The rabbinate remained composed of men of very varied quality, few of whom continued in service for a sustained period.[13]

Into this void of religious leadership and learning, Rabbi Amram Blum came as a flashing meteor, both in the glory and brevity of his Argentine career.[14] A prodigy of the *yeshivah* and a fiery exponent of religious orthodoxy, Blum marked a point of radical discontinuity with the tradition of Argentine rabbinical leadership. Advocates and detractors alike may well have wondered if Blum's arrival in Argentina was divine recompense for the rabbinate of Henry Joseph.

Blum was the scion of an eminent rabbinical family in Nagykároly, then part of the Austro-Hungarian Empire. As a child, Blum excelled in talmudic study, and he was only sixteen upon receiving rabbinical ordination (*semikhah*). The honor was still greater for coming from Rabbi Joseph Elimelech Kahana, a renowned Talmudist who awarded only three such ordinations in his entire life.

Blum left his native town to study under Rabbi Soiffer in the large Hungarian *yeshivah* at Pressburg (now Bratislava). Within three years, he became dean of the rabbinical school at Klausenburg, in Czechoslovakia. By the time he became engaged in 1938, at the age of twenty-six, he had earned the highest rabbinical orders, and his career appeared to have boundless promise.

All Blum's plans suddenly changed after the Fascist shadow eclipsed his native Hungary. He managed to obtain a rare visa for Palestine in 1938, but his Czechoslovakian fiancée had to attempt to join him via an illegal emigration operation arranged by the Jewish Agency. Two Yugoslavian vessels were to carry out the mission, transporting some 800 young people; but the government abruptly denied any responsibility for them, and they were turned back at Bratslava. This catastrophe for the would-be fugitives occurred on Passover, the Jewish feast of liberation.

Blum arrived in Palestine in December 1938 and, with great difficulty, obtained from the Jewish Agency a certificate visa for his fiancée. This accomplishment suggested both his prestige and his persistence, for it required a unique departure from the Jewish Agency's policy of issuing such visas only to blood relatives of immigrants. In April 1941, Blum's fiancée arrived in Palestine on a transport filled with refugees. The couple married on June 2 of that year.

Blum settled in Jerusalem, where he founded a synagogue and a school called Nahalat Shiva. He became better known, though, for his appointment by the British government as chaplain to the Jewish prisoners in Palestine. Most of these were political prisoners, often arrested simply for publicizing Zionist sentiments. Many were ill treated by the British, and some were tortured for possible information about terrorist groups like the Stern Gang. All prisoners lived in appallingly unsanitary conditions.

Given the discouraging circumstances of his ministry, Blum acquitted himself well. Beyond his efforts to sustain the morale of the prisoners, he intervened regularly with British officers to implement minor but inspiriting changes in camp life. Notably, Blum arranged for the religious prisoners to receive kosher food in their quarters.

At the close of the Second World War, Blum's restless energy led to new challenges. First he traveled to Europe at the request of the Grand Rabbi of Palestine, to minister to the remnants of the Jewish people. While serving in Europe, he discovered the need for spiritual leaders in the Jewish communities of Latin America. One reason for Blum's special interest in this cause was the presence in Latin America of many Jewish refugees from the Holocaust, whose condition required first-hand examination and aid. He soon left Europe to join the rabbinate in Argentina.

Blum became the spiritual leader of a Syrian Jewish congregation in Buenos Aires. His famed linguistic talents—he spoke Hungarian, German, Hebrew, French, Yiddish, Italian and, later, English—enabled him to absorb Spanish with little trouble. This was vital in serving the Sephardic membership, which spoke Arabic, Spanish, and some Italian, but of course knew no Yiddish.

During his first years in Argentina, Blum was in a most unusual position. A man steeped in Ashkenazic tradition, he headed a major Sephardic congregation. A preeminent talmudic scholar in a community of few rabbis, he was still a minor figure in the *kehillah,* which was directed by earlier-settled residents.

Blum channeled his energies into strengthening Jewish education, reflecting his *yeshivah* training and orientation. He became spiritual leader of a Jewish day school and reorganized and improved it so that its president soon appointed him dean as well as tutor. Under Blum's supervision, the school accommodated over 200 students through the eighth grade. Blum simultaneously opened a *"yeshivah"* in his own home, providing Jewish instruction along with two other rabbis.

Relations between Blum and his Sephardic congregants proved an interesting experiment in cultural compromise and commitment. Blum's willingness to speak Spanish and Italian to his congregants was a point in his favor. Virtually all other Ashkenazic rabbis spoke only in Yiddish. Another virtue in Sephardic eyes was Blum's obvious superiority in Jewish learning. Blum's fierce concern for the welfare of individuals in the Sephardic community gained additional admirers. At the same time, however, his devotion to Orthodoxy and, more important, to Ashkenazic tradition caused more than one altercation.

Blum's tenacious adherence to Ashkenazic custom, or *minhag,* was perhaps etched most sharply when a Sephardic Jew requested permission to put a photograph of his wife on her gravestone. The reader might well assume that the result was a casual nod and a fond farewell from Blum and nothing more. In fact, the act in question is not forbidden by Jewish Law. It is, however, forbidden by Ashkenazic custom, which in Eastern Europe became indistinguishable from *halakhah* (Jewish law). To Blum, this sufficed as a reason to refuse the request, and no amount of pleading by the Sephardic Jew could change his mind. A day later, the Sephardic Jew returned to the rabbi's office with a gun and threatened Blum with dire consequences if a photograph were not placed on his wife's grave, and quickly! Little did the desperate man know how unshakable was the will of Blum, who considered this a test of his integrity to Judaism and God's will. He refused the violent man's demands. Against such resolve, the Sephardic Jew was reduced to despair and eventually, regaining a cool head, begged the rabbi's forgiveness.

Incidents like the one above, though seldom as dramatic, strained to the limit—and often beyond—the affection of many congregants for Blum. Few could deny that he was a rabbi of the first magnitude in knowledge, accomplishments, and even compassion, but some saw in his attitude toward Jewish law a parochialism that at times overcame his better qualities.

Blum's transformation from a relatively obscure though respected rabbi into a preeminent community figure curiously pertained less to his spiritual qualifications than to his political ties. His participation in Jewish delegations to the Argentine government led to a friendship with President Juan Perón. Perón liked Blum's energetic personality and immense intelligence, and he sought his knowledge and advice regarding the Jewish community.

Blum also was favored by Perón's wife, Eva, whose political influence was second only to that of her husband. Their most widely known meeting occurred in 1949 at a gathering of Jewish and government representatives. Eva had wanted a picture taken with an official in the *kehillah* as a matter of good public relations. Blum, a tall and impressive-looking man, was singled out for the photographic honor, and the unlikely couple posed for a striking picture, which appeared in all the national papers.

As Blum's visits to the Peróns became more frequent, his influence with both the government and the *kehillah* rose sharply. Leaders in the Jewish community noted with amazement and even awe that one of the *kehillah*'s minor officials held regular access to the highest circles of national power.

Blum focused his influence primarily on furthering his surpassing concern for Jewish education. He persuaded Perón to permit establishment of a Department of Jewish Studies in the University of Buenos Aires School of Philosophy and Letters. Blum chaired the department from its founding in 1948 and also taught a course at the university. Though not the first college course in Jewish studies—the Catholic university at Salvador appears to hold that distinction—the one taught by Blum quickly became the most widely attended and discussed.

Blum's widow recalled the precipitating event in his decision to foster such a department: "One day a student at the University of Buenos Aires who also attended the rabbi's Sephardic congregation told him that the university students had voted their opinions on whether or not God exists, and he had cast the only positive vote. Rabbi Blum felt more strongly than ever that young people did not know enough about Judaism and needed deeper instruction."

Blum's course was among the more popular university offerings. His imposing figure and incisive personal style made him a commanding lecturer, and his knowledge of Judaism was clearly masterful. His first talk created pandemonium at the university, not for its content—it was an introductory course on Judaism—but for its unexpected following. The large classroom was so crowded that for the first time in anyone's memory at the university, loudspeakers were set up outside so that students turned away from the doors could still listen to the rabbi. Thereafter, Blum regularly enjoyed a large and enthusiastic audience.

Blum's Jewish star was ascendant. In 1952, the Ashkenazic community offered him the post of spiritual leader of the Temple Paso, the largest and most important synagogue in the nation. By this time, Blum's work in education, excellence in T ..1ud, and above all his friendship with Perón combined to make him the logical choice for heading the Argentine rabbinate. The AMIA formally elected Blum to this post within a short time of his departure from the Syrian congregation to lead the Temple Paso.

Blum's greatest service as Grand Rabbi may have been in mediating with Argentine officials on behalf of the Jewish community. Individuals still recall Blum's timely intervention in numerous and varied circumstances. One man related how Blum convinced the chief of police to grant an immigration visa to a Jew who formerly had been unable to obtain one and whom the DAIA had been unable to help. Blum's well-known friendship with Perón doubtless instilled his every word with added cogency.

Menachem Blum relates that his father once spared an Orthodox Jewish family from an autopsy of the husband, who had been killed in a train accident. Autopsies are forbidden by Jewish Law but required by Argentine law in cases where the full cause of death is unknown. Blum suggested to police authorities that the cause of the man's fall onto the tracks was easily explained: "Because the man was an Orthodox Jew, a *shohet* from Mendoza, he strictly followed the command to keep a head covering at all times. He would not even travel eight steps without one. The roaring train, creating great winds in the station as it approached, caused the man's hat to blow away and he had to recover it." Thinking first of the hat and only too late of the origin of this powerful wind, "he attempted to retrieve his head covering and perished in the effort." It is the sort of logic that would have drawn Enrique Dickmann from his grave in protest against "Orthodox superstition." Nevertheless, as an elderly member of the community who recalled the incident said, "If you've ever seen a *'shohet* from Mendoza' or wherever, then you know it could really happen." Blum ultimately managed to obtain permission from the authorities to have the man buried without first having an autopsy.

The demands of the Grand Rabbi's position, combining severe loyalty to Jewish tradition and delicate diplomacy toward government officials, afforded Blum tremendous satisfaction. It was pride well deserved, for many Jews saw in him a uniquely effective champion of their civil and religious rights.

This period of Blum's career did not end happily, however. He made enemies among all sectors of Jewry, even the strict Orthodox. One community leader described Blum as "a man to keep a grudge, as I discovered from personal experience." Another claimed that Blum enriched himself by using his ties to Perón to obtain government permission to import and sell expensive American automobiles. The less religious resented his insistence on the strictest interpretation of Jewish law, regardless of the attitudes of the people or the circumstances involved. Most important, perhaps, was the resentment of many community leaders who were overshadowed by Blum's flamboyant personality and his closeness to the Argentine president.

Perón's fall from power in 1955 in effect doomed the position of Rabbi Amram Blum. The AMIA and the DAIA led a successful campaign to drive Blum out of office, denouncing him for his link with the country's former dictator.

Even today, Jews tend to recall with strong disapproval that Blum said a prayer for the soul of Eva Perón, who died of cancer in 1952 at the age of thirty-four. This act caused resentment partly because it involved the rabbi's participation in a Roman Catholic religious service. Some also questioned the propriety of blessing the memory of Eva Perón in any service, for she had been a dangerous and unstable demagogue and, at times, inimical to the Jewish community.

The more blatant charges against Blum, still given wide currency in the *kehillah,* do not seem valid. Certainly he was no mere puppet of the Argentine president. He remained dedicated to the welfare of the nation's Jews throughout his tenure as Grand Rabbi. Moreover, Blum held the rare distinction of refusing to join the Perónist Party—on the grounds that his religious position required

126

a nonpolitical stance—and still retaining his professorship in the wake of Perón's seizure and "reform" of the universities. In short, Blum's successful relations with Perón involved no discernible sacrifice of courage or integrity.

The decision to say a prayer for Eva Perón was, according to Blum's son Menachem, a necessity. It was at a time when the entire nation was according her frenzied adulation. Had Blum spurned President Perón's request for him to say a short and fairly innocuous prayer for his all but canonized wife, it would have irresponsibly placed the Jewish community in jeopardy from embittered Argentine mourners.

In the general reaction against Perón and Blum in 1955, neither Blum's numerous contributions to the *kehillah* nor his proven devotion to Judaism protected him from a wave of abuse reminiscent of the rabbinate of Henry Joseph. The officials of the Temple Paso would not even permit Blum to conduct the rites for the Day of Atonement because "he had collaborated with the former government and accepted a professorship in the School of Philosophy and Letters."

Blum decided not to prolong the fight and resigned as Grand Rabbi. He eventually settled in the United States, where he acquired doctorates in history and Semitic languages and served as rabbi for congregations in Los Angeles and Cleveland. Blum died in Cleveland in 1970, at the age of fifty-seven.

Like Henry Joseph, Argentina's first Grand Rabbi, Blum was never fully understood in his lifetime. Perhaps his great complexity made that impossible. A friend of Blum's who knew him in Palestine and later in Cleveland said of him, "Blum had no intellectual equal. He was therefore a very lonely man. . . . Fanatical? That was his image, but let me tell you that inside Blum was a rebel. You know, there was a Jewish tradition in Eastern Europe of never speaking Hebrew in ordinary conversation, only Yiddish. Do you think Blum saw any sense to that? All right, but he represented not only his own religious feelings but the traditions of an entire community. He was the *Grand Rabbi* and so he spoke in Yiddish to everyone. And when he asked for me on the phone—we'd call each other several times a week in Cleveland—it would be in Yiddish, too. But when we spoke to each other, he used Hebrew, which he pronounced with a beautiful Sephardic accent, as they do in Israel."

127

Whatever his faults, Blum gave greatness to the Argentine rabbinate. And if he was racked with inner doubts about aspects of Jewish tradition, at heart he loved Judaism and the responsibilities of the rabbinate, personal as well as ritual. He was at once Argentine Jewry's leading sage and its most zealous defender.

Since the departure of Blum, there have been several successive Grand Rabbis of the Ashkenazic *kehillah*. Of these, David Kahana has had the greatest impact, as well as the longest tenure (1965–75). Like Blum, Kahana is a product of European Orthodoxy. He was born in Russian Poland and served as chaplain for the Jews in the Polish army after the Second World war.

Kahana moved to Israel and in 1950 was appointed chaplain of the Israeli Air Force. (The extent of this honor may be seen in the fact that another occupant of this position, Shlomo Goren, subsequently became Chief Rabbi of Israel's Ashkenazic community.) In 1965, Kahana answered the call to fill the void left by Argentina's departing Grand Rabbi, Jacob Fink. After serving in the office for ten years, Kahana returned to Israel and was replaced by another Israeli, Menachem Fitterman.

A product of the *yeshivah* culture of Eastern Europe—as well as the holder of a doctorate in psychology—Kahana is a strictly observant Jew who adheres to a rigorous interpretation of the *halakhah*. During his tenure, for example, he felt compelled to reject the plea of a Jewish father to permit his young son, killed in an accident, to be buried in the Jewish cemetery. The boy's mother was Catholic, also making the boy a Catholic, according to Jewish law. Kahana therefore could not accede fully to the father's request but permitted the burial adjacent to the Jewish cemetery in a section reserved for children of mixed marriages.[15] However, Kahana's conception of Judaism also includes a prominent place not only for *halakhah* but for *aliyah,* and this served to enhance his stature among young Argentine Zionists unattracted to religious Zionism.

During a wide-ranging discussion in Kahana's home in Buenos Aires, not long before he left the country, the courtly, white-bearded rabbi conveyed an abiding concern to preserve and magnify a sense of Judaic tradition. Although he speaks Spanish and some English, for example, he insisted that the interview be conducted only in Hebrew or Yiddish, which he called "Jewish languages."

128

Kahana showed himself to be acutely aware of the Argentine Jewish tendency to minimize the religious element in conceptions of Jewish identity. Asked to compare this community with the one he had once served in Poland, Kahana's first reaction was a perfunctory, "There is no comparison." Then, more humorously, "All right, there is: they speak Yiddish, they have the same foolishness, the same mannerisms, what-have-you. But"—and here his words became somber, a voice from another era—"there is nothing more. Here, they don't have the knowledge. Every Jew in Eastern Europe studied in a *heder,* in a Jewish school. They were filled to the brim with Jewish knowledge, history, Torah, and Talmud. There were a great many schools. And there was no Jew who did not know how to read and write Hebrew. The majority here cannot even write Hebrew. We won't even speak of public prayer or how to use a *siddur* [prayer book]."

Kahana's personal eminence did not significantly raise the stature of the rabbinate itself. This remains a marginal institution in the *kehillah,* reflecting the poor showing of the religious parties in each of the AMIA elections. Hope that the rabbinate will become a more energetic and effective institution is contingent upon the graduates of Argentina's rabbinical seminaries. Until the present, almost all Argentine rabbis have been born and educated abroad—in the United States, Israel, and Europe. Unless the *kehillah* increases the number of its seminaries, the rabbinate will lack the strength to affect the mainstream of Jewish community life. Outside Buenos Aires, for example, there was not a single rabbi throughout the country until one was sent to Rosario in the summer of 1972. It is a vicious cycle that deprives the community of spiritual leaders who might educate the children and create an environment in which new leaders can emerge.

Bet din

Two AMIA departments deal with religious affairs. Aside from the rabbinate, there is also the *bet din,* or rabbinic tribunal, which functions according to the same principles used by the Jewish tribunals in the earliest days of the Diaspora. The *bet din* acts as a unifying force in the community, as both the Conservative and

Reform movements adhere to its judgments rather than form their own courts. This is especially important when one considers that the Orthodox recognize only the *get* (divorce) that strictly conforms to *halakhah* and regard children of marriages that follow an "invalid" *get* as illegitimate and cut off from the community.

The rabbinic tribunal is still attended by devoted Jews in preference to non-Jewish secular courts. It has successfully resolved hundreds of cases, and even Argentine secular courts have upon occasion recommended the tribunal to its litigants. The *bet din* tries only cases between members of the Jewish community. It operates with no binding authority except its own prestige and moral weight, but its judgments are generally heeded by the contesting parties. Increasingly, the *bet din* has presided over cases between Jewish institutions and cases involving both institutions and individuals.[16]

Religion in the interior

If religion is losing its grip on Jewish culture in the major Argentine cities, it is flourishing there in comparison with the state of religious Judaism in the small centers of the interior. Matters have worsened since historian Jacob Shatzky wrote this assessment in 1952:

The small communities have difficulty celebrating nuptial ceremonies, for lack of religious officials. The functioning of synagogues is similarly impeded by the lack of cantors. The number of *shohetim* diminishes from year to year. There are still communities in the provinces that observe *kashrut* and must renounce the consumption of meat for lack of a *shohet*. . . . Only the great temples can count on a permanent cantor and others hire a religious cantor for the great festivals. In general, the position of religious functionaries is not very prosperous and only a diminishing number of them can live on the salary of a *shamash* [synagogue attendant] or *shohet*.[17]

Moisésville alone of the colonies has excellent facilities for Jewish education, including one of the most important rabbinic seminaries in the country. Its dedication to Judaic tradition reflects the determination of its earliest immigrants, one of whose leaders

First Jewish Argentine Congress at Teatro Nuevo, 1916

Seminar for Teachers of Hebrew, ca. 1940

First Building of the Oldest Synagogue, Buenos Aires,
Congregación Israelita de la República Argentina

*Sociedad Hebraica Argentina Theater in Buenos Aires, Seating
Capacity of 1,000*

*AMIA Building, Buenos Aires, Where Several Vital Jewish Agencies
Are Located*

*Building of Di Yidishe Tsaytung, Buenos Aires, the Daily Jewish Newspaper,
No Longer Published after 1974*

sent the following message to the Jewish communities of Eastern Europe via a Hebrew newspaper:

We do not want for the moment, to ask for any other aid but the delivery of seventy copies of the Pentateuch and some twenty copies of the *Zohar*, 220 copies of prayer books, some twenty commentaries on the Talmud, 200 books of Psalms, phylacteries, *mezuzot*, everything which can be useful . . . in strengthening our religion. . . . Perhaps hemostatic drugs can also be sent for use after circumcision—in order to stop the flow of blood, since these cannot be obtained here.[18]

Aside from the rock of Jewish continuity presented by Moisés-ville, the colonies are slowly losing their Jewish identity. While in the early 1960s, the rate of religious intermarriage was only about 15 to 20 percent overall in the *kehillah*, in some communities of the interior it soared to 33 percent and higher.[19]

Zalman Wassertzug, the prominent Yiddish writer and AMIA official, observed in 1966 that there was very little hope to save these communities, which "are slowly dissolving. . . . The few families that live there languish in a slow social agony."[20]

Clearly, given the concentration of people, resources, rabbis, and educational facilities in Buenos Aires, if there is to be a renaissance in Jewish religious learning and traditional observance, it must come from the community of the capital and radiate from there to the remnants of the interior communities.

The liberal movements

Recent years have witnessed the first major signs of new religious forms in the *kehillah*. The most striking developments have been the growth of the Conservative and Reform movements, which have provided Argentine Judaism with much needed philosophical and institutional vigor.

Conservative Judaism is the larger of the two liberal Jewish denominations in Argentina. It originally developed in Europe during the nineteenth century, largely as a reaction against extreme liberal elements within Judaism. In Argentina, though, Conservative Judaism arose before the Reform movement and responded instead primarily to the limitations of Orthodoxy in meeting the needs of the *kehillah*.

131

The philosophy of Conservative Judaism stresses the historical development of the Jewish people and their need to adapt to new circumstances while conserving basic values and beliefs. In the secularized and nationalistic Argentine *kehillah,* this emphasis on Jewish history rather than divine revelation has given the Conservative movement an intellectual appeal unmatched by Orthodox Judaism.

During the late 1950s, Guillermo Schlesinger became the first Argentine rabbi to move his congregation officially into the Conservative fold. Schlesinger's move had especial symbolic significance, for he was the elder statesman among Argentine rabbis, while his synagogue, the Congregación Israelita, was the oldest Jewish institution in the country.[21] To aid in developing the new movement, Schlesinger obtained the services of a young American rabbi, whose leadership would soon become practically synonymous with Conservative Judaism in Argentina.[22]

Marshall Theodore Meyer, then a recent graduate of the Jewish Theological Seminary of America, was not quite thirty years old when he arrived in Buenos Aires in 1959, as assistant to Rabbi Schlesinger. He quickly gained a reputation for energetic administration, as well as for a rare personal rapport with many Jewish youth. Meyer increased the use of Spanish in the synagogue services and added other features to draw young members. This interest in Jewish youth led him to establish the first South American branch of Camp Ramah, the name for a network of Hebrew-speaking Conservative Jewish summer camps in the United States. He also insured Conservative Judaism of firm educational roots by founding the Latin American Rabbinical Seminary in 1962.

Meyer left the Congregación Israelita in December 1962 to preside over the newly formed congregation at Temple Bet-El, the first fully Conservative synagogue in Argentina. Together with a rabbinical colleague, Marcos Edery, he soon guided Bet-El to a membership of over 500 families and a record of leadership in Jewish education, cultural activities, concern for youth, and the promotion of interfaith cooperation. By the early 1970s, the Conservative movement in Argentina counted 2,200 families in four congregations and appeared destined for still further expansion.[23]

Reform Judaism, totally absent from Argentina for most of the *kehillah*'s history, took tentative root there during the 1960s. Like the Conservative movement, Reform Judaism originated in Europe as a response to the emancipation of the Jews in the nineteenth century. Early Reform leaders sought to interpret Judaism as a "modern" religion easily integrated into the life of a good, patriotic citizen. Concomitantly, Reform Judaism minimized Jewish national consciousness. However, after the terrors of the Holocaust and the creation of the State of Israel, Reform Judaism moderated its views on Jewish nationalism while retaining its modernizing, liberalized attitude toward religious tradition.

In Argentina, where many Jews feel a general sense of identification with their Judaic heritage despite a disinclination toward strict observance of the Mosaic Law, Reform Judaism would appear to be a movement of great popular potential. Yet in its initial stages, Reform Judaism was a movement largely transplanted from abroad.

American-trained religious leaders have played a crucial role in Argentine Reform Judaism since its inception in 1963; its first temple was completed in 1965. Rabbi Haim Asa inaugurated the religious activities of Temple Emanu-El, the main Reform temple in Buenos Aires. His successor, Rabbi Rifat Sonsino, wrote the first Argentine books on Reform Judaism. Rabbi Leon Klenicki, who guided Temple Emanu-El until 1973, continued Sonsino's efforts to publicize the movement. In particular, Klenicki became known for his energetic campaign to gain greater acceptance for the Reform movement among other, more traditional sectors of the *kehillah*.

Reform Judaism in Argentina has been especially concerned with sponsoring cultural and intellectual programs, including numerous seminars on religion and lectures by both rabbis and youth leaders. The movement also participates in an exchange program enabling Argentine youths to live for six months with an American family affiliated with a Reform temple. The American-based National Federation of Temple Youth provides scholarships for this program.[24]

Klenicki asserted in 1969 that Reform Judaism faced a critical period in Latin America and that "Reform's success here in Buenos Aires will mean success in the rest of the continent."[25] He added that the Reform movement's most urgent needs were for more rabbis to share work he described as "overwhelming"; for publications on Reform Judaism in school texts, printed magazines, and a Reform Passover *Haggadah*; and for increased coordination of Emanu-El with other branches of Reform Judaism in Argentina.[26]

The Reform movement in the early 1970s included 920 families in its three congregations and, like the Conservative movement, seemed likely to continue its growth.[27] Klenicki, who privately acknowledged the difficulties of establishing a new and very different Jewish movement in the Argentine *kehillah*, also stressed that it was an essential task. He believed that "Reform Judaism in Latin America has a great future, it is *the* answer to the identification crisis of the new generations . . . the only road to spiritual salvation and vital meaning."[28]

Denominational trends

The efforts of Conservative and Reform leaders to attract previously uninterested families, especially younger members, is perhaps the critical variable in the development of religious Judaism in Argentina. A look at American Jewish trends, though, may provide balance to predictions that these liberal denominations will soon predominate in the religious life of the community.

The history of Jewish religion in the United States has shown that denominational surges tend to run in cycles. The high tide of Reform Judaism in the late nineteenth century receded before a gradual movement on both ends of the religious spectrum toward Conservative traditionalism, in fact if not in name. Similarly, predictions during the 1960s of an irresistible push by the Conservative movement to displace Orthodoxy have become more muted in the 1970s. Instead there has been a renewed emphasis among many religious Jews on the scrupulous observance of Jewish law and custom.

The lesson for Argentine Jewry is that no one approach to Jewish religious expression is likely to meet all the varied needs of the community. Therefore, it is doubtful whether a single denomination or movement will exert a lasting hegemony among the rank and file of the *kehillah*.

Possibly the success of the liberal religious movements will stimulate the Orthodox to experience a cultural and educational renewal, as well as a more manifest concern for the needs and loyalties of younger Jews. The future of religious Judaism in Argentina may still depend in large part on the resiliency of the Orthodox movement, to which a majority of religious officials, congregants, and institutions retain at least a nominal allegiance. For the present, though, the Orthodox have developed neither the mass base nor the cultural creativity such as they once enjoyed in Eastern Europe. Therefore, it has been left to the liberal denominations, at least temporarily, to provide for the continued vitality of Argentine Jewish religious culture.

5   EDUCATION

"Education, education, education!" Dr. Moisés Goldman, the seventy-year-old veteran leader in the *kehillah,* used these words to answer my question of what was most essential for the future of Argentine Jewry.[1] Few other leaders disagreed with his emphatic order of priorities. Yet today Jewish education is dying in Argentina. It is a crisis that has menaced the community, and ever more severely, since the time of the first Jewish settlers.

Roots of the problem

The earliest efforts of the Jewish Colonization Association (ICA) in the field of education set an enduring pattern of neglect of talmudic and biblical learning. The ICA created the first schools in 1894, four centers parallel to American Jewish day schools, which devote equal time to secular and religious subjects. The actual attention paid to these two areas was rather less equally apportioned in the ICA schools. For the secular curriculum, the ICA followed the government syllabus and hired capable personnel from the Alliance Israélite Universelle. These educators were knowledgeable and influenced by the Enlightenment's ideals of rationalism and progress. An altogether different and dismal situation applied with regard to the hours of religious instruction. These classes were patterned after the East European *heder,* an inspiration that all but guaranteed the failure of Jewish religious learning in Argentina.

In contrast to the *yeshivot,* revered for their cultivation of razor-sharp analysis and subtle exegesis, the *heder,* or Jewish primary

137

school, was much less honored. A Jewish proverb in Eastern Europe declared: "Two things it is never too late to do: to die and to teach in a *heder.*" The classes featured a mixture of drudgeries, including endless oral repetitions, severe discipline and, above all, lessons that failed even to suggest a point to the memorization of Hebrew phrases that no one understood. Solomon Maimon, a brilliant Polish scholar and philosopher in the late eighteenth century, left a vivid impression of these schools in his memoirs:

[The *heder* master] was the terror of all young people, "the scourge of God"; he treated those in his charge with unheard-of cruelty, flogged them till the blood came, even for the slightest offense, and not infrequently tore off their ears or beat their eyes out. . . . All under his discipline became either blockheads or good scholars. . . .

[Biblical passages] are explained in school, and these with every possible grammatical blunder. Nor can it well be otherwise. For the Hebrew must be explained by means of the vernacular. But the vernacular of the Polish Jews is itself full of defects and grammatical inaccuracies; and so the Hebrew language, which is learned by its means, must be of the same stamp. The pupil thus acquires just as little knowledge of the language, as of the contents of the Bible.[2]

The emotional strains on the children in the *heder* were predictably severe. Those with considerable resilience were toughened mentally, if not enlightened intellectually; but more sensitive souls among the students were sometimes unable to learn by or even cope with the *heder* routine.

The deterioration of the *heder* from a folkschool into a sort of correctional school by the nineteenth century is captured in an anecdote by Shmarya Levin, who spent his childhood in a Polish *shtetl.* It was a custom, Levin writes, after performing an initial ceremony, for the father to wrap the child of *heder* age in a prayer shawl and carry him in his arms all the way to the school. The mother did not come along, as this was considered man's business. Levin observes, "It was as if some dark idea stirred in their minds that this child was a sacrifice, delivered over to the *heder*—and a sacrifice must be carried all the way."[3]

One may well ask what point there was to these primitive institutions. The religious would have responded that the point lay in the subsequent schooling that the *heder*-educated youth received.

The intense dedication to religion and education carried these children through the rigors of their first phase of learning. When these youths came out of the *heder* and into the world of Talmud and *pilpul* (dialectical analysis), they were prepared to study long hours and memorize large portions of commentaries. The *yeshivah* refined the intellects that devotion and *heder* made strong. Naturally, all the many brilliant rabbinic teachers wanted to serve in the only place that challenged their skill and knowledge—the prestigious *yeshivah.* But the *heder,* with all its weaknesses, was an integral part of Jewish education in Eastern Europe.

The tragedy of Jewish education in Argentina is that the *heder* became almost the *only* institution of religious learning. What even many pious Jews long considered a sad but necessary prelude to the spiritual and intellectual delights of the *yeshivah* now moved into the front lines of defense of the Jewish cultural heritage. It was a hollow parody of Jewish learning in Eastern Europe and could not suffice to transmit its rich cultural traditions.

Disillusion with the schools was rapid, and the distracting demands of life in the colonies speeded the process along. The schools were remote from many homes, and the unpleasant prospect of a horseback ride during the Argentine winter discouraged many children from attending school for weeks at a time. Then in summer most children had to help their families with the harvest. The parents came to lose interest in supporting or using the Jewish schools, and the student population declined steadily.

The failures of the ICA schools meant a failure for almost all Jewish religious instruction. More than 90 percent of the students between 1890 and 1910 lived in the agricultural centers. Even by 1928, when the ICA no longer possessed the resources to maintain its hold on Jewish education, youths from the colonies still formed 65 percent of the Jewish schoolchildren.[4]

Leaders in the ICA were as frustrated as the colonists with the results of the school system, which was fast becoming an unacceptable financial burden. In 1914, the ICA relinquished official control over its network of schools, and a brief period of local autonomy ensued. Within three years, however, the ICA encouraged the Jewish Congregation in Buenos Aires to form a new entity, the Va'ad Hahinukh Haroshi (Head Education Office), to assume control of all schools. The new organization adhered to the general patterns earlier drawn by the ICA.

At first glance it is bewildering that the great majority of schools remained for so long under the direction of a single institution. This was, after all, a community with a faction for every occasion and for every side of a social or cultural issue. One important reason for the ICA's long and effective domination of the schools is its financial superiority over any of the smaller community societies. A possibly more significant explanation, though, is that the ability of the ICA to control the schools resulted from indifference to traditional education among members of the community. The secular currents building in the *kehillah* had left the old educational patterns deeply unsatisfying. Yet initiatives for new forms of education, stressing nonreligious facets of Judaic experience, proceeded too slowly to fill the void. As a result, the colonists quarreled over Zionism, socialism, indeed almost every other issue in community life, but passively accepted the ICA control over traditional Jewish instruction and with equal passivity witnessed the steady deterioration of Jewish learning.

Ideological upheaval

The ICA's attempts to channel Jewish education into Western forms—rationalist, anti-Zionist, anti-Yiddish, and politically conservative—broke down during the late 1920s and early 1930s. The initial cause relates less to the emergence of rival educational networks—these could scarcely sustain themselves—than to the ICA's gradual abdication of administrative and economic responsibility for the schools.

The triumph of the ideological movements compatible with the East European experience was largely ignored at the time because it coincided with a nadir in Jewish educational activity. Until the early 1920s, the schools enjoyed a tenuous stability but little organizational progress. Despite the continued population increase, the number of students was scarcely greater in 1923 than it had been in 1913. Then, during the 1920s, a downward trend set in. The gradual withdrawal of ICA funds and a general lessening of interest in the schools resulted in a student enrollment one-third less in 1929 than in 1923.[5] With the onset of the Depression in

1929, the schools met disaster. Budgets strained to the limit, and many more centers were forced to close because of insolvency. The Argentine dictatorship that came to power in 1930 ordered many others shut as well, fearing subversive influences among schools founded by Socialist elements. In 1934, the ICA formalized the catastrophe by officially ending all aid to the Argentine community. The following year, enrollment figures plunged to their lowest point, 1,553 students in all Jewish schools.[6]

The mid-1930s marked a period of consolidation for the new school networks. The major movements—Zionist, Socialist, Communist—all weathered the financial and political storms that had decimated their ranks and began to expand their educational centers a little at a time. By 1940, aided by a return of economic stability, the Jewish schools counted more students (4,343) than were enrolled prior to the Depression (3,401 in 1928).[7]

The administration of the schools also stabilized. The Central Education Office, successor to the ICA, continued to direct the provincial centers, while the AMIA officially assumed control of education in Buenos Aires. Both of these central coordinating organizations maintained strict detachment from schools run by any extremist parties that might embarrass the larger community.

The strongest Zionist party in Argentina, the labor Po'alei Zion, also made the most determined efforts to create educational institutions independent of ICA direction. In 1908, they founded a Jewish school that strongly inculcated their leftist-nationalist ideology. They also established the Borochov network of schools in the 1920s with the same purpose. The schools' name honored the great Jewish idealist Ber Borochov, whose synthesis of Marx and Herzl placed him as the foremost intellectual figure among left-wing Zionist groups.

After losing most of their students and centers in the first years of the Depression, the Po'alei Zionists revived their school system in 1934 by forming the Sholem Aleichem network. This was a line of schools organized by the left-wing group Tsentraler Veltlekh Yidishe Shul Organizatsie (ZVISHO—Central Organization of Jewish Secular Schools).

Other Zionist schools complemented the efforts of the Po'alei Zionists. Schools named for the poet Haim Nachman Bialik provided a dual Hebrew and Yiddish approach to Jewish nationalist

141

education. The exclusively Hebrew-speaking school, Nahman Gesang, honored the Argentine Jewish Zionist (1868–1944), who fought to make Hebrew an integral part of Jewish life and learning. Herzlia and Tel Aviv schools also shared these values.

The Bund, or Jewish labor organization, in 1931 contributed the Gezelshaft far Yidishe Veltlekhe Shuln in Argentine (Association of Jewish Secular Schools in Argentina). This network included one of the largest schools in Buenos Aires, named after the Yiddish writer, Isaac Leib Peretz. The Bundist schools naturally wove their brand of Socialist politics deeply into the curricula, and teachers conducted all classes in Yiddish, the heart of Bundist Jewish identity.

The Jewish Communists broadcast their party line in a series of schools named, perhaps inevitably, Mendele Mocher Sforim. The choice symbolizes the deference that the most varied sectors of the *kehillah* gave to both the Yiddish language and its Old World exponents. Since the Po'alei Zionists already basked in the prestige of Sholem Aleichem and the Bundist schools claimed the glory of Peretz, the Communists were quick to appropriate the revered memory of Mendele Mocher Sforim, the third preeminent European master of Yiddish prose.

The Communist schools, like their other organizations, were ostracized by the rest of the community and were persecuted by the Argentine government. Despite these grave disadvantages, they remained a vigorous force in spreading Yiddish culture. By 1944, the Communist school network boasted several kindergartens, five elementary schools, and two high schools, having a total attendance of approximately 900 students. Enrollment reached over 2,000 during the 1950s, and several of its schools still operate today.[8]

Zionism remains the dominant chord in the ideological tones of the Jewish schools. It is an inextricable part of the curricula in most centers and receives the wholehearted support of the Central Education Office in Buenos Aires. Thus, the community has broken fully from its Western mentors in the ICA and given full expression to its own ideological ethos.

Levels of instruction

Jewish education in Argentina has been practically synonymous with elementary instruction. There was no institution for higher education in the *kehillah* for its first fifty years. Since 1940, the community has attempted to fill that void with teacher's seminaries, *yeshivot,* and other higher level schools, but the gap remains more imposing than the advance.

The first wonder of Argentine Jewish education—the Teacher's Seminary—appeared in 1940 under the sponsorship of the AMIA. The seminary was really a secondary school whose graduates would generally become teachers at an elementary level, but given the previous state of Jewish education this was no small achievement. The secular and Jewish nationalist leanings of the seminary led the Jewish Congregation in Buenos Aires to found a similar institution, the Institute for Jewish Studies, which assumed a more traditional and religious orientation.

The original Teacher's Seminary, known as the Midrasha, is the outstanding institution in secondary education, having graduated 900 teachers from 1940 through 1965. It operates in Buenos Aires but accepts students from the interior as well. Nearly 70 percent of the teachers in the Jewish schools of Greater Buenos Aires have graduated the Midrasha, and all high school teachers are required to matriculate there. In 1966, 350 students enrolled in its classes.[9]

During the early forties, the community constructed its first *yeshivah,* Hafetz Haim, under the direction of the religious party Agudat Israel. Classes began in 1943; by 1951 they included four teachers and thirty-five students. After decades of only *heder* schools, this represented a dramatic advance in the community's educational system. Yet the "miracle" of Hafetz Haim appears in a more naturalistic light if one considers that by East European and American standards, the term *yeshivah* should be applied loosely to the Argentine model. The advanced talmudic study that forms the heart of a *yeshivah* training was altogether lacking at Hafetz Haim in its early years; later some Talmud classes were added but not on a very sophisticated level.[10]

Hafetz Haim did contribute a major innovation in the practical area of providing student support. This had been a problem for the European *yeshivot,* where families of the students were seldom well-off and the youths had little sustenance for such intensive thought. Usually, they lived on bread and tea; meat was available only on the Sabbath. "Eating days," during which time *yeshivah* lads dined at some villager's home, was a common arrangement but somewhat awkward and even uncertain. During the 1890s, food shortages actually led to a student strike at one *yeshivah.*

Hafetz Haim instituted a wholly different approach to feeding the students. During the first half of the school day, it taught each student a trade, like watchmaking, textile-weaving, and so forth. Each month it deposited a certain sum of money in a treasury for the student. At the end of the course of instruction, the student would have some small capital to establish a business of his own. The excellent planning behind this approach reaped fine results and enabled this institution to graduate three of the first five rabbis educated in Argentina.[11]

The success of Hafetz Haim inspired new experiments in higher education. A second *yeshivah,* Makhon Lelimudei Hayahadut (Institute for Jewish Studies), commenced in 1945. Its directors soon after converted it into an advanced day school designed to serve as a teacher's seminary. Morning classes in Hebrew were followed by instruction leading to a secular baccalaureate. Yet religious life did not dissolve with the noon dismissal. Formal study complemented a religious existence within a communal life-style, which featured traditional celebration of Sabbath and festival days. The school included a synagogue on its grounds and, unlike the old ICA schools, this institution accorded equal priorities to religious and secular education. The six-year course of instruction culminated with the licensing of all graduates as teachers in the AMIA's primary schools.[12]

Yeshivot on a more advanced level than those of the 1940s remained a major community goal in higher education. During the early 1960s, two such centers began operating in Buenos Aires. They were designed to train potential rabbis and therefore to give fuller instruction than the various teachers' seminaries.

The recent achievements highlight the growing role of the

Conservative movement in the *kehillah*. It complemented the Orthodox Yeshiva Gevoha with its own Latin American Rabbinical Seminary in 1962. By thus sponsoring one of the two foremost institutions of religious learning, Conservatism wedged itself firmly into the center of the *kehillah*'s cultural life. Rabbi Marshall Meyer directed the seminary with vigor and steadily expanded its curriculum and faculty.

A happy ending to the story on higher education still would require a largely different set of facts. The community as yet has no Jewish school comparable with the best American or Israeli institutes. Rabbi Meyer admitted this candidly in 1970:

In reality, at least for the while, the name of Seminary is in some sense inexact, since the institution does not have sufficient resources to cover the full field of rabbinical studies. It is for this reason that the graduates of the Seminary do not receive the title enabling them to practice as rabbis until after having completed their training at the Jewish Theological Seminary in New York, or, if they wish, at the Hebrew University in Jerusalem. Therefore, up to the present moment, the Seminary is really a pre-Seminary, and will remain so until it possesses enough qualified professors to assume the responsibility of guaranteeing [the education needed for] *semichah* or rabbinical ordination.[13]

The same limitations apply substantially to the other Argentine Jewish schools of higher learning.

More discouraging than simply the limited scope of *yeshivah* education is the small number of students for whom it would make any difference. In 1967, for example, the total number of graduates from Jewish secondary schools in Buenos Aires was 126.[14] The plummeting totals of student participation beyond elementary education may be seen in the figures in Table 8. (Also see Table 9.)

The problem of dropouts is staggering. Of the students who attended the first grade in Buenos Aires in 1960, only 4.2 percent survived the rather mild academic rigors of elementary school to complete the sixth grade. This figure was obtained from classes through the mid-sixties, before the educational crisis actually lowered the proportion of those enrolled in the Jewish schools.[15]

An American scholar on Jewish education recently stated that "at least 3,000 hours of religious instruction are needed before Jewish schooling has any lasting impact." This would be equivalent,

Table 8: Extent of Jewish Education in Argentina, 1963

| Type of School | Buenos Aires | | Interior | |
	Schools	Pupils	Schools	Pupils
Kindergarten	56	5,090	28	998
Elementary	58	8,163	56	3,263
Secondary	9	818	8	233
Yeshivah	3	122	– –	– –
Teacher Seminary	2	282	1	139
College	1	92	– –	– –
TOTAL	129	14,567	93	4,633

SOURCE: Moshe Kitron, "Yahadut America Ha-Dromit Ubayoteha" (Latin American Jewry in Our Time), *Bitfutzot Hagola* (Winter 1964), p. 157.

for example, to attending Hebrew school approximately eight hours a week for nearly ten years.[16] By these standards, "higher education" in the *kehillah* has scarcely begun to make an appreciable impact.

The interior communities

The days of provincial hegemony in the *kehillah*'s schools are past. Now, over three-quarters of the students reside in Buenos Aires, and administration is centralized in the federal capital. Educational conditions are particularly disturbing in the remaining interior communities, where only 32 of some 140 Jewish localities have any formal centers for Judaic instruction.[17]

The centers in the interior have always varied widely in their ability to sustain Jewish culture. During the 1950s, for example, only 13 of its 85 schools (20 of which were kindergartens) reached the fifth grade. Yet there were bright exceptions wherever a cohesive religious and organizational life still prevailed after four or five decades of settlement. Resistencia, a city of 240 Ashkenazic families in Entre Ríos, is a particularly notable case. In sharp contrast to the usual 15 to 20 percent figures for student attendance, fully 70 percent of the Jewish children attended Resistencia's Hebrew schools in 1952. The community also maintained a beautiful building that included a fine Judaica library and a credit cooperative, which supported community educational activities.[18] More re-

Table 9: Lineal Depiction of Extent of Jewish Education in Argentina, 1963

Type of School	Total Number of Students (in Buenos Aires and the interior)
Kindergarten	+++++++++++++++++++++++++++++
Elementary	++++++++++++++++++++++++++++
	+++++++++++++++++++++++++++
Secondary	++++
Yeshivah	+
Teacher Seminary	++
College	+

NOTE—Each symbol represents 500 students. This chart is a lineal depiction of information in Table 8, above.

cently, one can point to the unusual situation in Córdoba, whose Jewish community faces the relatively few economic troubles that plague the *kehillah* in Buenos Aires. Córdoba's Jewish community recently spent close to a million dollars on a Jewish day school on the secondary level. Of its school-age children, 25 percent enroll in some Jewish classes, a low figure in itself but considerably higher than the proportion of Jewish children attending school in Buenos Aires.[19] In still other communities, usually small and close-knit, Jewish school attendance is out of all proportion to comparable statistics in the capital and larger interior cities. In Paraná, for example, 83 percent of all school-age children attend Hebrew school.[20]

In higher education, the interior boasts only one major institution, but this is quite impressive. The teacher's seminary in Moisés-ville is among the prime educational centers created in the expansionist era of the 1940s. Ten elementary school teachers graduated its first classes in 1949, and the school eventually taught over 200 students each year. The seminary gradually expanded into the interior, with branches in Córdoba and Rosario. It is unique among the country's Jewish secondary schools for its primarily religious orientation. In 1966, 120 resident students and 85 commuters enrolled in its classes. Almost all the teachers who have come from this school are native-born, and many have spent a year in Israel.[21]

The wide variations in the interior schools nevertheless tend

147

to cluster around a general pattern of inadequate Jewish education. The primary problem is that the central administration for all the schools, located in Buenos Aires, is itself unable to support fully even the classrooms of the capital. The result has been to let the interior communities wither, except those isolated pockets of wealth or social resiliency that can endure independent of outside aid. Because of crises within the Buenos Aires *kehillah,* it appears highly unlikely that this neglect of the interior will be substantially remedied in the near future.

The worsening condition

The recent history of the educational system has been bleak, though the 1950s had augured better times for the community's schools. Instead, administrative crises, bankruptcy, and enrollment plunges have highlighted Jewish education.

During the optimistic era of the 1950s, school construction accelerated. Most were "supplementary" schools, which gave only Jewish instruction, either before or after a four-hour session of Argentine elementary school. Modest rented locations disappeared, and a network of impressive, spacious, and comfortable buildings steadily took their places. This modernization spurred more parents to send their children to Jewish schools for at least a few hours each day.

The efforts to establish new educational institutions still lacked a central plan. Some neighborhoods in dire need of schools were ignored in the construction of school buildings, while other districts with less urgent needs but more energetic leadership or greater budgetary resources were able to modernize existing schools and establish new ones. Busing programs began in the *kehillah* to ameliorate these conditions, bringing students to new schools from every part of Buenos Aires. Educational costs rose concomitantly and fund-raising, too, had to reach new levels, as the Israeli scholar Haim Avni describes:

Committees of communal workers headed by their presidents, secretaries, and treasurers assumed the burden of the day-by-day running of the schools. Children's parties in every school were turned into social and cultural events for parents and community workers alike, and annual

148

"fairs" and celebrations were planned to help mobilize funds for the schools, all of which in the course of years became routine events in the life of the community.[22]

The need to coordinate school construction and curricula and the challenge of low attendance by students led the two giant institutions of education in the *kehillah* to merge in 1956. The Va'ad Hahinukh Haroshi (Head Education Office) of the interior provinces and the Va'ad Hahinukh (Education Office) of the AMIA for Buenos Aires formed a controlling committee called the Va'ad Hahinukh Hamerkazi Be-Argentina (Central Argentine Education Office). It supervised all Jewish schools except those of the Sephardic and German Jews and the Communist-directed schools. The community funded the schools run by the central committee, through grants from the AMIA, contributions by Jewish credit cooperatives, and tuition payments by parents of the students.

The results of administrative restructuring were mixed. Innovations were impressive in several areas, such as the nonpolitical federation of Hebrew school parents begun in 1964 to stimulate interest in Jewish learning. The group, called Horim (Parents), sponsors annual conferences between parents and teachers, and hosts lectures, study groups, and other projects. The *kehillah*'s leaders hope that groups like Horim, which personally involve the parents of school-age children, may help overcome the apathy that has for so long hindered the development of a sound Jewish educational system.

A recent achievement in administrative unity is the Casa de la Educación Judía, dedicated by the AMIA in April 1969. Perhaps inspired by the prestigious and popular Sociedad Hebraica Argentina, the Casa's directors established a major center of Jewish learning for all Buenos Aires, drawing upon the resources of the Midrasha Teacher's Seminary, the Maimonides Secondary Day School, the Midrasha Ha-Ivrit (a postsecondary school of 228 students), the Instituto for training kindergarten teachers, and the AMIA's central library of 17,000 volumes. The Casa serves over 800 students in their respective Jewish schools.[23]

Problems of coordination remained, however, during the 1960s. The president of the Education Office, Hayim Raichemberg, declared in 1966 that the entire educational network required restructuring. He urged that small schools in the same districts of the federal capital merge immediately, "since only half the city's 24 primary schools had the required minimum number of students for the proper functioning of the school's morning sessions."[24]

These chronic structural difficulties were merely the prelude to a sudden hammer-blow to the educational system, which shattered both its organizational pattern and its financial resources. In 1967 the minister of education introduced in Buenos Aires the *doble escolaridad* program. This meant that the public school day would extend from early morning to late afternoon instead of having two shifts for the children. Under the original system Jewish education was almost exclusively "complementary," giving some three to four hours of Judaic instruction during that time of the day when the child did not have public school classes. In 1968 many Argentine schools implemented the longer school day for the new semester, and thus affected many Jewish children. Though not its intention, this measure threatened to ruin the *kehillah*'s whole system of education.

The first reaction by the Education Office was to petition. It asked that Jewish students affected by this system be permitted to transfer to other schools where *doble escolaridad* did not yet apply. On the whole the petitions were well received, and the authorities showed an understanding of the problem.[25] The transfer of many Jewish children followed, so that they could continue their studies in the complementary Jewish schools. Yet this was not a long-term solution.

The Jewish community in Buenos Aires resolved to prepare its schools for teaching standard secular curricula as well as Jewish subjects. This policy had long been practiced successfully by Jewish centers in Rosario, Córdoba, Mendoza, and other interior communities. Its advantages were considerable. Day school education would help curb the dropout rate from purely Jewish schools. It would also increase the prestige of Jewish education, as Haim Avni writes, "by eliminating the contradictions and confusion aroused among the pupils by their having to study within two different educational systems which were at times even opposed to each other."[26]

An intimidating array of problems barred the long route be-

150

tween the *kehillah*'s new policy and its implementation. Vastly improved school buildings were suddenly obliged to appear and begin operation. This near impossibility had to be matched by the acquisition of new principals and 100 more teachers, in order to obtain official government recognition as a legitimate private school network. The community found it necessary to hire many non-Jewish faculty to teach secular subjects. This, too, presented the serious problem of maintaining a Jewish atmosphere and integrating secular and Hebrew departments in the Jewish schools.

There was the additional and formidable task of insuring adequate enrollment in these new schools. The caliber of education had to be raised above old levels in order to impress sufficiently both government officials and the parents of Jewish school children. Moreover, the community needed funds merely to maintain reasonable prices to parents sending their children to the *kehillah*'s schools. Argentine public education was free on all levels through the university, but Jewish education was expensive, ranging from about 40 dollars a month for each child in kindergarten to about a 100 dollars a month for a high school student.[27]

The *kehillah* acted quickly in a variety of ways to meet these challenges. To obtain more teachers, the AMIA created a Teacher's Institute for Community Day Schools. To aid parents of Jewish schoolchildren, the Education Office awarded 1,000 scholarships to students transferring from Talmud Torah to day schools. It also raised monthly subsidies to schools for each enrolled student to cover part of the costs for new programs. "Included in the 1969 AMIA budget," the *American Jewish Year Book* stated, "was also an allocation of 17 million pesos for scholarships and subsidies for Jewish summer camps." The total number of pupils in the first two years of the new programs increased by 2.5 percent. To support them, officials made appeals continually and nearly imposed a "voluntary education tax" on the Jewish community.[28]

The rapidity of the change wrought by the *kehillah* is startling. In 1961 there was only one day school in all of Greater Buenos Aires.[29] Six years later, less than 30 percent of the schools were integral. But by the end of the decade more than 70 percent of the Jewish schools offered a day school education.[30]

The crisis had clearly spurred the community to its finest hour in education and organization, but the cost was staggering. Under the best of circumstances, the *kehillah* might have weathered it, but a general collapse of the national economy struck first.

Jewish teachers were among the hardest hit by the inflationary spiral, which in the 1970s seemed to acquire a life of its own, defying the best efforts of Argentine ministers to bring it under some control. The payment of substandard salaries to teachers in the Jewish schools was, even before this economic disorder, a notorious chronic debility in the Jewish educational system. Given the limited funds of the *kehillah,* the policy of keeping down the wages of its teachers is defensible from a short-range view; but it has been responsible for an acute shortage of trained instructors.

It is significant that a major source of dropouts in the educational system is in the faculty's own ranks. Turnover in personnel is demoralizingly high and impedes development of a stable, let alone strong, educational system. Most faculty members have less than five years of teaching experience; only one-fifth have taught in schools for more than a decade.[31]

The low salaries attached to these teaching positions is the prime cause of faculty defections. The typical teacher in a Jewish school is a young woman, usually in her early twenties and looking for a temporary source of income either to bear the cost of university education or to supplement her husband's income. The pro-male sex bias of Argentine society encourages women to take jobs of this nature, not sufficiently remunerative to support a family but useful as a way to help make ends meet. Few men would take such work, and even at present nearly nine of every ten teachers in the Jewish school system is female. When their husbands are well established, their career in the Jewish schools generally ends. A curious sidenote is that the *machismo* factor in Argentine society prevents these women, who have acquired experience if not affluence in their teaching roles, from strengthening Jewish learning in higher-paid directorial posts. These are disproportionately filled by men, as high as 65 percent in 1962 and 44 percent even by the end of the decade.[32] The combination of poor wages and conservative social mores thus militates against developing and retaining truly capable educators.

How to attract potential teachers even for a few years is no easy matter. The *American Jewish Year Book* reported in 1963 that "of the approximately forty graduates" in that year from the Institute for

Jewish Studies, "only seven or eight planned to enter the teaching profession."[33]

Entering the decade of the seventies, the Jewish school teachers faced an intolerable situation. Not only was inflation siphoning their meager incomes, but the hard-pressed Education Office prepared to dismiss a possible 300 of the 948 teachers in the capital and its suburbs for lack of classrooms in which to practice. When the teachers vehemently protested, the Education Office assured them that "only a hundred would be without work," a pledge that brought few cheers to the faculty ranks.[34]

In June 1971, the desperate teachers went on strike against the school system for four days, demanding a 30 percent wage increase, a cost-of-living provision against further loss of purchasing power from inflation, and job security. Though early in June it had seemed as if educators in the general school system of Argentina would strike for similar demands, the teachers in the Jewish schools were left alone in their strike action, and they obtained only half their claims. The raises were hardly adequate except to drive the Education Office further into debt.

The finishing blow to the education budget was not long in coming. The folding of the credit cooperatives in 1972 collapsed the remnants of a self-sufficient community school system. The *kehillah* had already met disappointment in attempting to relieve its financial pressures by appeals for funds, including a voluntary education tax. These efforts, despite massive publicity, yielded only modest revenues. The collapse of the long-faltering cooperatives was simply the coup de grace to the fund-raising campaign for the day schools.

With the schools verging on dissolution, the Jewish Agency in Israel and the Joint Distribution Committee of the United States aided the AMIA with huge loans. The Israeli government, interested in Jewish education in the Diaspora and the potential it presents for *aliyah,* directed the Bank Le'umi in 1971 to lend the AMIA 1 million dollars for educational purposes only. The loan is payable over the next ten years at 4 percent interest.[35] The Joint Distribution Committee added 650,000 dollars to the AMIA's educational budget as a grant. Also in 1971, the AMIA subsidies to Jewish schools totaled about 2 million dollars. But the crisis presents no foreseeable recovery. The Bank Le'umi found it necessary in 1972 to lend another 1 million dollars to Argentine Jewish education.[36]

The comatose state of Jewish education in Argentina currently shows little sign of improvement, despite the valiant efforts of the *kehillah* in the past decade. Amid declining student enrollment and the wreckage of the financial situation, community initiatives have been limited to isolated and small-scale projects. The vulnerability to cultural erosion will therefore continue to grow while the community seeks new ways to salvage its schools and with them, Judaic tradition.

6 SEPHARDIM

The Sephardic communities

Jorge Luis Borges, the famed Argentine author, recounts that a distant relative, an Italian Jewish engineer named Jorge Suárez, brought the first horse-drawn tramcars to Argentina. Suárez also engaged in one of the earliest and most brazen experiments in Jewish-Christian relations in that country. Borges recalls that

Suárez was a guest at General Urquiza's "palace" in Entre Ríos, and very improvidently won his first game of cards with the General, who was the stern dictator of that province and not above throat cutting. When the game was over, Suárez was told by alarmed fellow guests that if he wanted the license to run his tramcars in the province, it was expected of him to lose a certain amount of gold coins each night. Urquiza was such a poor player that Suárez had a great deal of trouble losing the appointed sums.[1]

Suárez was only one among the many Sephardim, or Jews of Spanish descent, who have helped to mold the character and history of the modern Argentine Jewish population. Sephardim today compose about one-sixth of the Jews in Argentina, or between 70,000 and 90,000 persons.[2] They are a distinctive minority, organized into communities separate from those of the numerically predominant Ashkenazim, or Jews of Northern and Central European origin.

The Sephardim in Argentina represent a great diversity of Jews from different nations. Their collective name, Sephardic, derives from the Hebrew word for Spain, where a portion of Jews

155

settled in the first century C.E. following the destruction of the Second Temple in Jerusalem. After Spain expelled its Jewish population in 1492, these Sephardim sought refuge in England, Holland, various Mediterranean lands, and the Americas. By extension, the name Sephardic has come to include (and is used here to denote) Oriental Jews, or all Jews living in the Balkan countries and Moslem nations influenced by medieval Spanish or Arabic culture.

During the nineteenth century, worsening conditions for Jews in Arabic lands encouraged further migrations. Some of these Jews traveled to Argentina, at first only individually and then as part of larger, organized groups of settlers. The first immigration occurred in 1875, more than a dozen years before the Russian Jews on the *Weser* put into port at Buenos Aires.

Charles de Foucauld, a traveler in Morocco in the latter part of the nineteenth century, noted among the conditions which led Jews to leave,

the obligatory [and discriminatory] black slippers, the special taxes on assimilated Jews at tolls and ports and on their pack animals, the obligation to march barefoot in the towns, and the crowding of the hovels in the ghetto.[3]

Once in Argentina, the Sephardic Jews—like their Ashkenazic brethren—found increased opportunities for economic advancement. Today the majority of the Sephardim form a middle class of businessmen, artisans, and white-collar employees. They are especially well represented in the textile industry, certain branches of which are commonly known as "Sephardic" occupations. The manufacture of silk clothing, for example, is a specialty among Sephardim from Arabic lands.

Comparisons of wealth among Sephardic and Ashkenazic Jews have yielded varying assessments, but analysts tend to agree that the two groups enjoy a rough parity in economic attainments.[4] This is plausible based on the criterion of estimated average per capita income among Sephardim and Ashkenazim. Yet differences emerge when one focuses on the distribution of wealth within each group. A somewhat greater diversity appears to exist in the living standards of the Sephardic Jews than among the Ashkenazim. A recent study of Sephardim from Turkey and the Balkans cautions against exaggerating this widely asserted phenomenon; but impressionistic evidence from both interviews and personal observation suggests that it is significant.[5] In particular, poverty and menial employment appear more widespread among Sephardim from Arabic nations than among any other group of Jews in Argentina. Yet the affluence of certain elements among Sephardic Jewry is such that the overall economic strength of the Sephardim may be fully equal to that of the Ashkenazim.

The differing Ashkenazic and Sephardic patterns of economic development are only part of a comprehensive range of factors that have distinguished and isolated the two subgroups of Argentine Jewry from each other. Divergences in liturgical tradition, language, Judaic perspectives, secular involvement, and educational patterns all contribute to a mutual exclusiveness that the Sephardim appear to desire at least as strongly as the Ashkenazim.

The successive waves of Sephardic settlers were self-consciously independent of the Ashkenazic Jews already established in Argentina. The experience of the first Sephardic group, from North Africa, set the pattern for this exclusive behavior. Initially, they were forced to rely on existing Ashkenazic organizations, but left them as soon as they achieved a modicum of financial independence. In 1891 these Jews founded the Congregación Israelita Latina, in part to retain their distinctive Sephardic traditions in chanting Jewish prayers. From this first move toward autonomy, these Sephardim gradually formed a completely separate system of organizations. This included a cemetery and burial society, assuring an independent source of income for their other institutions.

The Sephardic population itself is divided according to the origins of the various immigrant waves. Four distinct communities emerged in Buenos Aires, the result of small differences in culture and custom and the tendency of people from the same area to cluster together. One scholar compared their separate social institutions to the Ashkenazic *landsmanshaften,* or immigrant societies, formed according to town or region of origin.[6] The Jews from Aleppo, for example, until recent years kept a community completely separate from that of the Jews from Damascus, although both cities are located in Syria and have virtually no fundamental cultural differences.

Geographical distinctions by country of origin have been mirrored in the physical layout of Sephardic neighborhoods in the capital. Thus, the Moroccan Jews settled in the oldest part of the capital, in the South; those from Rhodes gathered in Colegiale; Turkish immigrants lived in the Villa Crespo; those from Aleppo concentrated in Once, Flores, and Liniers; and those from Damascus, in Flores and Barracas. These residential patterns still resist changes that are more than gradual.

The first Sephardic community to establish itself in Argentina originated in Tangiers in Spanish Morocco. Today, there are still some 500 Moroccan Jewish families, of which about 300 belong to the central communal institutions established in the late nineteenth century. Their close-knit organizational structure includes three synagogues, a social club, and a small secondary school attended by about thirty students. These Sephardim, however, are now the smallest and most assimilated Sephardic group in Argentina. Their influence has been eclipsed by Sephardim coming to Argentina early in the twentieth century from the Balkans and the Middle East.

The distinctive Syrian Jewish communities are also the two largest Sephardic groups. Some prefer to designate these Jews as Oriental rather than Sephardic, because the origins of their communities in Syria antedate by centuries the arrival there of some Jews exiled from Spain.[7] Yet the Syrian Jews in Argentina themselves affirm their identity as part of a larger Sephardic tradition, even while zealously maintaining separate institutions, as do the other Sephardic immigrant groups.

The Jews from Damascus are the dominant Sephardic group in Argentina, numbering some 3,500 families in Buenos Aires alone in 1968. They still congregate in the organizations created by their forebears in 1913, namely the Sephardic Jewish Association of Culture and Welfare and the Sephardic Jewish Association of the Sons of Truth. These Jews boast an unusually vital communal life. In addition to four synagogues and four social clubs, their leading school, Maimonides, is among the largest centers for Jewish education in the country. The community also maintains its own cemetery and recently assured itself of diversified sources of income by copying Ashkenazic cooperative arrangements. Apart from revenues from burial frees, the community also operates an insurance agency and an agricultural cooperative.

The Jewish immigrants from Aleppo constitute the second

largest Sephardic community in Buenos Aires, some 2,500 member families in 1968. Most of these trace their roots to northern Syria, near Turkey, but other Sephardim also participate in this community. The Aleppano *kehillah* came to include Jews from the Caucasus and from Palestine during the 1920s and 1930s, because of its strong appeal to religious Jews seeking traditional institutions.

The roof organization of the Aleppano community is known as the Sephardic Jewish Association. It originated in 1913, the year in which their brethren from Damascus built their separate communal institutions. The *kehillah* includes a separate cemetery, seven synagogues, two kosher social clubs, and a secondary school with an enrollment of 500 pupils.

Ladino-speaking Jews constitute the fourth major group of Sephardim in Argentina. They come from Turkey, Rhodes, Italy, Bulgaria, and the Balkans. Their Ladino dialect is a variant of Spanish that, for example, Cervantes employed when he wrote *Don Quixote* and that the Spanish still spoke at the time of the expulsion of the Jews in 1492. Since then, only minor additions in vocabulary (Hebraicisms) and differences in pronunciation—no more distinct than the peculiarities of Castilian and Latin American speech—divide Ladino and modern Spanish.

The Ladino-speaking Jews founded their central organization in 1914 but forged a fully unified community only after the heavy Balkan Jewish immigration during World War II. The old and new settlers formed the Sephardic Jewish Community Association in 1942. By 1954 the community included five synagogues in different areas of the capital and maintained two cemeteries. Like the other Sephardic groups, they also fostered numerous fraternal clubs throughout greater Buenos Aires. In 1968, the community counted 2,365 member families in the capital, which constituted the great majority of Ladino-speaking Jews in the nation.

The different Sephardic communities cooperate with each other in some important, if limited, areas. This is exemplified by the accord reached by the first communal leaders over the use of burial fields. The provision of religious burial services afforded each community with the income needed to sustain its various activities. Therefore, the primary institutions of the four Sephardic groups entered a pact to help each other maintain exclusive ownership over cemeteries and the facilities for religious burial. In this way, the communities were able to centralize control over a vital aspect of Sephardic tradition and to insure a reliable source of funds for the future.

Despite such constructive attempts at mutual assistance, the Sephardic communities prefer full autonomy to unity in most areas of Jewish activity. Consequently, the periodic efforts to centralize various Sephardic groups and campaigns have thus far had only minor impact. The first decades of Sephardic settlement, for example, witnessed the creation of the Comité Sefaradí to collect funds for Israel on behalf of all Sephardic organizations. The Ladino-speaking Jews soon left this committee, however, and formed their own roof organization for Sephardim, Delegaciones de Entidades Sefaradís Argentinas. Both groups proved little more than loose federations unable to persuade other Sephardic institutions to accord them real authority.

The desire for unity has also stumbled against barriers of geography and simple inertia. Haim Avni describes a typical effort to consolidate communal institutions when in October 1964 the Ladino-speaking Jews celebrated the fiftieth anniversary of their *kehillah*:

At the festive assembly which then took place, after two days of discussion in committees resolutions were passed which included detailed proposals for efficient concentration of educational, religious and welfare activities within the framework of a board of communities, which was to unite not only the communities in the capital and its vicinity, but also the communities in the towns of the interior. In spite of the enthusiasm and the exaltation of this convention, the Sephardi board of communities did not materialize.[8]

The resistance to consolidation has left Sephardic life in the care of small local institutions that in effect constitute a series of semi-independent communities.

The social club, even more than the synagogue, is the essential unit of Sephardic communal life. Unlike the Ashkenazic counterparts, the residence societies that have all but died out, the Sephardic clubs have maintained vigorous activity. Together with Sephardic Zionist organizations, the clubs promote efforts in education, social welfare, and Jewish culture.

Recently the clubs have added a new dimension—sports.

160

Many clubs have large buildings with gymnasiums and sports fields, as well as kosher dining facilities and grand ballrooms. The preference for clubs of this type stems in part from their utility in attracting Jewish youth and in this way minimizing intermarriages. The clubs have also helped in a broader way to bind the generations and curtail geographic dispersal. In recent years, the social clubs have even served to facilitate contact among different Sephardic groups. They are thus accomplishing, by social mixing and marriage, the Sephardic unity that the central communal institutions have never achieved.

Sephardic culture

The vital force sustaining Sephardic Jewish identity is a devotion to religious observance and tradition. Although the extent of this devotion varies with the different immigrant groups, the majority of Sephardim in Argentina are clearly more attached to religious Judaism than are the Ashkenazic communities from Russia and from Germany.

The Syrian Jews are especially dedicated to religious Judaism. Their synagogues are filled each Sabbath, and they own most of the shops in Buenos Aires, which close to observe the Jewish day of rest. Behor Issaev wrote in 1962, "A walk through Paso Street and a visit on Saturday to the temples in Once, filled with men and women of all ages, suffices to show that this [religious] fervor continues in the heart of the 'Alepina' community."[9] A less visible but equally important measure of their religiosity is the fact that the Sephardim are known to buy most of the kosher meat sold in Buenos Aires, although they form only a small portion of the total Jewish population.[10]

The Ladino-speaking community is also religious, though more flexible and diverse in its forms of observance than are the Syrian Jews. Their main synagogue, Shalom, affiliated with Conservative Judaism in the 1960s, is unique among Sephardic temples in Argentina. Rabbi Aaron Angel, director of the large Sephardic day school Maimonides, introduced the bat mitzvah at Temple Shalom, the first such ceremonies to be performed in Argentina.[11] The bat mitzvah, for girls twelve years of age, is the equivalent of the bar mitzvah ceremony widely practiced among American and other Jews, wherein a boy of thirteen formally accepts responsibility for keeping the Mosaic law. Generally, he symbolizes this passage to manhood by chanting a portion from the Prophets in the Old Testament. For the traditional and patriarchal Sephardim, such rites for women remain rare.

Only in the small community from North Africa has secular involvement managed to eclipse religious sentiment. Because they lacked trained religious leaders since the beginning of the twentieth century, the Moroccan Sephardim steadily drifted away from religious traditionalism. Their memories of the secularized French culture in Morocco and their growing economic prosperity in Argentina also led them to become complacent, resulting in a decline in their commitment to Judaic ritual and study.

The assimilationist trends among the Moroccan community in Argentina led one of its officials to write a public protest in 1929. Benjamin Benzakan warned of a growing alienation from Judaism and noted that many Moroccan Jews were desecrating the Sabbath, eating non-kosher food during religious ceremonial meals, and intermarrying with ever greater frequency.[12]

The Moroccan community received an added sense of purpose in 1948 when the creation of the State of Israel spurred *aliyah,* and the appearance of a youthful leader named Saadia Benzakan gave new interest in the synagogue. However, these developments only slowed, but could not reverse, the trends earlier denounced by Benjamin Benzakan. Today, the Moroccan community, alone of the Sephardic groups, still refuses to reject members involved in mixed marriages, while assimilation erodes the community more rapidly than it does the other Sephardic centers.

The Moroccan experience is anomalous among the Sephardic immigrant communities largely because the other Sephardim were comparatively unaffected by assimilationist forces while in their countries of origin. Therefore, they found it easier, once in Argentina, to maintain a commitment to Judaic tradition and to the preservation of their particular communal identities.

In addition to the strong family ties that militate against the breakdown of religious tradition, Sephardic religious leadership has been vigorous for many decades. During the 1920s, when the new immigration introduced a strong antireligious sentiment, Rabbi Shaul David Sithon, spiritual leader of the Jewish community from Damascus, effectively rallied the forces of Jewish traditionalism. Sithon is most noted for his controversial decision to prohibit conversion to Judaism in the Argentine Republic.[13] He enacted this ruling with the concurrence of Ashkenazic rabbis, including Rav Kook, the Chief Rabbi of Palestine at this time. This stricture was intended to bolster the community in its struggle against the white slave trade, because many Argentine males sought to appease their kidnapped wives—usually Jewish women sold by the slavers—by converting to Judaism. Naturally their conversion was insincere, their marital status worse than dubious, and the whole process of conversion a disgrace upon the Jewish community. Although the slave trade perished in the 1930s, the prohibition of conversion is still in force in both the Argentine Sephardic and Ashkenazic communities.

Strictly observant and traditional leaders like Sithon have continued to prevail in Sephardic communal life. Of the fifteen Orthodox rabbis in Buenos Aires in 1970, four were Sephardic, a proportion nearly twice that of Sephardim to Ashkenazim among Jews in Argentina.[14] The difference in leadership accurately reflects the relative importance of religion among the mass of individuals in the two Jewish groups.

Despite this commitment to religious tradition, however, the level of Jewish learning is not high. In part, this mirrors the general decline of Sephardic cultural achievement following the exile from Spain and settlement in more backward nations. Traditionalism gradually began to substitute for a deep grasp of Judaic knowledge rather than reinforcing it. The limits of Jewish learning among Sephardim in Argentina are ably summarized by Behor Issaev:

[Their] traditionalism is not supported by a very profound knowledge either of sacred Scripture or Talmudic literature. On the contrary, nearly total ignorance reigns in the community, as much in religious theology as in modern Jewish philosophy. Of the Jewish literary movements of the nineteenth century, it is difficult to discover any influence. Neither the Enlightenment . . . nor the literature from Mendele and Gordon to Bialik, let alone writings in Yiddish, have penetrated the Sephardic communities. Peretz, for example, is absolutely unknown even to this day, and Sholem Aleichem is known occasionally, by name alone.[15]

Conceding a definite Ashkenazic bias to the above evaluation, it is clear nevertheless that a low level of Judaic knowledge is the case for most Sephardim—as indeed for most Jews—in Argentina.

Jewish education is of varying quality in the Sephardic communities, each of which controls its schools through separate educational commissions. No central organization comparable to the Ashkenazic Va'ad Hahinuh exists to coordinate Jewish learning among the Sephardim. Nevertheless, according to a survey of Argentine Jews in 1952, the percentage of Sephardic children who received some Jewish education actually exceeded that of Ashkenazic children.[16]

Of the Sephardic groups, the Moroccan Jews have the weakest system of religious education. The synagogue-supported Talmud Torah attracts a very low proportion of school-age children in the community. The Jews from Syria and the Ladino-speaking Jews also had severe problems for many years in building effective systems of Jewish education. The Syrian Jews faced the added handicap of language difficulties, for it was not always easy to find knowledgeable teachers who spoke fluent Arabic. This was an important matter because the schools, like the Yesod Ha-Dat created by the Jews from Aleppo in 1908, originally functioned wholly in Arabic.

The Jews from Aleppo led the Sephardic advances in religious education during the early part of the twentieth century. By 1939 they owned a large school whose enrollment reached some 500 students. Its teachers came from Israel, and it was among the first Argentine Jewish schools to teach modern Hebrew. The Ladino-speaking Jews created their own modern Hebrew school in the early 1950s, known as Adat Yeshurun. The Jews from Damascus maintained three schools in Buenos Aires during this time, including one that offered an "integral" education combining general and Judaic curricula.

Sephardim have accepted a number of modern ideas in the content and methods of education over the past decade. There has been a trend among the different communities toward including secular as well as religious instruction in their educational program. The Maimonides Day School of the Jews from Damascus, for example, became an "integral" institution only during the 1960s; it provides a Jewish and a general education to more than 700 students. Among the Ladino-speaking Jews, integral primary schools

164

have superseded the old Talmud Torahs, which taught only Jewish subjects. Special attention is still accorded religious learning, but in most of the schools, secular curricula are included at least through the first four grades.

Despite the progress made by the Sephardic schools, the level of Jewish education remains low. The schools have reached only a small proportion of the youth in any of the four communities. There is, moreover, a strongly entrenched cultural parochialism among many Sephardim that constricts knowledge of both Jewish and general developments.

This parochialism is least severe among the two smallest Sephardic groups, the Moroccan and the Ladino-speaking Jews. Almost from their arrival, the Jews from Morocco rapidly adjusted to Argentine society. Though poor, they were well educated, far beyond the average for non-Jewish Moroccans. Some were even hired as teachers for the new Ashkenazic settlements. The ICA employed them because, unlike the East European immigrants, the Moroccan Jews spoke Spanish fluently upon arrival. Thus, even while these Jews were fast losing hold of their traditional culture, they acclimated with surprising ease to the new conditions in Argentina.

Some Ladino-speaking Jews show an even more pronounced degree of Western acculturation. They received their education in the French schools of the Alliance Israélite Universelle. As a consequence they absorbed secular Western culture in addition to their religious learning.

Many of the most secularized Jews among the Sephardim trace their origins to Bulgaria and Greece. Zionist currents from Russia influenced the Bulgarian Jews, while in Salonica, intellectual currents from Paris invigorated this Greek center of Zionist activity. The Elnecavé family, which has long been eminent in Argentine Jewish publishing, is among this Sephardic element.

Yet both the Moroccan and Ladino-speaking communities make up only a small portion of the Sephardim in Argentina. The cultural isolation of the Sephardim most deeply affects the communities from Damascus and Aleppo, at once the most observant and least acculturated of the Sephardim.

The majority of Sephardim tend to be more insulated than the Ashkenazic Jews from the larger Argentine society. Both Jewish

THE JEWS OF ARGENTINA

groups, for example, have their own tribunals for adjudicating intracommunal disputes; but the Ashkenazim often refer instead to national courts, especially in business matters. The Sephardim do this rarely, preferring their own arbitrating panels.

Little about the Sephardic community is reported in the Yiddish press, nor is anything to be found in the general Spanish publications. A Sephardic press does not really exist. Aside from *La Luz* and *Israel,* the latter antedating all other Jewish magazines in the capital, there are no Sephardic publications other than the monthly bulletin of the Delegaciones de Entidades Sefaradís Argentinas, sent free to all who contribute to its activities.

The lack of channels for the spread of information to the masses of Sephardim has impeded the development of a wider political consciousness. Many Sephardim remain apathetic to secular involvement of any sort, and this aversion extended to the Syrian rabbi Isaac Schehebar, who refused to answer any questions about his community on the grounds that "it would be improper for me, as an official of the community, to say anything about it."[17]

The development of Zionist activity among the Sephardim, especially in the past two decades, has perhaps been the most important way in which these Jewish communities have gained in secular awareness and involvement. Most Sephardic immigrants to Argentina were largely apolitical, in contrast to the spirited Zionist and Socialist movements among the Ashkenazim. Increasingly, though, Sephardim have organized Zionist programs in the social clubs and, to a lesser extent, by forming separate organizations for this purpose. Today, the Zionist clubs have at least yearly programs of conferences and cultural events relating to Israel. Many clubs also include libraries with abundant literature on the Jewish State.

The Comité Sefaradí exercises its most vital influence in the community by helping to coordinate Zionist groups, many of which are in their incipient stages. Among the organizations under its auspices is La Acción Sionista Sefaradí, the largest Zionist institution in all the Americas. This center sponsors courses in Hebrew, contributes to the development of Sephardic schools, and organizes conferences and festivals fostering Zionist sentiment.

The social role of the Zionist organizations may be at least equal in importance to its cultural contributions. The annual Purim ball sponsored by Keren Kayemet illustrates this added dimension to the Zionist activities. At this festival, girls from the various Sephardic youth organizations compete for the title of Queen Esther. This celebration is one of many arranged by Zionist groups in which Sephardic youth are enabled to congregate in a Jewish atmosphere.

Sephardic Zionist activity blossomed during the 1960s, partly as a result of the Arab-Israeli war in 1967. The decade marked the creation of the Organización Sionista Sefaradí which plays several important roles in the Zionist movement. Its official organ, *Crónica Sefaradí* (Sephardic Chronicle), publicizes Zionist activities in the Sephardic community. The organization also sponsors symposia on such themes as "Current Ideologies within Zionism," attracting many Zionist groups throughout Buenos Aires. Perhaps most important, the Organización Sionista Sefaradí has helped, through both publicity and annual financial contributions, to foster *aliyah* among the Sephardim. In 1969 alone, some two hundred Sephardic Jews from Argentina settled in Israel, a figure which in proportionate terms approximated the Ashkenazic contribution to *aliyah.*

While these trends clearly suggest an impressive awakening of Zionist activism among the Sephardic Jews, it is important not to mistake this for the largely secularized and politicized Zionism prevalent in the Ashkenazic Jewish centers. Israeli emissaries have frequently traveled to Argentina for the purpose of encouraging the Sephardim to establish Zionist parties parallel to those of the Ashkenazim, but the results have been meager. For even in the present day, Zionism in the Sephardic communities is still based less on awareness of modern Jewish history and the daily events of world politics than on religious sentiments. Indeed, Sephardic Zionism retains features of the deeply religious, messianic yearnings for Zion that characterized much of medieval Hebrew poetry and literature among Sephardic Jews in Moslem Spain.

Zionism may therefore be seen to have a twofold significance in Sephardic life. On one hand, it is a source of secular involvement and activity for a people many of whose members have been long accustomed to treating the outside world with passivity and indifference. At the same time, it is a development that coexists with and even revolves around the religious traditionalism that characterizes Sephardic Jewry in Argentina.

167

Interior Sephardic Communities

Sephardic centers in the interior of Argentina are disappearing. There are sixteen such centers outside Buenos Aires. They include such major cities as Córdoba (the largest Sephardic center in the interior), Rosario (the second largest), La Plata, Corrientes, Tucumán, Salta, Santa Fe, and Mendoza. Each population center has fifty to five hundred Sephardic families. In all, there are an estimated 1,500 Sephardic families outside Buenos Aires.[18]

The Sephardic communities in the interior are more, and in some cases completely, integrated with the Ashkenazic communities than are the Sephardim of the capital. In most instances there is close contact and interaction between the two Jewish groups, though separation still exists in synagogues and cemeteries. In Rosario, Tucumán, and Mendoza, the two cultures have established joint communal frameworks. An important reason for this is the lack of Sephardic (and in many cases Ashkenazic) leadership in the interior, leaving the communities little choice but to band together.

The paucity of religious leadership has had disturbing consequences. In Rosario, with a little less than two hundred Sephardic families, the community has built three synagogues. Not one of them has a rabbi and it is difficult for any of them to assemble a *minyan,* the religious quorum of ten men, even on the Sabbath. This situation typifies the Sephardic condition in the interior.

Nissim Elnecavé, the Sephardic editor of *La Luz,* tells of attending Sabbath services in the newest Sephardic synagogue in Rosario, built in 1963. When called to the Torah, he found the congregational leader reading from a book, instead of the sacred scroll that Jews use all over the world. He asked the leader why he was not reading from the Torah scroll and learned that the man could not read Hebrew well, and not at all without vowels.[19] These are the pronunciation markings common in basic Hebrew instruction, but as incongruous for use in reading the Torah as if a concert pianist were to refer to a chart of basic notes during a performance.

Sephardim in the interior suffer an abysmally low level of Jewish education and, what is most likely a related phenomenon, a high rate of intermarriage. Sephardim in the interior communities

168

are even more accepting of intermarriage than the Ashkenazim, whose marriages to Catholics often reach well over one-third of all weddings in the smaller Jewish centers. In 1966, the Sephardic synagogue in Corrientes hosted the wedding of an Ashkenazic man to a Catholic woman, after the Ashkenazic synagogues of the city refused to marry the couple.[20]

It is apparent that the Jewish communities of Buenos Aires must help revitalize the centers of the interior, both Ashkenazic and Sephardic, if these communities are to continue to exist.

Change

"The Sephardim are, of course, more superstitious than the Ashkenazim," a Jew of Russian origin and a leading official in the Ashkenazic community confided to me. Many other Ashkenazim echo such opinions, especially in disdain for the Sephardim who come from Arabic lands. The Sephardic head of the Society of Argentine Jewish Women, Deborah Manassen de Lang, was "amazed to find the change in attitude toward Sephardic Jews" upon moving from her native Holland to Buenos Aires. "In Holland we were respected as a prosperous, cultured element of the community, but in Argentina many Ashkenazim look down on Sephardim as poor, ill-educated cousins."[21]

It is true that Sephardic Jews, in Argentina as elsewhere in the world, have yet to recapture fully their distant era of greatness in Spain under Islamic rulers. The Jews in that period, which climaxed during the late twelfth century, were never wholly free from discrimination, but they were valued by their Moslem hosts for their trade, artisanship, and learning. The foremost Sephardic Jew of this and any other era, Moses Maimonides, dramatically enhanced Judaic knowledge with a monumental work on the Talmud and a series of brilliant theological expositions in *The Guide of the Perplexed.* He also gained renown as a physician to the royal court and as an author of numerous medical treatises. Maimonides thus epitomized the achievements of Sephardic Jews, who kept the Mosaic commandments, encouraged Judaic learning, and flourished within the Islamic society as highly acculturated members.

After the expulsion of the Jews from Spain, the exiles entered nations whose cultures were often not nearly so advanced as that of the Islamic rulers of Spain or even of their Christian successors. This was especially true of Jews who settled in Morocco, Syria, and other Arab countries that had not maintained the glory of their medieval ancestors. As before, Jews played an important economic role in the society, but their progressive and worldly tendencies were muted by a less hospitable social climate and by the general backwardness of these nations, which had scant technology, primitive economies, and wide illiteracy.

This legacy has affected, in varying degree, the Sephardic groups in Argentina. Many Sephardic Jews still lead insular lives, speaking mainly Arabic, avoiding politics, maintaining close patriarchal ties, and living more simply than most Ashkenazim. Yet this image of the Sephardic Jew is becoming ever more incongruous with the living patterns of thousands of Argentine Sephardim and with the trends of recent years.

Marked acculturation has been evident among younger members of the Sephardic communities. A recent study of the Ladino-speaking Jews showed that the present generation tends to be less involved in Jewish communal activity but more advanced in the general society than was the previous generation. Heads of member families in the central organization, the Sephardic Jewish Community Association, are generally older (averaging fifty-two years) and contain a higher proportion of foreign born (50 percent, mainly in Turkey) than the heads of nonmember families (averaging thirty-eight years and with only 18 percent born abroad). The nonmember families also boasted twice the proportion of university graduates as were among the member families (26 to 13 percent).[22]

Sephardic acculturation still is gradual, and it has not led simply to assimilation, as the above study also indicates. Most of these Ladino-speaking Jews are registered in the official central society. Over one-third of nonmembers say that they associate with some Jewish institution. The outside society has, however, begun to act upon these Jews with greater force than at any time in the past.

One sign of these changes is the tendency to rely less exclusively on the Sephardic social clubs for group activities than in the past. The membership of the clubs decreased during the early 1970s and so, too, did their range of programs. Many clubs still meet the needs of young Sephardim, but others have become only a meetingplace for older women to play cards. A director of one such club said in 1972, "I think and hope that this is a temporary phase due primarily to bad times economically. The general interest in clubs of this type—to bring boys and girls together, to have basketball and other games, and to do this in a Jewish atmosphere, is still strong."[23] It would appear, however, that growing cultural interests outside the Sephardic community as well as economic problems are responsible for this trend.

New ideas among the Sephardim are evident in their methods of business and fund-raising. For many years the conservative Sephardic mentality would not permit any cooperative organizations in their community, such as existed among the Ashkenazim. When one was finally established, the Banco Cooperativo, it was unsuccessful. During the sixties and seventies, though, there has been growing interest in such institutions, notably among the Syrian Jews. Three cooperatives have thus far enjoyed success, symptomatic of wider changes being wrought within the Sephardic world.

Distinctions between Ashkenazic and Sephardic school systems have also blurred in recent years. Neighborhood patterns of the Ladino-speaking community, for example, have shifted so that their main Hebrew school, Shalom, is now attended primarily by Ashkenazic pupils. Among the other, much less mobile Sephardic groups, there is still an increasing trend for children to attend, in sizable numbers, the integrals schools founded by the Ashkenazic community. In Bialik primary school there are eighty Sephardic children, and in Theodore Herzl, Sephardic children are learning some Yiddish along with their Ashkenazic friends.

It should be emphasized that by no means all of the Sephardic claims to modernity and achievement are the result of copying Ashkenazic patterns and institutions. The Sephardic image today must include, for example, the Club Oriente, a social center and kosher restaurant rather more opulent than its leading Ashkenazic counterpart, Sucat David. Both places, in fact, are owned by an energetic Sephardic Jew who leases Sucat David to Ashkenazic management but personally supervises the Sephardic establishment. The Club Oriente caters to a clientele rather different from many of the Jews who frequent Sucat David. It is true that both centers tend to attract respectable and educated middle-class people. Yet the Sephardim, in general, appear a wealthier and even more intellectual group, whose members will discuss Jewish affairs and world events with equal knowledge and avidity, while consuming shish kebob, deep-fried beef *kibes,* and other Arabic specialties. Luxuries like baked apples, extraordinary casseroles, and even specially piped water, vastly superior to that served in most other Argentine restaurants, impress the visitor with a sense of aristocratic splendor reminiscent of Sephardic Jewry's golden age in Islamic Spain.

The myth of the primitive Sephardim clashes most sharply in the author's mind with memories of a visit with Eli Ben Veniste, a soft-spoken and highly intelligent business executive in his thirties. His spacious and finely decorated home was in the elegant neighborhood of Belgrano. The family's meals were prepared and served, on this occasion, by a maid, and the many courses were unsurpassed in variety and attractiveness by any Jewish center.

Ben Veniste's company that evening included a group diverse in both ages and backgrounds; but all these Sephardim were supremely well educated. His children and guests managed a combination of Spanish, English, Hebrew, and Portuguese, and this linguistic melee ranged over such subjects as clinical psychology, the merits of *aliyah,* and monetary fluctuations and their relation to Argentine economic policies. In these discussions, even the teenagers displayed a sophistication scarcely paralleled in the United States.

The Ben Venistes and many patrons of the Club Oriente and other centers are among the cultural patricians of Argentine Jewry, the potential kernels of another Sephardic golden age. In all probability, though, they will first assimilate into the wider pool of Ashkenazic Jews. Although the Sephardic and Ashkenazic communities continue to maintain largely separate institutions and activities, "intermarriages" between the two groups are fast increasing. Currently they constitute only 14 percent of all Jewish weddings but fully 70 percent of Sephardic ones.[24] In the coming decades, this phenomenon will likely dissolve the insularity that has long characterized much of Sephardic Jewry. It is leading, in Argentina as elsewhere in the world, to a gradual merger of two great Judaic traditions.

PART THREE

THE COUNTRY

7 ACCULTURATION

Jewish acculturation in Argentine society has been rapid and conspicuously successful. Jews today form only 2 percent of the nation's population of over 25 million people. Even in Buenos Aires, where Jews are most heavily situated, only one in twenty *porteños* (townsmen) is Jewish. Yet Jews have influenced Argentine economic development, progressive political movements, and cultural activity beyond all proportion to their demographic strength.

Economic activity

Jews have played a crucial role in the industrialization and modernization process in Argentina, partly because they arrived precisely when the liberal oligarchy was attempting to pull the nation out of its economically backward state, and partly because they brought certain key economic skills in greater proportion than other immigrant or native groups.

During the late nineteenth century, government leaders encouraged cultivation of new lands to increase the agricultural surpluses needed to finance budding industry. The government also welcomed immigrants in urban areas who provided cheap labor for new factories. Jews were particularly helpful in both areas. Their agricultural colonies displayed excellent planning and innovations. Jews soon began earning numerous prizes at Argentine agricultural fairs for the quality of their dairy and grain produce.[1] They introduced products like sunflower seeds, which rapidly became staples of export activity. The government was sufficiently impressed with

175

the administration of these centers to adopt their procedures for all government-sponsored colonies in recent decades.[2]

Jews also contributed in two areas essential to the initial process of industrialization: finance and textile manufacture. The first Jewish financial operations were of course small-scale affairs, for the immigrants generally had very modest resources. However, the widespread use of different kinds of cooperatives enabled the Jewish community to pool resources in order to maximize their utility. Peddlers, for example, could offer a wide variety of merchandise to customers because they transacted almost all their operations on credit. Businesses expanded far more rapidly than had each storekeeper depended solely on his own meager supply of capital; as businesses prospered, the financial institutions also proliferated. For decades thereafter, well over half of the cooperative societies in Argentina were Jewish-owned, and most others were patterned on the early Jewish models.[3]

Textile manufacture traditionally provides the first area of industrial opportunity for societies attempting to break out of an agriculturally based economy. This industry is suitable for such nations because it requires little technology, the resources needed are generally plentiful and accessible, and organization can be flexible, often employing small labor forces in each place of manufacture. Jewish immigrants, many of them skilled tailors and cloth cutters in Russia, quickly entered the textile industry in large numbers upon arriving in Argentina. Their progress parallels that of American Jews who established or greatly expanded many of the present garment centers in cities like New York and Los Angeles. They frequently began as workers in sweatshops, cutting and sewing patterns for minimal wages. The more successful and enterprising started small independent businesses and hired less fortunate coreligionists as assistants. In Argentina as in the United States, this skilled proletariat rapidly emerged as a class of largely independent tradesmen. Today the streets of Once and other mainly Jewish districts are lined with shops offering a tremendous variety of goods in leather, fur, cloth, and so forth.

Jews were also among the leaders in diversification of industry. Many began as importers, taking advantage of their trading connections with the nations from which they had emigrated. Then, to

176

supplement their incomes or to defray costs of importing a variety of spare parts, they began to produce many of the products they once purchased from abroad.

The fluid state of the Argentine economy facilitated this rapid entry by Jewish entrepreneurs into almost every major industry. A look at the United States during its period of heaviest Jewish immigration highlights the significance of the timing of the Argentine Jewish settlement. As early as the 1880s, and certainly by 1900, the American economy was among the most industrialized and technologically advanced in the world. The corporate avenues open to Jewish penetration were accordingly more limited than was the case in Argentina. As late as 1936, *Fortune* magazine's well-known study of Jewish life in America showed that Jews "figured hardly at all in capital goods industries such as steel, coal, transportation equipment, electrical goods, oil, rubber, and the manufacture of automobiles."[4] By contrast, in Argentina at this time almost all these industries were comparatively underdeveloped and awaiting new initiative from any quarter. Jews were therefore able to play important roles in "new fields such as plastics, the chemical and pharmaceutical industries, the automobile industry, electrical goods and electronics, and a large part of heavy industry. Jewish companies, often very large ones, existed within the new industries after World War II to supply the local market. Jews also engaged in all aspects of the building industry," notably the skyscraper construction during the 1960s.[5]

Today a comprehensive listing of "Jewish" goods, whether produced or imported, would require a separate volume of forbidding size. In addition to the many textile enterprises that continue to expand, Jews are currently well represented among firms producing heavy machinery (Arbena represents the American Tool and Die Company), chemicals (Simselovich Drug Firm), food products (Goldstein Breads), ships (Samuel Gutnisky Corporation), and construction materials such as lumber (Jaime Liebling Company) and steel (Mauricio Silbert)—these represent only a small sample. The diversity of fields and of firms within each field is striking.[6]

A particularly important test of national modernization is the communications industry. Jews have accelerated Argentine devel-

opment in this field in numerous ways, including the virtual creation of its television industry. Not only have Jews been prominent
among network leaders, but businessmen such as the Werthein
brothers and Jaime Yankelevich were responsible for bringing the
first televisions into the country. Jewish-owned firms like Dinamix
currently are spreading the availability of television to the general
public and thereby aiding social and educational integration within
the nation.

Jews have played a similarly preeminent role in publishing. An
Italian Jewish family headed by César Civita directs Editorial Abril,
the largest magazine publishing firm in Argentina. Another Jew,
Jacobo Timerman, has established a variety of innovative publications. Timerman's creations include *Primera Plana* (Front Page),
which in 1961 became the first Argentine weekly newsmagazine,
and *La Opinión,* a sophisticated journal which has been likened to
the French daily *Le Monde,* but which also displays strong Zionist
views. Timerman's overt pro-Israeli position led to death threats by
right-wing terrorists in 1974, but he continued his efforts in the
forefront of Argentine journalism.[7]

The Jewish niche in the Argentine economy presently comprises three main roles: commercial wholesaling and retailing; professional services; and technology. The three areas reflect the rapid
progress Jews achieved since coming largely as lower-class workers.
If, for many years, the words Jew and peddler were virtually synon-

Table 10: Class Groups in Argentine Society, 1961

Classification (by class)	General Population (in percent)		Jewish Community (in percent)
Upper	4.2	(0.7)	– –
Middle (independent)	54.1	(6.6)	51.5
Middle (dependent)		(32.9)	45.0
Lower	41.7	59.8	3.5
TOTAL	100.0	100.0	100.0

SOURCE: Adapted from "La nupcialidad de la kehila de Buenos Aires, estudio
estadistico," *Annals,* III, p. 75. Source for figures for Jewish community and for
general population, first column, is Gino Germani's statistical survey in 1961, cited
by Carlos Alberto Erro in *La Nación,* March 5, 1961, figures for general population (in parentheses).

ymous to many Argentines, this stereotype melted with the rapid transformation of the community from an older generation of itinerant merchants and workers to a younger one of professionals and better-established shopkeepers. Over half of all Jewish workers are now self-employed businessmen, whereas the once-large Jewish proletariat has, by Argentine standards, practically disappeared. As can be seen in Table 10, the proportion of Jews in the middle classes (professionals, entrepreneurs, skilled laborers, and white-collar employees) far exceeds that of the general population.

An AMIA study in 1963 gives a more complete breakdown of the Jewish role in the economy, revealing large clusterings around professional, entrepreneurial, and clerical occupations. (See Table 11.)

Among the younger generation of Argentine Jews, about one in six enters a profession requiring a university degree. This passion for education distinguishes Jews from other immigrant groups in Argentina. Even lower-class Jews coming from Eastern Europe were highly literate upon arrival, and only the linguistic transition slowed their educational achievements in their adopted land. Today, at least one-sixth of all university students are Jewish, eight times the proportion of Jews in the general population.[8]

Jewish professionals favor medicine, engineering, economic science, and pharmacy and biochemistry, compared with the preferences of non-Jewish professionals. (See Table 12.) Yet relatively few Jewish professionals enter legal service, partly because the Argentine legal system militates against the advancement of Jews, especially in promotions to important judicial positions at the national level. This has indirectly encouraged the tendency of educated Jews to enter medicine, and more than three out of every ten Jewish professionals work as physicians.

The predilection for medical study, traditionally strong among Jewish communities throughout the world, grew especially intense during the early years of colonization, when the difficult ocean voyages and rough conditions in the interior resulted in a series of epidemics, including hepatitis and typhoid. The desperate need for doctors in this period is seen in the almost mystical veneration accorded the physician Noé Yarcho. It is significant that Yarcho, a man intensely active in community life and a multifaceted idealist,

179

THE JEWS OF ARGENTINA

Table 11: Occupational Distribution Among Members of the Jewish Community of Buenos Aires, 1961–67

Occupation	Number of Family Heads	Percent
Professionals (university degrees)	165	15.6
Teachers, artists, and intellectuals	11	1.0
Business and industry	334	31.6
Technicians	78	7.4
Jewelers	37	3.5
Marroquineros (leather craftsmen)	14	1.3
Carpenters and polishers	5	0.5
Tailors and dyers	16	1.5
Butchers and bakers	5	0.5
Furriers	8	0.6
Tapestry-makers	4	0.4
Shoemakers	2	0.2
Employees (clerical and similar)	231	21.8
Brokers	19	1.8
Workers	3	0.3
Graphics workers	6	0.6
Textile workers	26	2.5
Metallurgy workers	5	0.5
Transport workers	5	0.5
Workers in footwear	2	0.2
Other wage occupations	5	0.5
Students	48	4.5
Retired and pensioned	1	0.1
Not specified	28	2.6
TOTAL SAMPLED	1,058	100.0

NOTE—Sample population: 1,058 couples married between 1960 and 1962 at the Temple de Paso, Temple de Libertad, and the *kehillah* of Buenos Aires.

SOURCE: Adapted from "La nupcialidad de la kehila de Buenos Aires," *Annals,* III, pp. 88–89.

is still remembered above all else for his devotion to medical healing.

In addition to professional services, the very high educational level attained by the Jewish community accelerated another major part of the modernization process—technological advancement. Many developing nations depend almost totally upon outside technical as well as economic assistance, but Argentina early established a solid and expanding core of native-born scientists, economic analysts, and other technical specialists. In view of the great proportion of Jewish university graduates, it is unsurprising that Jews serve prominently in all these special fields.

Jewish research achievements are most impressive in the medical-related sciences, in bacteriology, biochemistry, and so forth. Beyond the undisputed preeminence of the Jewish Hospital in Buenos Aires, both in patient care and research facilities, individual Jewish discoveries have been prolific. Examples of Jewish contributions to medical research would fill volumes and in fact have done so, for there are separate Jewish scientific journals, as well as general ones, to keep pace with the achievements of Latin America's Jewish research leaders.[9]

Jews have also been conspicuous among the roll call of eminent economic and social theorists. A striking example of the nation's reliance on Jewish technical expertise even during periods of

Table 12: Distribution of Professionals, 1963

Career	All Argentine Professionals (in percent)	Jewish Professionals (in percent)
Medicine	26.8	30.4
Engineering	15.9	16.2
Economic sciences	11.5	16.2
Pharmacy and biochemistry	5.2	9.9
Exact sciences	5.3	6.3
Law	12.3	6.9
Odontology	11.6	7.8
Architecture	4.4	2.5
Obstetrics	5.5	– –
Others	1.5	0.4
Not specified	– –	3.4
TOTAL	100.0	100.0

NOTE—Sample: 18,854 for general population; 204 for Jewish population. Figures for Jewish professionals were compiled in 1963 by the AMIA; figures for the general population were taken from a national survey, cited in the same source.

SOURCE: Adapted from "La nupcialidad de la kehila de Buenos Aires," *Annals,* III, p. 80.

181

anti-Semitic reaction is the career of Abraham Heller. This economist served as adviser to the minister of the interior during the liberal government of Hipólito Yrigoyen in the 1920s. The administration also commissioned Heller to reorganize the Banco Hipotecario Nacional, which he accomplished with exceptional speed and success. When Yrigoyen fell from power in 1930, Heller's prestige was such that the ultraconservative and xenophobic new president, General José Felix Uriburu, retained him as an adviser and made him a delegate representing Argentina in ten international congresses on economic problems. Since then, Jewish economic advisers have been present in most Argentine administrations, including some which have disdained their presence in official governing capacities.

The Jewish roles in finance, commerce, the professions, and technological innovation have helped to make Argentina the most industrialized, wealthy, and modern state in Latin America. Ironically, anti-Semitic groups in Argentina routinely villify Jews for "parasitic" draining of the economy, rumors that have spread alarmingly in the past two decades as the economy continues to disappoint popular expectations. The roots of this stagnation lie not with any social sector, however, but with the flagrant mismanagement of resources during Juan Perón's rule in the forties and fifties. Many Argentines still credit him with modernizing the country through all manner of government projects, but his policies actually ruined golden opportunities for development. Perón squandered the nation's huge gold surplus after the Second World War by investing in numerous enterprises that held high political but small economic value, including excessive and indiscriminate construction projects that often served as monuments to Perón and little else. With similar disregard for economic repercussions, he paid workers inflationary increases to tighten his hold on their support. By the time Perón fled the country in 1955, the economy had been wrenched badly off its promising course of rapid modernization and growing prosperity.[10]

Today, the luster of the once-confident Argentine economy has almost vanished. Years of union strikes, featherbedding, wage increases unsupported by gains in productivity, mismanaged government investment, and the haphazard nationalization of industry have created economic chaos.

182

The peso, long valued between five and ten to the United States dollar during the 1940s, began a downward spiral that reduced its worth so drastically that by the early seventies it took well over a thousand to obtain a single American dollar. As this book went to press in mid-1978, Argentina was the world's leader in inflation, with an annual rate of well over 100 percent.

Another indicator of adversity is the fate of the beef supply. Although the nation is famed for its cattle and savory steaks, the Argentines themselves find beef difficult to obtain. The government, in search of a cure for economic stagnation, banned domestic sales of beef on alternate weeks in order to export more. At one point in 1972, the government extended this ban to two weeks at a time, but popular protest made enforcement too dangerous to attempt. The *semana de no carne,* or week of no meat, nevertheless became an accepted fact of life for most Argentines.

Jews, far from profiting from these economic troubles, have been among the groups hardest hit by them. This is partly because they are concentrated in areas most affected by instability and panic—the small businesses and financial institutions.

The decline in Jewish economic fortunes merely traces in sharper form the dangerous financial trends throughout the post-Perónist years. As credit tightened and inflation eroded purchasing power, small businessmen found it difficult to maintain their enterprises. This precipitated a mass run on banks and cooperatives, many of which were bankrupted by the rapid withdrawal of funds. The withdrawals and bankruptcies in turn accelerated the panic and led in the 1970s to the insolvency of a great proportion of the Jewish cooperatives. The military government intervened in 1972 to take over the cooperatives, either closing them altogether or directing them so as to ensure "regular" transactions. The fall of these institutions ruined businesses in desperate need of loans to help them survive the worsening instability. The Jewish community still suffers acutely from these conditions, while the Argentine economy as a whole shows little sign of dramatically increasing business confidence or ending the crippling strikes and shortages impeding recovery.[11]

It is astonishing that after these long bouts with economic ills and the concomitant political strain, Argentina remains by far the strongest Latin American nation in gross national product, per capita income, and most other standards of economic strength. Brazil alone rivals its economic potential, and that nation is still approaching those levels of prosperity that Argentines have long enjoyed. In this context, the Jewish contribution to Argentine development is most clearly observed.

Literature and other cultural media

Argentina, ever receptive to contributions by foreign settlers, reflects considerable Jewish influence in its cultural expression. The titan of Argentine literature, Jorge Luis Borges, seasons many of his tales with Jewish themes and characters. He confides that the Hispanic Jewish poet, Rafael Cansinos-Assens, was the single strongest influence on his literary style. This man "had studied for the priesthood," Borges relates, "but having found the name Cansinos in the archives of the Inquisition, he decided he was a Jew. This led him to the study of Hebrew and later on he even had himself circumcised." Borges adds, "I still like to think of myself as his disciple."[12]

It was Borges who, as director of the National Library, pressed to have a Judaica section added in recognition of the cultural force Jews represented. He described Jews and Argentines as cultural brethren in that they shared the same source of creativity. Just as the Jew throughout history has been a part of and still apart from Western culture, enabling him both to assimilate and innovate, so the Argentine has this opportunity with European traditions.[13]

Jewish writers have added directly to Argentina's literary heritage, enriching its explorations of immigrant life and the complex process of cultural adaptation. Many writers also focused attention on different marginal elements in Argentine society, whether in urban slums or neglected interior communities, thus giving new impetus to social reform movements.[14]

Alberto Gerchunoff is the country's most celebrated Jewish author. He was born to Russian immigrants in Entre Ríos and commemorated that colonizing era with a novel of twenty-six tales called *Los gauchos judíos* (The Jewish Gauchos). Published in 1910 while Gerchunoff was still in his twenties, the book became a classic of Argentine literature, an epitome of immigrant hopes and challenges.

Los gauchos judíos is above all a labor of love and faith. Gerchunoff believed passionately that the new settlers would become productive and patriotic Argentines, differing only in their religious tradition. The prologue captures his sense of a new era by comparing the emigration from Russia with the exodus out of Egypt. Gerchunoff exhorts Jews to celebrate their journey to freedom in the Argentine colonies as a new Passover tradition.

Gerchunoff's life was no less adventurous than that of the characters he described in his tales. He was a peddler, student, and manual laborer before turning to journalism. He began writing for the great liberal daily *La Nación* in 1910. Later in the same decade he traveled to Europe on a cultural mission, representing the progressive administration of President Roqua Saenz Peña. Gerchunoff's circle of friends included some of the greatest names in Argentine letters—Robert Payró, Leopoldo Lugones, José Ingenieros, Ricardo Rojas, Manuel Gálvez, and Emilio Bécher. He was popular not only for his literary attainments but for a droll, congenial, and satiric manner. Manuel Gálvez portrayed Gerchunoff in one of his novels under the name Orloff, a trenchant figure, both sarcastic and yet kindly, in a deeper way.

The Orloff depicted by Gálvez was never in truer form than at the scene of a lavish social function to which Gerchunoff had been invited as representative of *La Nación.* He gave his card to the official at the entrance, who ceremoniously called out the name on the card to the prestigious, exclusive circle of guests and then whispered to Gerchunoff, "Title?" Gerchunoff, without hesitating, responded *"Judío!"* Years later, the writer Silvano Santander mused on the incident that, aside from the practical jest, Gerchunoff had taken an expression that had been abused by countless pejorative uses and infused it with nobility.[15]

Gerchunoff revealed a fervent idealism in a series of essays on Don Quixote entitled *La jofaina maravillosa* (The Marvelous Washbasin). The theme pervading these pieces is that it mattered little that Don Quixote's helmet was merely a washbasin, so long as he stayed true to his convictions. There was much of Gerchunoff in his Don Quixote. A political radical, Gerchunoff fought for the rights of free expression and dissent as founder and head of the Argentine Writer's Association, and as editor of *La Nación.* Although initially Gerchunoff heralded the benefits of assimilation and even cultivated a neo-Christian mysticism, his horror at Hitler's madness

185

catalyzed the resurgence of his Judaic sentiments, and he zealously embraced the cause of Zionism. During the last decade of his life, Gerchunoff met with political leaders across Latin America to seek support for a Jewish state.

Gerchunoff's novels today are standard works in classrooms throughout Argentina. Streets and even a railway station in Entre Ríos bear his name, and major government officials attend ceremonies honoring his memory. Gerchunoff's prestige extends—as would please him most—equally as *argentino* and *judío*.

The most prestigious living Argentine Jewish writer is Israel Zeitlin, who under the pseudonym of César Tiempo idealized the harmony of Argentine and Jewish cultures in a series of books, poems, essays, and columns. More than Gerchunoff, Zeitlin glorifies the Jewish religious tradition. His *Para la pausa del sabado* (For the Sabbath Rest, 1930), won the First Municipal Prize of Buenos Aires for poetry. Other collections of poems, including *Sabatión Argentino* (1933) and *Sabadomingo* (Sabbath Sunday, 1938), also sympathetically explore the religious reasons for the Jewish day of rest. Zeitlin whimsically calls himself "a mad singer of the Hebrew *barrio,*"[16] though he is equally at home in other *"barrios,"* writing many essays for both *La Nación* and *La Prensa.* When President Perón nationalized *La Prensa* in 1949, Zeitlin became director of the widely read "Literary Supplement."

A cofounder and first secretary of the Argentine Writers' Association, Samuel Glusberg is the quintessence of the cosmopolitan thinker who still affirms his Judaic heritage. His literary pseudonym, Enrique Espinoza, reflects his admiration for Spinoza and Heinrich Heine and his intent to draw from Jewish and non-Jewish traditions. The Russian-born writer came to Argentina as a child of seven and is among the most prolific Latin American journalists, editing two literary reviews, *América* and *Babel,* and a great number of critical essays. In 1924, at the age of twenty-six, he wrote his masterpiece, *La levita gris* (The Grey Coat), a collection of tales of Jews coping with life in Buenos Aires. Glusberg later edited his prestigious journal *Babel* while living in Santiago, Chile.

The versatile intellectual, Carlos Grünberg, taught Spanish literature, practiced law, translated Heine, and edited a literary journal of his own creation, *Heredía.* Grünberg's magnum opus, titled *Mester de judería* (Expression of the Jewish People), is among

186

the most highly praised works on Judaism in Argentina. The book first appeared in 1940 during the Holocaust, and the style was fiercely polemical, protesting the world's barbarity against the Jews throughout history. Grünberg also peppered his work with refutations and slashing attacks against his critics in Europe and the Americas. Jorge Luis Borges praised the book in a foreword, writing that "Grünberg, a poet, is indisputably Argentine."

Among the better-known Argentine poets is Lázaro Liacho, previously cited for his tales of Jewish immigrant life in the farm colonies. Liacho later gained national recognition for such collections of verses as *Bocado de pan* (Morsel of Bread, 1931) and *Pan de Buenos Aires* (Bread of Buenos Aires, 1940). He sought especially to portray relationships between Jews and Christians in Argentina. In more recent years, with works like *Entre diós y satán* (Between God and Satan, 1966), Liacho turned to biblical, religious, and metaphysical themes.

Numerous Jewish social critics used literary forms as vehicles to promote their ideals for reform. One of the first and most successful was Isaac Kaplan (1878–1976), known as the father of Jewish cooperativism in Argentina. Kaplan's family left a town in Byelorussia to settle in the colony Clara when he was fifteen. There he helped establish the second Jewish cooperative in the country, working with the famous physician, Noé Yarcho, and Yarcho's brother-in-law, Miguel Sajaroff.

Kaplan viewed the cooperative as more than an economic innovation. He believed it could serve the most altruistic purposes, and he expounded his philosophy in a series of articles for the colonies' monthly journal *Kolonist Kooperator,* which he also edited for over a quarter-century, from 1921 to 1947. Kaplan also turned to drama to express his ideas, with the play *La necessidad es ingeniosa* (Necessity Is the Mother of Invention). His clearest exposition of cooperative ideals is *Vadamecum del cooperativistas,* a sort of catechism of the movement published by the central agency for all Jewish cooperatives. Even Kaplan's fiction, however, was designed mainly as polemic, much as Edward Bellamy subordinated the narrative of his classic political novel, *Looking Backward,* to an analysis of his utopian vision.

Kaplan's works advocated a class theory of behavior but lacked the venom of some Marxist tracts. If he gave special praise to the

187

working classes, it was not because they would destroy their oppressors but because they would be the first to perceive the blessings of cooperativism. He wrote in *Vadamecum,* "Cooperativism grows naturally, casting its roots in the ranks of those who have found life's great teacher: misery, where there exists natural comprehension, sincerity, and the desire to improve things continually. In this lies the secret of its success." Kaplan summed up the cooperative movement as "the practical expression of economic justice . . . a means for constructing a better world."[17]

Kaplan's prestige as the leading theorist of cooperativism extended even to government circles. The Argentine minister of agriculture more than once appointed him to aid in planning government policy toward the colonies, both Jewish and non-Jewish. Kaplan also became a spokesman in Parliament for the interests of the colonists, helping to guide into passage laws that promoted their agricultural activity and security.

Another Socialist writer, José Pavlotzky, dramatized the plight of settlers in his native Chaco Province in the novel, *Esta tierra es mía* (This Earth Is Mine). He focused, too, on the mistakes of rural legislation that compounded the difficult times faced by the pioneers. His work was the basis for a film on the Chaco settlers and stirred new interest in the lives of the frontier communities.

Pavlotzky's work belongs to a long tradition of Argentine novels of man's fight with nature and the brutal existence of rural life. Increasingly, though, new settings have occupied the attention of major writers, and novelists from the rapidly urbanizing Jewish community have strongly contributed to the new literary trends. The Jewish writer, Bernardo Vertibsky, is perhaps the most distinguished exponent of the still-emerging genre of Argentine literature on the turmoil and problems of the city.

Vertibsky's works burn with a moral intensity and social protest that give him a special niche in Argentine fiction. His first major work, *Es difícil empezar a vivir* (It Is Difficult to Begin to Live), won the honored Ricardo Güiraldes Prize for his sensitive portrayal of Jewish life in Buenos Aires in the years from 1933 to 1941, when fascism was on the rise at home and in Europe. Pablo Levinson, the story's main protagonist, is a Jewish teenager both curious and critical, living amid corruption, anti-Semitic injustices, and social and educational crises. Much later, Vertibsky wrote *Villa miseria tambien es América* (The Slum Is Also America), revealing the envy of the lower classes toward their affluent countrymen. The book's probing of deep-rooted social problems and its narrative skill earned Vertibsky the Alberto Gerchunoff Prize for fiction.

Among the younger social critics, Bernardo Ezequiel Koremblit is prominent for erudite and subtle analyses like *La torre de marfil y la política* (The Ivory Tower and Politics), which examines the role of the intellectual in working for reform. The Argentine writer, Alfonso Reyes, wrote that Koremblit's work "will be difficult to surpass." Another critic called it "an exceptional book; written by an artist, unfolding the dramatic work of an intellectual."[18] As this literary acclaim descended, Koremblit assumed the post of director of the Sociedad Hebraica Argentina. In an era when third-generation Jewish intellectuals increasingly are turning away from the *kehillah,* Koremblit's course is particularly noteworthy.

Beyond broadening the social vision of Argentine literature, Jews have added a new genre: psychological drama. Its leading exponent was a native-born *entreriano* (one born in Entre Ríos Province), Samuel Eichelbaum (1894–1967), hailed as the foremost Latin American playwright. Eichelbaum wrote his first major work at the age of twenty-five, the beginning of a prolific career of several dozen plays and additional writings. In 1930, eleven years after his earliest effort, he received the Municipal Prize of Buenos Aires for his play, *Tormenta de dios* (Torment of God). Then in 1937 he won the same coveted award for his play *Señorita.* In both plays, Eichelbaum used the plot mainly as a framework for his penetrating insights into the hidden motivations of human actions. Eichelbaum wrote only two plays on Jewish themes, *El Judío Aarón* and *Nadie la conoció nunca* (No One Ever Knew Her), both comedies. He also wrote a short story "Una buena cosecha" (A Good Harvest) set in Rosh Pinnah, a Jewish colony in Palestine. Eichelbaum's works were generally devoid of overt ethnic themes and concentrated instead on universal human dilemmas and desires. What Vertibsky did for the Argentine literary perception of social conflict, Eichelbaum equalled with his insight into the soul of the individual.

Jewish writers have fashioned the main but by no means only bridges between immigrant and native cultural traditions. Jewish

189

painters and sculptors, musicians, and other artists have blended elements of both worlds while gaining recognition in the larger Argentine society.

Many Jewish artists have transplanted new European styles to Latin America while expressing both Judaic and Argentine settings.[19] The Polish-born immigrant Moses Faigenblum, who came to Argentina in 1928, gained distinction both as a painter and calligrapher. He illustrated and styled the Hebrew lettering for an edition of the Passover *Haggadah.* He did similar work for the *Song of Songs* and the treatise *Cuzari* by Judah Halevi. In his oils, Faigenblum especially portrayed scenes of Jewish worship, of Buenos Aires, and of Warsaw under the Nazis. Faigenblum also experimented with ceramics and collages of colored paper on plain surfaces to achieve some of his most striking work.

One of the first exponents of abstract constructivism and kinetic art in Latin America is a Czechoslovakian-born Jew named Gyula Kosice. This naturalized Argentine, just now in his midfifties, helped found two art journals (*Arturo,* in 1944, and *Invention,* in 1945). Kosice also has written numerous articles about his plexiglas creations and on the use of light and movement in sculpture. He more recently has worked in Paris, where in 1957 his works formed the first exhibition of hydraulic sculpture in France. Six years later, he directed an exhibition of kinetics and other Argentine art at the Museum of Modern Art in Paris.

Kosice has had many prominent disciples in his so-called Madi group. Martin Blazko, born in Germany in 1920, moved first to Poland in 1933 and then to Argentina in 1939. His work stresses the relationship between plastic form and structure, and it has achieved international recognition, including prizes from the London Institute of Modern Art (1952), the gold medal at an Argentine exhibition at Brussels (1958), and numerous national distinctions. Blazko's creations are displayed in several museums across the country.

Another German-born Jew, Pablo Hanneman, earned critical praise in Argentina since settling there in 1937, for his work in plastic forms, sculpture, and woodcarving. He has innovated with images in concrete and declared that this is the only true link with architecture. Hannemann founded an art school in Argentina in 1955 and worked with two other architects to organize the first

Israeli industrial exhibition in Argentina. His work reflects Jewish themes, including the Holocaust, as in his *Cámara de gas* (Gas Chamber).

A sculptor born in Paraná in Entre Ríos Province, Israel Hoffman is known for his impressionistic originality and devotion to popular and folkloric themes. His creations include *El Pescador* (The Fisherman), *El Viejo* (The Old Man), *El Chico Entreriano* (The Boy of Entre Ríos), and others. Hoffman also directed the Museum of Arts in his native Paraná until his death at the age of seventy-five in 1971.

Mauricio Lasansky's *Nazi Drawings* recall the horror of the Holocaust through simple yet moving pencil sketches. The work, completed in 1967, added to this native Argentine's already superlative reputation in his field. He was born in Villa De Voto in 1913, of Polish immigrants, and studied at the Academy of Art in Buenos Aires. Later, he became head of the Free Fine Arts School in the capital and established what became the most prestigious graphic arts workshop in the world. Lasansky's original method of color printing and his imaginative engravings have garnered over seventy prizes internationally. At present, he teaches in the United States at the University of Iowa and is also a consultant to the Guggenheim Foundation.

Among Jewish painters who excel both as craftsmen and innovators, Carolina Muchnik is prominent for her expressionist work. Adherent of a school of artistic "magic and fantasy," her works have been praised in Europe, where she has given exhibits in Paris, Brussels, and other cities. Her paintings are noted for a unique quality of mystery, in which reality mixes with darker touches of the unknown.

Internationally famed Estela Albertal specializes in portraits, a field in which she has also written several studies. Her interest in French painting led to a national radio program in which she lectured regularly on the subject. Albertal's portrait of Domingo Sarmiento established her reputation in Argentina, while her works have been acclaimed in France as well. Among her other accomplishments are a number of murals reflecting historical and literary themes.

The tragic life of the painter Moritz Minkowsky yields both beauty and pain. Born deaf and mute in 1881, Minkowsky studied

191

art first in his native Poland and then in Paris. He was a close colleague of Modigliani, Chagall, Braque, Dali, and Picasso. However, many of these strong-minded titans of the avant-garde soon disparaged Minkowsky's ideas and he left Europe for Argentina. All his paintings reflect the pain and desolation of the ghetto. His figures have compressed lips, and are mute and sad. Even the deep beauty of the youths in his paintings is poisoned by the anguish seen in embittered expressions, a reminder of the tragedy of East European Jewry. Minkowsky's haunting talent inspired numerous young artists, before his death at age forty-nine; his deafness prevented him from perceiving an oncoming car.

Another Jewish painter influenced by the Holocaust is Wolf Bandurek, born in 1906 in Poland. His work was exhibited in Danzig (1932) and Paris (1934), where one of his oils won an award. After settling briefly in Paraguay, he moved to Argentina in the 1940s, continuing his artistic themes of human desperation before the evils of life. One of his most famous paintings, *El Bajur de Yeshivah* (The Yeshivah Youth), shows a religious boy with eyes wide from shock at the brutality of the Nazi invaders. Bandurek also tried to capture on his canvases the ideal of Sabbath worship, using an expressionistic style to highlight the emotional quality of his work.

In music as in art, Jews developed and blended many traditions. Classical European composition in particular has attracted a disproportionate number of Jewish musicians. Pianists Raúl Spivak, who played to acclaim at Carnegie Hall, and the prodigy Daniel Barenboim are two among many brilliant examples of this devotion. Barenboim, son of a former teacher at the Vienna Music Academy, was already widely renowned in Argentina while still in his early teens, before leaving to study music in Rome. He later settled in Israel and has since achieved even greater fame both as a pianist and conductor.

Jewish folksingers in recent years are fusing elements from many musical origins and performing to warm popular receptions. Isabel Aretz has added to the songs and dances that have become a part of Argentine folk culture. She has made many trips into the interior to meet demands for her renditions of songs, both collected and original. Even more exotic is the music of Dina Rot, an attractive singer of East European descent who performs in Ladino, the

Sephardic dialect. Journalist Marsha Taylor records, "Falling easily on the ears of native speakers of Spanish, the Dina Rot songs were a hit with both Jews and non-Jews, when presented at several private theatres and at the Sociedad Hebraica Argentina."[20]

Traditional Jewish melodies survive in Argentina, partly through the activities of composers for choirs. Jacobo Fischer, among the most original of these musicians, won national recognition with symphonic arrangements for Jewish themes. *Sulamit* (1929) received a prize for composition, and *Tercera Sinfonia* won second prize from the National Commission of Culture in 1941. Fischer's Hebraic melodies honored the poems of Judah Halevi, the Talmud *(Tres piezas sinfónicos según el Talmud),* and the writings of the unofficial poet laureate of Argentine Jewry, César Tiempo.

The greatest Jewish composer in Argentina died almost unknown. Colman Saslavsky proved in his brief lifetime that ill fortune could triumph over the most remarkable talent. Saslavsky lost both his parents while still a child in Bessarabia, Russia, and lived upon the charity of the local Jewish community. As a youth, he alternated *yeshivah* study with music lessons and showed uncommon facility with a variety of instruments. Saslavsky wrote articles on Hebrew melody for the Jewish press and made the acquaintance of the leading cantors of the region. His fame reached to Kishinev, the capital of Bessarabia, where he was made orchestral director of the main synagogue.

Russian pogroms spurred Saslavsky to espouse Zionism, and his grief at the news of Herzl's death in 1904 led him to compose a funeral march for the Jewish leader. The Jewish community in Austria invited him to direct the composition in Vienna, but Saslavsky wanted to leave Europe altogether, in part because of the worsening anti-Semitism. Feeling unable to travel to North America, he instead settled in Argentina. It was the worst mistake of his life.

Saslavsky arrived in 1905 in Buenos Aires and worked as a Hebrew teacher and synagogue cantor for 50 pesos a month. During the High Holy Days, he directed a temple choir of twelve voices. He also found time to compose, study, and play various instruments; but the new environment was not to his liking. Saslavsky's creativity suffered from the sad fact that his reputation, so rapidly ascending in Europe, appeared to have dissolved in this new community.

After two years in Buenos Aires, embittered by the lack of recognition, Saslavsky moved to the countryside in hope of a change of fortune. This merely accentuated his basic frustration, for his musical abilities were even less appreciated in the struggling colony of San Antonio. Moreover, his new work as a farmer left him completely dissatisfied. Saslavsky began regularly commuting great distances to Buenos Aires to direct holiday services. These trips marked a resurgence in his musical activity and in his prestige as composer and director of liturgical choirs. When he conducted a concert by a mixed choir in the Yiddish theater Olympia, he appeared to have regained his former stature in Europe. Yet his hopes received another crushing blow. The mixing of sexes in religious gatherings offended many traditional Jews, and they arranged to have Saslavsky's choir banned from further performances.

Again Saslavsky succumbed to melancholy reflection and a desire to create for a more appreciative audience. An offer soon came from outside Argentina, for many Brazilian Jews remembered Saslavsky's reputation from their youth in Europe, and they invited him to arrange and conduct the music for their main synagogue in Rio de Janeiro. Saslavsky instantly seized this opportunity, setting sail for Rio in a ship owned by a Greek naval company. The ownership may appear trivial, but to Saslavsky the consequences were staggeringly important, for "incorrigible romantic, he forgot a small detail: his documents."[21] Brazilian port officials unfamiliar with Saslavsky's liturgical achievements stubbornly concentrated their attention on his lack of identification. They prevented him from disembarking and obliged him to remain on the ship, which slowly pulled away from the harbor and sailed toward Greece. Saslavsky arrived suitably demoralized and also destitute. He wandered for months over the Greek isles until, at last, a Greek Jewish family gave him support to travel to France. From Marseilles, he wrote to his former neighbors in San Antonio to send his passport to Montevideo in Uruguay, as he intended to return there en route to Argentina. Several more months of hapless peregrinations followed before Saslavsky again found his way to the modest *chacra* he owned in San Antonio.

Saslavsky's productivity increased as his melancholia deepened. He composed arrangements inspired by the trials of Mena-hem Mendel Beilis and Alfred Dreyfus, and dedicated music to various Jewish figures, including Sholem Aleichem, whom he par-ticularly admired. Saslavsky became evermore peripatetic, alternat-ing his farming chores in San Antonio with Bible and Talmud instruction in Moisésville, while also finding the time to direct liturgical music in many Argentine towns. Yet he lived in constant poverty because he neglected to charge for many of his services and was ignored by community charities since, unlike some other colo-nists, he at least possessed a *chacra.*

Saslavsky placed all his hopes in his son Herzl, a prodigy in music. At age nine Herzl died of an illness. Saslavsky himself died shortly afterward, brokenhearted, at the age of forty-eight.

Saslavsky's reputation rose dramatically since his death, as evi-dence of his creative and prolific work continues to surface. Yet even today this evidence is still largely indirect. Many works remain lost, others preserved only anonymously, so that the full extent of his contributions to music in Argentina may never be ascertained. The tragedy of his career, gone so sharply awry, is well summarized by the title of an account of his life: "Colman Saslavsky, the Forgot-ten Cantor."[22]

An art form that Jews have done much to help popularize in Argentina as in many other nations is chess, the "royal game" of imagination and logic. The recent exploits of the charismatic and idiosyncratic champion, Bobby Fischer, of the United States, pro-pelled chess into a much broader public reception than ever before, and it is at last gaining wide admiration as a most challenging aesthetic form. Like many of the towering figures in chess, from Emanuel Lasker and Wilhelm Steinitz in the nineteenth century to Mikhail Botvinnik and Boris Spassky in the present, Fischer is of Jewish descent. The same is true of some of the most brilliant Argentine masters, whose immigration from Europe helped to make the country into a major chess power.

The finest chess player Argentina has ever known and one of the immortals of the game is a Jew now in his sixties, Moshe Najdorf (1910–). He is famous for playing forty-five games simul-taneously without sight of board or pieces. He kept the positions for each game in his mind and called out his moves to each opponent, who of course referred to a chessboard in the style of more mortal combatants. Najdorf's vision of the imaginary pieces swirling in his mind was sufficient to defeat easily almost all his adversaries.

Najdorf left his native Warsaw for Buenos Aires in 1939 after completing a tournament there and learning of Nazi aggression against Poland. He Hispanicized his name from Moshe to Miguel but still joined the AMIA in Buenos Aires. Najdorf for many years was a prime contender for the world chess championship, and his best games include victories over Fischer and several other world champions, including Boris Spassky of the Soviet Union. His games are noted for their delightful inventiveness and bold attacking play. One of these contests, against an opponent named Glucksberg, ranks among the very finest displays of combinational skill ever seen in tournament competition. One noted American master and critic altogether "resigned" his composure and declared, "The striking series of brilliancies initiated by Black's [Najdorf's] thirteenth move compares favorably, I believe, with any combination ever played over the board."[23]

Najdorf as recently as 1970 participated in a major tournament held in Buenos Aires. Bobby Fischer also played in this tournament en route to a spectacular return to regular chess competition following a two-year period of sullen, nearly total withdrawal. Fischer easily captured the first prize, but the sixty-year-old Najdorf, well past his best playing years, managed to hold the American genius to a draw. He was one of only four players in a field of eighteen to do so.

Ironically, Najdorf has been overshadowed throughout his brilliant career by an American Jew, also of Polish origin, named Samuel Reshevsky. Reshevsky is one of the very few masters who adheres strictly to Orthodox Jewish Law, even at the cost of subsisting on fruit and nuts during tournaments where kosher food is difficult to obtain, as in the Soviet Union. Reshevsky's greater fame and celebrated Jewish observance reflect in microcosm the sad eclipse of Argentine Jewry by their brethren to the north.

It may be added as an epilogue to the interaction of immigrant and native Argentines that the artist most closely linking Jews and non-Jews is not a writer, painter, scientist, or musician, but a television performer named Adolfo Stray. He is the star of a program called *Don Jacobo,* roughly comparable to the American television comedy series, *All in the Family.* As Marsha Taylor observes, *"Don Jacobo's* main attraction is its hero, a wealthy Jewish businessman who has coped since 1969 in mangled accent-tinged Spanish with the generation gap, intermarriage, and other touchy subjects. To judge from continued high ratings, the series exerts a pull on Jewish and non-Jewish audiences alike." Neither as Don Jacobo nor in real life does Stray at all disguise his Jewish heritage, and indeed after one show, close to the High Holy Days, he briefly addressed his fellow Jewish citizens in Yiddish over national television. Stray comments on his image, on screen and off, that in forty years he has never been made to suffer because of his Jewishness.[24] Through humor, caricature, and a very human vulnerability, Stray has created a Jewish character that Argentines not only smile at but with whom they also identify—the greatest cultural exchange one can achieve.

Politics

Jewish political activity in Argentina has been preponderantly oriented toward movements for greater popular participation in politics and for wider distribution of wealth. This represents in part the enthusiasm so many Jewish immigrants carried from Russia for the creation of democratic socialist utopias. It represents also the long Judaic commitment to social justice, bonded by religious tradition and long persecution.

The progressive outlook of the Jewish community has clear similarities with the liberal democratic sentiments of most American Jews, but the parallels are by no means complete. The Jews in Argentina retain a more intense Socialist ethic, evident in their centralized welfare organization, cooperative institutions, and powerful support for Socialist-Zionist parties. Yet Argentine Jews wield less political power than their American coreligionists, despite the greater solidarity of the former community in other ways. One cause for this is the greater concentration of Jews in key American cities. New York, for example, is well over 25 percent Jewish, whereas Buenos Aires is scarcely 5 percent Jewish. Another explanation for the relative lack of power is that Catholic Argentines have not accepted the idea of Jewish political influence as fully as has the American population. The retention, through several revisions of the Constitution, of the ban against electing a non-Catholic president symbolizes this conservatism in Argentina. Perhaps the main factor, though, is that so much of the *kehillah*'s energies are absorbed by campaigns against anti-Semitism, a far more serious problem than in the United States. The concern with anti-Semitism also leads the community to avoid any appearance of group pressure on general political issues, in contrast to American politics, where ethnic solidarity and appeals are accepted and even celebrated publicly by candidates of both major parties.

The extreme reluctance by Argentine Jews to assert themselves as a pressure group, with common legitimate interests, is typified by an incident from the election campaign of 1958. That year marked the liberalization of the political system, which had been run by the military faction for three years. The relaxation of political restraints had noticeable benefits for Jews. Almost every major party included some Jewish candidates, and party spokesmen vied with each other to produce the most grandiloquent speeches on behalf of Israeli-Argentine relations. On the left-wing, Alfredo Palacios of the Socialist Party told Jewish audiences of his visit to Israel during the period of the Sinai campaign. On the right-wing, the Conservative Party leaders recalled that Jewish settlement had been facilitated "thanks to the immigration laws of the old Conservative Governments."[25] Rather than relishing this newfound political strength, as Argentina moved from military to civilian democratic rule, the Jewish community was appalled. The Argentine Jewish Institute for Information published an appeal in all the leading newspapers, asking political parties not to make special approaches to Jews for votes in the elections. The appeal asserted that Jews had no collective ties motivating their decisions at the polls.[26] It was, in effect, a repudiation of ethnic political power. In the United States this would be incomprehensible, and even in Argentina the repudiation was in no clear way a result of wider political or social exigencies in the nation at large. Perhaps after long persecution and with continued feelings of insecurity, the Jewish community simply could not adjust to this role reversal of being courted instead of crushed. Its response was to shrink from the light of this new opportunity as if it were, in some nebulous but deeply feared way, ultimately dangerous.

Argentine Jews also do not fully share the political patterns of other Argentine immigrant groups. It is true that Italian and Spanish settlers initially spanned the leftist political spectrum, including many anarchists and syndicalists. Yet as these immigrants gained relative economic security under Perón, most quickly shed their radical ideology and soon became locked into more economically and socially conservative positions. Many enthusiastically submitted to authoritarian regimes in exchange for whatever economic largesse they could obtain. As a result, Perón drew some of his most solid support precisely among these immigrant groups. Jews have, on the contrary, tended to fear authoritarian governments too much to support them actively, even when those governments pursued policies that objectively favored, or at least spared, their economic interests.

Jewish radical politics took root immediately with the first settlements from Eastern Europe. These movements tended not only toward socialism but toward Zionism and a strong patriotic attachment to Argentina, their adopted land. Unsurprisingly, it was a Jewish Socialist, Augusto Kuhn, who in 1890 organized the first Argentine celebration of the successful colonial revolts against Spanish rule.

The Jewish left was not at all a united front. The first Jewish union, Centro Obrero Israelita, formed in 1897, was so moderate that even some employers joined. Its central interest was mutual aid, and in this respect the progressive views of all elements of the community served to mute class tensions. However, there were also sufficient numbers of Jewish Communists, Syndicalists, and Anarchists to induce a leading journal of the extreme Left, *La Protesta,* to devote an entire news page to the Yiddish language. Another major left-wing paper, *La Vanguardia,* was largely Jewish-run and published numerous Yiddish articles.

As immigration from revolutionary Russia increased, Jewish unions and leftist parties and publications proliferated. Yet their leaders tended to be gradualists, like Isaac Kaplan, whose reforming vision was completely pacific. Most affluent Argentines, however, especially the ruling elite, not only disapproved of such movements but dreaded them. It mattered little that the vast majority of leftist groups adhered to nonviolent means of dissent; the shadow cast by the few extremists totally darkened their image in business and government circles.

The first sign that all Jews would bear the notoriety achieved by the handful of violent left-wing activists came in 1909. A seventeen-year-old Jewish anarchist named Simon Radowitzky felt a calling to avenge personally the brutal police repressions of his comrades in anarchy. His solution was to hurl a bomb at Chief of Police Ramón Falcón and his assistant. Radowitzky's aim was accurate, and with one blow he set back his cause immeasurably. Three thousand hapless workers in the vicinity suffered deportation or imprisonment. Other Jewish anarchists took refuge in London, in preference to imprisonment or possible execution. Radowitzky himself was sent to jail for ten years until pardoned by President Yrigoyen, after the liberal journal *Crítica* organized a campaign in his favor.

Radowitzky's action swelled anti-Semitic feelings among the *criollos.* On May 14 and 15, 1910, they released their fury against the Jews in a full-scale pogrom, beating and raping many in the Jewish quarter of Buenos Aires. These atrocities were merely a prelude to the butchery known as the *Semana Trágica,* or Tragic Week, of 1919. What began as a labor-management conflict became an outlet for barbarism whose random violence found only one common victim, the Jew.

Labor discontent and business fears of communism both crested after World War I. The armistice truncated a period of rising wages and production in Argentina, long the beneficiary of an expanded wartime European market. Worker resentments rose visibly, with strikes increasing by more than 75 percent and the number of strikers by over 100 percent, between 1918 and 1919.[27]

Against the background of the Bolshevik takeover in Russia, the worker actions terrified Argentine conservatives. They perceived a gruesome specter of revolution more menacing with every labor strike. They also perceived a link between Jews and a diabolical Marxist plot to control Argentina. This impression drew support from elements in the Catholic church that viewed the Jew both as a parasite and deadly agent of social change. The leading cleric of Córdoba, Bishop Bustos, warned the populace of "the social revolution which threatens us," and other priests soon followed his lead to denounce first the "European" carriers of the Socialist disease and finally the "Jewish Marxists."[28] The chilling and logical consequences of these images exploded during the second week of January 1919.

Workers at a metallurgical plant in Vasena precipitated the events of the *Semana Trágica* by striking and destroying machinery. The government retaliated with police to "restore order," leaving five workers dead and forty wounded. Workers throughout the nation immediately responded with a general strike, which paralyzed the economy. Thus, in its initial stages the Tragic Week involved escalating class tensions but little overt race prejudice.[29]

Nightmares for the Jews began when the government repression of the workers merged with newspaper cries against "outside agitators," "Marxists paid by Moscow," and "the Jewish Bolshevik conspiracy."[30] The Jewish Socialist leader Pinhas Wald appeared in these headlines as the architect of a revolutionary government, ready to assume control of Argentina as dictator-president. At that point, violence sparked largely by police and right-wing agitators turned fully upon the Jews.[31]

Di Prese called January 10, 1919, the "day of assaults and night of murders."[32] Frenzied gangs rushed through the streets of Buenos Aires looking for Jewish centers to vandalize. They sacked the offices of the Socialist journal *Avangard*, Po'alei Zion, and the Jewish library Moses Hess. Other ruffians attacked and robbed bankers and cloth and fur merchants in the Jewish quarter. Pinhas Wald described the sanguinary activities:

Savage were the demonstrations of the "rich kids" who marched to the cry of "Kill the Jews," "Kill the foreigners," "Kill the Marximalists." . . . They stop a Jew and then from the first blows a stream of blood runs from his mouth. They order him to sing the national anthem. He does not know it; they murder him on the spot.[33]

All the while the police stood by, in perfect order, completely impassive.

Jews responded to the pogrom by protests, pamphlets, and representations to the president. Their most significant published appeal, by the combined heads of the Jewish organizations, was entitled "150,000 Jews: To the People of the Republic," urging an end to the violence against their fellow citizens.[34] Many Argentines joined these appeals, including the progressive politician Alfredo

Palacios, who said, "Jewish brothers—do not blame the Argentine people for the contemptible nature of a group of ignorant and vicious persons, whose acts will not be repeated. In our country you are under the shelter of justice and can rely on the deep and sincere affection of all upright people."[35]

The journal *La Razón* (Reason) justified its name by printing a plea by a Jewish official to end the anti-Semitic savagery, saying, "Once again the Jews are paying for the crime of being Jews. In many places of the world it is because we hate them; here it is because we confuse them with Marxists."[36]

President Yrigoyen's reaction was more guarded. The erratic leader was partly responsible for the antilabor policies contributing to the events of the Tragic Week. He received the Jewish delegation and assured them of his sympathy but voiced displeasure that their protests were made in the name of the Jewish community and not as Argentine citizens,[37] a subtle point to tax his indignation in view of the killings during the previous week.

The Tragic Week was a calamity for non-Jews as well as Jews. In all, some 700 people were slain and 4,000 injured.[38] But the Jews, whose ranks bore the brunt of police and civilian assaults, recognized that they above all were isolated in their adopted land. Distrusted by the lower classes as exploitative capitalists, they were loathed and genuinely feared as agents of communism by the business elite and government. The Tragic Week showed the Jews that important segments of society would turn on them as scapegoats in moments of social, economic, and political crisis.

The aftermath of the Tragic Week and the wave of conservatism which swept Argentina in the 1930s and early 1940s cast a pall over Jewish political activity for the next quarter century. There were some conspicuous exceptions even then. Enrique Dickmann, the leading Socialist politician among the Jewish immigrants, continued to serve in Parliament during the most reactionary military regimes. Dickmann had joined the Socialist Party in 1895, three years before entering the School of Medicine at the University of Buenos Aires. In the next decade, he became closely acquainted with the founder of the Socialist Party, Dr. Juan B. Justo, and in 1914 won election to the Chamber of Deputies, a position he held for the next twenty-four years. He also edited the Socialist daily *La Vanguardia* and represented the party in several international

202

congresses. A writer of extraordinary versatility, he produced his best-known works in defense of human rights, such as *Contra el odio de las razas* (Against Racial Hate). In 1943, at the height of a new wave of anti-Semitic activity, both in and outside the government, Dickmann dared to read in the Chamber of Deputies a bill that proposed to ban all racial and religious discrimination. Dickmann observed in his speech that Argentina was a country of immigrants from its beginnings and suggested that there is in its blood "a bit of Semitic leavening, which is historically and socially the catalyst of holy and fertile rebellion."[39]

Dickmann's career during the 1930s and 1940s symbolized a new emphasis by Jewish political activists on political freedom and tolerance, in contrast to the stress during earlier decades on economic justice. This shift in priorities continued to pit them against the dominant political trends, which in the 1930s led not only to a closed oligarchical system but to military control of most political activity.

Among those Jews who dared to defy the authoritarian system, Gregorio Topolevsky was a marked man. Russian-born and raised in Argentina, he gained fame as a medical specialist well before he became known as a dissenter. During the 1930s, he was arrested several times for openly protesting the government's repressive character. In 1937, Topolevsky saw a concrete opportunity to fight fascism in the Spanish Civil War and joined the idealists from several continents who volunteered for the Loyalist forces. Topolevsky returned to Argentina in time to witness the rise of a new authoritarian figure, Juan Perón. Undaunted by bitter past experience, Topolevsky criticized the government's disregard for individual liberties and again, in 1951, he suffered imprisonment for his opposition.

One must note, of course, that most Jews, like other Argentines during this time, eschewed overt dissent against the dictatorships of the thirties and forties, particularly the Perónist government. Perón personally was never an ideological anti-Semite and always welcomed obeisance from any quarter. For the small number of Jews who supported him, Perón was fair, even generous by past standards. Yet most Jews merely acquiesced to his rule without ever joining the special Jewish organization he created to draw the *kehillah* into support for his regime.

Perón's fall in 1955 marks the beginning of a series of attempts to restore democratic civilian government to Argentina. Yet only the brief administrations of Arturo Frondizi (1958–62) and Arturo Illia (1963–66) have given the nation's liberal and democratic elements wide freedom and a measure of success. These administrations naturally witnessed the greatest political activity by Argentine Jews in the past two decades.

One of the more fortunate political developments for the Jewish community during this time was the factionalization of the Radical Party in 1958. The Radicals, who despite the name are the major group for moderate reform in Argentina, divided over questions of personal leadership rather than ideology, and formed two separate Radical parties. This afforded the Jews greater flexibility in choosing candidates, despite their general commitment to moderate progressive parties. This, in turn, increased the Radicals' incentive to heed the Jewish vote.

Frondizi's Unión Cívica Radical Intransigente party assiduously courted Jewish voters and nominated Jews as gubernatorial candidates in two provinces in the elections of 1958. Frondizi himself numbered several Jewish aides for many years, and he retained them in government during his presidency. David Blejer had been legal adviser to the Argentine Agrarian Institute during the 1950s and developed a close rapport with Frondizi through his work for the Radical Party. When Frondizi reached the presidency, he appointed Blejer undersecretary to the minister of the interior. Shortly thereafter, in February 1959, Frondizi chose Blejer as his minister of labor, marking the first time in Argentine history that a Jew held a full ministerial position in the cabinet. Subsequently, Blejer received the prestigious post of ambassador to Mexico, in which capacity he served until 1961.

Mariano Weinfeld also linked his political fortunes to Frondizi's success and became an intimate adviser to the president. Born in Buenos Aires in 1905, he studied medicine before becoming involved in reform politics during the 1930s. Weinfeld was twice a candidate for national deputy of Jujuy Province and served as a delegate to the liberal Comité Nacional Partidario for twenty consecutive years beginning in 1938. In 1952, he was chosen treasurer of this organization's executive board, then headed by Frondizi. Four years later, he advanced to the key position of secretary of the executive board, in which capacity he worked closely with Frondizi on numerous political matters. Upon Frondizi's victorious campaign in 1958, Weinfeld became an honorary adviser to the president, accompanying him on travels to Europe, Asia, and North America.

Arturo Illia's administration also included several Jews, most notably the irrepressible Topolevsky. After Perón's fall, his fortunes had revived briefly, and he served as President Pedro Aramburu's ambassador to Israel. Then in 1958, after the Radical Party divided into two competing factions, Topolevsky supported Ricardo Balbín of the Unión Cívica Radical del Pueblo against Frondizi. Both candidates were veteran reformers and democrats, but Frondizi proved more skillful in a crucial respect—politics. He made a secret deal with the Perónistas to secure the necessary plurality for election, and Topolevsky was not among the politicians who could count on his favor afterward. Topolevsky reentered the government in 1963, when Illia appointed him general director of social welfare in the Ministry of Communications.

David Schapira was prominent during both the Frondizi and Illia administrations. A native of the Jewish colony Carlos Casares, he was elected senator for the Province of Buenos Aires in 1958 and chaired the Senate Public Health Committee. He later reached his greatest fame in the National Chamber of Deputies. Yet his and other Jewish political careers came to a sudden end in 1966, when the military *junta* that deposed Illia purged liberal elements in the government and suspended all democratic politics.

With the return of Perón in 1973, the Jewish role in politics took a more complex turn. Many in the Jewish community reacted coolly to Perón's ambitions, but Perón managed to forge a strange alliance with the Polish-born businessman, José Ber Gelbard, who afforded critical support to Perón's presidential candidacy.

Gelbard entered Argentina as a child in the early twenties and worked his way from peddling to a prosperous commercial career. He first met Perón in 1947 when the Argentine president visited Catamarca Province to meet local representative groups. Shortly thereafter, Gelbard played an active role in bringing business elements closer to Perón through creation of the Entrepreneurs' Central Federation. The organization dissolved in 1955 when Perón was deposed, but Gelbard remained a sought-after intermediary between Perón in Spain and diverse military and political factions in Argentina.[40]

Gelbard was already a millionaire by the time Perón returned to Argentina and used his political influence and financial reputation to line up previously hostile commercial sectors behind the Perónista campaign. With Perón's decisive victory in 1973, Gelbard, considered a "moderate" in Perón's entourage, became a vital linchpin in the new Justicialista coalition. He kept the business community's support, or at least acquiescence, while Perón drew his major strength from the more conservative labor unions. The aging Perón no longer wished to shake the country with social and economic reforms comparable to those in his first administration nearly thirty years earlier. At that time, Perón took for granted his left-wing followers but preferred to side with the more stolid bloc of workers who had continued to support him fanatically during the decades of his exile.

As Perón drifted toward the Right, he realized the need for a man of great technical expertise to stabilize the economy and set a new course of development. He chose Gelbard as minister of finance, possibly the most important position ever held by a Jew in the Argentine government. Gelbard faced an almost impossible task and tackled it with characteristic intelligence and energy. He drafted a wage-price freeze system which Perón quickly instituted, and began to restore Argentina's international credit rating. Gelbard's greatest coup came shortly after the European Common Market refused to give Argentina special tariff consideration in its imports of beef. Gelbard responded by successfully negotiating favorable trade agreements with both the Soviet Union and Communist China, thereby spurring Argentine agricultural productivity and generally raising the hopes of Argentine businessmen for a significant recovery in the near future.

Gelbard's technical wizardry drew international admiration. The respected journal *Latin America* marveled at the rocketing volume of exports that insured Argentina a huge trade surplus for 1973 and added that "there can be no doubting the positive effect of having an economy minister . . . who has a clear understanding of what he is trying to do, and a clear mandate to get on with it."[41]

Gelbard had reached close to the pinnacle of power, but as often happens in politics, obstacles proliferated as the summit came in view. Though Gelbard was working economic magic given the problems he inherited, he could in no way limit the political dimensions of Argentina's distress. The terrorist violence continued unabated, and organized labor rebelled against his wage-price guidelines.

Gelbard's most difficult problem was in having the outside track in the vicious jockeying for Perón's attention and favor. Perón was especially close to two people: his minister of social security, José López Rega, and his wife and vice president, María Estela (Isabel) Martínez de Perón. López Rega, a conservative and unscrupulously ambitious politician, saw in Gelbard a rival whom he had to eliminate from the government. Beyond several predictable denunciations of Gelbard's economic policies, coupled with appeals to Perón to be more generous to the workers, López Rega also resorted to anti-Semitic tactics to undermine Gelbard. He alleged, in February 1974, that the presence of Jews in government made it difficult to negotiate with the Arab nations.[42] The remark clearly applied to the only Jewish government official of consequence, the vulnerable Gelbard. López Rega had another advantage over Gelbard in that he exercised inordinate control over Isabel Perón. With the death of Juan Perón in July 1974 and the succession of his wife to the presidency, Gelbard's position became ever more fragile.

During the summer of 1974, López Rega maneuvered to fill new posts in the cabinet with political allies, further isolating his primary rival in the government. The finance minister continued his political balancing act with consummate skill in the months that followed, but his base of support steadily wore thinner. Popular speculation on Gelbard's longevity was captured deftly by the magazine *Cuestionario,* whose August issue featured on its cover a caricature of Gelbard tremblingly walking on a tightrope. Just over two months afterward, Gelbard slipped fatally from his tenuous perch in government.

The collapse of the wage-price guidelines during mid-October signaled the end of Gelbard's viability as finance minister. On October 21, shortly after Isabel Perón announced a 13 percent wage increase, dooming his anti-inflationary policies, Gelbard resigned. He recognized that López Rega's appeal to the conservative trade unions had succeeded and that his own long-range designs for economic recovery had been jettisoned. Gelbard prudently remained a loyal minister even in resignation. He voiced no criticism of the government or any of its members and said only that his decision was motivated by a desire to serve "the national process."[43]

Gelbard's ouster indicated the darkening political climate as much as it did the rejection of his economic policies. During his tenure as finance minister, he had tried to moderate López Rega's attempts to repress political dissent. With Gelbard gone, López Rega used a combination of martial law, police measures, and mass mobilization techniques to increase his personal power. His repressive policies, as much as his anti-Semitic statements, revealed the continued insecurity of the country's Jewish population.

The tide of repression continued to build even after López Rega's growing list of personal and ideological enemies added his name to the flurry of resignations from Isabel Perón's disoriented government. When she, too, finally yielded power to a military *junta* in 1976, the right-wing reaction to national instability was complete. Among the first actions taken by the *junta* was to purge all national figures whom they regarded as potentially discomfiting to their authoritarian designs. They initially exiled only one—José Ber Gelbard.

Like Gelbard, who stood valiantly if futilely between López Rega and his repressive schemes, the Jews as a group remain a committed element in support of political democracy and antimilitarism. Yet alone they are unable to control or even limit the antidemocratic surges that reflect the prevalent political climate as well as an integral part of the national heritage. In this sense, Gelbard is as much a symbol of Jewish vulnerability as he is of the historic Argentine Jewish attachment to a free and open society.

The pattern of Jewish acculturation, in sum, reveals an array of achievements in economic, cultural, and political spheres. This picture is marred, however, by the failure of Jews as a group to obtain full popular acceptance as Argentine citizens. The root causes of this continued state of insecurity deserve fuller exploration. It is clear, though, that in adjusting to a society inspiring both hope and fear, the Jews have offered a vital and original influence to the course of Argentine development.

8 THE ROOTS OF ANTI-SEMITISM

Argentina has proved to be less a shelter for Jews than for anti-Semites. It is, in this respect, something of a Noah's Ark of bigotry, preserving every major type and group of anti-Semite in the world over the past century. The Nazis, the Arab League, extreme elements of the Left and Right, and periodic repression by the government itself have all contributed to the perpetual insecurity of the Argentine Jew.

Yet many Argentines, both Jews and non-Jews, deny that anti-Semitism extends beyond fringe organizations of hate. The journalist Arturo Jauretsche summed up a widely held opinion of his society with the comment, "In reality, there is no climate of anti-Semitism, but only certain individual anti-Semites."[1]

There is considerable evidence for Jauretsche's claim. Even under the current *junta,* the position of Argentine Jews compares favorably in many ways with that of millions of Jews elsewhere in the world. Argentine Jews have not known, for example, the kind of sustained and systematic government efforts to undermine Jewish culture and identity that has long menaced Soviet Jewry. Jews in Argentina have been able to affirm and perpetuate their heritage largely free of government interference. They are equally free to emigrate to Israel or other countries.

Most Argentine administrations in the past thirty years have been moderately Judeophilic in their rhetoric and at least neutral in their policies toward Israel and toward the Argentine Jewish community. Past presidents have made a practice of sending periodic greetings to the *kehillah* through the DAIA's chosen officials.

209

Civilian politicians have competed vigorously and openly for the "Jewish vote," treating Jews as an integral part of Argentine democratic traditions.

The press in Argentina has been, on the whole, even more aggressively outspoken on behalf of Jewish civil rights than the government. In particular, the great dailies like *La Razón, La Nación,* and others have energetically defended the principles of toleration and minority rights. To cite only one typical example, *La Prensa* responded to anti-Semitic remarks by the Syrian ambassador to Argentina in 1969 with an editorial vehemently denouncing "his indiscriminate attacks against the Jewish collectivity as such, not against any determined attitude or person, but against 'the Jews,' which assumed a form of racism and can only bring as a consequence resentment and aggression among ethnic groups."[2]

Relations between the Jewish community and the Argentine media were especially encouraging during a period of extremist violence in 1960. Máximo Yagupsky, a leading editor of *Judaica*, wrote then:

Argentine newspapers gave a great deal of space to the news of the anti-Semitic manifestations. Most of them condemned such outbreaks when they first appeared here, pointing out that such racial hate is alien to Argentine sentiments.[3]

Unfortunately the evidence is far from exhausted by the positive side of relations between Argentine Jews and non-Jews. Scholarly studies and personal observation both support the belief that anti-Semitism in Argentina is not merely a dangerous social disease, but it is also highly contagious.

A scholar named Enrique Pichón-Rivière conducted a survey in 1964, in which a sample of 500 Argentines indicated their attitudes toward Jews in different social roles, and revealed widespread anti-Semitic feeling. (See Table 13.)

The military, with its legacy of German training and narrowly conceived nationalism, emerges as more intransigently anti-Semitic than the civilian sector, but both display significant anti-Jewish tendencies. Half the civilian respondents would object to having a Jewish educator for their children; and three persons in ten would not want a Jew for either a working companion or personal friend, simply because of his ethnic background.

210

Table 13: Argentine Acceptance of Jews in Different Social Roles, 1964

Category of Social Acceptance (I would accept a Jew as a:)	All Civilians (in percent)	Low Income Only (in percent)	Military (in percent)
Neighbor	80	85	43
Fellow worker	73	78	36
Teacher for my children	49	58	29
Lawyer	58	70	29
Doctor	72	74	22
Personal friend	68	78	29
Spouse of a close relative	52	54	14

NOTE—Sample: 500 subjects, including 440 civilians, 60 military personnel. Often, the civilian category would be broken down to include a low-income group (of less than 5,000 pesos monthly) or 264 subjects.

SOURCE: Enrique J. Pichón-Rivière, "Los prejuicios raciales en la Argentina," *Nueva Sión,* January 31, 1964.

What qualities do Argentines attribute to Jews? The same sociologist, Pichón-Rivière, reported the following traits most frequently given by his respondents. (See Table 14.)

The military again forms the more anti-Semitic group. The purely negative images they conjure of Jews (avaricious and unscrupulous) mesh with their hostile answers in the previous part of this survey, in which nearly 80 percent rejected the possibility of having a Jewish friend.

The qualities mentioned by civilians (industrious and intelligent) appear surprisingly complimentary in light of the substantial numbers who objected to Jews as teachers (51 percent), friends (32 percent), lawyers (42 percent), and so forth. A possible explanation

Table 14: Qualities Argentines Attributed to Jews, 1964

Percent Mentioned by Civilians		Percent Mentioned by Military	
Industrious	45	Trading and dealing	83
Skillful	42	Avaricious	78
Trading and dealing	42	Hypocritical	44
Intelligent	39	Unscrupulous	44
Progressive	32		

SOURCE: Adapted from Enrique J. Pichón-Rivière, "Los prejuicios raciales en la Argentina," *Nueva Sión,* January 31, 1964.

for this apparent contradiction is that the characteristics cited do not pertain to character, morals, or patriotism, but rather are qualities needed to rise above others in society.

Scholars have disputed the relationship between social and economic levels and the extent of anti-Semitic feeling in Argentina. Two studies during the 1960s by a Harvard sociologist named Gino Germani and a scholar for the DAIA, Joaquin Fischerman, explored the problem but reached conflicting results.

Germani's study indicates that the lower classes in Argentine society—the working masses who so fervently supported Juan Perón—contain a much larger proportion of anti-Semitic persons than do wealthy and prestigious families in the uppermost levels of Argentine society. (See Table 15.)

Germani's data contradict earlier theories that Argentine anti-Semitism is largely an upper-class phenomenon. The results also apparently conflict with historical evidence linking anti-Semitic acts with incitement by upper-class elements. Germani explains his results in terms of two distinct kinds of anti-Semitism. "Traditional" anti-Semitism is found in the laboring classes and includes popular stereotypes of Jews, often ill defined and largely unconscious. The upper classes, by contrast, contain fewer anti-Semites but these tend to be "ideological," forming more complex and precise stereotypes of Jews as conspirators and exploiters. Such anti-Semites frequently reflect authoritarian desires.[4]

Table 15: Anti-Semitism Among Different Social Sectors 1962

Social/Economic Position	Proportion of Anti-Semites, 1962 (in percent)
Upper class	6.9
Upper middle class	18.3
Middle middle class	18.7
Lower middle class	19.2
Upper lower class	27.7
Lower lower class	27.6

NOTE—Sample: 2,078 subjects chosen from the metropolitan area of Buenos Aires.

SOURCE: Adapted from Gino Germani, "Antisemitismo ideológico y anti-semitismo tradicional," Comentario, 9, 34 (December 1962), p. 60.

Fischerman discovered a very different correlation between class and anti-Semitism: the higher an Argentine's social and economic position, the more likely he or she is to hold unfavorable attitudes toward Jews. His findings are subdivided to account for "ethnocentric" respondents who display strong prejudices against ethnic groups generally; in both subgroups, however, the same correlations exist between class and frequency of anti-Semitic sentiment. (See Table 16.) Fischerman's research results are defended and Germani's implicitly rejected by another Argentine scholar, Juan José Sebreli, who suggests that it would be illogical for the largely first- and second-generation workers to be narrowly nationalistic.[5]

Germani's two-tiered approach to explaining anti-Semitism in Argentina appears the most sound and accords with this writer's personal observations. Of course, Sebreli's explanation of why the working classes should not be anti-Semitic is wholly rational—but this is a quality that, in their dealings with Jews, anti-Semites themselves never achieve.

Theories about the bases of anti-Semitism in Argentina have been as varied as on the issue of which groups are most prejudiced against Jews. Sebreli's polemic-tinged writings on the "Jewish question" form the most brilliant and ambitious analysis of the subject.[6] Although he sees varied causes of anti-Semitism, he stresses the racism and xenophobia that have their roots deep in Argentine culture. Sebreli observes that these sentiments gripped even the nation's "liberal" leadership during the nineteenth century:

Table 16: Anti-Semitism Among Different Social Sectors, 1967

	Percent of Anti-Semites	
Social/Economic Position	*Non-ethnocentric*	*Ethnocentric*
Upper class	33	66
Middle class	30	62
Lower class	19	50

NOTE—Sample: 1,000 subjects chosen from the metropolitan area of Buenos Aires. (There were 791 respondents to this question.)

SOURCE: Adapted from Joaquin Fischerman, "Ethnocentrismo y antisemitismo," *Índice,* no. 1 (December 1967) p. 20.

The belief in the superiority of the white race is so dominant in our thoughts that already in 1878 when the Chinese were nearly unknown in our land, [Domingo] Sarmiento warned of the "yellow peril," [asking] "how to contain that human surge and to avoid having an inferior race dispossess and take the work away from the superior one, and Asia would again recover America whose inhabitants, the Indians, are decidedly Mongols."[7]

Sebreli notes that even the founder of the Socialist Party in Argentina, Juan Justo, wrote his magnum opus, *The Realization of Socialism* (1922), for an audience of "white men" only, in which he extolled "the historical importance of military efforts against the Indians." It was thus a small step for Justo to write another essay entitled, "Why I Do Not Wish to Write for a Jewish Publication," in which he charged the Jews with opposing the formation of a national consciousness by their stubborn refusal to abandon their Jewish heritage. Sebreli concludes that no matter how "progressive" the political faction in Argentina, racism and ethnic prejudice are at the core.[8]

Jews never received the needed opportunities to assimilate, Sebreli writes. Those who, like Justo, assailed Jews for impeding the growth of Argentine nationalism ignored the discrimination by native Argentines that compelled Jews to retreat into their cultural tradition. A similar phenomenon occurred with the Italians in the early years of Argentine immigration. These cultural peculiarities disappeared, however, when the children of the settlers found opportunities to assimilate during the first decades of the present century. With the Jew, this did not happen except for the period of mostly civilian rule from 1945 to 1966, and even in these years there were times of acute anti-Semitism. "Therefore," Sebreli comments, "it is not to be wondered that there persists among the Jews this enclosure within their own tradition."[9]

Sebreli's provocative critique offers a valuable point of departure for exploring the roots of Argentine anti-Semitism. Two facets of his argument, however, invite question. First, there is the salient irony that Sebreli, who so sharply dissects the deeper prejudice in the "liberal" mentality, himself defends Judaism only as the unfortunate consequence of persecution. In this he differs from the liberals he describes, mainly in his more sophisticated approach to inducing the Jew to abandon his cultural particularism. Sebreli's implicit solution to the "Jewish question" in Argentina would be to let the Jews gradually assimilate, casting off their "cultural peculiarities" for the belated benefits of social equality and tolerance. This way has indeed tempted many Jews in Argentina and throughout Jewish history, but always there have been Jews who sought to preserve their distinctive heritage even at the risk of "provoking" resentment among the non-Jewish population. It is the treatment society accords these Jews that is the acid test of its tolerance.

Sebreli's primary emphasis on xenophobia and racism to explain anti-Semitism in Argentina is also open to doubt. Clearly these are important causes, as he cogently demonstrates, but Jews appear vulnerable to far deeper hostility than a generalized dislike of alien social elements. For in a nation filled with ethnic and immigrant groups, the Jews are indisputably the group most subject to popular antipathy.

Germani's conservative findings, for example, show that Jews are ill regarded by a far greater proportion of Argentines (22.1 percent) than are Poles (9.5 percent), Romanians (8.0 percent), Germans (7.0 percent), French (6.3 percent), Italians (4.4 percent), Spaniards (3.5 percent), and even compared with the "exploitative" North Americans (14.0 percent) and English (10.6 percent). A mere 2.9 percent of the respondents indicated a dislike for "foreigners" as a group.[10] A similar poll by Pichón-Rivière asked the respondent if he would desire to block various ethnic groups from entering Argentina. (See Table 17.)

It is significant that even the Germans, who in Argentina have

Table 17: Proportion of Argentines Who Would Bar Immigrant Groups: Opinion Among Three Subgroups, 1964

Foreign Group	Civilians (in percent)	Low-Income Civilians (in percent)	Military (in percent)
Italians	7	11	11
Spaniards	4	7	11
Jews	26	23	72
Germans	8	8	6

NOTE—The results pertain to Question 1, Part 3, of Pichón-Rivière's survey.
SOURCE: Adapted from Enrique J. Pichón-Rivière, "Los prejuicios raciales en la Argentina," *Nueva Sión,* January 31, 1964.

215

preserved their cultural and kinship ties at least as zealously as the Jews, incurred far fewer negative responses than did Jews in this survey.

Why then has Argentine racism focused so intently upon the Jews? Many Argentine Jews who talk about this issue do not single out racism, nationalism, the military, or even the Nazis as the deepest problem. Rather, they point most frequently to a highly respectable and therefore dangerous source of anti-Semitism—the Roman Catholic church.

Clerical anti-Semitism is a far different and less potent phenomenon than its counterpart in the days of Spanish rule. Increasing numbers of priests have evinced interest in interfaith dialogue and cooperation. The eminent Catholic journal *Criterio* and numerous prelates have been in the vanguard of campaigns to preserve human rights and oppose violence against Jews and other Argentines. Yet these important signs of progress cannot wholly shield the fact that ingrained religious prejudice against Jews remains a powerful social malady.

Even in this largely secularized society, over 90 percent of the population is Catholic, and most Argentines are receptive to some degree to the influence of religious leaders. Dr. Lázaro Rubinson, then president of the Argentine Zionist Organization, put the matter succinctly when I asked if Catholicism affected the Jewish position in Argentine society: "Catholicism is often nominal here. As a whole Argentines are not very religious, but this is sometimes sufficient to raise anti-Semitism. In *this,* too many are more than sufficiently religious."[11]

Sermons are a prolific and effective source of anti-Semitic stereotypes, often transmitted in unconscious fashion. The image of the Jewish "Christ-killer," for example, is a theme especially conducive to prejudice. Some four in ten Argentines believe that the true Christian can never forgive the Jews for having crucified Jesus, according to a study in 1964 by Pichón-Rivière. Among lower-income groups, nearly half (46 percent) hold this conviction.[12]

Equally troublesome is the fact that some of the most extreme anti-Semites in Argentina have been clerics in good standing. Julio Meinvielle, for example, whose writings vie with the most twisted statements by Joseph Goebbels, never experienced more than occasional conflicts with church leaders regarding his anti-Semitic con-

216

duct. In 1962, at the height of his attacks against the Jews, Mein-vielle was permitted to use a Catholic university as a forum for a speech, and he remained a fully ordained priest in the nation's capital. A more dangerous anti-Semite, Alberto Ezcurra Uriburu, combined fervent Catholicism and anti-Semitism with the tacit approval of the church, which ordained him as a priest in December 1971.

For most clerics, the strident hatred of Jews that marked an earlier era of Latin American history is past, but subtler prejudices have survived. A recent archbishop of Buenos Aires, Antonio Cardinal Caggiano, exemplified the new clerical anti-Semitism, coated in public with a veneer of religious brotherhood. Caggiano piously deplored anti-Semitism as un-Christian when hooligans were engaging in vicious actions against Jews early in the 1960s.[13] Welcome as such a declaration was, it turned out that the archbishop had been casting stones a bit hastily. Shortly after, a Jewish scholar, looking through a Christian journal, came across Caggiano's private remarks on Jews, which were in a rather different vein from his official statements. It appeared that in the interest of peace and toleration, Jewish and Christian citizens were joining an association promoting brotherhood and mutual respect, the Confraternidad Judío Cristiano. Caggiano all too readily perceived a peril to good Catholics; to the relief of reactionary elements throughout the church, he addressed his lower echelon clerics: "This type of activity produces a profound danger for those who participate in it. It appears well to remind our priests and faithful, in the manner that each cleric deems most fitting, of the decree of the first Argentine Council [which banned several "dangerous" and heretical societies]. . . . To these organizations can be added: the association commonly known as the Friends of Israel, which has been prohibited wherever it exists among us."[14]

The DAIA and other organizations were appalled by this frightening, even ludicrous denunciation of brotherhood by such an influential figure; they denounced Caggiano's statements and their implications for Jewish security. Instead of denying or retracting the statement, a church spokesman named Augustíne Luchía Puig defended it and claimed that it was seen as anti-Semitic only because it was viewed "with typically Jewish criteria." He went on to explain, in the heart of his apologia, "In effect a Jew can be

217

Marxist, indifferent in matters of religion, can even have none at all, and always will be considered by the Jewish community as a member of that community. The unifying link of the members of the people of Israel has some time ago ceased to be strictly religious. The only link universally accepted by them at present is a racial one."[15]

These "assurances" understandably failed to calm many in the Jewish community. Nissim Elnecavé, writing in *La Luz,* expressed the widespread indignation over Puig's remarks in a stinging editorial:

What anti-Semite has ever confessed that he was one, save Hitler and his henchmen? God save us and keep us from comparing Cardinal Caggiano and his defender, Luchía Puig, with Hitler and his followers. But the fact is that behind such teachings there could come in strange ways a Hitler.[16]

Although some in the *kehillah* were inclined to excuse Caggiano's remarks as simply an isolated intemperate statement, Caggiano himself would prove them sadly mistaken. Indeed he surpassed his past anti-Semitic conduct with a new declaration in late 1972, at a mass in the Buenos Aires Cathedral attended by Syrian, Egyptian, and Lebanese ambassadors to Argentina. The mass took place shortly after the tragedy of the Munich Olympic massacre of eleven Israeli athletes by Palestinian terrorists. Caggiano found no cause to comment on this butchery, but the Israeli retaliation against terrorist camps within Lebanon appeared to abrade his skewed moral sensibilities. At the well-publicized mass, Caggiano sermonized on behalf of "the victims of the attack in Lebanon." He left the cause of this attack unmentioned; instead he stressed that the Israeli policies could not be tolerated, for "the Church rejects these acts . . . violative of human rights and the laws of God."[17]

The anti-Semitism in the church is so deeply embedded as to be almost involuntary. An example is the behavior of Monseñor Gustavo Franseschi at a reception given in his honor by the Israeli ambassador to Argentina, Dr. Arie L. Kubovy, in 1956. Monseñor Franseschi, just returned from a visit in Israel, was introduced in glowing terms by the eloquent Kubovy to some five hundred guests at the Israeli embassy. Kubovy referred to the generous spirit of his invited speaker of honor "whose relationship toward the Jews is not merely one of tolerance, because tolerance presumes a certain

218

masked deprecation," which certainly was unworthy of this most illustrious prelate. As it happened, Franseschi was scarcely disposed to earn the epithet "tolerant." He said, in a spirit of unwonted and unwanted generosity, that according to Deuteronomy "the children should not pay for the sins of the fathers" and so "we will not attempt to make the Jews of today pay for the crucifixion of Christ." Kubovy was chagrined, but Franseschi's paternalism was merely one of many manifestations of ecclesiastic reluctance to accept Jews on a par with other, Catholic Argentines.[18]

A similar and more recent debacle featured Father Azpiazu, a tireless worker for closer Argentine-Jewish relations. At an address to B'nai B'rith in Buenos Aires, Azpiazu talked of Jesus in Israel and began subtly missionizing to his audience, apparently in total disregard for the sensibilities of his Jewish listeners.[19]

Missionizing also assumes more overt poses. The late 1950s witnessed a successful campaign by conservative and nationalist lobbies to reinstitute compulsory Catholic instruction in the public schools. This development required Jewish as well as Christian pupils to attend classes in Catholic religion, catechism, and "Christian morality." The government made a dispensation to children who wished to be excused on religious grounds, but this generosity was only apparent. A woman in her late twenties recalled her school days at that time, "I was embarrassed to leave my classmates. I did it anyway because my parents told me to and I did not want to have Judaism attacked in school. But it made no difference because if you didn't go to classes in Christianity you had to go to classes in general morality instead." I ventured the opinion that this seemed fairly innocuous and she countered, "Yes, that was the idea, but in fact these classes were filled with references to Christian themes of salvation and the like. Only the name of the class was changed." After much effort by the organized Jewish community, in conjunction with other liberal and anticlerical groups, the government eventually rescinded its ruling. Still, the precarious condition of nonsectarian democracy and pluralism was fully illuminated for all who dared see it.

While cultural prejudice forms the core of Argentine anti-Semitism, extremist ideologies crystallize the often nebulous resentments into vivid stereotypes.[20] In the past, anticommunism or xenophobia provided the primary focus for agitation against the

Jews. Currently the sine qua non of anti-Semitic polemic is the denunciation of "Zionist imperialism," a guilt-relieving euphemism that also coincides well with Third World opposition to Israel. The Argentine who harbors prejudice against Jews yet wants to consider himself tolerant and even idealistic can excoriate Zionist machinations while denying anti-Jewish feelings.

An unsurpassed example of the anti-Semite masquerading as anti-Zionist is Brigadier General Gilberto Hidalgo Oliva, best known for his open letter in 1964 to the president of the DAIA, Dr. Isaac Goldenberg. Oliva earned a prominent shrine in the crowded pantheon of Argentine anti-Semites with this remarkable substitute for reasoned communication:

The Argentine people hold you Zionists responsible for the calamitous crisis—economic, political, social, and spiritual—through which we are presently passing. . . . Monopolists first and foremost . . . dastardly acts of embezzlement. . . . Zionism has set to work, wielding the double hammer of Freemasonry and atheistic Communism. . . . A frontal attack against the primary unit—the family. . . . Zionist imperialism. . . . The present intolerable Zionist dictatorship . . . is it just a coincidence that you Zionists hold all the key positions in the present Cabinet? Could any Argentinian, even in jest, call this government—though perhaps nominally run by [President] Illia and [Vice-President] Pereta—*our* government? . . . Let Zionism call off its deceitful game! Let it beware! We Christian citizens know how to strike back, despite the forgiveness in our hearts.[21]

Extremist ideologues like Oliva are especially prone to distort economic conditions in order to exacerbate anti-Semitic feelings already present in society. Argentine Jews have long been vulnerable to the slander, so common throughout Jewish history, that they are exploiters of the people. During the early period of Jewish settlement, for example, when Jews were being hunted down in the streets as "maximalist revolutionaries" trying to overthrow the capitalist order, they were simultaneously villified as parasitic capitalists oppressing the Christian masses. Students in the higher grades of primary school and secondary school studied textbooks like *Argentina, la tierra,* which reported that Jews were expelled from European countries because "they monopolized the sustenance of other peoples" and because "they are filthy." "In Russia there live more than six million Jews who are all fish-peddlers, bar-keepers, and usurers," while "in Galicia the Jews monopolize all commerce and suck the blood of the Polish people." One book charged that "Moses, dressed in swallow-tail coat, pince-nez, and white tie [referring here to Baron Hirsch] brings the expelled Jews to Argentina, to create here a new Palestine," and that once in Argentina "the Jews try to bring their parasitism and their diseased love of money, elements which have brought upon them the hatred of Europe."[22]

More recently, the cry against "exploitative Jews" became particularly fierce during the early sixties, in the aftermath of scandals implicating a minority of Jewish as well as non-Jewish bankers. Jewish community groups promptly repudiated the offending religious brethren whose deeds were deemed a disgrace to upstanding Jewish citizens. Nevertheless, Jews as a group were widely blamed for the nation's economic and social ills. One banker lamented this tendency: "If there are a hundred thieves in Argentina and they find one who is a Jew, everyone says, 'It is the Jews who are taking the money from Argentina.' "[23]

The very success with which Jews have integrated into Argentine economic life provokes resentment. Sebreli illuminates this point: "I have heard very frequently the modest employee, who has at great effort bought his Fiat 600, designate the Valiant that he cannot buy as the 'car of the Jews.' Jews are accused of being unscrupulous climbers who do not have the right to be a 'true gentleman.' "[24]

The irrational, often contradictory charges regarding the Jewish economic role in Argentina seem to be more an outlet for anti-Semitic feeling than a cause. When Jews first came to Argentina they were scorned as peddlers. Jews now well established in business and the professions are scorned as nouveau riche. In the last analysis, it appears that they are scorned not as peddlers, shopkeepers, bankers, or doctors, but as Jews.

The leading anti-Semitic propaganda machine among Argentine extremist groups is the Arab League. This organization far outstrips the many Nazi groups in the volume and sophistication of its writings. Most Argentines, even those with some prejudice against Jews, tend to disdain Nazi elements as crude and barbaric. Yet the Arab League's more refined and carefully calibrated propaganda assaults against the Jews have had some impact in a society all too receptive to anti-Semitic arguments.

The significance of the Arab League in Argentina might not immediately impress the American observer, because in this country Arabs wield far less political power than Jews. Never has a candidate for major office tailored his views to court the "Arab American" vote, a short and sure route to political defeat and popular opprobrium. In Argentina, though, the Syrian and Lebanese Arabs actually outnumber the Jewish population by a substantial margin. Estimates range between three-quarters of a million to 1 million Arabs, or about one in every 25 Argentine residents. The Arab League is the most militant element in the community, is largely foreign directed, and superbly well financed. Its intensive anti-Zionist activities have made it the single most feared organization among the DAIA leaders, who believe it to be responsible for heightening anti-Semitism in the country. As the director of the DAIA, Marcos Barborosch, said, "When you have all these lies hitting, hitting, hitting at the people, something is liable to penetrate."[25]

The rare exceptions in the media's generally cordial relationship with the Jewish community have caused more concern than the typically offensive propaganda campaigns of either the Nazi groups or the Arab League. A recent and sensational example is the controversial airing of "Rapprochement of the Arab States Toward Latin America," telecast in 1974 on the nation's official network, Channel 7. The DAIA charged that the program's three guests were all obsessively anti-Semitic and were prodded by the moderator, Perla de la Vega, into making the most extreme statements against Jews. After Channel 7's managers declined to provide a tape of the program for "technical reasons," the Jewish Telegraphic Agency managed to obtain a private recording that verified the substance of the DAIA's charges in shocking detail. It is questionable whether the quick-witted Miss Vega was more than a provocative interrogator, but it is indisputable that her guests sought to villify Zionism and even Judaism per se in the most unrestrained terms. One guest called Judaism that "talmudic capitalistic-rabbinic religion . . . antisocial and anti-Christian." Another claimed that Zionists had "organized commandos in Argentina for the moment when Israel will suffer a military blow, to strike by surprise in Argentina and establish a secessioned [sic] Jewish State here."[26]

Most fortunately for the Jewish community, such programs remain unrepresentative of most network fare. The tendency of television and other media has been to provide a responsible picture of the nation's Jewish citizens. The exceptions to this pattern, while dangerous, serve more as a call to vigilance than to despair.

How do Jews perceive their image in Argentine eyes? The most striking reply to this question came from a visiting Uruguayan Jew, who spends much of his time in Argentina. "Here, people shout 'Jew' and profanity in the same breath. The children, too, even before they know what the words mean. Oh, it comes naturally, you hear it all the time." Just then, a Mr. Weinstein was paged by the hotel secretary. "You hear that name," the Uruguayan continued, "then you think 'dirty Jew.' That's how you're conditioned here."[27]

A more common response is that anti-Semitic elements are a serious threat, but that most Argentines do not share such prejudices. I spoke to a librarian in Córdoba's Jewish archives who told me:

The Talmud says that if you are cooking some food and something un-kosher accidentally falls into the pot, if it is only a sixtieth of what is in the pot, you may call it kosher. It is the same in this country. We have some crazy people here, Nazis, others, but the Argentines as a people are still "kosher."

A German Jew, who spoke with fear and contempt of the church and of the Fascist organizations for their anti-Semitic activity, nevertheless had no ill feeling toward Argentines: "They see us not so much as better or worse but as different. I know of one Argentine who didn't even know that Jews believe in God. We are somewhat exotic to them, but I think so are the Italians here, and so forth."

The synagogue official and community historian, Daniel Rubinstein, related, "When I was in the army, I met no discrimination from my fellow soldiers. Also, as an engineering student, I met no discrimination." He added that once an Argentine who felt he had been cheated by a Jew told him, "All Jews are exploiters." However, in general the people were not anti-Semitic.

A surprising number altogether denied the existence of anti-Semitism in the nation, even when confronted with contradictory information. One youth recalled only with reluctance that yes, his teacher gave him more demerits in school because he was a Jew, "but not all the children called me names." A middle-aged man, typical of many Jewish respondents, claimed that the society was not anti-Semitic because "Jews are just citizens like the rest."

It is easy at first to believe these people who insist that anti-Semitism is largely a myth in Argentina. Yet as I traveled through the country, I saw a large swastika painted near a synagogue in Rosario; a charming salesgirl in Córdoba innocently offered me a book translating as the infamous anti-Semitic pamphlet "Protocols of the Elders of Zion"; coming back to Buenos Aires, I found that one of the major synagogues had been bombed. Equally disturbing were the continued rumors of a "Patagonia plot," an absurd anti-Semitic story of a supposed Jewish conspiracy to take southern Argentina by storm. The tale should have succumbed to bored disbelief within the first week of its concoction, but instead it whirled its way across the nation for months afterward.

One thinks also of the six hundred eminent intellectuals, Perónista leaders, and union officials, from the leader of the leftist Third World Priests, Reverend Carlos Mujica, to the conservative figure Sánchez Sorondo, all of whom signed an advertisement in the journal *Clarin* denouncing the Jewish State as inherently usurping, racist, aggressive, and expansionist.[28] One remembers, too, that despite the heralded liberalism of the political parties, a Perónist deputy, Juan Carlos Cornejo Linares, created a stir in 1964 with a call for investigation of Zionist activity in Argentina. Linares thought it an open issue whether Zionism is "striking at the very roots of our nationality" and undermining the existence of the country.[29] Amid the lively debate over the value of Linares's proposal, a Jewish congressman introduced a motion to investigate the increase in anti-Semitic activities then deluging Argentina. His motion failed to muster a quorum for discussion.[30]

The Jews who focus on the many progressive aspects of Argentine society without, however, facing the other, harsher reality of widespread and persistent anti-Semitism, suffer a pernicious form of blindness recurrent in Jewish communities in the Diaspora. They parallel in some degree the optimistic German Jews of the 1930s who, with even less reason, believed that as good citizens they would be allowed to achieve full acceptance by their fellow nationals. History has shown, however, that to shy from vigilant awareness of prejudice is a false luxury that Jews can never safely grasp. For Argentina's Jews, this realization offers the most genuine basis of hope for the future in a nation of both opportunity and peril.

9 PERÓN AND THE JEWS

Juan Perón was the most powerful leader in Latin American history during his rule of Argentina from 1946 to 1955. As with so much Perón did, his actions toward Argentina's Jewish community set a host of precedents. The complex interplay of his overtures to and manipulation of the *kehillah* led most importantly to greater Jewish participation in the larger society.

Perón's early career gave little sign of future accommodation with the Jews. Although Perón was not an ideological anti-Semite, his rise to power, as part of a military *junta* from 1943 to 1945, was tightly linked to Fascist principles and support. Perón himself idolized the Italian Fascist dictator, Benito Mussolini.[1] As the minister of labor, Perón carefully avoided offending Jews in his public speeches, but he at least tacitly encouraged his lieutenants in their rabble-rousing efforts against the Jews. Jew-baiting provided a frequent and successful tactic for attracting the masses to Perónista rallies and heightening the emotional intensity of these crowds.

If Perón personally had no anti-Semitic or right-wing convictions, the *junta* he served and on which he based his ambitions teemed with such ideologues. Prominent among Perón's Fascist colleagues in government during this period was Gustavo Martínez Zuviría, who became the minister of justice and education in 1943. Martínez Zuviría's only proven quality prior to this appointment was a talent for writing rabidly anti-Semitic novels. Under the pseudonym Hugo Wast, he produced some of the most infamous anti-Semitic literature on the continent, including *El Kahal, Oro* (Gold), and *Myriam la Conspiradora* (Myriam the Conspirator).

227

Martínez Zuviría also demonstrated his general authoritarian biases as director of the National Library, during which time he suppressed classics he considered too liberal for public view.

To the dismay of the Jewish community, Martínez Zuviría and fellow Fascists in the government fulfilled the worst expectations of repression and prejudice. Anti-Jewish legislation passed easily on August 19, 1943, including a ban on kosher meat-processing in municipal stockyards of the capital; Jewish newspapers and other publications were shut down, on the pretext that the national censor would read only Spanish and that the Jews obdurately wrote much of their literature in Yiddish. By October, no Jewish printing house remained in operation in all Argentina.

The severity of anti-Semitism repelled the American government, then in the midst of a worldwide struggle against Fascist tyranny. President Franklin Roosevelt voiced "misgivings at the adoption in this hemisphere of action obviously anti-Semitic in nature, and of a character so closely identified with the most repugnant features of the Nazi doctrine."[2]

The Argentine government humored Roosevelt by rescinding its prohibition of Jewish publications but otherwise continued its discriminatory policies. For example, the federal interventor of Entre Ríos, who enforced national laws in the province, announced that no Jewish or Masonic benefit society charters would be renewed.[3]

Violence against Jews accompanied the attacks on Jewish culture. A journalist reported that two of Perón's police "stood approvingly by" while hoodlums painted on the sidewalk, "Kill a Jew and be a patriot!"[4] Another correspondent wrote that "alarm and even terror are beginning to spread in the Jewish quarter because for some time all gatherings of Colonel Perón's followers have been a signal for some action against Jews."[5]

This fear grew on more than rumors and rallies by agitators. Synagogues across the country were subject to periodic bombings, and few Jews were safe from assaults by anti-Semitic gangs. Invariably, the terrorist perpetrators of such crimes would find an easy shelter of government approval and popular indifference.

As Germany's defenses crumbled before the Anglo-American armies, Perón, adept at whistling many different tunes, toned down

"Deutschland, Deutschland" and began a tentative rendition of "Yankee Doodle." Accordingly, he took pains to show that he was not an anti-Semite, though he still would take no measures to protect Jews from either Fascist marauders or the widespread discrimination he had helped to inflame. Within seven months of the German surrender, he discovered publicly that those participating in anti-Semitic demonstrations "are outside all democratic standards and cannot be regular members of any Argentine political force."[6]

Fascists dropped from the ranks of government officials, quietly but steadily. Martínez Zuviría himself was ousted as early as February 1944, though he had managed to do much harm during his tenure in the cabinet. As the last of the Axis powers unconditionally surrendered, the pace of Argentine efforts to appear democratic quickened noticeably. Government ministers hastened to express their shock and revulsion at anti-Semitic activities, reflecting Perón's new liberal outlook. General Felipe Urdapileta, the minister of the interior, publicly instructed the federal police chief to suppress anti-Semitic riots in the fall of 1945. The general added, "The recent lamentable expressions of anti-Jewish feeling have done nothing but earn the repudiation of all responsible sectors of public opinion, and the most complete disapproval of the Government, which considers such expressions foreign to Argentina's spirit of tolerance and justice."[7]

For the next several years, Perón danced several political waltzes with the *kehillah,* a most reluctant partner. He praised the new Jewish State, while abstaining in the United Nations vote to establish such a state. He expressed his sympathy for the Jewish refugees from European barbarism yet limited Jewish immigration. He spoke of his warm regard for the Argentine *kehillah* yet attempted to rival the DAIA by imposing a Perónista organization upon the entire Jewish community.

Perón's pro-Jewish rhetoric did make a positive contribution despite the inconsistency of his speech and actions, because rhetoric was such an integral part of his leadership. The Argentine president was a dynamic, charismatic figure who symbolized the pride and vitality of the nation. His open acceptance of the Jews as a valuable element in Argentine society helped cool the anti-Semitic impulses simmering in the country. Few could fail to be moved by impassioned speeches like the one Perón delivered to a Jewish delegation in March 1949:

Let my first words be to give praise to the noble people of Israel and to the nascent nation representing them. . . . We Argentines are a new people, born of agreement of civilized nations scarcely a century ago. Your race represents the age-old Hebrew people, who were separated from their land by an unjust fate, living for two thousand years across all the stretches of the earth, giving to humanity an example of what moral values are worth to a race that has survived both time and adversity. A magnificent example for new peoples. . . . I want to conclude by asking God for the greatness and prosperity of the reborn nation of Israel, that our prayers may reach Him, that its prosperity be eternal, and that Jews in all the world have there a heart beating in a place on this earth where this persecuted race may find the peace to which all men have the right.[8]

Perón's quasi-rabbinic sermons were unfortunately counterbalanced by condescension toward Jews as a group. He acted like a European prince protecting "his" Jews. In a speech on July 5, 1951, he praised the Jew for his humility: "When a Jew comes to ask that his rights be respected, he does this humbly, without arrogance and without pressing that he have justice. This demonstration is for me, appreciating the soul of men, the greatest quality that a man can have who claims his rights."[9]

Perón's stand on the issue of Jewish rights was often glaringly hypocritical, especially in regard to the activities of anti-Semitic groups. A deluge of anti-Jewish periodicals prompted a protest by the *kehillah* in May 1950, petitioning the superintendent of Buenos Aires to prohibit the printing, circulation, and sales of the "Protocols of the Elders of Zion" and Henry Ford's "The International Jew." Each publication is a classic of irrational yet widely accepted argumentation against the "exploitative" Jew. When the spread of these virulent pamphlets continued unchecked, the DAIA directly requested Perón to take action. His unctuous reply gave small comfort to all but the most gullible listeners. "Fortunately," he rejoiced, "the periodicals mentioned in your above-cited letter in no way represent the national sentiment, despite the fact that they enjoy the unconditional benefits that stem from freedom of the press which the laws of our country assure everyone."[10] Perón was in fact a zealot in eliminating freedom of the press in Argentina and installing government-controlled journals in place of critical papers. However, Perón's disingenuous reply to the *kehillah* ended discussion. As a result, anti-Semitic literature enjoyed wide distribution throughout Perón's years as president.

Government duplicity was also apparent in the matter of Jewish immigration. Perón's expansive claims of sympathy and aid provided for Jewish refugees were merely examples of rhetorical inflation run wild. One of the main stumbling blocks to Jewish immigration during the 1930s and 1940s was the technical illegality of settlement in Argentina without prior display of identification certificates. Naturally, many Jews who fled Europe with the urgency of the Hebrews rushing from Egypt lacked the time and the means to prepare such documentation. Despite Perón's assurances of his government's understanding, the DAIA was still protesting to the Argentine government about the harassment of these refugees even after Perón fell from power:

In their flight from that great horror of the terrible conflict, they were not able to provide the documentation that the law requires. But their settlement has been affirmed in the long run, since it is based on peaceful and constructive settlement, and the efforts of their labor, the constitution of a family, and the birth of Argentine children, linked irreversibly to the land that received and protected them in their development, giving them the opportunity of remaking their lives, far from the persecution and horrors that they left. Let us remove these artificial impediments and declare amnesty for all those already forced by circumstances to enter the country without strict adjustment to the legal fine points.[11]

The DAIA tactfully omitted mention of Perón's willingness to overlook moral as well as legal scruples in admitting Germans, many of them war criminals, in the years after World War II. Although these Fascist elements remained largely quiescent under Perónist rule, their presence made the contrast with Jewish immigration policies all the more bitter to the *kehillah*.

Perón's approach to the refugee problem was neither pro-German nor anti-Semitic but simply cynical. The impoverished Jewish refugees could not provide the incentive of large bribes such as those of the often-wealthy Germans used to influence Perón's policies. Moreover, Perón found that immigration restrictions policies. Moreover, Perón found that immigration restrictions afforded a way to manipulate the *kehillah,* and so was reluctant to ease the procedure.

Perón also sought to control the *kehillah* directly, by creating the Organización Israelita Argentina (OIA). Headed by the loyal Perónista, Pablo Manguel, the OIA routinely praised everything Perón did, from its very first message in 1947 till the end of Perón's regime in 1955.[12] Perón in turn tried to raise the prestige of the OIA by sending all his messages of goodwill to the Jewish community through that organization. He took every opportunity to indicate that the OIA was the one Jewish group fighting for democracy and minority rights. Perón commented in 1949 on his revision of the Argentine Constitution:

We have in our reformed Constitution, Article 26, which bars racial divisions in our land. But *Señores,* I want to do justice to the truth. The inclusion of that clause we owe to the initiative of the OIA, which, through its president, our friend [Sujer] Matragt, worked for its acceptance.[13]

Perón's dual manipulation of the *kehillah* through immigration restrictions and the puppet group OIA converged when he invested the OIA with authority to screen out Jews "unfit" for citizenship. Even applicants who were close blood relatives of Argentine citizens had to secure immigration visas through the OIA. This patronage prize to the Perónist Jewish group actually made Jewish immigration more, rather than less, difficult; for alone among Argentine immigrants, Jews needed approval by two authorities, including the regular government agency for admitting new settlers.

Government relations with the Jewish community were further complicated by the unpredictable presence of Perón's wife, "Evita." María Eva Duarte de Perón often appeared to be the "first person" as well as "first lady" in the government, an almost inexplicable anomaly in a male-dominated society. Once scorned as a lower-class actress of dubious talent and less virtue, she had an inner Geiger counter for power, which she pursued with a will unmatched by Perón himself. Hers was the iron character around which Perón wrapped his flexible ambitions, as became evident in the wake of a military coup deposing him in 1945. While Perón went to pieces and begged for his life, Evita treated the *junta's* officers to an obscenity-filled shouting tantrum that so nonplussed them that they released the "mad" woman. The plotters answered for their good deed; for Eva Perón had always been more histrionic than hysteric. Left alone, she deserted her tantrums for the tactics of organizing mass demonstrations, securing the aid of Cipriano Reyes and other Perónist labor leaders. The ensuing rioting outside the capital building compelled the *junta*'s vacillating officers to restore Perón to power in order to avert a possible civil war. Relieved, but not beyond words, that his life was to be spared, Perón eloquently assured the frenzied masses in the street below that he was boldly determined to lead them as before. The equal political partnership of the Peróns was sealed in these events, months before their belated marriage officially legitimized Eva's status.

In Eva, the *kehillah* dealt with a caricature of Juan Perón. She moralized politics by freely excoriating the rich and other perceived enemies of the workers. She also personalized politics by resorting to extra-legal methods to intimidate opponents. Her democratic and demagogic tendencies were both so forceful that it is problematic whether even she could distinguish them. Certainly both traits were strongly evident in her behavior toward the Jewish community.

Ever alert to the political value of public posturing, "Evita" became better known than her husband for fiery speeches on behalf of all suffering Argentines. She called for equal rights eloquently and with apparently genuine passion, often before specially invited Jewish delegations. Yet her policies toward the *kehillah* were so volatile and often irresponsible as to overwhelm her efforts to appear as its benevolent guardian. Eva's vindictive and deadly pursuit of the well-known Jewish family, the Groismans, revealed her darker side at its most frightening.[14]

The Groisman affair stemmed from Eva's attempts to extort business contributions to the Maria Eva Duarte de Perón Social Aid Foundation, which the government both subsidized and managed. The foundation, as Eva was quick to boast, enabled the construction of schools, hospitals, and inexpensive hotels. Knowledgeable observers whispered that the foundation also provided funds to enhance the Perón's private political and economic fortunes.[15]

Many businessmen gave large sums of money to Eva's cause, less influenced by philanthropic than prophylactic considerations.

This subtlety eluded the Groismans, managers of the prominent Mu-Mu candy factory in Buenos Aires. Long-brewing friction between the Groismans and "Evita" came to a head when her foundation ordered some 10,000 dollars' worth of candies to send to poor children at Christmastime—in her name. The Groismans complied with the order, then sent a bill for their wares to the outraged wife of the president. As a friend of the Groismans recalled, "They were prepared to offer a discount, of course, but what Eva Perón wanted was simple extortion for what was really a political purpose. So they insisted on payment." Their decision was momentous and proved completely disastrous.

Eva already had reason to dislike the Groismans, for one of the brothers, a lawyer for the family business, was a well-known Socialist leader in the anti-Perónist opposition. Whether the Groisman brothers' demand for financial compensation marked the snapping point of Eva's patience or whether it merely served as a pretext for striking at anti-Perónist activists is uncertain. What is clear is the thoroughness with which Eva vented her fury.

Government "inspectors" suddenly visited the factory and publicly announced that the Groismans' factory teemed with rodents. They warned that the chocolate candies being sold to school children were poisonous, an indictment that even the most zealous anti-Semite would have found difficult to improve.

Immediately following these charges, government agents advanced on the factory, evicted the Groismans and their employees, and closed down all operations. Fully 700 workers were thrown into unemployment, the Groismans themselves were ruined, and the *kehillah* sent into consternation. For "Evita" was the patron saint of the Argentine masses, and her accusation against a Jewish family for literally poisoning the nation was the material of which pogroms are fashioned.

The four Groisman brothers urged the heads of the community to contest the injustice to their business, but these officials were extremely reluctant to confront the Peróns. The DAIA offered a large sum for legal defense of the Groismans, but no lawyer wanted to take this quick way out of the profession by courting Perónist disfavor.

The Groismans refused to concede. After vainly appealing to many community officials, they visited Rabbi Blum, known even then for his acquaintanceship with Perón. He was precisely the sort of man the Groismans had been seeking, for he assured them of his determination to confront Perón if necessary to restore their business.

Blum first met with the *kehillah*'s leaders and promptly incurred a unanimous rejection of his plans. Though he argued that they could not stay aloof from the fate of the Groismans, other leaders were less combative. They warned that if he attempted to see Perón despite their disapproval, he should on no account claim to represent any other official or institution in the *kehillah*. The senior rabbi of the community, Guillermo Schlesinger, was more explicit. He suggested that Blum, a newcomer in Argentina, should stay out of politics altogether.

The community leaders were by no means callous to the plight of the Groismans. The situation was exceedingly complex and dangerous. If the Jewish community approached Perón and branded Eva's charges as false, the result might well have been to incense the president against other sectors of the community. This would have risked government repression and anti-Semitic rioting. The misfortune of the Groisman brothers would then have paled before the anguish of hundreds and thousands of Jewish citizens. To many community leaders, Blum was idealistic but myopic, a man of blind courage threatening to provoke a major catastrophe in order to save one family's business.

The guest list for a party Blum arranged, following his meeting with the *kehillah*, revealed his strategy. Among the persons invited were the minister of culture and the three owners of the Mu-Mu chocolate factory—Lázaro, David, and Emilio Groisman. Blum brought all four together during the celebration and helped explain the Groismans' position. He also asked the minister for an audience with Perón. Shortly thereafter, the Argentine president agreed to receive the rabbi, and their meeting occurred just after the holy days of the Jewish New Year.

The long period intervening between the factory's closing and Blum's talk with Perón added two major developments to the situation. Most important was the death of Eva Perón, who succumbed to cancer at a very young age. Her passing obviously simplified Blum's task. Yet the lapse of over a year markedly increased the difficulties inherent in reopening the factory, and several in Perón's inner circle were disposed against the Groismans' appeal. Therefore, Blum's problems remained considerable.

The meeting began well, with Perón greeting the rabbi warmly. As they talked, the president appeared taken with Blum's unique courage. Blum reportedly said to him, "I speak from concern for the 45,000 Jewish families in Argentina, who are extremely worried and anxious because of this case. You can use your prestige and influence to help and assure the Jewish community." Perón made a token gesture by calling in his minister of commerce to discuss the file on the Groismans. The minister, a man of suspected anti-Semitic leanings, warned that any attempt to reopen the factory would take many months, that the business had been closed so long that repayment of the 700 unemployed workers complicated the case, and so forth. Perón appeared ready to assent to the minister's judgment, and the rabbi feared he had lost his case for the Groismans. Before leaving, however, he added to Perón that Yom Kippur was approaching—the holiest of days for the Jewish people. "On that day, God forgives us all that we did during the year," the rabbi said. "I beg you, then, to take this opportunity to forgive them also and allow me to take this message to the congregants on this holy day. It will lighten the spirit of the whole Jewish community."[16]

Blum's desperate and brilliant psychological appeal succeeded. Perón took in the praise and the drama of bestowing a major favor upon the Jewish community at this paramount religious occasion. Perhaps he was sincerely moved by Blum's eloquence; perhaps he believed that through Blum he could expand both his popularity with and influence over the Jewish community. Whatever Perón's motives, which must remain speculatory, the result was a triumph for Blum and the Groismans. Perón and Blum together announced over the radio just before Yom Kippur that the Groismans would be permitted to reopen their chocolate business. With Perón's flair for the dramatic, this was kept secret till the time of the broadcast, and the Blum family heard the good news for the first time when the president and the rabbi spoke on the radio.

The Groisman affair epitomized the Perónist treatment of the Jewish community. While not explicitly anti-Semitic, the Peróns nevertheless often jeopardized individual and collective Jewish interests by their volatile behavior. At the same time, they remained open to entreaties by representatives of the community. Indeed, the sole consistency in Juan Perón's policies toward the *kehillah* was his willingness to listen to whoever could appeal most skillfully to his self-interest.

The balance sheet of Perón's opportunistic behavior toward the Jews is by no means fully negative. Discounting his often hollow rhetoric, one is still struck by the number of precedents Perón dared to set in the sphere of Jewish rights and privileges.

Perón defied long-standing Argentine convention by opening sensitive government positions to qualified Jewish applicants. Aristocratic families had long considered diplomatic careers exclusively within their province, but in 1949 Perón chose a Jewish member of his Justicialista party, Pablo Manguel, as the first Argentine ambassador to Israel. Another Jew, Liberto Rabovitsch, received appointment as a federal judge, although previously it was almost inconceivable that a Jew could rise so high in the judicial hierarchy.

Perón set a third major precedent on Jewish appointments by selecting Abraham Krislavin as subsecretary to the minister of the interior. Not until 1959, with the appointment of David Blejer as minister of labor and social security, would a Jew reach higher in government circles.

Jews also exercised responsible functions within the Justicialista party organization. Most eminent among these officials was a member of the Chamber of Deputies, José Alexenicer, who rose to leadership of the Perónist party in the key city of Córdoba.

The army, a bastion of anti-Semitic sentiment, also felt the effects of Perón's public commitment to ending all racism in Argentina. Jewish soldiers had long been slighted routinely by anti-Semitic officers, a policy reaching to the highest echelons of the armed forces. Yet at Perón's insistence, in 1952 the army actually granted official leave to all Jewish soldiers during the High Holy Days of Rosh Ha-Shanah and Yom Kippur, for the first time in Argentine history.

Even Perón's dictatorial whimsies, pernicious in themselves, became dissociated from anti-Semitic overtones. His repression of dissident newspapers, for example, involved no special effort, open or covert, to weed out Jews or blame them for his actions, despite the visibly large role of Jewish journalists. This was most evident after Perón nationalized the premier Argentine daily, *La Prensa,* in

237

retaliation for its bold criticism of his regime. Perón had hoped simply to intimidate it through political pressure and harassment, but *La Prensa*'s editors rejoined in aggressive editorials, "We do not need mentors or tutors or prophets or redeemers or protectors or saviors. Let nobody govern or try to govern unless he has been freely and spontaneously called by the people to govern."[17] Perón ended his debate with *La Prensa* in 1951 by ordering it closed. He claimed with unadulterated falsity that *La Prensa*'s workers had struck against the management, necessitating his intervention. Eventually he reopened the paper under the leadership of his union subordinates. To head the prestigious literary supplement of *La Prensa,* a most sensitive position, the administration selected a talented Jewish writer, César Tiempo. Perón made no attempt to justify his war against the journal by conjuring images of Jewish conspiracy in the media.

Aside from the Groisman chocolate factory episode, the Jewish community enjoyed a period of relative security and prosperity under Perón's benign neutrality. At the time he was deposed in August 1955, his record on Jewish rights was in many ways admirable. Sebreli perceptively writes, however, that "despite these conspicuous facts, liberals remain committed to portray Perónism as anti-Semitic in order to accord more closely with their absurd Hitlerian analogy. . . . The most regrettable part is that the very Jewish bourgeoisie who believed this image and were generally anti-Perónist never ceased to take advantage of all the benefits that the regime brought them."[18]

Sebreli is accurate in asserting that many Jews who did well economically and were otherwise unhindered by Perón's regime still opposed him, inwardly if not actively. An editor of a Jewish magazine explained:

During the reign of Juan Perón there was not one single case of anti-Semitic assault. After, under Aramburu, Frondizi, and Illia, there were anti-Semitic attacks and leaflets by the thousands. But during the reign of Perón, we were in a state of terror, because we did not know when the dictator would fall on us. There was a state of intimidation.

The majority of Jews resented Perón, not so much for his attitudes toward Jews as for his authoritarian style of governing Argentina. Jews who had fled Russia and Germany knew too well the dangers of living under a dictator, even one disposed—for the moment—to seek Jewish support. Moreover, Perón's undemocratic tendencies attracted support from extremist elements who were dangerous to the Jews. It took several years for Perón to separate his government from the country's leading anti-Semitic groups and he never did this completely, even through the last years of his life.

Jews tend to recall the Perónist era as a time of irresponsible government, a tragic period of Argentine history for the whole nation. One businessman told me, "He gave a lot of things away, he gave everything away to the masses, but he did not know how to govern or to manage the economy. As for the Jews, I think we were very, very lucky." I asked if he meant because of Perón's protection. "No, we were lucky in spite of Perón. It was a great time for a pogrom but we had none."

The intellectual community also had reason to distrust Perón, as a Jewish professor described:

Perón made a shambles of the universities with his—he called them "reforms." He wanted to get the leftists but he ruined many other teachers. Now you know that we [Jews] are a large part of the student body and faculty, so when Perón came in with his troops and his new laws, we were hurt badly. Now Perón probably couldn't care that we were Jews, but with repression it just happens that Jews suffer the most. And those who don't —well, they worry about the next time, and with good cause.

The negative opinions of Perón were not unanimous. Some admitted that small businessmen benefited from Perón's impartial encouragement of all industry and commerce. Jewish youth looked with new pride and ambition as opportunities appeared in once-forbidden areas of government service. Above all, leaders in the *kehillah* acknowledged that if they were careful to humor Perón he would generally respond benevolently. A veteran official in the Jewish community related: "Once a Jewish women's organization wanted to send clothes to Israel. Their efforts met all sorts of obstacles until they agreed to label each box, 'a donation of Eva Perón.' Then it all went well. If you spoke well of Perón, he would do anything for you."

Though Perón was not the Judeophile he portrayed to the leaders of the *kehillah,* the last ten years of his life were far from an unrelieved curse upon the Jewish community. Certainly Perón was more favorably disposed toward the Jews than were the military rulers who preceded him in the years from 1930 to 1943. And, ironically, the succession of democratic presidents, alternating with military officers from 1955 to 1977, showed less inclination or ability to hinder anti-Semitic outbreaks than did Perón during the previous decade.

Given the fact that Argentina's Jews have lived in continual vulnerability, they were fortunate that Perón's particular type of demagoguery led him first to seek popularity with everyone rather than to make scapegoats of anyone. One need not ignore his dictatorial and expedient style of government in order to realize his many positive accomplishments in integrating Jews into the wider community on a basis of equality. With all his flaws, Perón still evolved into a president who was one of the most benevolent toward the Jewish community in modern Argentine history.

Anti-Semitic Slogans in Buenos Aires, 1960

(Look *Oct. 23, 1962*)

Argentine Nazis Salute, 1962

(**Look** *Oct. 23, 1962*)

Street Sign Defaced, 1962

Desecration in Jewish Cemetery, 1968

10 ANTI-SEMITISM DURING AND AFTER THE PERÓNIST EXILE

The Nazi threat

The intensity of extremist violence under Perón's successors dashed the hope that anti-Semitism would shrink into an ugly relic of Argentine history. Instead, with the fall of Perón, who had monopolized the means of terror in Argentina, underground hate groups suddenly swelled in numbers and boldness.

The Nazis and similar Fascist groups multiplied during this time. They bombed synagogues, defaced Jewish property with painted swastikas, and slandered Jews in leaflets and pamphlets. Many of these groups found veteran leadership for their Fascist programs through the participation of Nazi war criminals. These directors of Nazi schemes for genocide against the Jews and other groups had escaped the Allied authorities after World War II and were enjoying a safe haven from world justice inside Argentina.

Latin American nations, accustomed to receiving political and other refugees and generally unsympathetic toward the practice of extradition, offered an ideal sanctuary for hundreds of Nazis when the German Wehrmacht and the Reich it guarded collapsed in 1945. Argentina in particular made an inviting refuge because of the influence of a large and wealthy minority of German descent.

The moral onus for admitting many known Nazis among the German immigrants rests primarily with Juan Perón. His successors, however, followed similar considerations of diplomatic, political, and economic pressures in leaving this element of Argentine society largely undisturbed.

241

The German community in Argentina, which had long maintained personal and ideological links with kinsmen in Germany, helped to facilitate immigration by fellow nationals. The community's lobbying influence derived not only from its economic strength but from the sympathy shown by the Argentine armed forces, which were largely German-trained, and by the upper classes. Even today, according to sociologist Julio Adin, the Argentine Germans "exert a considerable influence on wide circles of the local aristocracy who are dazzled by German organization, discipline, and culture and prize a German governess as educator for their children above all things."[1]

Argentina's heavy economic dependence on Germany also influenced its policy toward immigration. Before the Second World War, Germany ranked third after the United States and Great Britain in investments and industrial holdings in Argentina. During much of the war, Germany surpassed even Great Britain in its importance to the Argentine economy. Most significant for the future, German technicians were playing a key role in Perón's plans to develop Argentine light industry and arms production.

Corruption smoothed the remaining rough edges in the Argentine immigration policy. Perón in particular saw an opportunity to share the riches amassed by Europe's leading plunderers. He therefore made lucrative deals with Gestapo officers and other agents of Hitler's Reich. An adviser to Perón, one Dr. Klingenfus, arranged the details, which involved the provision of forged identity passes to the Nazis and the transfer of much of their wealth to Perón's own coffers. The Nazis who thus entered Argentina included some of the worst criminals against humanity.

Martin Bormann is the world's most wanted fugitive from justice. West German authorities have long had a standing offer of 100,000 marks (about 25,000 dollars) for information leading to his arrest. As the chief bureaucrat in the Nazi government, Bormann reached a pinnacle of power overlooked only by Hitler himself. Even many of Hitler's directives trace ultimately to Bormann's influence.

Bormann took with him to Argentina a murderous past. As head of the Nazi party apparatus, he issued all important orders regarding concentration camps and killings. While his colorless personality and loyalty to Hitler led one historian to call Bormann

242

"Hitler's shadow," the dedicated Nazi-hunter Simon Wiesenthal suggests that the description "Hitler's evil spirit" comes closer to the truth.[2]

Wiesenthal and others suspect that Bormann is still living in Argentina or perhaps at present in neighboring Chile, but they cannot apprehend him. Assuming he is alive, in his late seventies, Bormann's connections with powerful German families in Latin America afford him ample protection against disclosure and arrest.

Hundreds of "Bormanns" over the years have been wrongly identified and reluctantly released, most of them in Argentina and a few in other Latin American nations. The most accurate though still tentative identification is from May 1964, made by a contact for Wiesenthal. He used a wartime photograph of Bormann to identify a man who called himself "Bauer" living in the Paraguayan capital of Asunción. There he used to meet regularly with a certain Mengele, the name of another notorious war criminal who fled originally to Argentina.

Josef Mengele, second only to Bormann on the Allied list of wanted war criminals, carved a niche of unparalleled infamy as the chief "doctor" of Auschwitz. Wiesenthal writes of him:

The physicians who practiced in the concentration camps didn't attempt to heal patients, but acted on the theory that the most effective remedy for a headache is to cut off the patient's head. . . . I have the testimony of a man who had seen Mengele throw a baby alive into a fire. Another man testified that Mengele once killed a fourteen year old girl with a bayonet. . . . Mengele was the perfect S.S. man; he would smile at pretty girls while he sent them to death. In front of the Auschwitz crematorium he was once heard to say, "Here the Jews enter through the door and leave through the chimney."[3]

The Argentine government eagerly overlooked Mengele's past indiscretions. He settled in Buenos Aires in 1952 and, under a range of aliases from José Aspazi to Lars Ballstroem, once again pursued the practice of medicine. He lacked a license but not the approval of the Argentine police, and so he encountered no problems. When Perón was overthrown, Mengele panicked and fled to Paraguay. Soon, however, he learned that the factors motivating Perón to show leniency toward the Nazis applied with equal force under his successors. Mengele returned to Buenos Aires, and convinced that the world no longer cared to bother about Nazi misdeeds, he eventually reassumed his real name.[4] This, at last, was a blunder, but only a minor one. West Germany requested his extradition in order to try him for his crimes at Auschwitz, but Mengele's powerful friends in West Germany and Argentina saved him from justice. German families in Argentina learned in advance from contacts in West Germany that Mengele would be arrested, and quickly warned him. Tacuara, an ultranationalist group, also intervened for Mengele, persuading the police to act with all deliberate delay. Mengele need never have worried in any case. Since the close of World War II, his family was highly respected in Argentina, where it controlled a half interest in Fadro Farm KG, SA, a local assembly plant for German-made tractors, capitalized at 1 million dollars. With this economic leverage, coupled with his important friendships in the Argentine German community, Mengele's escape never was in doubt.[5]

West Germany delivered a second demand for Mengele's extradition in January 1960, an effort that proved as futile as the previous one. He continued to live in Latin America, staying in nearby Paraguay, where he was guarded against Israeli and other agents by national troops and four private bodyguards, and with a reward of 15,000 dollars offered by the West German government for his capture. It appears certain the reward will never be collected.

Argentine Nazis were heartened by the presence of one of the Reich's masters of destruction, Adolf Eichmann. He was the ultimate efficiency expert for murder, coordinating plans for the arrest, transport, and slaughter of millions of Jews throughout Europe. His zeal in this endeavor is numbing in its unfathomable detachment from all moral sense or human feeling. Once, upon concluding an inspection of Theresienstadt concentration camp, he remarked to nearby inmates, "Jewish death lists are my favorite reading matter before I go to sleep."[6] After the war, Eichmann settled in Argentina, was joined quietly by his relatives, and enjoyed a prosperous and comfortable life amid the sympathetic Argentine German community.

The security these leading Nazis enjoyed and the rise of violent extremist groups reflected, in part, the Argentine government's moral lassitude toward issues of anti-Semitism. During the reign of President Pedro Aramburu from 1955 to 1958, virulent anti-Jewish magazines and books received continued immunity from government prosecution. The Aramburu administration piously cited Article 14 of the Constitution, which grants to all citizens the right "to publish their ideas in print without censorship."[7]

Although the government considered the issue of anti-Semitic slander a suitable line of defense for the right to free expression, it apparently viewed Jewish culture as outside the radius of protection. The *kehillah* protested to President Aramburu against consistent government harassment of its cultural activities. The government based its hostile stance on an edict dating from 1941, hardly a vintage year for Jewish rights in Argentina, that required exclusive use of the national language "in all demonstrations and assemblies." This ruling in effect banned Yiddish from Jewish ceremonies, though it was the language used by most Argentine Jewish institutions and was an essential part of the community's cultural identity.[8]

President Aramburu's response to the *kehillah* was ambiguous and discouraging. He denied that the edict of 1941 was discriminatory because it applied equally to all Argentine citizens. He added that it was necessary "to facilitate the integration [of different groups] into the nation. . . . Furthermore, the use of Spanish is obligatory among all inhabitants of the country, whether citizens or foreigners." At the same time, Aramburu concluded, the edict was certainly intended to authorize foreign languages "when artistic, cultural, or religious reasons make that indispensable."[9] This, of course, violated the spirit of the edict as Aramburu had just interpreted it. In short, the use of Yiddish by the *kehillah* might continue but in the same state of jeopardy and uncertainty as before.

Aramburu brushed aside other complaints of anti-Semitism with equal insensitivity. The DAIA reported to the government that many city hospitals routinely excluded Jewish medical students. Aramburu refused to consider the charges, preferring instead to repeat the cynical statement of the Department of Social Aid and Public Health blandly denying the possibility of discrimination.[10]

The DAIA also continued to exchange complaints for government denials on the sensitive issue of Jewish immigration. The government not only threatened penalties and possible deportation for the illegal Jewish refugees from Europe, but according to the

245

DAIA, created "a total prohibition of entry by Jewish immigrants into our country." Aramburu casually asserted that religion was not a factor in immigration quotas, but peremptorily refused to reexamine policies toward accepting Jews desperate to leave Russia and Eastern Europe.[11]

Aramburu himself probably was not necessarily anti-Semitic. Rather, he was indifferent to the problems brought by the DAIA, preoccupied as he was with the manifold problems of the Argentine economy and with building a stable political coalition. As a result, Jewish rights were slighted by the government and trampled upon by Fascist groups little hindered by local or national law enforcement.

The seizure of Eichmann and the rise of Tacuara

The election of the Liberal democrat, Arturo Frondizi, in 1958, gave Jews new hope of a champion of their civil rights. Initially, this hope appeared justified by Frondizi's appointment of a number of Jews as officials and advisers in the new administration, despite strong right-wing criticism. Yet little more than two years into Frondizi's presidency, the confidence succumbed to a new reign of terror precipitated by stunning news from Jerusalem: Adolf Eichmann, the elusive mass murderer of 6 million Jews, had surrendered to Israeli agents in Argentina and was in Israel awaiting trial.

The seizure climaxed a persistent search crossed with setbacks and frustration. The Israeli who led the manhunt, Tuvia Friedman, was a former inmate of a German concentration camp. "He saw his family battered to death with Nazi rifle butts and he saw countless other Jewish men, women, and children shot, burned and turned into fertilizer and laundry soap."[12] Friedman dedicated his life to bringing Nazis to justice, but his main quarry was always Eichmann. Through the subtle detective work of Simon Wiesenthal, the most resourceful and successful hunter of Nazis, Friedman was able to complete his mission.

Wiesenthal exploited the most slender thread of evidence to identify Eichmann correctly. Eichmann's father died in 1960, and although Adolf Eichmann himself made no appearance at the funeral, his four brothers all attended. Two of Wiesenthal's aides perched behind large and distant tombstones and took excellent pictures of the Eichmanns. Wiesenthal studied these and a prewar picture of Eichmann, and with a genius born of obsession, he managed at last to construct a composite picture of what the aging Eichmann should resemble. He gave this sketch to two Israeli agents who would not specify to him their precise mission. However, the astute Wiesenthal noted that this meeting followed by only a few months Argentina's expressed reluctance to extradite Josef Mengele to West Germany. Wiesenthal realized that the frustrated Israelis had despaired in the efficacy of relying on international concern with these Nazi criminals.[13]

Israeli agents acted on May 11, 1960, intercepting a late middle-aged man called "Ricardo Klement" as he returned from work on the outskirts of Buenos Aires. They identified him aloud as Adolf Eichmann and asked if he was prepared to face trial in Israel. Perhaps fearing a worse fate otherwise, he agreed. On May 23, Israeli Prime Minister David Ben-Gurion informed the world that Eichmann was in the Jewish State, awaiting action by a high court on charges of mass murder.[14]

The Argentine government was incensed. President Frondizi threatened to cut diplomatic relations with Israel and urged the United Nations Security Council to brand Israel an aggressor. The Security Council quickly convened in June, and the United States and France joined in rebuking the Israelis. The one major power to defend Israel, though cautiously, was the Soviet Union.[15] Though generally pro-Arab and anti-Israel, the Soviets were influenced by deeper considerations in this case. Apparently, first-hand experience with Nazi butchers afforded a more sober, sensitive perspective on the moral and legal issues at stake.

With many nations, Eichmann's crimes held minor consideration compared with the weighty issue of what would constitute a fitting censure of the Israelis. This was the heart of the Argentine position. Mario Amadeo, the Argentine ambassador to the United Nations, accused the Israelis of disdaining international law for private purposes. The agents involved "had no doubt whatsoever as to the fact that it was illegal, as is proved by the clandestine manner in which they operated." Amadeo suggested that if Eichmann had entered the country under false pretenses, so had many Jewish refugees. He added that "Argentina has always liberally

247

received refugees from every quarter, and if our liberality in this field has sometimes brought us more than one disadvantage, it is a price which we are always ready to pay." Amadeo concluded with the warning that Israel's actions, if repeated, would endanger international peace and security, and he demanded reparations by the Israeli government.[16]

Golda Meir, then Israel's foreign minister, responded to Amadeo that "this isolated violation of Argentine law" must be "seen in the light of the exceptional and unique character of the crimes attributed to Eichmann on the one hand, and the motives of those that acted in this unusual manner on the other hand." She described Eichmann's atrocities and asked: "Is it not inconceivable that Eichmann has enjoyed freedom during all these years? That he has not been brought to trial? Is not this a violation of the sovereignty of the spirit of man and of humanity's conception of justice?" Mrs. Meir also noted Amadeo's mention of illegal Jewish immigrants and expressed her astonishment that he "found it possible and appropriate to speak in one and the same breath of Eichmann and his victims." She stressed that Israel had apologized to Argentina for formally violating its laws and asked that this be put in its "proper perspective."[17]

The proper perspective of world opinion again weighed Jewish lives on a special scale and found them wanting. The Security Council supported the Argentine charges against Israel and directed Jerusalem to make reparations, by a vote of eight to nothing. The United States, Great Britain, and France supported the resolution. The Soviet Union, torn between its commitment to the Arab States and its disgust for the Argentine complaint, abstained altogether. Its abstention was echoed by the Polish delegate, the only other nonaffirmative vote in the council.

Argentina did not lack dissenting voices, as increasingly this introspective people pondered their nation's complicity in harboring Eichmann and other war criminals for so long. La Prensa editorialized: "Our country became a favorite refuge of Nazi and Fascist elements that sought to escape the punishment they deserved and live here secretly until the memory of their acts was forgotten. . . . These persons did not come here to seek asylum from unjust reprisals but to hide in most cases abominable crimes." That

Argentina could be "pointed out as the country of choice of such human scum" called for "a reaction by our collective conscience."[18]

The Argentine journal *El Mundo* went even further in defense of the Israeli act. "How can we not admire a group of brave men who have, during the years, endangered their lives in searching throughout the world for this criminal and who yet had the honesty to deliver him up for trial by a judicial tribunal instead of being impelled by an impulse of revenge to finish him off on the spot?"[19]

Others questioned the fitness of Mario Amadeo's moral perspective in judging the Israelis, for Amadeo was himself suspect of having supported the Nazis. In 1946, the United States Department of State had identified him in an official publication as a wartime "trusted collaborator of the Sicherheitdienst," the Nazi intelligence service. When questioned by the Jewish Telegraphic Agency during the controversy over Eichmann, Amadeo replied, "No comment." Comments did follow from other quarters, however. Arthur Mathov, a member of Parliament from the Argentine Radical People's Party, charged that "Doctor Amadeo cannot be our spokesman at the United Nations, having been himself an enthusiastic follower of Hitler."[20]

Even more damning to Amadeo's contention that Argentina would try Nazi criminals on its own was a revealing court case in July 1960. The Federal Court of Buenos Aires rejected a request by Czechoslovakia for the extradition of Jan Durcansky, a mass murderer during the Nazi occupation of that country. The court ruled that Argentina's statute of limitations guaranteed immunity from prosecution after fifteen years and thus barred trial for Nazi war criminals taking refuge in Argentina.[21]

The increasing disaffection of many Argentines with their government's handling of the Eichmann affair, coupled with a succession of Israeli apologies (though Eichmann remained securely in a Jerusalem prison), mollified the government's position toward Israel. The two nations resumed normal relations in August 1960, and a month later Buenos Aires featured an Israeli exhibit of biblical and other Jewish items. The Israelis hoped that the exhibit would also minimize repercussions to the Jewish community in Argentina as a result of the Eichmann affair.

The reconciliation between Argentina and Israel was not sufficient to prevent a quantum jump in the level of anti-Semitic activity in Argentina. Incidents of fire-bombings, beatings, and also more dangerous assaults increased sharply in 1961 and again in 1962. The Jewish community came under siege from a lunatic fringe whose deeds and numbers swelled like a river overflowing its banks during a heavy rain.

The most infamous of the violent organizations was Tacuara, whose name derives from the lance wielded by the *gauchos* of the nineteenth century. Tacuara first formed in 1930 as an ultranationalistic society, but in the 1940s Perón coopted it into the Perónist youth movement. Then in the late 1950s it rose on the crest of a wide campaign for compulsory Catholic instruction in public schools. Tacuara's "spiritual founder," a Jesuit priest named Julio Meinvielle, attracted the admiration of right-wing listeners with charges that Jews were undermining the national morality by their opposition to a union of church and state.

Meinvielle's whole life was an unstinting crusade against the windmill he perceived as the Jewish menace to world civilization. Baldish and scholarly, Meinvielle lined his modest apartment in Buenos Aires with books and piles of documents. The mention of Jews in any conversation would catalyze him into a state of high excitability, and he would speak loudly and rapidly on the subject. Jews "were linked with large-scale Communist movements" and had subverted the departments of medicine, economics, and philosophy in the University of Buenos Aires to further their nefarious operations.[22]

To immortalize his theories on the Jews, Meinvielle wrote a classic work of irrational invective, *The Jew in the Mysteries of History,* which established him as the Hugo Wast of Argentine "nonfiction" writing. Meinvielle's thesis was that a perpetual conflict between Christians and Jews existed because of the determination of Jews to rule the world through both capitalism and communism, a paradoxical combination in no way suspect to this passionate anti-Semite.

Tacuara's unholy alliance of fascism with Catholicism, which shocked the sensibilities of most Argentines, can be gauged from its manual of doctrine. The manual suggested three non-Argentines whose names would make fitting slogans and titles for new Tacuara branch organizations. The names were Benito Mussolini, Jesus Christ, and Adolf Hitler.[23]

Tacuara and similar groups exacted a heavy toll in lives and property, focusing almost exclusively on Jewish targets. Almost every week brought news of another terrorist attack on an innocent civilian or a bombing of a religious center. Such attacks had occurred even before the Israelis apprehended Eichmann, but his capture appeared to serve Tacuara as a rallying cry for vengeance against Jews everywhere.

Perhaps most alarming was the government's indifference toward controlling the flood of violence. A gang attack on two Jewish youths on the day of the Jewish New Year in 1961 went unpunished. So too did a bomb and gun assault that same year against the non-Jewish Frey Macho theatre in Buenos Aires, the Argentine Press Association, and the University of Buenos Aires School of Philosophy. Extremists struck at all these institutions because they either had Jews in substantial numbers or were considered linked to some Jewish subversive plot, according to statements left by extremists themselves. These assaults typified hundreds more that occurred during the early sixties.[24]

Frondizi's inaction during the mounting anti-Semitic activity resulted partly from his insecure hold on the police and partly from preoccupation with his own political survival, which was even more insecure. Frondizi did create some difficulties for Tacuara, though. Several of its leaders were questioned and some members jailed on charges of violating national security.

March 1962 brought more ominous news for the Jews. Frondizi, by his softness toward the Peronistas and his failure to revitalize the Argentine economy, unwittingly united the army's several factions against his administration. The military leaders first requested his resignation, then compelled it. They replaced him with Senator José María Guido as provisional head of the nation pending new elections in 1963.

Guido's regime gave Tacuara and other groups complete liberty to wage their campaign against the Jews. The young student leader of Tacuara, Alberto Ezcurra Uriburu, admitted to a journalist, "Tacuara is treated much better under this Government than under President Arturo Frondizi's regime."[25]

Fascist organizations thrived in this hospitable moral climate.

251

Twenty-seven major anti-Semitic incidents marked the first half of the year 1962 alone.[26] Nazi rallies dotted the country, often allying with Tacuara's "soldiers." Their meetings recall images of Germany during the 1930s, which marked the level of Tacuara's mentality. The scholar Julio Adin observed one of these rallies:

The stage was flanked by 300 young men in khaki shirts and military outfits. They cheered the speaker, shouting: "Kill the Jews, hang the Jews!" Some of them wore the Tacuara badge—a red and black flag with a Maltese Cross in the Center. Others bore *tacuaras* (rods), flying penants depicting the same symbol. Former S.S. members display the Maltese Cross at their meetings too. During the rally, shouts were directed against the USA, the ruling class and the democratic system, as well as against the Jews.[27]

Tacuara and its allies plunged to their lowest depth of infamy in June 1962 with an assault on a Jewish coed at the University of Buenos Aires:

One morning recently as nineteen year old Graciela Narcisa Sirota was waiting for a bus to take her to her classes at the University of Buenos Aires, a grey station wagon with three young men in it pulled over to the curb. One of the youths got out, rushed at Miss Sirota, and knocked her down with a club. When she came to later, she was lying on a wooden table in a strange room, and the upper half of her body was bare and afire with pain. Two of her abductors were calmly burning her with lighted cigarettes. The third appeared, holding a knife. Bending over, he carefully incised a three-inch swastika on her right breast, then leaned close to her ear and explained the attack: "This is in revenge for Eichmann." Dumped beside a railroad track, Miss Sirota somehow found her way home, and was treated for brain concussion, shock, second-degree burns and multiple contusions.[28]

Almost as grisly was the response by Argentina's law enforcers to this atrocity. Graciela Sirota's father went to the police, only to be cross-examined unsympathetically and turned out of the office. Shortly afterward, the identity of the three youths became a matter of open knowledge and one even boasted of his revenge against Jewish crimes. Despite this brazen confession, the federal police chief, Enrique Green, refused to file charges and suggested that left-wing Jews were pandering false allegations in order to subvert the fabric of Argentine society. Green stated that such complaints about anti-Semitism were "exaggerated and exploited by the Communists," and he continued his policy of ignoring anti-Semitic assaults.[29]

The Jewish community united in its outrage at both the attack on Graciela Sirota and the tacit approval of the crime by police authorities. The DAIA urged Jews to stop work for half a day on June 28. The response was overwhelming: almost all Jewish workers walked off their jobs at the appointed time and virtually all Jewish-owned businesses closed. Many non-Jewish Argentines did their country credit by participating in the work stoppage along with the Jews.

Among the Jewish businesses closing for the boycott was the restaurant owned by Graciela Sirota's father. He "bitterly recalled that he had donated blood to victims of the recent collision between a train and a school bus, and 'I do not remember anyone asking me if my blood was Jewish,' he said."[30] His disillusion and cynicism characterized the bulk of the Jews in Argentina, especially toward the Guido government. The president promised stern measures against anti-Semitic offenders, but the assaults continued, and the prisons were noticed to be suspiciously free of even the self-confessed bomb throwers and other "avengers."

A minority in the government shared the Jews' concern. Minister of the Interior César Androgué vehemently deplored the Nazis and the assaults. He himself had once been tortured by neo-Nazi marauders, and his empathy with the Jews was powerful and genuine. At the same time, he had to show caution despite his official control of the Federal Police. His power was only nominal because he had to contend with military officers who might topple a government they perceived as antinationalist. Nevertheless, given the political static he faced, Androgué worked diligently to increase police vigilance against anti-Semitic offenders.[31]

Raul Angelini, head of Federal Coordination, the equivalent of the United States FBI, protested the inadequate measures against anti-Semitism by resigning on July 2, 1962. The precipitating cause of his action was the police passivity after a gang attacked two Jewish youths and branded them with swastikas. Angelini accused his superiors, namely Chief of Federal Police Enrique Green, of systematically dismissing charges against obvious perpetrators of violence.[32] Angelini's action was laudable, but it left the police force more homogeneous in its attitudes than before.

After a summer of violence and mounting protest by Jewish and non-Jewish groups, Guido announced that he was considering a measure to outlaw movements promoting racial and religious discord.[33] Though such a law eventually was decreed, it bore little relation to the actual state of affairs. Ten days after the Guido administration assured the visiting president of the B'nai B'rith, Label A. Katz, that groups like Tacuara would be banned, a gasoline bomb exploded in front of the new Community of Israel Temple. Two girls emerging from the temple suffered wounds from shotgun blasts.[34]

Some members of Parliament openly deplored the deepening tragedy of violence and government irresolution. The president of the Argentine Chamber of Deputies, Frederick Fernández de Mondarin, protested the unspeakable crimes regularly committed, while another deputy declared, "If I were a Jew I would have volunteered to help catch Eichmann." A Jewish representative in the Chamber of Deputies, Zenan Goldstreich, warned, "I do not come here to defend the Jews whose tragic history is free of crime and violence toward others; I come to defend our Argentine democracy which is in peril because of anti-Semitism."[35]

The Arab League and the rise of anti-Semitism

The succession of the liberal Arturo Illia to the presidency in July 1963 was a small improvement—very small, though, as events unfolded. During Illia's administration, anti-Semitic activities occurred at the rate of nearly one a day. A DAIA official told journalist Mauricio Dulfano that

in 1964 alone, more than 300 specific incidents were registered with the DAIA. The range includes: physical assaults; sniper shooting; fire and tar bombs thrown at synagogues, schools and private houses; desecration of cemeteries; mail and phone threats; etc.[36]

Terrorist thugs climaxed another wave of violence in February 1964 with the murder of Raoul Alterman, a Jewish student who lived in Plaza Once. Gangmen from Tacuara and the Nationalist Restoration Guard entered his home and shot him to death. They placed a note near his body, claiming revenge for the murder of three syndicalist leaders at the hands of Communists. Alterman's bereaved parents received another letter from the Nationalist Restoration Guard a week later:

We do not kill without cause. Your son was slain because he was a Jewish Communist dog. If you are displeased, go back to Judaea, your own country, with all the other Jewish dogs and oppressors. What are all of you doing in our land? We are sick and tired of your pleas and complaints to the Government, paid for by the DAIA and other bodies![37]

Eichmann, the rallying symbol for so much anti-Semitic activity, was executed in Israel on May 31, 1962, after an extensive trial; but he did not die unmourned. Two years to the day after he was executed, his second son, also named Adolf, took up the fallen fasces and organized the National Socialist Party of Argentina. Wearing black jackboots and a red armband with a black-velvet swastika, the twenty-four-year-old fanatic intoned, "The one thing I can do in order to mark this second anniversary is to sit facing the swastika flag and meditate over the fact that my glorious father did not die in vain. His death opens the way for all who strive towards a better society." In case any doubted as to his means of reaching utopia, he vowed to destroy "the oppressive rule of international Zionist Jewry."[38]

The leading organization in the constellation of anti-Semitic forces during Illia's presidency was the Arab League of Latin America. This organization began operations in Buenos Aires in 1955, the year it expanded its propaganda efforts to include areas of the Jewish Diaspora. Under the guidance of Hussein Triki, one of the Arab League's top officers, the Argentine branch required scarcely a decade to become the major source of anti-Semitic literature in the nation.

Triki had had ample preparation for his work in Argentina. During the Second World War, he had collaborated with the Nazis in Tunisia, manufacturing propaganda bulletins against the Allies. As the Anglo-American soldiers pressed the Nazis across the North African sands, Triki retreated to Paris and Berlin to play a leading role in Maghreb, an Arab-run organization that promoted the Nazi war effort.

Triki churned out a barrage of anti-Jewish distortions as head of the Arab League in Argentina. At the same time, he performed incredible intellectual acrobatics to avoid being called an anti-Semite. Triki insisted that he did not despise Jews but wanted only "to fight international Zionism, the common enemy of the Argentine and Arab peoples."[39] The average Argentine citizen, however, could barely distinguish the blurry border Triki drew between anti-Zionism and anti-Semitism, a border that Triki regularly transgressed.

Primitive anti-Semitic stereotypes were the main ingredients in Triki's recipes for effective anti-Zionist propaganda. He restirred charges from the "Protocols of the Elders of Zion," which he cited to reinforce his arguments, equivalent to Goebbels' "documenting" anti-Semitic charges with quotations from Hitler's *Mein Kampf.* Triki could also rise to subtler levels in attempting to disparage the Jews. For example, he wrote that President John F. Kennedy "went to his death without blinking an eyelid. He will join the ranks of the martyred saints, alongside Count Folke Bernadotte [the UN official slain by members of a Jewish terrorist group in Israel in 1948]."[40] Although Triki did not directly accuse the Jews of complicity in Kennedy's murder, the subliminal superimposition of the slayings, amid more open charges against the Jews, made a potent anti-Semitic innuendo.

Triki allied the Arab League with the country's strongest Fascists. He defended the Nazi, General Enrique (Heinrich) Rauch, when his behavior as minister of the interior drew outcries from civil libertarians and led ultimately to his forced resignation. Triki blamed the Jews for the downfall of the Nazi minister, whom he characterized as a qualified public servant. Triki also upheld the murderous acts by Tacuara and the National Restoration Guard, which were merely countering "Zionist terrorism." Always he stressed the fantasy that the root of all evil was a Zionist conspiracy. "If the state of Israel did not exist," he told an audience in 1964, "Argentina would not be in the deplorable condition that it finds itself."[41]

The Arab League reached its full stride in Argentina during the early and mid-sixties. Triki exploited the plethora of anti-Semitic groups (as did his successors after 1964) by arranging combined rallies for many Fascist organizations. At one such meeting of these spiritual kinsmen, Triki deprecated Jewish strength in the world (never troubled by the demands of consistency, he also frequently cited the "Protocols" to prove their overwhelming strength) and recalled the huge ratio of Arabs to Jews. When Triki added, erroneously, that there were but 6 million Jews throughout the world, his Nazi supporters broke in with alacrity, "Thanks to Hitler! Thanks to Hitler!"[42]

Triki finally overstepped his Argentine welcome when his increasingly strident, unrestrained rhetoric became acutely embarrassing to the Argentine government. His visa expired in 1964, and the Illia administration, to its credit, ordered him to leave Argentina.

Triki fought the expulsion directive with all the resources at the Arab League's command. A dinner in his honor for the purpose of influencing the government to extend his visa took place in April at the Honori Patria club, the social center of the Argentine Arab community. Among the 150 guests, as noted by Julio Adin, "were the elderly Nazi-Fascist and former governor of Buenos Aires Dr. Manuel Fresco; Isaias Juan Nogas, a member of parliament; Juan Luco, president of the Perónist parliamentary faction; a number of other Perónist deputies and various nationalist and Perónist figures."[43]

The Illia government held firm on Triki's case, but the Arab League itself continued its pernicious propaganda activities. General Esam Helmy El-Masry assumed leadership of the league in August 1964 and promised to uphold "the same patriotic activity" as had his predecessor. The anti-Semitic language of the Arab League's Spanish-language pamphlets remains undiluted.

President Illia clearly meant to defend the liberal order, but his inability to do so became ever more apparent. Tacuara and other Fascist groups grew increasingly brazen in their terrorist and propaganda campaigns. The wide measure of freedom and security that they enjoyed led DAIA officials and other Jewish leaders to a state of near despair in the Illia government. *Di Yidishe Tsaytung* charged that all major political parties (except the Progressive Democratic Party) maintained a "strange silence" on the activities of the country's Fascist groups.[44] Nissim Elnecavé, in *La Luz,* accused the government of trying merely to explain away the problem of anti-Semitism rather than eradicating its worst manifestations.[45]

Officially, the government was energetic enough. It banned

Fascist groups as of November 1964, but actual conditions were unchanged. One particularly absurd Nazi action, in February 1965, hints at the Fascists' sense of security in Argentina. The younger Adolf Eichmann ordered some of his thugs to rip down a street sign near the main airport because it displayed STATE OF ISRAEL. Up in its place beamed a new sign with the greeting STATE OF ADOLF HITLER.[46] Innocuous amid the hundreds of anti-Semitic crimes perpetrated by the Nazis, this act of unwitting self-parody still reveals how totally ineffective Illia's measures were in cowing such groups. The Nazis in fact proved more entrenched than Illia himself, when in June 1966 the military staged a coup d'etat and ended civilian democratic government.

President Onganía and the military repression

If many Jews believed that their security had reached a nadir under the Illia administration, General Juan Carlos Onganía, the new president, proved that matters could still worsen. Onganía and his colleagues in the armed forces seized power when they concluded that Illia was too ineffectual to reorganize Argentine economic life. The new military government determined that Argentina needed above all a diet of austerity and authority. On every level, the first victims of this repressive policy were the Jews.

The very fact that the military controlled the government disconcerted the Jewish community. The armed forces had a long elitist tradition with powerful overtones of anti-Semitism that remain strong to the present day. Jewish officers have been all but unknown in the military since the early twentieth century, while Fascists have been proportionately more numerous here than in almost any other sector of Argentine society.

Bigots parading stripes and insignia have played leading roles in Argentine anti-Semitic movements since General José Felix Uriburu took power in 1930. It is significant that General Gilberto Oliva, whose intimidating letter to the DAIA in 1964 accused Zionists of every crime from theft to treason, did not write as a lone fanatic. A prestigious member of the air force, he enjoyed strong support from his comrades in anti-Semitic epithets. His letter was hailed, for example, by the group The 29 Oathtakers, to which Oliva belonged. The members were all prominent air force officers who swore to fight the enemies of their Fascist ideals.[47]

The German-trained army also had anti-Semitic leanings but neither so pronounced nor uniform as in the air force. Nazi officers continued into the 1960s to exercise a malevolent influence on the officers. During the early sixties, for example, German-born General Rauch was active in behalf of Argentine Nazis. In 1963 he received the opportunity to express his hate when he was appointed minister of the interior for a brief period. Rauch used this critical position to crusade for "better morals and a national purge of economic crimes," which he undertook with Gestapo-like zeal. Secret police arrests became the order of the day, and twelve persons—ten of them Jews—were imprisoned without even a preliminary hearing. Rauch accused them of whatever came into his mind —fraud, smuggling, or communism. By a dubious coincidence, the victims included several of Rauch's journalist foes who had criticized his Nazi leanings. The government compelled Rauch to resign within a short time, and the prisoners were all freed. Rauch nevertheless maintained his popularity among army leaders; in elections to select a new leader of the prestigious officers' organization Circulo Militar, Rauch received one-quarter of the ballots.[48]

The worst fears of the Jewish community were justified by Onganía's first months as president. He nullified two decades of Jewish political integration by effectively removing all Jews from positions in government, whether as officials or advisers. He appointed in their places only Catholics of established lineage, in order to cleanse the government of presumed subversive foreign elements.

The venomous factions of the extreme right wing appeared to be the upright groups Onganía favored for his new, pure coalition. Mario Amadeo, a supporter of the National Restoration Guard and an inveterate anti-Semite, became a frequent companion to Onganía after an absence of five years from government circles. The confirmed anti-Semite, Enrique Horacio Green, was given control of the Buenos Aires police force. His ties to Onganía were reinforced by his status as a brother-in-law to the Argentine president. Green marked his new promotion by arbitrarily arresting a respected Jewish municipal official, Bernardo Jaroslavsky. There were no substantial charges accompanying the act, which shocked but did

259

not surprise. Another of Onganía's appointments was Secret Service Director Eduardo Argentino Señorans. He was remembered by Jewish leaders for his brief tenure as secretary of war in 1963, during which time he had shielded members of Tacuara from arrest for anti-Semitic violence.

During the first year of the Onganía administration, Tacuara and other ultranationalist groups enjoyed a free hand against their victims. Only two days prior to a meeting with concerned Jewish leaders at which Onganía denied allegations of anti-Semitism in the government, his minister of the interior, Enrique Martínez Paz, conferred with Tacuara's high-ranking officer, Patricio Errecalte Pueyrredón. Such an act would be comparable with an American president's dispatch of a cabinet member to reassure the imperial wizard of the Ku Klux Klan that the government understood its needs and aims. Pueyrredón concluded after this meeting that "the National Revolution has begun on the debris of the liberal system," and pledged his unwavering support for the patriotic movement led by General Onganía.[49]

During July 1966, the Onganía administration conducted raids in Plaza Once and the Calle Libertad, both largely Jewish business areas in Buenos Aires; arrested eighteen officials of Jewish credit cooperatives; and seized several Jews in raids on ships reportedly selling contraband goods. It was also during this time that Jaroslavsky, in the Department of Public Works and Urban Development, was imprisoned.[50]

The blow to the credit unions also affected indirectly but severely many small industries and businesses that, again, were largely Jewish. The government cited possible smuggling and fraud as the reasons for the raids, but many suspected that they were carried out to appease commercial bankers who complained of competition by the Jewish credit unions. The apparently deliberate avoidance of non-Jewish businesses in the government raids belied Onganía's public disclaimers of anti-Semitism. Eventually, the Jewish businessmen were freed for lack of substantive charges against them; the blame for these violations of civil liberties was cast on some "overzealous government officials."[51]

Doubtless the most overzealous official in Onganía's regime was the notorious Enrique Green. Green's power expanded when Mario Fonseca, the federal chief of police, accorded him free reign to conduct that dangerous plaything of authoritarians, a "morality campaign." Toward this end, Green "ordered the police to check the documents of people under 22 on the street at night, announced his intention to ban the mini-skirt, decreed that night clubs be brightly illuminated 'so that the sex of people can be distinguished,' and initiated a vigorous campaign against driving violations." "The root of the trouble," Green mused on the problem of immorality, "is liberal atheism, which we will fight." He believed that "liberal atheism is out to destroy the pillars of Argentine society and has eroded respect for religious and moral principles and historic tradition."[52]

Late in July, Onganía and Fonseca detected a deadly threat to national security in the operation of the University of Buenos Aires. This university has, almost by itself, consistently guaranteed Argentina a preeminent reputation in higher education throughout Latin America. The government dreaded, however, what it considered the subversive influences of the educational system and decided to strike decisively. Police attacked university students and professors to the shouts of anti-Communist and anti-Semitic slogans. They brutally beat persons merely walking along the campus.

An American professor at the university, Warren Ambrose, reported that he

had been in the Dean's office for a few minutes, with a group of some twenty professors, when they heard heavy footsteps in the hall. Then they began to feel the effects of tear gas. On entering the corridor, the professors encountered a group of police officers, swinging batons and shouting curses, who pushed them into another section of the building. They were then forced to stand facing the wall with their hands over their heads, after which they were instructed to leave the building, one at a time.[53]

Over half the 2,000 faculty members resigned in protest at this disgrace. The eminent mathematician, Rolando V. García, former dean of the Faculty of Exact Sciences at the university, began legal proceedings against Police Chief Fonseca. García stressed the anti-Semitic overtones of the assaults and said that despite the complete lack of resistance by students and faculty, "all of us were beaten without compassion."[54] An editorial in the *New York Times,* which also found its way into several Argentine papers, aptly called the repression a reminder to "the world of the similar tactics used by Hitler's stormtroopers in the 1930s."[55]

Stung by these criticisms, the government nevertheless acted only against the victims, not the perpetrators, of ultranationalist violence. On August 14, a Jewish student who had a cross cut on his body by Tacuara thugs was actually arrested and imprisoned together with other students and teachers. Argentine and American students banded at the United Nations three days later to denounce the Onganía regime. Signs read, STOP AID TO MILITARY DICTATORS and NO MORE ANTI-SEMITISM IN ARGENTINA. A twenty-eight-year-old physics student, Daniel Wini, warned of clear signs of the existence of anti-Semitism in Argentina and condemned the government for harboring known Tacuara agents within its ranks.[56]

In late August, a Jewish professor wrote of the situation in deep despair:

We remain disconcerted and a little bit like cornered rats, wanting to leave or escape without knowing where or why. They are taking revenge and the accumulated hatred is oozing out of them. If you walk through the streets of Buenos Aires you would not notice anything; it is as if nothing had happened and behind us a strange people are destroying, little by little, the work of many generations. The only entity which has functioned in this country, with all its contradictions, has been the National University. . . . I fear that this country is condemned, at least for many years. . . . After having meditated on the matter sufficiently, I have decided to leave . . . although at times, from a barbaric desire, I want to assume my part in the fight.[57]

The situation remained tense for opponents of the dictatorship and for Jews of all political persuasions. At first, Onganía answered only indirectly the charges made against him by Argentine and American sources. Though anxious to appease the court of world opinion, he still could not bring himself to repudiate anti-Semitism openly. At length he held a press conference in which he guaranteed the protection of minority rights and declared that the government "will prevent Communist action and that of any other extremism."[58] The listener could interpret as he liked whether the danger of extremism came from Tacuara or from Jewish subversive exploiters.

The Onganía government appeared to respond most fully to

liberalizing pressures from outside Argentina. American demonstrators, journalists, and politicians all exercised a moderating effect on Onganía's policies. Senators Robert F. Kennedy and Jacob Javits of New York made especially strong protests against Argentine anti-Semitism and urged President Lyndon Johnson to withhold recognition of the Onganía government until Jewish rights were again respected. The Jewish High Holy Days marked a symbolic change in Onganía's approach to the Jews; he offered a pacific gesture in the form of a letter publicized in the Argentine papers, in which he wished good tidings to the Jewish community.[59]

Onganía's sudden cordiality was admittedly incongruous both in the light of past actions and amid continued anti-Semitic terror in Argentina. Nevertheless, it was the beginning of a new phase in Onganía's administration in which government hostility was slowly but steadily deflected away from Jews and liberal dissenters and focused instead on the ultranationalist groups such as the Tacuara.

The results of this new trend in government attitudes and actions were not easily spotted. For example, in 1967 it was noted that 142 of the 313 recorded incidents of anti-Semitism throughout the world occurred in Argentina.[60] By 1968, the anti-Semitic tide was still strong, but definitely ebbing. The American Jewish Committee reported in October 1968 that despite sporadic incidents, Argentina was noticeably freer of anti-Semitism than at any other time in Onganía's rule.[61]

It should be realized that this newfound security was relative. Just a month before the American Jewish Committee's reassurances, the whole Israeli Trade Fair and exhibition of Israeli art works in Buenos Aires fell victim to a "sporadic incident." A firebomb planted inside the main building ruined 1 million dollars' worth of property in a fire that raged for three hours. Including the cost of the art works, the building, and customs duties paid to the Argentine government, the total loss was 1.5 million dollars. The fair itself was beyond salvaging and never reopened.[62]

The overall trend in Onganía's administration encouraged Argentine critics mainly for the increased vigor with which he suppressed terrorists. It was a performance neither Frondizi nor Illia had come close to matching in their administrations. This was not because Onganía suddenly saw the merits of Jews, still less of dissenters, but because he became, for a time, a successful authoritarian ruler. He disdained the fringe organizations of the Right and Left as vexatious competitors for power, and as commander-in-chief of the armed forces, he possessed the means to discourage them. In this way, Onganía's regime resembled that of Juan Perón. Once secure of his own command, his dangerous alliance with right-wing zealots lost its utility and yielded to his desire to impose political stability. Thus the dictator, Onganía, indirectly afforded Jews more physical security than any of the democratically elected leaders in 1950s and 1960s were able to do.

Onganía's ability to maintain a fair degree of order and tranquility collapsed during 1969. Social forces that he had previously managed to intimidate but not satisfy suddenly surged against him in mounting student and labor unrest and violence and a sharp increase in terrorist activities. Rioting in major cities led the armed forces to remove Onganía in June 1970, and only nine months later to depose his successor, General Roberto Levingston. General Alejandro Lanusse took the presidential oath of office in March 1971 to confront the same economic shambles, labor hostility, and political chaos that, in the phrase of the Jewish official Paúl Warszawski, "changed this one man, Onganía, from a good President to a very bad one." Amid these deteriorating conditions, apparently beyond the competence of government to overcome or even contain, the Jews once again emerged as scapegoats for the nation's ills.

The return of Perón

Walter Beveraggi Allende is a professor of political economics at the University of Buenos Aires Law School. He became better known in November 1971 for his open letter to José Rucci, the general secretary of the country's largest union, setting forth theories of Jewish conspiracy beside which Father Meinvielle's rabid polemic appears as so much reasoned congeniality.

Allende's letter accused the Jews of "a veritable genocide of our people." He charged that Jews had arranged the nation's general strike earlier in the year. He also hypothesized that they timed this strike for Yom Kippur so as to divert attention from their monopolistic control of the nation's finance and economy. These allegations merely whetted anti-Semitic appetites for the main charge: that a document just uncovered proved a Jewish plot to convert the southern third of Argentina, known as Patagonia, into a Zionist state to be named Andinia.[63]

Allende's absurd charges nevertheless gained immediate national interest and received front-page attention in several major dailies.[64] Thousands of reprints of his letter reached all social sectors, and in January 1972, an attorney in Tucumán Province, Exequiel Avilla Gallo, charged a federal court to expose the Jewish Zionist high command "with the aid of all security organs and intelligence organizations of the Armed Forces, federal and local police."[65]

Helping Allende to spread his gospel of hate was the new head of the Arab League in Chile and Argentina, Yusaf Albandek. Formerly, he had lived in the United States, where he engaged in vicious propaganda activities. He left the country in 1950 when the Anti-Defamation League of B'nai B'rith exposed his links to prominent anti-Semites. In 1971, he established new headquarters in Chile. According to Rabbi Morton Rosenthal of the Anti-Defamation League, Albandek was "the major force behind the new virulent anti-Semitic and anti-Israel campaign in Argentina."[66]

Another widely distributed tract blaming the Jews for Argentina's social, economic, and political woes attracted adherents with the forged seal of the respected religious society the Sisters of the Sacred Heart. The society publicly repudiated the tract and its allegations against the Jewish community, but these denials scarcely commanded the attention of the apocryphal document itself.[67]

The wave of anti-Semitism carried well into 1972. Jewish leaders received anonymous letters threatening "reprisals" against Argentine Jews. In Bahía Blanca, 420 miles from Buenos Aires, allegations spread that "international Zionism" was responsible for the death of Eva Perón. In two other cities, Tucumán and Resistencia (800 and 650 miles, respectively, from Buenos Aires), public meetings condemned the "Zionist conspiracy" of Allende's vivid imagination.[68]

During this same year, Argentina received electrifying news that intensified the already frenzied atmosphere—Juan Perón and the ruling Argentine officers were seriously negotiating terms for his return to Argentina.

From exile in Madrid, Perón had retained a strong hold on both his political organization and his mass base of support among the workers. Yet for most of the period between his overthrow in August 1955 and the country's last presidential election in July 1963, his party had been legally barred from appearing on the national ballots. The party faithful, which consistently included more than one-third of the nation's voters, countered this restriction by casting blank ballots to show support for Perón. The result was to embarrass and weaken the successive administrations.

During the 1970s, the economic and political tensions simply became unmanageable by the ruling military officers. Popular discontent and terrorist violence reached unprecedented levels. Perón was fortunate in not having to preside over the collapse, which he as president had done so much to bring about. His name rang through the nation's streets as militant crowds proclaimed him Argentina's sole salvation. The military *junta* led by General Alejandro Lanusse was apoplectic over this popular clamor, but as the nation disintegrated amid strikes and riots, there seemed little choice but to extend overtures to the aged Perón.

For the Jews, Perónist history was dangerously repeating itself. During his new bid for power in this unstable nation, Perón's lieutenants frequently found it profitable to add to the atmosphere of anti-Semitism by collaborating with known Fascists and stirring workers to violence. One of Perón's top aides, Senator Andres Framine, openly made noxious diatribes against the Jews.

Jewish leaders asked Perón to clarify his position. "Anti-Semitism is totally alien to Peronista ideology," he obliged. Perón added that anti-Semitism divided the people and wasted precious energy in needless struggles. "Whatever problem is raised between Jews and Arabs in Argentina is artificial. Both Jewish and Arab communities are perfectly integrated in our country and live in harmony. It is very dangerous and undesirable to transfer to Argentina the Middle East conflict, which can be solved if the great powers wish it."[69]

Perón also responded to Jewish complaints about anti-Semitic statements by Perónist leaders. He addressed his comments to Dr. Noé Davidowich, one of three Zionist delegates questioning his position, in a letter published by the Argentine press:

While it is true that those persons [slandering the Jews] are connected with our movement, they have no authority to do what they are doing in the name of the National *Justicialista* [Perónist] movement. They themselves are responsible for and represent only their personal position. The National *Justicialista* movement has proved faithfully—through a tradition of more than a quarter of a century—that it is alien to any racist feelings. . . . It is my duty to assure you in the name of our movement, that in its political activities there is no room for any kind of anti-Semitism.[70]

Perón's skillful handling of the issue was in character. He repudiated anti-Semitism without rejecting the support of known anti-Semites. Perón was not about to compromise his chances for political success by too strong a condemnation of any of his deputies and senators, and so Perónist-fanned violence against Jews continued, despite the calming letter to Davidowich.

Then in July 1972, Perón seemed suddenly to enter political senility with an incredible statement about foreign conspiracies, in an interview given in Madrid to an Argentine colonel. Perón warned of "the great international synarchy, manipulated from the United Nations, where there are Communism, capitalism, Judaism, the Catholic Church, . . . and Masonry. . . ."[71] In other times, such a flagrant attack on respected as well as marginal elements in society might have cost Perón dearly. In volatile Argentina in the 1970s, though, the remarks scarcely slowed his momentum and in some ways possibly increased it.

I asked a Jewish journalist whose father had been a prominent member of the *kehillah* during Perón's earlier rule, if he thought that a return to power by Perón would be a disaster for the Jewish community, in view of Perón's recent ravings. "No, I don't think so necessarily," he replied, and added that Perón's character was brought out fully during the crisis over the Groisman's chocolate factory. "You see, Perón isn't really anti-Semitic and never has been. He just wants to be courted." Perhaps the man also had his doubts, though, because he hastily remarked, at the end of our discussion, "Please don't report my name. You see, you go, but I stay here."

The event once thought impossible—the political resurrection of Perón in Argentina—appeared ever more likely and essential as the year 1972 continued to explode with new violence. In Mendoza, a beautiful city in western Argentina, noted for its wine and its political conservatism, there occurred a scene that might have been Berlin in 1933. Torches were waved in the brisk night air while a crowd chanted rhythmically and melodically for the return of Perón. When police tried to disperse them, the defiant crowd became a mob, and gunshots rang out. The chaos that ensued left three people shot to death. This was in July, scarcely a month after police had killed two students in a clash at the University of Buenos Aires and prior to more violence in other major cities of the country. Everywhere, block after block, wall after wall, posters and handwritten slogans formed a graffiti campaign of gargantuan proportion. Curiously, while the signs often read PERÓN VUELVE! (Perón Returns!) and PERÓN O MUERTE! (Perón or Death!), the most popular sign did not even mention Juan Perón at all. The sign instead featured a picture of his late wife, Eva, in a characteristically kinetic pose, and with the defiant (if sadly inaccurate) words, EVITA VIVE! (Evita Lives!).

The Jewish community divided on the issue of Perón's bid for power, but most Jews had strong reservations about the prospect of a new Perón administration. The business sector, especially the wealthier executives, were afraid of Perón, partly because of his unpredictability, partly because of his past incompetence in managing the economy. Most elderly Jews remembered the first Perón regime with limited affection and were reluctant to repeat the experience. Among younger Jews, with no bitter memories of Perón's repressive policies toward the universities, support for his political ambitions ran much higher. The DAIA, of course, held to its firm principle of political neutrality and avoided an official stand on the issue. The DAIA official, Marcos Barborosh, voiced hope in a private conversation that if Perón gained the presidency he would safeguard the rights of the Jewish community and prove open to its needs, as in the past.[72]

Perón's party participated in the elections held in March 1973 and the results, as anticipated, were a complete triumph for the Justicialista movement. Héctor Cámpora, representing Perón, won a comfortable majority of the vote, then resigned so that new elections could be held, with Perón and his young wife, María Estela Martínez de Perón, running for president and vice president, respectively, on the Justicialista ticket. Perón won handily to complete a personal revival worthy of Lazarus, disproving the pundits who had claimed that he was too old and content in Spain to challenge Argentina's military dictatorship.

268

The fanfare accompanying Perón's victory spectacularly exceeded the achievements of his brief second reign from March 1973 till his death in July 1974. Perón was not able to restore the once-great progress of the economy or arrest the wave of strikes and riots that had crippled the nation in his absence.

At the time Perón died, his policies toward the Jewish community were still unclear. Though Jews awaited anxiously for Perón's political weathervane to settle in its new direction, it continued to move, or feint, in all directions at once. In April 1973, Cámpora declared on Perón's behalf that "Argentina won't be anti-Semitic."[73] In June, Perón personally praised the Jewish role in Argentina's development.[74] Yet he also moved to please the Arab League and the oil-producing states of the Middle East, arranging for Walter Beveraggi Allende, of "Andinia" notoriety, to make a goodwill tour of several Arab countries. It was part of a general campaign to improve relations with these nations, which intensified with the Arab oil boycotts of many countries after the war with Israel in October 1973.

Perón's increasingly pro-Arab and anti-Israel foreign policy affected his domestic attitudes toward Jews. Early in his administration he appointed Jews as well as Catholics to government offices. Yet under pressure from the Arab League, Perón wavered. In March 1974 he tacitly approved the charge by a key member of the cabinet, José López Rega, that the large numbers of Jews in government were a stumbling block to the national interest, which required closer ties with the oil-rich nations. At the same time, Perón kept the Jewish finance minister in his inner councils, despite the strong pressures from conservative Peronistas to purge him and other Jews from government offices.

The future course of Perón's actions toward the Jews was probably unknown even to Perón himself. He had never been shackled by ideals, let alone by dogma. Had he lived and ended the epidemic of riots and assassinations while invigorating the economy, then he might well have dissociated his movement completely from anti-Semitism and bid for stronger Jewish support. Such was his policy in the forties and fifties once he felt secure enough to jettison the destructive, rabble-rousing elements in his loose-fitting coalition.

Unfortunately, the short-lived Perón administration gave little promise of rapid achievement, which may also be said of Perón's successors. Although the transfer of power to his politically inexperienced widow was orderly, the tensions in Argentina became greater than ever under her sad, confused reign. The military coup that deposed her in late March 1976 was almost inevitable and widely accepted, given the total paralysis into which her administration had fallen.

Now that the shibboleth of "bringing back Perón" has proved insufficient, a new shibboleth may well be sought. And as one Jew made cynical from long experience remarked, "When the economy is sick, a Jewish villain makes a good placebo for the nation."

The continuing danger

Events in Argentina during 1976–78 have been disheartening in the extreme. The military *junta,* in its zeal to eliminate suspected left-wing dissidents, awarded Fascist groups free reign to prey upon "undesirables." Inevitably, Jews rather than terrorists became the most vulnerable targets of this policy. Self-appointed "death squads" were soon roaming the country with impunity, murdering prominent liberals, trade unionists, intellectuals, and Jews of every occupational and political background.

Terrorist bands like the Argentine National Socialist Front brazenly flaunted their Nazi leanings. Freed captives of such groups reported that their tormentors "sang Nazi songs and shouted slogans against the Jews." A former prisoner recalled seeing a portrait of Adolf Hitler on the wall when his blindfold was briefly removed.[75] The activities of these extremists were supportively flanked, moreover, by a proliferation of Nazi writings selling briskly in Argentine newsstands. Most popular in 1976 was a new edition of Hitler's *Mein Kampf.*

Not since the Onganía regime a decade earlier had the Fascist banner flown so closely beside the national flag. Although international pressure led the *junta* to issue a nominal ban on overtly pro-Nazi publications in September 1976, this token gesture for external consumption received scant enforcement. The same Nazi tracts, an observer commented, "had considerable readership within the armed forces and backing from some generals."[76]

In this atmosphere of intolerance and repression, a wave of

anti-Semitic incidents engulfed the nation, evoking memories of darkly similar incidents during the sixties. In June, a physician named Salvador Akerman was gunned down in the street for being a Jew. His assailants anonymously telephoned newspapers that Adolf Eichmann had again been avenged. In August, the son, daughter, and daughter-in-law of poet Juan Gelman were kidnapped by armed civilians in Buenos Aires. It was reported that the daughter had been seriously ill and the daughter-in-law pregnant. Earlier in the same month, Israel protested the arrest of five nationals in Córdoba, suspected of subversion for their participation in a seminar on Zionism.

I asked a Jewish woman who had left Argentina in October 1976 about the danger faced by both Jews and non-Jews from guerrillas and government forces. "Not even Catholic priests are safe now from guerrilla attacks," she said,

but if you are a Jew, you are compounding your troubles many times. There is, of course, the blind shooting; then there is the violence that hits Jews because they make up a large part of targeted groups like the intelligentsia; and there is the killing by the really open anti-Semites. And all of it is worse than anyone fully knows. When you want information about your missing friends and relatives, the word everywhere is, "Don't ask, or you may be next to disappear."

Some within the Jewish community insist that the current danger is not really a result of anti-Semitism. They tend to argue that the nation as a whole is passing through an inevitable period of stern rule because of the excesses of the left-wing guerrillas. The Montoneros and other revolutionary groups have necessitated a certain amount of preventive security measures by their wanton butchery of civilians and government officers alike. Jews are disproportionately involved in the revolutionary movements, and so it is to be expected that many of those killed or arrested by the military also will be Jewish. In general, however, only Argentines suspected of subversion have been targets of the government forces.

Yet after every allowance is made for disruptive social conditions and the conspicuous presence of Jews in leftist guerrilla groups, one still finds that the government policies betray a strongly anti-Semitic character. The pattern of events since 1976 suggests that the mere fact of Jewish identity can stimulate government

271

mistrust, if not active harassment. Some government officers seem
to believe that most Jews are at least sympathizers with the revolutionaries, although only a tiny, ostracized minority of all Argentine
Jews are either Communist or violent. Moreover, each well-publicized arrest of a Jewish figure contributes to the tendencies within
Argentine society to link the terms "Jewish" and "subversive." The
result is a vicious anti-Semitic cycle of suspicion and persecution,
exacerbating an already perilous situation.

While some blamed the repression and anti-Semitism on the
junta's nominal leader, General Jorge Rafael Videla, life was
scarcely more tranquil for this "moderate" among his fellow officers. Videla's claim to office narrowly survived several assassination
attempts by left-wing guerrillas and assorted challenges by right-
wing military officers. The latter group desired still more energetic
prosecution of the government's war against guerrillas and other
dissidents.

In 1977, it became evident that Videla was less a totalitarian
ruler than a desperate interest broker among competing military
factions, many of whom were rabidly anti-Semitic. While Videla
still resided in the presidential Casa Rosada, policy initiatives increasingly came from extremist officers in the navy and in the First
Army Corps defending—or menacing—Buenos Aires Province.

As the junta's repressive actions mounted, Jews above all other
groups found themselves in unprecedented danger. They were not
only brutally assaulted by freely operating extremist bands but were
increasingly singled out for public slander by the government.

The escalating harassment entered a new and ominous phase
in April with the so-called Graiver scandal. The government
charged that a well-known Jewish banking family, then headed by
the late David Graiver, was subsidizing terrorist activity. The un-
proved accusations concerned Graiver's Banco Comercial de la
Plata, alleged to have accumulated nearly 18 million dollars in
ransom money from guerrilla kidnappings.

Whatever truth may be found in these charges, the sordid
nature of the government's actions in the Graiver case is already
established. The case against Graiver is based on the replies by a
captured guerrilla leader under torture to the quite possibly leading
questions of security agents. Then, too, observers have questioned
the suspicious convenience with which the Graiver affair has en-

abled the *junta* to implicate many of its most prestigious and troublesome opponents. Among those that the *junta* has tried to discredit for having obtained funds from Graiver's banking operations are former presidents Alejandro Lanusse, arrested for his connection to Graiver, and Isabel Perón, already under close government guard.

Public response to the Graiver scandal included the feared cross-currents of anti-Semitic slogans and rumors. Elements in the media exacerbated this inflammable situation by stressing the Jewish names of some of the key persons involved in the scandal. Channel 11 on Argentine television was a major offender with a sarcastic editorial that inquired, "Very Argentine, these names, aren't they? Not all the country is like this. The rest is honest."[77]

The Graiver case also served as a springboard for the military to move against predominantly Jewish economic interests. Under pressure from Videla and other officers, the Graiver family divested itself of shares in a major newsprint plant it had managed jointly with the government. Soon after, Jacobo Timerman, the editor of *La Opinión,* was arrested without explanation and his paper confiscated. Timerman was a staunch Zionist and also a key supporter of Videla's hopes to maintain an "open society" despite the war against the guerrillas. On both counts, he was anathema to the more extreme officers in the *junta.* The fact that Graiver had invested funds in *La Opinión* appeared to be the pretext for the arrest, but after months in prison Timerman had yet to discover the nature of the charges against him.

The momentum of economic war against largely Jewish interests proved self-sustaining, even without the Graiver affair to provide a covering rationale. In May, the military confiscated Aluar, the aluminum processing plant in which José Ber Gelbard was a major shareholder. The loss of Aluar was perhaps the most substantial blow to the Jewish community since the Graiver affair errupted.

The seizure of Aluar was at least in part a way of striking at Gelbard, then an expatriate living in America but still feared as a possible rallying focus for an antirightist coalition. Until the time Gelbard died in October 1977, at the age of sixty, he was ardently sought for "trial" by the Argentine government for various crimes against the state.

The embers of the Graiver and Aluar affairs were still glowing

273

fiercely when the *kehillah* staggered with the news that its American Jewish Committee office was closing under duress, after twenty-nine years of operation. The immediate cause was the forced departure of the organization's representative in Argentina, Jacobo Kovadloff, whose family left for the United States after harassment by government security agents.

The tragic victimization of Kovadloff marked a sinister precedent in the choice of Jewish targets by extremists in the *junta*. Previously, such harassment of Jews was either random or else directed at leaders at least marginally connected with opposition to the government. Kovadloff, however, was respected in Jewish and many non-Jewish circles as a humanist long concerned with interfaith toleration and almost wholly untouched by partisan politics. Moreover, while he worked for an American-affiliated group, he was scarcely vulnerable to the same xenophobia that plagued the foreign-born Gelbard, for example. For Kovadloff's Argentine roots traced back several generations to the Barón Hirsch colony in Entre Ríos.

Kovadloff evinced confidence in the Argentine people and government even after the terrorism that compelled his move to America. He deplored the repression caused by "elements of a Nazi-Fascist mentality and ideology" who had "infiltrated into the government itself in high positions." Yet he expressed "the hope that the authorities in power would seek to control the right-wing extremists."[78]

It became increasingly apparent as the year unfolded that the right-wing extremists were to a large degree the real authorities in power. Nehemias Resnizky, leader of the DAIA, was still defending the government against charges of anti-Semitism in late July 1977 when his son was kidnapped. Resnizky's quiet appeal to moderate elements in the government led within a week to the return of his son—in a car known for its use by government security agents. Resnizky blamed the kidnapping on "obscure and pogromist forces," but such forces were clearly finding inspiration in the actions of the *junta* and its security network.

Forecasting the Jewish community's situation is a highly speculative endeavor. As Kovadloff commented shortly after arriving in New York, "Episodes and incidents flow so fast that any predictions as to the future would be hazardous."[79] Beyond the daily and even monthly ebbs and flows, however, one can entertain only the most limited hope for the *kehillah* and for the country as a whole.

The economic dislocations behind much of the nation's turmoil remain severe, including the problems of inflation, labor unrest, poor resources management, and the uninviting atmosphere for business investment. The currently dormant political parties have already exposed their inability to grapple with these problems, most recently during the brief and dismal Perónist reign in the early 1970s. As for the military, divided and as yet unable to crush the guerrilla resistance, it long since proved Lanusse's recent statement that officers lack the training to govern a nation.

The most roseate expectation for Argentine recovery would allow a decade of slow, painful progress toward moderate economic health and political stability. Whether this occurs under a civilian or a military regime or, as events have shown to be more likely, an alternation of these, the challenge to salvage Argentine society from its present morass will remain monumentally difficult for years to come.

For the Jews, as the repressive situation possibly takes some tentative turns for the better, the temptation will arise once more to dismiss or minimize past anti-Semitic horrors as a sad aberration. Those with a sense of their community's history—and the larger history of the Jewish people—realize, however, that such "aberrations" are all too likely to haunt them again.

275

EPILOGUE: A GENERATION OF THE DESERT

The editor of a respected Jewish journal in Buenos Aires told me of his intent to resettle in Israel, lamenting, "Jewish life in Argentina will disappear within fifty years." His dark assessment of the community's future typifies the opinions of a wide and growing spectrum of Argentine Jewish leaders.

Why has this giant among Latin American Jewish communities instilled such foreboding and pessimism among many of its most active members? In part, anti-Semitism in a variety of malevolent forms is responsible. Even more worrisome, though, to many in the *kehillah* is the continuing disintegration of Argentine Jewish identity that now places cultural survival in imminent jeopardy.

This crisis of cultural continuity was presaged as early as 1895 by a meeting between Theodore Herzl and Baron Maurice de Hirsch, who by his death had committed several million British pounds to his belief in the possibility of Jewish life in Argentina. The ambitious philanthropic plans touted by Hirsch, exemplified by his idea to transport millions of oppressed Russian Jews to the Argentine hinterlands, left the usually visionary Herzl unimpressed. The baron, Herzl admonished him, was simply throwing away his money.[1]

The original mission of Argentine Jewish settlement envisioned by Hirsch faded long ago. The idyllic vision of a pastoral Jewish community has been swept aside by the urban-centered migrations during the 1930s and after. For all but a remnant of Argentine Jewry, the rural pioneering spirit that characterized the first settlers has become only a memory.

277

The shrinking of the Jewish farm settlements need not have imperiled Judaism in Argentina. However, all other pillars of Jewish identity have steadily eroded as well. A major reason, perhaps the prime one, is that Jewish education for the young is minimal—and decreasing. No more than 12 percent of all Jewish youth attend any form of Jewish school.[2] Even this figure is generous, for it includes many kindergarten children and obscures the fact that all but a very few students drop out after three years of the most basic schooling. This situation is a stark contrast with most other Jewish communities in the Americas. Moshe Kitron wrote in 1964 that in the area spanning Chile and all lands north through Mexico, "between 60 and 85 per cent of all Jewish children now receive a Jewish education."[3] The most pessimistic reports on Jewish education in the United States give the proportion of school-age children receiving some instruction at over 80 per cent.[4]

When I suggested to Grand Rabbi David Kahana that intermarriage might be a danger to ethnic survival in the *kehillah,* the white-bearded scholar replied sadly, "No, not intermarriage; the great danger is ignorance of Judaism!" He continued somberly, "I do not see in the schools that exist today a path for the maintenance of the Jewish people. The teachers are not knowledgeable. . . . I therefore feel that unless there is a change with regard to education, with regard to instruction, we will end up very bitterly. And this is *the* problem, just education."[5]

Religious tradition was among the first casualties of the educational debacle. Argentine Jews have long been relatively indifferent to religion. Yet even the weak roots of Orthodox *shtetl* patterns have shrunk noticeably. A survey in 1967 of young married couples in the prominent cultural center Sociedad Hebraica Argentina revealed that fewer couples (57 percent) than their parents (72 percent) kept any religious traditions or ever attended synagogue (39 percent compared with 57 percent of the parents).[6]

In the absence of a strong religious or educational tradition, the bulwark of Argentine Jewish identity has long been anti-Semitism, fueling movements for Jewish nationalism and communal solidarity.

One Jewish leader called anti-Semitism "the greatest protector of Judaism we have here. The Jew who sloughs off his past wakes up to an exploding bomb or catches an insult prefaced with *'judío'* and remembers who he is once again."[7] This is no longer the whole truth, however. There are signs that anti-Semitism has begun to exercise a potent effect in quite a different direction, illustrated by the following incident. While Juan Perón was still exiled in Madrid, he warned his fellow Argentines to beware of international conspiracies—Catholic, Jewish, even Masonic. Later that same month, when I attended a film on Perón's life shown in Buenos Aires, several young Jewish companions joined the audience in wildly cheering the ex-dictator. Turning aghast to one of my friends, I asked how he and other Jews could applaud such a dangerous man. "Oh, he doesn't mean us," my companion reassured me—"just the Zionists."

This striking detachment from Jewish identity is not at all exceptional among younger Argentine Jews; rather it reflects a widespread attempt to be "pure Argentines." In Rosario, for example, a young Argentine, discussing attitudes toward Jews, confided to me that he had some friends who were Jewish. Later he added the passing comment, "and my parents also are Jewish." The notion that this accident of birth into a Jewish family may have affected his own status as well never surfaced in the conversation.

Much of this unthinking rush to assimilate is the product of anti-Semitic propaganda barrages that work their greatest emotional damage on those many Jews already isolated from their cultural background. These anti-Semitic campaigns frequently attack Jewish Marxism, Jewish capitalism, or Zionism rather than Jews per se. The distinction, of course, is artificial and only thinly veils anti-Jewish prejudice. To some Jews, however, it is a reasonable and even acceptable perspective. This attitude is reinforced by the respectability that anti-Semitic charges command in Argentina. The natural reaction of many Jews is to drift further from a heritage they perceive as stigmatized.

University-centered currents of nationalism and radicalism further undermine Jewish identity. The implacable hostility of left-wing groups toward Israel exerts tremendous pressures on young Jews to prove their exclusively Argentine loyalties. A Jewish Perónist expressed the attitudes of many Jewish students in declaring, "The new society has no room for Jews or Zionists."

Not only have many Jews succumbed to the appeal of the university leftist movements, but they have also influenced them in a major way. Jews form more than one-sixth of the university student body, a proportion eight times as great as their percentage of the general population. Their representation in student government is even more pronounced, reflecting an intense concern with social problems. According to a recent survey of students at the University of Buenos Aires, Jews maintain more strongly than non-Jews (58 percent to 30 percent) that student participation in university government is essential to preserve its democratic character. Over half the Jewish students (56 percent) believe that the universities should assume active positions on the country's political issues, compared with one-third of the non-Jewish students.[8]

The political activism of these youths appears to accelerate their alienation from all things Jewish. In talking with many students, I learned that a majority saw Judaism not only as an accident in their lives but as a barrier to social justice.

These Jews, naïvely idealistic and alienated from their heritage, readily enter crusades to cleanse the world, beginning in the streets of Jerusalem. One of the brightest Jewish students I met was a biochemist named Natalio. We disagreed on whether one could be both a good Jew and a patriotic radical, and he explained to me intently, "We are fighters for the legitimate rights of the Third World. Israel is not a part of this world, but rather a threat to it. So to claim you are a Zionist and an Argentine is hypocritical."

Another student, perceiving my discomfort at such polemic, softened the approach, "Suppose I call myself Jewish. I am still Argentine, that is the way I feel. There are so many important issues to work for, how will calling myself Jewish help me to accomplish any of these things?"

These attitudes are often reinforced by an astounding optimism about the nature of Argentine society that tends to make one forget the innumerable terrorist groups, the virulent propaganda of the powerful Arab League, and the fact that almost half the incidents of anti-Semitism in the world occur in Argentina alone. A second-year university student told me, "There is not real anti-Semitism among youth, and anti-Semitism as a whole is diminishing across the nation. Religion is less important than it was. We are all Argentines; we will eventually merge into one people."

Occasionally, Jewish students admitted that anti-Semitic feeling did exist, even at the university, but mitigating explanations generally followed. One of the leaders of a student political group at the University of Buenos Aires said, "Not every organization wants Jews, it is true—at least as leaders—but we must realize that our real enemy is on the right. Tacuara and their kind are really rightists and these are the most violent and the most anti-Semitic. The Left is only against Israel." I suggested that this might still inflame anti-Semitic feelings among Argentines who could not sharply distinguish Jews from Zionists. "We are not denouncing a people, but a state of mind that leads to imperialism," one of my listeners corrected me. "Obviously there is danger of confusion, but only as long as many Jews insist on blindly following Israel."

Even among those who belong to Jewish organizations, radical influences have eroded support for Jewish causes. At the community's celebration of Israel's twenty-fifth anniversary, in May 1973, the speaker of honor, Itzhak Navon, a member of the Israel Knesset (now president of Israel), suddenly had to confront some 5,000 disruptive youths. Most were left-wing members of the leading Zionist youth organization, Confederation of Argentine Jewish Youth, who opposed Israeli "intransigence" on Middle East peace negotiations. These youth booed Navon, while their spokesman charged the local organizations with "communal bureaucracy" and demanded "a just peace based on the evacuation of all occupied territory." The dissidents tossed leaflets into the stadium that proclaimed "the right of the Palestinians to self-determination."[9] What made the incident particularly agonizing to the community's leaders was that these were youth who identified themselves as Zionists. For what then could they hope from the many thousands more who did not?

The alienation of youth from Judaism is most easily discerned in the membership statistics of Jewish organizations. Of some 90,000 Jewish youth in greater Buenos Aires, less than 10 percent belong to any community institution. Even this small figure declines among university youth, where only a tiny fraction (4.3 percent) are members of Zionist organizations and very few more (5.8 percent) join Jewish groups of any kind. (See Table 18.)

The community appears woefully unprepared to wage the mas-

281

Table 18: Jewish Youth in Buenos Aires, 1971

Age Group	Number of Youths (in thousands)	Proportion of All Jewish Youths (in percent)	In Zionist Groups (in percent)	In All Jewish Groups (in percent)
10 to 14	26	29	8.5	12.7
15 to 18	22	25	13.3	15.8
19 to 25	39.6	45	2.6	3.6

SOURCE: Adapted from Bernardo Kligsberg, "La juventud judía en la Argentina, *Nueva Sión,* (special edition), September 1971, p. 2.

sive campaign needed to retain the loyalty of the succeeding generation. Yet it has had sufficient warning. Following a flush of enthusiasm for Israel in the first years of the Jewish State, it became apparent that the pioneering spirit among some Argentine Jews had not been effectively translated into a mass youth interest in Judaism. Rather, the Zionist "pioneer" groups remained isolated currents of activity in a general atmosphere of indifference to Jewish life. The situation was distilled by David Roizin in 1963 when he stated: "Our children generally have only a vague notion of the history of the Jewish people," and as they grow up they drift from Judaism through inertia and the demands of general studies and earning a living. Worst of all, the community "is doing little or nothing to attract the university students among us."[10]

The AMIA's attempts to combat these trends proved more impressive in the planning than in reality. In 1958 it created the Youth Department to promote Zionist, educational, and cultural activities. Not until 1961, however, did the department hire more than two regular youth counselors for their entire network of programs. This absence of trained leaders frequently resulted in the separation of youth activities from any Jewish content.

The AMIA restructured the programs and created a Youth Counselor Corps in 1962, but the basic weaknesses of its earlier approach persisted. An AMIA report in 1963 conceded that some organizations were even opposed openly to all Jewish culture or else showed "a surprising lack of comprehension regarding the reality of Israel."[11]

Funding problems exacerbate this already difficult situation. Despite the flurry of activity to create strong Jewish youth groups, the AMIA subsidies in 1970 to its Youth Department and all other youth programs barely reached 1 percent of its expenditures.[12] Moreover, when the educational system passed from crisis to catastrophe during the 1970s, the subsequent drain on community funds made tenuous even the low level of expenditures for youth work and other marginal priorities. This has contributed to a decrease in the number of youths in Jewish organizations and to the closing of numerous centers, most acutely affecting the crucial nineteen-and-over age group.

The failure of the youth institutions to coordinate activities in more than a minimal way continues to frustrate community officials. Paúl Warszawski, the young and very able assistant director of the World Jewish Congress in Argentina, said that

the youth panorama of Jewish life is a shambles. You have many institutions, pioneer movements, centers for youth, even the Youth Department and general institutions and God knows what, but the central roof body is very poor, it is eroded from the internal contradictions of all the youth groups. The administration of all these outer forces is not at all efficient.[13]

The Confederation of Argentine Jewish Youth, with representatives from all non-Communist youth groups, is the most recent attempt to give some coherence to the Jewish youth movements. Thus far, however, it has proved to be only one more paper hierarchy that has not worked in practice. The president of the confederation declared in 1971, "The blindness of the community in the face of this [crisis] is nearly absolute."[14]

The situation, however, is far more complex than one-sided or even mutual myopia. Argentine Jewish leadership over the years has constituted a dazzling roster of eminent professionals, writers, educators, biochemists, and so forth. Most work for the community without financial compensation, motivated only by the ideals of service to the community and the preservation of Jewish culture. Even the most capable leaders, though, are vulnerable to blind spots when fundamental values are at issue. Leaders in such circumstances often find the proper blend of resolution and compromise, idealism and pragmatism a supremely taxing riddle.

As for the youth there remain a considerable number who have not been caught up in the anti-Zionist currents of the universities. While they have not absorbed the Yiddish-centered, Old

World Judaism of their parents, neither have they completely lost an attachment to Jewish identity. These "floating Jews," between the two worlds of assimilation and tradition, are beginning to transform—and perhaps to save—the commitment to Judaism in Argentina.

The growing pains of this regenerative process have been severe both for those older Jews committed to East European traditions and for their children who are not. Often differences have sparked passions more destructive than creative. The birth of Reform and Conservative religious movements during the 1960s in Argentina illustrates this tension. Both movements have been far more popular among the youth than have the traditional synagogues. Yet the Orthodox elements prevailing in the *kehillah* received the new Reform congregation very much like antibodies attacking a foreign germ. *Mundo Israelita,* the influential Spanish weekly, assailed the Reform Jews for "dividing the community" and warned that this new group threatened to lead the Jews into a new kind of Protestantism and assimilation. Other Jewish newspapers and officials reacted similarly toward this intruding element. Rabbi Rifat Sonsino of the main Reform Congregation, Emanuel, despaired that the attacks would ever let up "until the people with more liberal ideas can explain what Reform Judaism is all about. . . . But I myself find it very hard to discuss the question with the majority of Jews here. Most of them don't consider us Jews."[15]

Most outward signs of hostility toward the new liberal movements have subsided in recent years, but the suspicions of these transplanted denominations, with their American-dominated leadership, persist in some quarters. In particular, the phenomenal popularity of the young American-born rabbi, Marshall Meyer, proved unsettling to many in the Orthodox community. A young member of Rabbi Meyer's Temple Bet-El recalled, "Ever since he came here he has spoken Spanish to us and called us *ché* [an informal address used among close companions]." This sharp contrast with the exclusively Yiddish speech of most rabbis further accented the divisions between the newcomers and the established community.

The rejection of Yiddish by even those youth interested in Judaism has been especially painful to many in the elder generation. For American Jews, who tend to regard Yiddish with nostalgia but little more, such passions over the preservation of this language may seem strange. In Argentina, though, Yiddish far more than Hebrew has been so intertwined with Jewish identity that many older Jews practically equate Yiddish with Judaism itself.

The decline of Yiddish in Argentina has accelerated in recent years, but it began several decades ago. In 1940, a writer in the twenty-fifth anniversary issue of *Di Yidishe Tsaytung* admitted that even in "bulwarks of Yiddish, like Moisésville or the colonies of Entre Ríos, the youth employ Spanish more frequently than Yiddish."[16] In 1946, Pinhas Wald, the elder statesman of Jewish Socialists and a distinguished writer in Yiddish, noted that this language, as everywhere else in the Americas, was losing ground to the vernacular.[17] And in 1950, a Jewish school director lamented to a journalist in *Di Yidishe Tsaytung,* "Youth do not read Yiddish. The moment they leave school, they lose their interest for Yiddish books."[18]

During the 1960s it became clear that the future of Yiddish in Argentina was very dark. A study by the AMIA of Jews in a suburb of Buenos Aires and in a town in the interior revealed that Yiddish has a base of support only among foreign-born Jews. Among these immigrants, approximately 40 percent write Yiddish either exclusively or in addition to Spanish and occasionally Hebrew. However, among native-born heads of Argentine Jewish families, nearly 60 percent write only Spanish, and less than 1 percent write only Yiddish.[19]

The steady inroads made by Spanish into the community's readership are reflected in the publication of 75 percent more books on Judaism in Spanish than in Yiddish, throughout the decade of the sixties.[20] During the "Jewish Book Month" sale in 1970, the purchase of Yiddish books (1,654) ran a poor third to the popularity of Spanish (13,047) and Hebrew (4,426) publications.[21]

The gradual replacement of Yiddish with Hebrew instruction in most schools dealt an agonizing blow to the advocates of Yiddish. Whereas Yiddish instruction was long the heart of the curriculum in a great majority of schools, the upsurge of Zionist sentiment in the sixties gave Hebrew a new importance that could not be overlooked by Jewish educators, desperate to increase student attendance.

The Yiddishists did not execute a particularly graceful re-

285

treat. One paper, *Di Yidishe Tsaytung,* even suggested that the turnover to Hebrew in school curricula was motivated by the opportunity to exploit visitors to Israel. "Truly, Hebrew today is a necessity for tourists," the paper commented, "and for tourists it is nothing to add to the cost of ocean or air travel one additional expense."[22]

In addition to these strategically placed marksmen in the major journals, the Yiddishists also possessed a hard core of administrators and teachers who did not surrender the ideal of imparting Yiddish instruction, despite the changing trends. Rachel Hendler, director of the Theodore Herzl Day School, gave a thoughtful explanation of why her school maintained Yiddish as a central feature of the curriculum:

There is a great part of our past in Yiddish. To understand this Jewish past you must know Yiddish—for Sholem Aleichem, Peretz, Mendele. This literature was created by the people from Europe—who are we to change this? They are the ones who went through concentration camps and gas chambers. If we can learn English, Italian, and French in this country, why shouldn't we learn Yiddish, our own language.[23]

The staunch defenders of Yiddish resemble an army doomed to eventual defeat, but whose soldiers occupy the field's key ramparts and show no sign of peaceful withdrawal. Influential elder statesmen of the AMIA like Zalman Wassertzug have tenaciously battled over many decades for the supremacy of Yiddish in community affairs. As recently as 1972 the ceremony for changing the directorship of the AMIA was conducted entirely in Yiddish, and the great majority of community assemblies still employ the language of their East European forebears.

The frequent attacks on Yiddishists for alienating the Spanish-speaking Jewish youth have provoked reactionary attitudes from many of the leading Yiddish journalists. After some youth protested the use of Yiddish in a ceremony by the main federation of Argentine Jewish organizations in 1969, Wassertzug retorted in *Di Yidishe Tsaytung,* "Instead of battling the Arab League, the youth make a 'pogrom' against Yiddish." He concluded this blistering essay with the acidic question, "What do you think of the heroism of our youth?"[24] *Di Prese,* Argentina's other major Yiddish daily, referred to the youth who attacked Yiddish as "Zionists of the left," "a fifth column which wants to destroy Jewish life and the State of Israel."[25]

The simplest expression of defiance by the "Old Guard" came from the talented editor of *Di Yidishe Tsaytung,* Itzhak Zudiker. When I suggested that many young Zionists preferred to learn Hebrew rather than Yiddish, he responded, "Then they can go to Israel. In Argentina, Yiddish has been the language of the Jew."[26]

Aside from the wrenching rejection of Yiddish, the growth of a militant Jewish nationalism has been the most important trend among the minority of youths concerned with Judaism. Younger Zionists tend to resent the Argentine-centered outlook of "establishment" Zionism, with its emphasis on fund-raising rather than settlement in Israel. A member of a pioneer movement which trains for kibbutz life in Israel recently declared, "I prefer to have a non-Zionist as president of the Jewish community, so I can battle with him ideologically, rather than an inconsistent Zionist."[27]

The Zionist fervor of these youths seems to exclude a concern with other aspects of Jewish history and culture. Among those few youths who claim to keep some Jewish traditions, a greater proportion keep the Passover holiday than do their parents.[28] One explanatory hypothesis is that Passover, of the various Jewish holidays, is the most strongly Zionist, with its central theme of Jewish liberation and return to Israel and its promise of "Next year in Jerusalem!" By contrast, the youths have virtually discarded purely religious traditions like the Jewish Sabbath. Most of these younger Jews also have little interest in the terrible challenge of the Holocaust, which the older generation and even young American Jews have made great efforts to memorialize. One youth counselor explained to me, "To think so much about the past is masochistic. We want to look forward, our commitment is to Israel."

Even this minority of concerned Jews, however, is less angry than adrift. Their sense of isolation, compounded of outside social pressures and inner doubt, is heightened by the intransigence of some community leaders toward the "apostate" youth. Paúl Warszawski, in urging a new community orientation toward the younger generation, warned that many young people with positive feelings toward Judaism felt estranged from the community because "our communication system with the youth is nonexistent. Aside from *Mundo Israelita* and *Raíces* [a Zionist magazine, now defunct], you haven't any contact with them."[29]

Bernardo Vertibsky's tale, "The Visit," written more than a quarter-century ago, captures the tension endemic to the meeting of foreign-born and native Argentine Jews. The protagonists of the story are an old immigrant woman and her grandson, whom she reproaches in elegiac tones:

What your mother did wrong was to have taught you no Yiddish. It doesn't matter that you are native to this country, all the same one must know it; it doesn't matter that it won't aid you in the profession you study, but one must know it. It is more important than anything else. I cannot forgive her for making you into *goyim*. And what is more beautiful than being a Jew? But you don't know in what world you live, and it is all the same to you.

Roberto seethes with inner pain and anger at his grandmother's identification of discarded external routine with a disinterest in any Judaic essence:

He was wounded by all the incomprehension it implied. However great his own lack of understanding toward his grandmother, hers toward him was at least as great. It grieved him more, because intimacy established in their conversation had inspired a better disposition toward her and even a desire to speak with her and seek answers to many questions. . . . But how explain to her that he was not so far away [from Judaism] as she believed? How explain anything?[30]

This mood of earnest, but aimless, wandering is perhaps epitomized by a letter, written in the furtive tones of a Marrano by a youth from Rosario, that appeared in a recent issue of *Raíces:* "I would like you not to publish my name. I am fourteen years old and my parents did not send me to a Jewish school. I want to make up for this lack, beginning a correspondence with some youth of my age who lives in Israel and who writes and understands Spanish. Would this be possible?"[31]

The rootlessness of such Jewish youths inspired a writer for the World Jewish Congress to conclude, "We are witnessing the advent of a 'generation of the desert.' "[32] Unfortunately, though, his study blurred all youth into a single renegade "tribe," destined for rapid ethnic extinction. Possibly this too precipitous judgment was colored by the Yiddishist perspective of the author, who saw—cor-

288

rectly—that the East European Judaism of the older generation is irreversibly diminishing.

While many Jewish youths have been simply swallowed up by the Argentine "New Left," others—cut off from Jewish knowledge, institutions, and observance—are still groping intently for new and viable forms of Jewish expression. Whether the elements of militant Zionism, liberal religion, and ethnic pride coalesce into a revitalized Jewish heritage or whether the forces of ignorance, isolation, and inertia lead ultimately to assimilation is still speculative. But from its beginnings, Argentine Jewry has been a burning bush of the modern Jewish world. Observers and its own leaders have long predicted its imminent consumption by Argentine nationalism and cultural decay. Yet this community has continued to exist and even to grow in the midst of all its perils. It remains for the "generation of the desert," whose values and patterns are still evolving, to determine whether this miracle is truly enduring.

SOURCES,
BIBLIOGRAPHY,
NOTES,
AND INDEX

SOURCES

ARCHIVAL AND INTERVIEW

BUENOS AIRES

Jewish Institutions

Central
Asociación Mutual Israelita Argentina
Federación de Comunidades Israelitas Argentinas
Asociación Israelita Sefaradí Argentina

Political
Delegación de Asociaciones Israelitas Argentinas
Organización Sionista Argentina
Brit Igunim Halutzim Be-Argentina
Organización Sionista Sefaradí Argentina

Cultural
Comité Judío Americano (American Jewish Committee)
Congreso Judío Mundial (World Jewish Congress)
Sociedad Hebraica Argentina

Welfare
Asociación Israelita de Bikur Holim
Hogar Argentino de Huérfanas Israelitas
Hogar Infantil Israelita Argentino

Educational
Va'ad Ha-Hinuh Ha-Merkazi (Central Education Office)
Escuela Theodore Herzl
Escuela Sholem Aleichem
Instituto Superior de Estudios Religiosos Judaicos
Midrasha
Seminario Rabinico Latinoamericano

Libraries
Alberto Gerchunoff (Sociedad Hebraica Argentina)
Biblioteca Nacional
Instituto de Estudios Superiores Judaicos
Instituto Judío Argentino de Cultura e Información
YIVO (Yidisher Visenshaftlikher Institut) records

Synagogues
Ahiezer Hahadascha
Congregación Israelita
Congregación Sefaradí
Gran Templo
Leo Baeck, Culto Israelita de Belgrano
Tiferet Bahurim

Youth
Campaña Unida Juvenil
Campaña Unida Pro Israel
Confederación Juvenil Sionista
Consejo Juvenil Judeo Argentino
Hazak Ve'ematz
Halutz Lamerhav
Macabi

Women's Organizations
Organización Sionista Feminina Argentina (WIZO branch)
Sociedad de Damas Israelitas de la República Argentina

Publications
Candelabro
Davar
Editorial Israel
Eretz Israel
Di Yidishe Tsaytung
Índice
La Luz
Nueva Sión
Raíces

Jewish Leaders Interviewed

Marcos Barborosch, an official of the DAIA

Rabbi Isaac Schehebar, Grand Rabbi of the Sephardic community

Nissim Elnecavé, director of *La Luz,* Argentine representative of the London *Jewish Chronicle*

Catalina Epstein, president of OSFA (Argentine branch of WIZO)

Itzhak Glaser, an editor, *Di Yidishe Tsaytung*

SOURCES

Isaac Goldenberg, chairman of the Congreso Judío Mundial and former President of the DAIA

Moisés Goldman, former president of the DAIA during the Perón regime in the fifties

Rachel Hendler, director of the Escuela Theodore Herzl

Rabbi David Kahana, chief rabbi of the Ashkenazic community

Alberto Lañado, president of Alliance Israélite Universelle

Deborah Manassen de Lang, president of Sociedad de Damas Israelitas Argentinas

S. Lotterstein, vice president of the Comité Judío Americano (Argentine branch of the American Jewish Committee)

Asher Mibashan, editor-in-chief of *Candelabro* and of the *Revista Editorial Israel;* representative of the Jewish Telegraphic Agency

Daniel Neuman, chairman of Latin American Confederation of Jewish Youth; leader in the Uruguayan Jewish community

Moshe Reskin, director of the Zionist youth organization, Halutz Lamerhov

Moshe Roit, editor of *Raíces*

Daniel Rubenstein, president of Tiferet Bahurim

Lázaro Rubinson, president of Organización Sionista Argentina

Lázaro Schallman, director of the Midrasha Library and historian of the Argentine Jewish community

Itzhak Tsudiker, an editor, *Di Yidishe Tsaytung*

Marc Turkow, president of the Congreso Judío Mundial

Paúl Warszawski, assistant secretary (director) of the Congreso Judío Mundial

Zalman Wassertzug, director of Federación de Comunidades Israelitas Argentinas and noted Yiddish essayist

INTERIOR COMMUNITIES

Rosario

Institutions

World Jewish Congress in Rosario, the equivalent of the DAIA, serves as the political arm of the Jewish community in Rosario

Asociación Israelita de Beneficencia, the equivalent of the AMIA, serves as the social organization of the community

Sociedad Hebraica Argentina de Rosario, supervises education, culture, and youth organizations

Vida Rosarina, the Jewish publication of Rosario

Interviews

Martin Lapidus, president of the DAIA and World Jewish Congress in Rosario

Sr. Segalovich, director of Asociación Israelita de Beneficencia

Rabbi David Eliezer Tabbachnik, the sole rabbi in the interior communities in 1972

Córdoba

Institutions

Central Unión Israelita

Asociación Sionista Theodore Herzl

Sociedad Hebraica de Córdoba

World Jewish Congress in Córdoba

Interviews

N. Goldman, president of the Central Unión Israelita

Daniel Chelmus, vice president of the Central Unión Israelita

Srs. Andersman and Kenanstein, directors of the Asociación Sionista Theodore Herzl

Natalio Kirchuk, director of the Sociedad Hebraica de Córdoba

SOURCES
Mendoza

Institutions

Beth Israel (synagogue)

Chaim Nachman Bialik Library

DAIA branch in Córdoba

Jewish Memorial Grounds

Macabi Summer Camp

Sociedad Israelita de Beneficencia

Interviews

Abraham Ofnaim, director of the Chaim Nachman Bialik Library

Raul Marchevsky, founder and Director of Sociedad Israelita de Beneficencia

Tucumán

Sociedad Unión Israelita de Tucumán

UNITED STATES

Archives and Libraries

American Jewish Archives on the Cincinnati campus of Hebrew Union College–Jewish Institute of Religion

American Jewish Committee in New York, Blaustein Library

Brandeis University, Goldfarb Library

Harvard University, Widener Library

Interviews

Rabbi Menachem Blum (March 1973, by telephone)

Mrs. Amram Blum (February 1975, conducted by Robert Murciano in Cleveland)

Jacobo Kovadloff (August 1977, in New York; November 1977, by telephone)

BIBLIOGRAPHY

The following bibliography is a selective list of the studies on Argentine Jewry that were of value in preparing this book. General works on Latin America, other Jewish communities, and Judaism are not included here; where such works make a specific contribution to this volume, they are fully credited in the Notes to the text.

Because the bibliography categorizes works solely by subject, the following may help guide the reader who wishes to select sources according to language: unmarked bibliographical references are in English; others are in Spanish (Sp.), Yiddish (Yidd.), and Hebrew (Heb.) and are so marked.

The reader who seeks a more extensive listing of titles on Argentine Jewry will profit by checking the references in three dissertations on the early community, two by Victor A. Mirelman and the other by Bernard D. Ansel (all three are fully cited below, in the section on Origins). Also recommended is the excellent detailed bibliography by Lázaro Schallman, "Fuentes de investigación sobre el judaismo argentino (bibliografía, archivos, y hemerotecas)," *Primera conferencia de investigaciones y estudiosos judeo-argentinos en el campo de las ciencias sociales y la historia,* Buenos Aires: AMIA, 1961. Schallman's work takes the reader through the major Spanish and Yiddish sources until the late 1950s. The reader is also invited to observe the references given in the Notes to the present volume, which include numerous specialized articles omitted in the bibliography.

The following abbreviations are used in the Bibliography and Notes:

Annals. The volumes of Yiddish and Spanish articles, editorials, and statistical studies on Argentine Jewry prepared and published by the Asociación Mutual Israelita Argentina (AMIA). The four volumes cited extensively in this study appear under slightly varying titles: in 1953 *(Anuario—vida comunitaria judía, 1953–1954)*; 1954 *(Anuario—vida comunitaria judía, 1954–1955)*, 1963 *(Cinco años de vida comunitaria judía, 1958–1962)*; and 1969 *(Anales de la comunidad judía de Buenos Aires, 1963–1968)*. They are differentiated in the Bibliography and Notes as I (1953), II (1954), III (1963), and IV (1969) after the title, *Annals.*

CJLA. Comunidades judías de Latinoamérica. Published by the American Jewish Committee in Buenos Aires. Editions in 1952, 1966, 1968, 1970, and 1974.

DAIA. Delegación de Asociaciónes Israelitas Argentinas

Primera conferencia. Primera conferencia de investigaciones y estudiosos judeo-argentinos en el campo de las ciencias sociales y la historia. Buenos Aires: AMIA, 1961. This is a series of specialized reports in Spanish on aspects of Argentine Jewish history and culture.

ORIGINS

Ansel, Bernard. "The Beginnings of the Modern Jewish Community in Argentina, 1852–1891." Unpublished Ph.D. dissertation University of Kansas, 1969.

Argentina, 50 años de vida judía en el país (also known as *Yoyvel Bukh* of Di Prese). Buenos Aires: Di Prese, 1938 (Yidd.).

Avni, Haim. *Argentina: Ha-Aretz Ha-Ye'uda* (Argentine: The Promised Land. Baron de Hirsch's Colonization Project in the Argentine Republic). Jerusalem: Magnes Press, Hebrew University, 1973 (Heb.).

Cohen, Jacob X. *Jewish Life in South America: A Survey Study for the American Jewish Congress.* New York: Bloch Publishing Company, 1941.

Elkin, Judith L. "Goodnight, Sweet Gaucho: A Revisionist View of the Jewish Agricultural Experiment in Argentina," *American Jewish Historical Quarterly,* 67 (March 1978):208–23.

Lewin, Boleslao. *Cómo fue la inmigración judía a la Argentina.* Buenos Aires: Editorial Plus Ultra, 1971 (Sp.).

———. *Los judíos bajo la Inquisición en Hispanoamérica.* Buenos Aires: Editorial Dedalo, 1960 (Sp.).

Liebman, Seymour B. *The Inquisitors and the Jews in the New World.* Coral Gables: University of Miami Press, 1974.

———. *Historia del tribunal de la Inquisición de Lima* (1569–1820), 1887. Reprint ed., 2 vols., Santiago de Chile: Fondo Histórico & Bibliográfico J.T. Medina, 1956 (Sp.).

———. *El tribunal del Santo Oficio de la Inquisición en las provincias del Plata,*

1899. Reprint ed., Buenos Aires: Editorial Huarpes, 1945 (originally published 1899) (Sp.).

Mendelson, José, ed. *Cincuenta años de colonización judía en la Argentina.* Buenos Aires: DAIA, 1939 (Sp.).

Mirelman, Victor A. "The Early History of the Jewish Community of Buenos Aires, 1860–1892." Unpublished M.A. thesis in history, Columbia University, 1969.

———."The Jews in Argentina, 1890–1930, Assimilation and Particularism." Unpublished Ph.D. dissertation, Columbia University, 1973.

———. "Jewish Life in Buenos Aires Before the East European Immigration (1860–1890)." *American Jewish Historical Quarterly,* 67 (March 1978):195–207.

Monin, José. *Los judíos en América española 1492–1810.* Buenos Aires: Biblioteca Yavne, 1939 (Sp.).

Schallman, Lázaro. *Historia de los "pampistas."* Buenos Aires: Biblioteca Popular Judía, 1971 (Sp.).

Schvartzman, Pablo. *Judíos en América.* Buenos Aires: Instituto Amigos del Libro Argentino, 1963 (Sp.).

Tenembaum, Juan L. "Las colonias agricolas judías en la Argentina," *Primera conferencia* (Sp.).

Triwaks, Hirsch, ed. *Cincuenta años de vida judía en la Argentina* (also known as *Yoyvel Bukh* of *Di Yidishe Tsaytung*). Buenos Aires: Di Yidishe Tsaytung, 1940 (Yidd.).

Winsberg, Morton. *Colonia Baron Hirsch—A Jewish Agricultural Colony in Argentina.* University of Florida Monographs: Social Sciences, no. 19. Summer 1963.

———. "Jewish Agricultural Colonization in Argentina." *Geographical Review,* 54, no. 4 (October 1964):487–501.

———."Jewish Agricultural Colonization in Entre Ríos, Argentina," in 3 pts., in *American Journal of Economics and Sociology.* "Some Social and Economic Aspects of a Venture in Resettlement," pt. 1, 27, 3 (July 1968):285–96; "Religious-Oriented Social Institutions Amid East European Ghetto Culture," pt. 2, 27, 4 (October 1968):423–28; "Economic Problems of Townsmen Resettled on the Land," pt. 3, 28, 2 (April 1969): 179–91.

COMMUNITY

"Argentina." *CJLA* (1974):21–83 (Sp.).

Avni, Haim. *Yahadut Be-Argentina* (Argentine Jewry). Jerusalem: Institute for Contemporary Jewry, Hebrew University, 1972 (Heb.). An English version of Avni's work is "Argentine Jewry," 3 pts. *In the Dispersion* —no. 12 (1971):128–62; no. 13–14 (1971–72):161–208; and no. 15–16 (1972):158–215.

Beller, Jacob. *Jews in Latin America.* New York: Jonathan David, 1969.

Davis, Moshe. "Centres of Jewry in the Western Hemisphere: A Comparative Approach." *Jewish Journal of Sociology,* 5, no. 1 (June 1963):4–26.

Horowitz, Irving Louis. *Israeli Ecstasies, Jewish Agonies.* New York: Oxford University Press, 1974.

————."The Jewish Community of Buenos Aires." *Jewish Social Studies,* 24, (October 1962):195–222.

Katz, Moisés. "Marev Eyropeyishe Yiden in Argentina" (Jews from Western Europe in Argentina), *Annals,* II:221–25 (Yidd.).

Kitron, Moshe. "Yahadut America Ha-Dromit Ubayoteha" (Latin American Jewry and Its Problems). *Bi-Tfutzot Ha-Golah,* 30/31 (Winter 1964):148–66 (Heb.). A slightly modified English version of Kitron's article is "Latin American Jewry in Our Time," *In the Dispersion,* no. 4 (Winter, 1964–65):53–78.

Lerner, Natan. "La vida comunitaria judía en Buenos Aires," *Primera conferencia* (Sp.).

————. "A Note on Argentine Jewry Today." *Jewish Journal of Sociology,* 6 (July 1964):75–80.

Litvinoff, Boris. *A Peculiar People.* New York: Weybright and Talley, 1969.

Maidanik, Marcos, ed. *Sefer Argentina* (The Argentine Book). Buenos Aires: Darom, 1954 (Heb.).

Monk, Abraham, and Rogovsky, Eduardo. "Dos investigaciones del departamento de estudios sociales del Comite Judio Americano," *CJLA* (1966):125–31 (Sp.).

"La nupcialidad en la kehila de Buenos Aires, estudio estadístico." *Annals,* III:53–99 (Sp.).

Rogovsky, Eduardo, et al. *La comunidad judía de Tucumán, estudio estadístico.* Buenos Aires: AMIA, 1963.

Rogovsky, Eudardo et al. "Estudio de actitudes, intereses, y opiniones de asociados a la Sociedad Hebraica Argentina," *CJLA* (1968):233–37. (Sp.).

Rosenswaike, Ira. "The Jewish Population of Argentina: Census and Estimate, 1887–1947," *Jewish Social Studies,* 22, no. 4 (October 1960):- 195–214.

Shatzky, Jacob. "Argentina," *CJLA* (1952):9–63.

Singer, Isaac Bashevis. "Di Kehila in Buenos Aires Is an Iberashung" (The Jewish Community of Buenos Aires Is Surprising), *Annals,* III:583–84 (Yidd.).

BIBLIOGRAPHY

SECULAR JEWISH CULTURE

Zionism

Herbst, Mordecai. *A Halber Yor Hundert Natsionale Geselshaftlikhe Arbayt 1905–1955* (Fifty Years of Communal Activity). Pamphlet issued by the Sociedad Unión Israelita Sionista de Santa Fe, n.d. (Yidd.).

Kitron, Moshe, "La aliya Latinoamericana en Israel," *CJLA* (1968):-143–55 (Sp.).

Kligsberg, Bernardo. "Sionismo y judaismo en la década del 70," *Nueva Síon,* 513 (March 10, 1970), supplement special edition no. 12, *La Comunidad judía en la Argentina* (Sp.).

Mibashan, Abraham. "Tsionism in Argentina," *Annals,* II:63–95 (Yidd.).

Regalsky, Marcos. "Politishe Shtremungen un Parteyen in Argentiner Yishuv" (Political Movements and Parties in the Argentine Jewish Community), *Yoyvel Bukh (Di Yidishe Tsaytung).* Buenos Aires: Di Yidishe Tsaytung, 1940, pp. 537–62 (Yidd.).

Judaic Literature

Amdurer, A. "Fertsik Yor YIVO in Argentina" (Forty Years of YIVO in Argentina). *Annals,* IV:434–40

Bronstein, Zvi. "Tsu der Geshikhte fun der Hebrayisher Bevegung in Argentina" (On the History of the Hebrew Movement in Argentina), *Annals,* IV:367–387 (Yidd.).

Horn, José. "In Yidishen Teater fun Buenos Aires" (Yiddish Theatre in Buenos Aires), *Annals,* IV:388–400 (Yidd.).

Kovadloff, Jacob. "La Sociedad Hebraica Argentina de Buenos Aires," *CJLA* (1966):180–85 (Sp.).

Regalsky, Marcos. "Beitrog tsu der Geshikte fun dem Eldsten Yidish Argentinishen Orgen," (Contribution to the History of the Oldest Organ of Jewish Opinion), *Annals,* II:281–296 (Yidd.).

Schallman, Lázaro. "Historia del periodismo judío en la Argentina," *CJLA* (1970): 149–73.

"Yidish Teater in Argentina," *Annals,* III:522–32.

RELIGION

"La Congregación Israelita de la república Argentina," *CJLA* (1970): 174–81.

Elnecavé, Nissim. "Radiografía de la vida religiosa judía en la Argentina," *La Luz,* 45, no. 1,000, supplement (March 1970):13–19 (Sp.).

Kahana, David. "Der Religezer Matsov in Argentina," (Religious Life in Argentina), *Annals,* IV:566–93 (Yidd.).

303

Meyer, Marshall. "Una decada de judaismo conservador en Latino-américa," *CJLA* (1970):182–93 (Sp.).

Rosenberg, Shalom, and Rubinstein-Novick, Daniel. "Instituciones y tendencias de la vida religiosa judía en la Argentina," *Annals,* IV:111–54 (Sp.).

Sonsino, Rifat. "La Congregación Emanu-el," *CJLA* (1968):221–26 (Sp.).

EDUCATION

Berlson, Meyer. "Yidish Shul Vezen in Provints in de Letste Finif Yor," (Jewish Education in the Interior in the Last Five Years), *Annals,* IV:509–22 (Yidd.).

Blejer, Abraham. "Problemas propios de la educación judía en el interior del país," *Primera conferencia* (Sp.).

Kaplanski de Caryevschi, Teresa. *La educación judía en la Argentina en 1970.* Buenos Aires: AMIA, 1971 (Sp.).

Rinkowitz, Yehezkel. "Perakim Le-Toldot Ha-Hinuh Ha-Yehudi Be-Argentina" (Chapters in the Development of Jewish Education in Argentina), *Sefer Argentina,* edited by Marcos Maidanik. Buenos Aires: Darom, 1954, pp. 105–54 (Heb.).

Sneh, Simha. "La red escolar judía en la república Argentina," *CJLA* (1968):129–42 (Sp.).

de Winter, Olga M. "La educación judía en la Argentina," *CJLA* (1966):-133–50 (Sp.).

Yagupsky, Máximo. "Di Yidishe Dertsiung in di Koloniyes un Provintsen" (Jewish Education in the Colonies and Provinces), *Yoyvel Bukh (Di Yidishe Tsaytung).* Buenos Aires: Di Yidishe Tsaytung, 1940, pp. 445–58.

SEPHARDIM

Elnecavé, David. "Los sefaradim en el mundo y en la Argentina," *Annals,* IV:181–86 (Sp.).

Elnecavé, Nissim. "Yehudim Sephardim Ba-Olam" (Sephardic Jewry in the World), *Bi-Tfutzot Ha-Golah,* 44/45 (Summer 1968):138–49 (Heb.).

———. "La comunidad sefaradí de habla española," *La Luz,* 45, no. 1,000 (March 13, 1970):39–40 (Sp.).

Issaev, Behor. "Los sefaraditas de Buenos Aires," *Annals,* II:11–18 (Sp.).

———. "La colectividad sefaradí bonaerense en el quinquenio 1958–1962," *Annals,* III:46–49 (Sp.).

"Mesa redonda sobre al tema: Puede promoverse un renacimiento en la vida judeo-sefaradí y como?", *La Luz,* no. 760 (September 23, 1960):-44–51 (Sp.).

Pessah, Alberto. "La asociación comunidad Israelita sefaradí de Buenos Aires," *CJLA* (1970):194–96 (Sp.).

Sidicaro, Luis. "La comunidad sefaradí de habla española," *CJLA* (1970):-197–202 (Sp.).

ACCULTURATION

General

Liebermann, José. *Los judíos en la Argentina.* Buenos Aires: Editorial Libra, 1966.

Economic

Benario, M. "Di Geshikhtlikhe Entviklung fun Yidishen Handel un Industrie in Buenos Aires" (The Historical Development of Jewish Commerce and Industry in Buenos Aires), *Yoyvel Bukh (Di Yidishe Tsaytung).* Buenos Aires: Di Yidishe Tsaytung, 1940, pp. 267–90 (Yidd.).

Kaplan, Isaac. "A Bisel Geshikhte fun Yidisher Kolonizatzye Un Freier Kooperatsiye," (Some History of the Agricultural Colonization and on the Free Jewish Cooperatives), *Annals,* II:167–89(Yidd.).

Scheps, Abraham. "El aporte judío a la economia argentina," *Primera conferencia* (Sp.).

Zudiker, Itzhak. "Unsere Kredit Kooperatives un Zeyer Entviklung far de Letste Yoren" (Our Credit Cooperatives and Their Development in Recent Years), *Annals*, IV:310–22 (Yidd.).

Literary

Horn, José. "Dos Yidishe Kultur Lebn in Argentina" (Jewish Cultural Life in Argentina), *Yoyvel Bukh (Di Yidishe Tsaytung).* Buenos Aires: Di Yidishe Tsaytung, 1940, pp. 459–78.

Kantor, Manuel. *Alberto Gerchunoff.* Buenos Aires, 1969 (Sp.).

Koremblit, Bernardo Ezequiel. "Cuatro escritores judíos en la literatura argentina," *La Luz,* 45, no. 1,000, supplement (March 13, 1970):-28–30 (Sp.).

Nesbit, Louis. "The Jewish Contribution to Argentine Literature," *Hispania,* 33, no. 4 (November 1950):313–19.

Santander, Silvano. "Tres personalidades judeo-argentinas," *Annals,* IV, 75–80 (Sp.).

Schallman, Lázaro. "La problemática de la literatura y el Periodismo judíos en el idioma del país," *Primera conferencia.* (Sp.).

Walsh, Donald. "César Tiempo: Argentine Poet," *Commentary,* 2, no. 1 (July 1946):51–57.

Weinfeld, Eduardo, ed. *Tesoros del judaismo,* X, *América Latina.* Mexico City: Editorial Judaica Castellana, 1959 (Sp.).

Zhitnitzky, L. "Der Yidisher Onteyl in der Argentinisher Kultur Kunst, un Visenshaft" (Jewish Participation in Argentine Culture, Art, and Science), *Annals,* III:477–512 (Yidd.).

Political

Dickmann, Enrique. *Recuerdos de un militante socialista.* Buenos Aires, 1949 (Sp.).

Solominsky, Nahum. *La semana trágica.* Buenos Aires: World Jewish Congress of Latin America, 1971 (Sp.).

Wald, Pinhas. "Yidisher Arbeter Bevegung in Argentina" (Jewish Workers Movement in Argentina), *Annals,* II:109–43 (Yidd.).

TOLERATION AND ANTI-SEMITISM

Adin, Julio. "Nationalism and Neo-Nazism in Argentina," *In the Dispersion,* 5/6 (Spring 1966):133–61.

Dulfano, Mauricio J. "Anti-Semitism in Argentina: Patterns of Jewish Adaptation," *Jewish Social Studies,* 31, no. 2 (April 1969):122–44.

Elnecavé, Nissim. "Hay un antisemitismo en profundidad—pero es intocable," in *La Luz,* three pts.: 41, no. 1,034 (July 16, 1971):5–11; 41, no. 1,035 (July 30, 1971):20; 41 no., 1,036 (August 13, 1971): 9–10 (Sp.).

Fischerman, Joaquin. "Etnocentrismo y antisemitismo," *Indice,* no. 1 (December 1967):17–24. (Sp.).

Germani, Gino. "Antisemitismo ideologico y antisemitismo tradicional," *Comentario,* 9, no. 34 (December 1962): 55–63 (Sp.).

Horowitz, Irving Louis. "Jewish Ethnicism and Latin American Nationalism," *Midstream,* 18, no. 9 (November 1972):22–28.

Perón, Juan. *El pensamiento del Presidente Perón sobre el pueblo judío.* Buenos Aires: DAIA, 1954 (Sp.).

Pichon-Rivière, Enrique. "Los prejuicios raciales en la Argentina." *Nueva Sión* (January 31, 1964) (Sp.).

Sebreli, Juan José. *La cuestión judía en la Argentina.* Buenos Aires: Editorial Tiempo Contemporáneo, 1971 (Sp.).

Viamonte, Carlos Sánchez. "La ofensiva antisemita," *Comentario,* 9, no. 33 (1962):3–6 (Sp.).

YOUTH AND TRANSITION

Avni, Haim. *Ha-No'ar Ha-Yehudi Ba-Universita* (Jewish Youth in the University). Jerusalem: Institute of Contemporary Jewry, Sprinzak Division, Hebrew University of Jerusalem, 1971 (Heb.).

"Comunidad judía: el 'establishment' y los rebeldes," *Raíces,* 2, no. 20 (July 1970):62–63 (Sp.).

"Cuatro años de labor del departamento de juventud de la kehila," *Annals,* III:31–34.

Elnecavé, Nissim. "La vida judía en el país: cómo será la comunidad judía en 1990?" *La Luz,* 41, no. 1,036 (August 13, 1970): 18–19 (Sp.).

Goldenberg, Isaac. "La decada del setenta en un continente en proceso de cambio: America Latina—las comunidades judías en el interrogante." Buenos Aires: World Jewish Congress, special edition no. 3, June 1972 (Sp.).

Kligsberg, Bernardo. "La juventud judía en la Argentina." *Nueva Sión,* special edition (September 1971) (Sp.).

Primera conferencia sobre identidad e identificación judía (based on an earlier survey by David Nasatir). Buenos Aires: American Jewish Committe, 1965 (Sp.).

"Qué clase de judí o quiere que sea mi hijo?" Buenos Aires: American Jewish Committee, 1971 (Sp.).

Rogovsky, Eduardo and Kovadloff, Santiago. "El problema generacional." *Annals,* IV:83–89 (Sp.).

Roizin, David. "Acercamiento de la juventud a la vida judía." *Annals,* III: 28–30 (Sp.).

Senkman, Leonardo. "Problemática de las nuevas generaciones del ischuv." *Annals,* IV:90–102 (Sp.).

NOTES

CHAPTER ONE

1. José Toribio Medina, *El tribunal del Santo Oficio de la Inquisición en las provincias del Plata* (1889; reprint ed., Buenos Aires: Editorial Huarpes, 1945) pp. 175–202, details the life and trial of Francisco Maldonado de Silva. An account in English of the martyrdom is provided by George Alexander Kohut, "The Trial of Francisco Maldonado de Silva," in *The Jewish Experience in Latin America,* Martin Cohen, ed., 2 vols. (Waltham: American Jewish Historical Society, 1971), II, pp. 39–55. The text quotations of de Silva's statements are based on the records of the Inquisition as reprinted in Medina, *Historia del tribunal de la Inquisición de Lima,* 2 vols. (1887; reprint ed., Santiago de Chile: Fondo Histórico y Bibliografico J. T. Medina, 1956, originally published in 1887), II, pp. 131–32.
2. Solomon Ibn Verga, *Shebet Yehudah,* ed. A. Shohat, (Jerusalem, 1947), p. 38.
3. Yosef H. Yerushalmi, *From Spanish Court to Italian Ghetto: Isaac Cardoso a Study in Seventeenth-Century Jewish Apologetics* (New York: Columbia University Press, 1971), pp. 39–40.
4. Ibid., p. 2.
5. José Monin, *Los judíos en la America española, 1492–1810* (Buenos Aires: Biblioteca Yavne, 1939), p. 128 (hereafter cited as *Los judiós*).
6. Medina, *El tribunal,* p. 141ff., discusses the Portuguese settlement in this region and the Spanish reaction.
7. Boleslao Lewin, *Los judíos bajo la Inquisición en Hispanoamérica* (Buenos Aires: Editorial Dedalo, 1960), p. 31 (hereafter cited as *Los judios bajo*), reprints a typical report of this nature.
8. Monin, *Los judíos,* p. 127.

9. Boleslao Lewin, *Cómo fue la inmigración judía a la Argentina* (Buenos Aires: Editorial Plus Ultra, 1971), pp. 31–34 (hereafter cited as *Cómo fue*), narrates the martyrdom of Juan Acuña de Noroña. The Inquisition's summary of the case, reprinted in Medina, *Historia,* II, p. 31, records: "Juan Acuña de Noroña, Portuguese, native of Lamego in Portugal, resident of Santiago del Estero en Tucumán, 55 years old, merchant, of Jewish descent [tried] for Judaizing apostasy, a denier [of the Christian faith], impenitent, heretic, who denied the immortality of the soul: he was burned."

10. Lewin, *Cómo fue,* pp. 30–31, relates the case of Alvaro Rodríguez de Acevedo.

11. Ibid., pp. 40–41, gives an account of Vitoria's life. Julio Caro Baroja, *Los judíos en la España moderna y contemporánea,* 3 vols. (Madrid: Ediciones Arion, 1962), II, p. 243, details Vitoria's Jewish ancestry.

12. Lewin, *Cómo fue,* p. 27. See also Boleslao Lewin, *Los León Pinelo, la ilustre familia marrana del siglo xvii ligada a la historia de la Argentina, Peru, América y España* (Buenos Aires: Sociedad Hebraica Argentina, 1942), pp. 5–14 (hereafter cited as Los León Pinelo) and, by the same author, *Mártires y conquistadores judíos en la América* Hispana (Buenos Aires: Editorial Candelabro, 1954), pp. 216–35 (hereafter cited as *Mártires*).

13. Lewin traces the life of Diego de León Pinelo in *Cómo fue,* pp. 27–29; *Los León Pinelo,* pp. 26–40; and *Mártires,* pp. 236–53.

14. Ricardo Levene, *A History of Argentina,* ed. and trans. William Spence Robertson (Chapel Hill: University of North Carolina, 1937), p. 157.

15. Antonio de León Pinelo's exploits are succinctly recounted in Lewin, *Los León Pinelo,* pp. 15–25.

16. Relevant demographic figures may be found in José Ingenieros, *Argentina* (New York: Consul General of New York, 1967), p. 89.

17. Registro oficial de la República Argentina (Buenos Aires, 1879), vol. 3, p. 92, item 189:5. Also see vol. 1, p. 177, item 360.

18. James Scobie, *Argentina: A City and a Nation,* 2d ed. (New York: Oxford University Press, 1971), p. 98.

19. Emilio Ravignani, *Asembleas constituyentes argentinas* (Buenos Aires: Jacobo Peuser, 1939), vol. 6, no. 2, p. 668.

20. Bernard Ansel, "The Beginnings of the Modern Jewish Community in Argentina, 1852–1891," unpublished Ph.D. dissertation, University of Kansas, 1970, p. 11 (hereafter cited as "Beginnings"), citing *Boletín del instituto de investigaciones históricas,* 7 (1928):307.

21. Ansel, "Beginnings," pp. 33–39, outlines Hart's early career.

22. Pablo Schvartzman, *Judíos en América* (Buenos Aires: Instituto Amigos del Libro Argentino, 1963), pp. 104–5.

23. Ansel, "Beginnings," pp. 53, 55, casts doubt on Brie's military achievements, including his role at Caseros, if any, and his subsequent service in the Paraguayan war. Lewin, however, unreservedly credits Brie with military heroism and various honors, citing documents held by Brie's descendants, in *Cómo fue,* pp. 74–75.

24. Bernheim's story is recounted by Ansel, "Beginnings," p. 42. The writer also notes the paucity of definite evidence regarding Bernheim's career.

25. Schvartzman, *Judíos en América,* pp. 103–7, relates the careers of the members of the family Navarro.

26. Ibid., p. 106.

27. Lewin, *Cómo fue,* p. 59. Article One of the law states: "The Catholic priests and the chaplains and pastors of the reformed faiths are entrusted with the civil registers of the inhabitants of the State, writing in them the baptisms, births, marriages, and burials transpiring in each parish, or among the individuals belonging to the religious community."

28. The phrasing and historical context of the law implies that only Christian dissidents were to receive dispensations. The existence of well over 5,000 British Protestants in Argentina in the early nineteenth century, some of whom were merchants prominent in the national economy, was the primary spur to the Argentine government at the time it extended religious tolerance through special legislation. The issue of religious freedom for Englishmen in Argentina had long been a delicate subject between the two nations. See Henry Ferns, *Great Britain and Argentina in the Nineteenth Century* (Oxford: Clarendon Press, 1960), pp. 77, 125–26.

29. Lewin, *Los judíos bajo,* pp. 99–100.

30. Ibid., p. 100.

31. Victor A. Mirelman, "The Early History of the Jewish Community of Buenos Aires, 1860–1892," unpublished M.A. thesis, Columbia University, 1969, p. 15 (hereafter cited as "Early History").

32. Ibid., p. 23, citing Isaac S. Emmanuel, *Precious Stones of the Jews of Curaçao* (New York, Bloch 1957), passim, pp. 484–86. Mirelman notes that the Jewish community of Curaçao was the closest one to Argentina with its own rabbinic leader.

33. Boleslao Lewin, "Esbozo de la historia judía en la Argentina desde 1580 hasta 1889," Annals, IV:52

34. Ansel, "Beginnings," p. 106, citing "La primera boda júdia en Buenos Aires," *Judaica,* 5 (1937):185–89, reprinting Navarro-

Viola's account in 1868. The same article reveals the remarkable liberalism of Navarro-Viola. Though a pious Catholic intent on maintaining church dominion over civil registers, education, and cemeteries, he commented on the Levy case: "This is a laudable precedent, in which, without breaking any principle, or making any innovations more or less dangerous like civil marriage, the laws that regulate us were interpreted with dignity and equity."

35. Lewin, *Como fué,* p. 63.
36. Irving Louis Horowitz, *Israeli Ecstasies, Jewish Agonies* (New York: Oxford University Press, 1974), pp. 141–42.
37. Louis Greenberg, *The Jews in Russia—The Struggle for Emancipation,* 2 vols. in one (New Haven and London: Yale University Press, 1965), 1:84.
38. Leo Pinsker, *Auto-Emancipation,* trans. D.S. Blondheim (New York: Maccabaean Publishing Company, 1906), p. 7.
39. Henry J. Tobias, *The Jewish Bund in Russia—From its Origins to 1905* (Stanford: Stanford University Press, 1972), p. 164.
40. Ibid., p. 251.
41. Ibid., p. 249.
42. The letter is reprinted in its original English version as it appeared in the *Jewish Chronicle,* August 2, 1889, p. 6. Its author identified himself only as "A.E.F." See also Yacov Rubel, "Argentina, si o no? ecos de la inmigración judía a la Argentina en la prensa hebrea de Rusia entre 1888 y 1890," *CJLA* (1974):280–81.
43. Mirelman, "Early History," p. 62, citing the editorial "L'immigration Juive," in *L'Union Française,* August 20, 1881.
44. Lazaro Schallman, "Antecedentes históricos y sociales de la fundación de la A.M.I.A.," *Annals,* IV:29–30.
45. Samuel Joseph, *History of the Baron de Hirsch Fund* (Philadelphia: Jewish Publication Society, 1935), p. 13ff., recounts the inception of the Jewish Colonization Association.
46. Maurice de Hirsch, "My Views on Philanthropy," *North American Review,* 153, no. 416 (July 1891):2.
47. José Mendelson, Genesis de la colonia judía de la Argentina (1889–1892)," *Cincuenta años de colonización judía en la Argentina,* ed. José Mendelson (Buenos Aires: Delegación de Asociaciones Israelitas Argentinas, 1939), p. 116. Also see Henry Joseph's account in the *Jewish Chronicle,* December 20, 1889, p. 8.
48. B. Stulbach, "Di Kehila fun Buenos Aires un ire Tetikeytn oyfn Religezengebit," (The Kehillah of Buenos Aires and Its Activity in the Sphere of Religion), *Annals,* III:236–37.

49. Lewin, *Cómo fue,* pp. 64–65.
50. Abraham Vermont, "Este trio ridiculoso," *La Voz del Pueblo,* June 17, 1905, cited in Ansel, "Beginnings," pp. 84–85. Vermont's career is charted by Lázaro Schallman, "Historia del periodismo judío en la Argentina," *CJLA* (1970):149–51.
51. Ansel, "Beginnings," p. 85, citing a letter by Joseph to the president of the *Congregación Israelita,* dated October 13, 1894.
52. Ibid., p. 60.
53. "La Congregación Israelita de la República Argentina," *CJLA* (1970): 176.
54. *Enciclopedia judaica castellana* (Mexico City: Editorial Judaica Castellana, 1948), 1:438.
55. Gregorio Vertibsky, *Rivera afán de medio siglo* (Buenos Aires, 1955), p. 122.
56. Lázaro Liacho, "La Tierra," *Tesoros del judaismo: América Latina,* ed. Eduardo Weinfeld (Mexico City: Editorial Judaica Castellana, 1959), p. 178.
57. Shalom Rosenberg and Daniel Rubinstein-Novick, "Instituciones y tendencias religosas de la comunidad judía en la Argentina," *Annals,* IV:116.
58. Morton Winsberg, *Colonia Barón Hirsch,* University of Florida Monographs: Social Sciences, no. 19, Summer 1963, p. 19 (hereafter cited as *Colonia Barón Hirsch).*
59. Juan Tenembaum, "Las colonias agricolas judías en la Argentina," *Primera conferencia,* is the primary source of information for the section on administration of the colonies. Tenembaum earlier gained national prominence as a specialist in designing scientific techniques of colony planning.
60. *Enciclopedia judaica castellana,* 1:440–41.
61. Tenembaum, *Primera conferencia,* p. 34.
62. Ibid., p. 13.
63. Winsberg, *Colonia Barón Hirsch,* p. 60.
64. Winsberg, "Jewish Colonization in Argentina," *Geographical Review,* 54, no. 4 (October 1964):500.

CHAPTER TWO

1. "American Jews and Israel," *Time,* 105 (March 10, 1975)p. 23.
2. Abraham Duker, "The Problems of Coordination and Unity," *The American Jew: A Reappraisal,* ed. Oscar I. Janowsky, (Philadelphia: Jewish Publication Society, 1965), p. 338.
3. Jacob Shatzky, "Argentina," *CJLA* (1952):19.

4. Natan Lerner, "La vida comunitaria judía en Buenos Aires," *Primera conferencia,* p. 13.
5. "Report of the Special Body of Experts on Traffic in Women and Children," (Geneva: League of Nations Publications, 1927), pt. II, p. 12.
6. Ibid., p. 17.
7. Victor A. Mirelman, "The Jews in Argentina, 1890–1930, Assimilation and Particularism," unpublished Ph.D. dissertation, Columbia University, 1973, p. 354 (hereafter cited as "The Jews in Argentina").
8. Jacob Simon Liachovitzky, *Zamlbukh* (Buenos Aires, 1936), p. 89ff., cited in Mirelman, p. 138.
9. Michel Hacohen Sinai, "Harav Reuben Hacohen Sinai," *Schriften,* no. 3 (1945):180, cited in Mirelman, "The Jews in Argentina," p. 135.
10. League of Nations Advisory Commission for the Protection and Welfare of Children and Young People, Traffic in Women and Children Committee, Minutes of the Sixth Session, Annex 8 (Geneva: League of Nations Publications, 1927), p. 125.
11. League of Nations, Traffic in Women and Children Committee, Minutes of the Tenth Session, Annex 7 (Geneva: League of Nations Publications, 1931), pp. 78–79.
12. Ibid.
13. Ibid., p. 75.
14. Jacob X. Cohen, *Jewish Life in South America: A Survey Study for the American Jewish Congress* (New York: Bloch Publishing Company, 1941), p. 99 (hereafter cited as *Jewish Life in South America*), citing Malick, *Menorah Journal.*
15. League of Nations Advisory Committee on the Traffic in Women and Protection of Children, Minutes of the Fourth Session, Annex 6 (Geneva: League of Nations Publications, 1925), p. 76.
16. League of Nations Traffic in Women and Children Committee, Minutes of the Tenth Session, Annex 7 (Geneva: League of Nations Publications, 1931), pp. 75 ff.
17. Ibid., pp. 76–77.
18. Julio L. Alsogaray, *Trilogia de la trata de blancas (rufianes—policía—municipalidad),* 2d ed. (Buenos Aires: Editorial Tor, 1933), particularly pp. 136, 164–65.
19. DAIA archives, sections 1602 and 1603.
20. Juan C. Mendoza, *La Argentina y la swástica* (Buenos Aires: Victoria, 1941), pp. 65–68.
21. Mauricio Dulfano, "Anti-Semitism in Argentina: Patterns of Jewish

Adaptation," *Jewish Social Studies,* 31 no. 2 (April 1969):135, cites a telling example of the way even liberal Argentines tend to disregard the DAIA as a serious institutional force.

22. Haim Avni, *Yahadut Be-Argentina* (Argentine Jewry), in Hebrew (Jerusalem: Institute for Contemporary Judaism, Hebrew University, 1972), p. 43.
23. On the subject of demographic trends, see Ira Rosenswaike, "Jewish Population of Argentina, Census and Estimate, 1887–1947," *Jewish Social Studies,* 22, no. 4 (October 1960):195–214.
24. Ibid., p. 204.
25. Morton Winsberg, "Jewish Agricultural Colonization in Argentina," *Geographical Review,* 54, no. 4 (October, 1964):491.
26. *CJLA* (1974): 24–25.
27. Sidney Goldstein, "American Jewry, 1970: A Demographic Profile," *American Jewish Year Book,* 72 (1971):38.
28. Ibid., p. 35.
29. Pablo Schvartzman, *Judíos en América* (Buenos Aires: Instituto Amigos del Libro Argentina, 1963), pp. 111–22.
30. Alberto Gerchunoff's short story, "El médico milagroso," appears in his novel *Los gauchos judíos* (La Plata: J. Sesé, 1910).
31. A thorough account of Di Tella's accomplishments and attitudes is Thomas C. Cochran and Reuben E. Reima, *Capitalism in Argentine Culture—A Study of Torcuato Di Tella and S.I.A.M.* (Philadelphia: University of Pennsylvania Press, 1962).
32. "The Organized Jewish Community of Buenos Aires—A.M.I.A.," *Dispersion and Unity,* no. 11 (1970):154.
33. "Las actividades de algunas secciones de la AMIA," *Annals,* IV: 211–12. The Department of Social Aid also assisted other, "special" categories of people in need, as listed in these pages.
34. *CJLA* (1970):27. Also see José Liebermann, *Los judíos en la Argentina* (Buenos Aires: Editorial Libra, 1966), pp. 214–17 (hereafter cited as *Los judíos*).
35. Interview with Deborah Manassen de Lang, August 10, 1972.
36. Rosa Resnick, "Problemas relativos al bienestar social de la comunidad judía de la Argentina," *Primera Conferencia,* pp. 4–7.
37. Cohen, *Jewish Life in South America,* pp. 95–96.
38. Israel Louis Horowitz, "The Jewish Community of Buenos Aires," *Jewish Social Studies,* 24, no. 1 (October 1962):213, charts the German communal structure, based on information from *Zehn Jahre Aufbauarbeit in Südamerika/Diez Años de Obra Constructiva en América del Sud* (Buenos Aires: Asociación Filantrópica Israelita, December 1943).

39. Moises Katz, "Marev Eyropeyishe Yiden in Argentina" (Jews in Western Europe in Argentina), in Yiddish, *Annals,* II:221–25, is the primary source for information in this section on the German Jewish community.
40. Liebermann, *Los judíos,* p. 196.

CHAPTER THREE

1. Boleslao Lewin, *Cómo fue la inmigración judía en la Argentina* (Buenos Aires: Plus Ultra, 1971), pp. 80–81.
2. John R. Spear, *The Gold Diggings of Cape Horn* (New York: G. P. Putnam's Sons, 1895), pp. 9–10.
3. Pablo Schvartzman, *Judíos en América* (Buenos Aires: Instituto Amigos del Libro Argentino, 1963), p. 82, citing Armando Braun Menéndez, *Pequeña historia fuegina* (Buenos Aires: D. Viau y cía., 1959).
4. Iaacov Rubel, "Argentina, si o no? Ecos de la inmigración judía a la Argentina en la prensa hebrea de Rusia entre 1888 y 1890," *CJLA* (1974):276 (hereafter cited as "Argentina, si o no?").
5. Bernard Ansel, "European Adventurer in Tierra del Fuego: Julio Popper," *Hispanic American Historical Review,* 50, no. 1 (February 1970):107, explores the possible causes of Popper's death.
6. Boleslao Lewin, *Popper: Un conquistador patagónico—sus hazañas, sus esoritos* (Buenos Aires: Editorial Candelabro, 1967), pp. 74–76. López went so far as to commit his literary reputation to the claim: "There are pages in Popper which, without exaggeration, remind one of the best in Edgar Poe and Mark Twain."
7. Moshe Davis, "Centres of Jewry in the Western Hemisphere: A Comparative Approach," *Jewish Journal of Sociology,* 5, no. 1 (June 1963):12.
8. Walter Laqueur, *A History of Zionism* (New York: Holt, Rinehart & Winston, 1973) synthesizes the interplay of Zionist factions in Europe, while Abraham Mibashan, "Tsionism in Argentina," *Annals,* II: 63–95, details the factional struggles among Argentine Zionists (Yidd.).
9. *Immigration to Israel 1948–1972,* pt. I, Annual Data (Jerusalem: Central Bureau of Statistics, special series, no. 416, 1973), pp. 20–24, Table 4.
10. Haim Avni. *Yahadut Be-Argentina* (Argentine Jewry) (Jerusalem: Institute for Contemporary Jewry, Hebrew University, 1972), p. 95.

11. *Encyclopaedia Judaica,* 9:536.
12. The section on phases of *aliyah* is based largely on Moshe Kitron, "La alia latinoamericana en Israel, " *CJLA* 1968:145–48.
13. Figures for Argentine *aliyah* in recent years are based on a bulletin, dated November 2, 1977, from the Israel Aliya Center, Inc., sponsored by the World Zionist Organization. In the last five years, the rates of settlement have been: 2809 (1973); 1625 (1974); 892 (1975); 1616 (1976); and 1896 (through October 1977).
14. Moshe Kitron, "Yahadut America Ha-Dromit Ubayoteha" (Latin American Jewry in Our Time), in Hebrew, *Bitfutzot Hagola,* 30/31 (Winter 1964):165.
15. Ibid.
16. Interview with Lázaro Rubinson, July 10, 1972.
17. Ibid.
18. Interview with Moshe Roit, August 7, 1972.
19. Natan Lerner, "La vida comunitaria judía," *Primera conferencia,* pp. 19 ff.
20. Fay Grove-Pollack, ed., *The Saga of a Movement: WIZO 1920–1970* (Tel Aviv:WIZO 1970), p. 133.
21. Abraham Monk and Eduardo Rogovsky, "Dos investigaciones del departamento de estudios sociales del Comité Judío Americano," *CJLA* (1966):128.
22. See Shmuel Rollansky, "Dos Yidishe Gedrukte Vort un Teater in Argentina" (Yiddish Writing and Yiddish Theater in Argentina), *Yoyvel Bukh* (Buenos Aires: Di Yidishe Tsaytung, 1940), pp. 327–418, for an analysis of Yiddish literary trends.
23. This section draws extensively on "Yidish Teater in Argentina," *Annals,* III:522–32.
24. Lázaro Schallman charts the evolution of the Yiddish press in Argentina in "Historia del periodismo judío en la Argentina," *CJLA* (1970):149–61 in particular.
25. Ibid., p. 154.
26. Interview with Marc Turkow, August 14, 1972. The story of the Jewish council meeting is based on the author's observation.
27. José Liebermann, *Los judíos en la Argentina* (Buenos Aires: Editorial Libra, 1966), p. 110.
28. Lázaro Liacho, "La Tierra," *Tesoros del judaismo: América Latina,* ed. Eduardo Weinfeld (Mexico City: Editorial Castellana, 1959), pp. 177–80.
29. Lázaro Schallman, "La problemática de la literatura y el periodismo

NOTES FOR PP. 111–19

judíos en el idioma del pais," *Primera conferencia,* pp. 32ff. (hereafter cited as "La Problemática"; and Schallman, "Historia del periodismo judío en la Argentina," pp. 163–68, treat Spanish Judaic journals.
30. Interview with Nissim Elnecavé, July 17, 1972.
31. Schallman, "La problemática," p. 34.
32. Boleslao Lewin, written reply to biographical questionnaire, in American Jewish Archives of Union Theological Seminary, Cincinnati.
33. Jacobo Kovadloff, "La Sociedad Hebraica Argentina de Buenos Aires," *CJLA* (1966):180–85.
34. Ibid., p. 183.
35. Schallman, "La problemática," p. 32.

CHAPTER FOUR

1. Jacob Beller, *Jews in Latin America* (New York: Jonathan David, 1969), p. 167.
2. Abraham Monk and Eduardo Rogovsky, "Dos investigaciones del departamento de estudios sociales del Comité Judío Americano," *CJLA* (1966): 128 (hereafter cited as "Dos investigaciones").
3. Nissim Elnecavé, "Radiografía de la vida religiosa judía en la Argentina," *La Luz,* special edition (March 1970): p. 17 (hereafter cited as "Radiografia").
4. Enrique Dickmann, *Recuerdos de un militante socialista* (Buenos Aires: La Vanguardia, 1949), pp. 43ff.
5. Monk and Rogovsky, "Dos investigaciones," p. 128.
6. Jacob Shatzky, "Argentina," *CJLA* (1952): 36.
7. Elnecavé, "Radiografia," p. 16. See also Lázaro Friedman, "Tres principios fundamentales en nuestra actividad," *Annals,* III:20, noting the proclamation by an AMIA spokesman that the AMIA had recently spent 30,000,000 pesos to acquire land joined to the cemetery of Tablada, a reserve of nearly ten hectares, which purchase he described as "an initiative of supreme importance."
8. *CJLA* (1974):58.
9. David Kahana, "Der Religiezer Matsov in Argentina," *Annals,* IV: pp. 566ff. See also Shalom Rosenberg and Daniel Rubinstein-Novick, "Instituciones y tendencias religiosas de la comunidad judía en la Argentina, *Annals,* IV:118.
10. Elnecavé, "Radiografía," p. 17, lists the rabbis in Argentina in 1970, arriving at the following pattern: Orthodox Ashkenazic (11), Orthodox Sephardic (4), Conservative Ashkenazic (2), Conservative Sephardic (1), Reform Ashkenazic (3).

The above pattern corrects a printing error in *La Luz,* which resulted in the inversion of the terms *Orthodox* and *Conservative.* Despite minor changes in subsequent years, the list is still suggestive of the state of organized Jewish religion in Argentina.

11. "La Congregación Israelita de la República Argentina," *CJLA* (1970): 178.
12. *La Luz,* special issue, no. 1,000 (March 1970): 37, assesses Schlesinger's contribution to the development of the *kehillah.*
13. *Memoria del presidente de la AMIA* (Buenos Aires: AMIA, 1945).
14. The following material on Amram Blum is based on two major sets of sources: newspaper files of the DAIA; and interviews with community leaders and with friends and relatives of Rabbi Blum, including a son, Menachem, and Blum's widow. Community leaders who ventured opinions on Blum have been left anonymous in these pages, at their request.
15. This and all subsequent uncited statements by Rabbi Kahana are based on an interview conducted July 29, 1972.
16. "Las actividades de algunas secciones de la AMIA," *Annals,* IV:206.
17. Shatzky, p. 35.
18. Rubel, "Argentina, si o no?" p. 284, citing a letter by Peretz Faigenboim, a leader of the colony of Moisésville.
19. Moshe Davis, "Centres of Jewry in the Western Hemisphere: a Comparative Approach," *Jewish Journal of Sociology,* 5, no. 1 (June 1963):-15; and *La Luz,* special issue, no. 1,000 (March 1970):16.
20. Zalman Wassertzug, "La kehila de Buenos Aires y el Vaad Hakehilot," *CJLA* (1966):147.
21. "La Congregación Israelita de la República Argentina," *CJLA* (1970):175.
22. For background on Rabbi Marshall Meyer's early life (until 1963), see his written reply to an autobiographical questionnaire prepared for the American Jewish Archives, Cincinnati. Meyer gives an account of the development of Conservative Judaism in Argentina, in "Una década de judaísmo conservador en Latinoamérica," *CJLA* (1970):182–93.
23. Elnecavé, "Radiografía," p. 18.
24. Rifat Sonsino, "La Congregación Emanu-El," *CJLA* (1968):221–26.
25. Leon Klenicki, "Reform Judaism in Argentina, 1968, and Projects for 1969," p. 6, American Jewish Archives.
26. Leon Klenicki, "Reform Judaism in Argentina, 1969," p. 8, American Jewish Archives.
27. Elnecavé, "Radiografía," p. 19.
28. Klenicki, "Reform Judaism in Argentina, 1968," p. 9.

CHAPTER FIVE

1. Interview with Moisés Goldman, August 2, 1972.

2. Solomon Maimon, *Autobiography,* trans. J. C. Murray (London: East and West Library, 1954), pp. 31–32.

3. Shmarya Levin, *Childhood in Exile,* trans. Maurice Samuel (New York: Harcourt, Brace, and Co., 1929), p. 45.

4. Haim Avni, *Yahadut Be-Argentina* (Argentine Jewry) (Jerusalem: Institute for Contemporary Judaism, Hebrew University, 1972), p. 89 (hereafter cited as *Yahadut Be-Argentina*).

5. Jacob Shatzky, "Argentina, *CJLA* (1952):43.

6. Avni, *Yahadut Be-Argentina,* p. 89.

7. Ibid.

8. *Encyclopaedia Judaica,* 6:456. Also see Avni, *Yahadut Be-Argentina,* p. 87.

9. *American Jewish Year Book, 1966,* 67:289. (Volumes of the *American Jewish Year Book* hereafter cited as *AJY,* and date of publication.) Also see *AJY* (1967), p. 278.

10. Shatzky, "Argentina" p. 47; Shalom Rosenberg and Daniel Rubinstein-Novick, "Instituciones y vida religiosa judía en la Argentina," *Annals* IV:121 (hereafter cited as "Instituciones").

11. Shatzky, p. 47.

12. Shalom Rosenberg and Daniel Rubinstein-Novick, "Instituciones," p. 121.

13. Marshall Meyer, "Una década de judaísmo conservador en Latinoamérica," *CJLA* (1970):188.

14. Simha Sneh, "La red escolar judía en la República Argentina," *CJLA* (1968):138. Also see Secretaria de Estado de Cultura y Educación, *Argentina, la educación en cifras, 1958–1967* (Buenos Aires, 1967), p. 47 (hereafter cited as "La red escolar judía").

15. *Encyclopaedia Judaica,* 6:456.

16. Harold S. Himmelfarb, "Jewish Education for Naught: Educating the Culturally Deprived Jewish Child," *Analysis,* 51 (September 1975):3, 9.

17. Abraham Blejer, "Problemas de la educación judía en el interior," *Primera conferencia,* p. 21.

18. Shatzky, p. 30.

19. Interviews with N. Goldman and D. Chelmus of the Central Unión Israelita; Baruch Braznin, *Cincuenta años de vida comunitaria judía en Córdoba* (Córdoba: Central Unión Israelita, 1966), p. 20, surveys Córdoba's progress in Jewish education.

20. *La Luz,* 41, no. 1,036 (August 13, 1971):18.
21. *Encyclopaedia Judaica,* 6:456.
22. Avni, *Yahadut Be-Argentina,* p. 92.
23. *AJY* (1970), p. 375.
24. *AJY* (1967), p. 278.
25. Sneh, "La red escolar judía," p. 135.
26. Avni, *Yahadut Be-Argentina,* p. 93.
27. *AJY* (1972), p. 435.
28. *AJY* (1970), p. 375.
29. Teresa Kaplanski de Caryevschi, *La educación judía en la Argentina* (Buenos Aires: AMIA, 1971), p. 8 (hereafter cited as *La educación).*
30. Avni, *Yahadut Be-Argentina,* p. 94.
31. Kaplanski, *La educación,* p. 28, 52.
32. Ibid., pp. 8-9.
33. *AJY* (1963), p. 278.
34. *CJLA* (1974):38.
35. *AJY* (1972), p. 435.
36. Interview with a director in the AMIA (anonymity requested).

CHAPTER SIX

1. Jorge Luis Borges, *The Aleph and Other Stories, 1933–1969,* ed. and trans. Norman Thomas di Giovanni (New York: E. P. Dutton & Co., Inc., 1970), p. 204.
2. Scholars differ on the number of Sephardic Jews in Argentina. The figure of 70,000 cited, for example, in *CJLA* (1974): 24, is the most common estimate, but other sources place the number much higher. David Elnecavé, "Los sefaradim en el mundo y en la Argentina," *Annals,* IV:183 (hereafter cited as "Los sefaradim"), and his son Nissim, in various studies, conclude that 90,000 Jews of Sephardic descent live in Argentina, of which 85 percent are in the greater Buenos Aires area and 15 percent in the interior.
3. Charles de Foucauld, *Reconaissance au Maroc* (Paris: Challamel et cie, 1888), p. 394, cited in Andre Chouraqui, *Les Juifs D'Afrique du Nord* (Paris: Presses Universitaries de France, 1952), p. 93.
4. See, for example, Luis Sidicaro, "La comunidad sefaradí de habla española en Buenos Aires," *CJLA* (1970):199, in particular. For comparison with the Ashkenazic community, see "La nupcialidad en la kehila de Buenos Aires," *Annals,* III, 23:75.
5. Sidicaro, "La comunidad," pp. 199–200, challenges the widely held view that the Sephardim contain disproportionately greater numbers of extremely poor and very wealthy persons than do the Ashkenazim.

17. Isaac Kaplan, *Vadamecum,* edition in DAIA archives, section 1035, p. 15.
18. Liebermann, *Los judíos,* p. 132, citing a review by Julián Marías.
19. The section on music and fine arts is based wholly on secondary literature surveying these fields, in view of the author's lack of expertise in appraising such works. Liebermann, *Los judíos,* pp. 165–183, offers a useful nonspecialist's survey of notable Jewish painters and musicians.
20. Marsha Taylor, "The Jews of Argentina: Facing the Second Coming of Perón," *The Times of Israel,* 1, no. 4 (March 1974):18.
21. Pablo Schvartzman, *Judíos en América* (Buenos Aires: Instituto Amigos del Libro Argentino, 1963), p. 135 (hereafter cited as *Judíos en América*).
22. Schvartzman, *Judíos en América* pp. 129–39, is the primary reference for the section on Saslavsky, Also see Bernardo Feur and Kalman Saslavsky, in Yiddish, *Argentiner YIVO Shriften,* no. 4 (1947).
23. I. A. Horowitz and the eds. of Chess Review, *The Golden Treasury of Chess* (1943; reprint ed. New York: Cornerstone Library, 1969), p. 11. Also see Julio Ganzo, *Historia general de ajedrez* (Madrid: Ricardo Aguilera, 1966), pp. 147–49.
24. Marsha Taylor, pp. 14, 18.
25. "Political Parties in Argentine Compete for 'Jewish Vote' in Elections," *Jewish Telegraphic Agency Daily News Bulletin* (hereafter cited as *JTA*), February 17, 1958, p. 3.
26. "Argentine Jews Stress Absence of Collective 'Jewish Vote, in elections," *JTA,* February 14, 1958, p. 4.
27. Rodolfo Puiggrós, *Historia crítica de los partidos políticos argentinos,* 2 vols. (Buenos Aires: Jorge Álvarez, 1965), II, p. 209.
28. *Di Yidishe Tsaytung,* November 25, 1918; and *La Nación,* November 25, 1918.
29. For details of the Vassena strike, see David Rock, *Politics in Argentina 1890–1930* (London: Cambridge University Press, 1975), p. 162ff.
30. Nahum Solominsky, *La semana trágica* (Buenos Aires: Biblioteca Popular Judía, 1971), pp. 16–17 (hereafter cited as *La semana trágica*).
31. Ibid., particularly pp. 15ff. , focuses on the impact of the *semana trágica* on the Jewish community.
32. *Di Prese,* January 15, 1919.

33. Pinhas Wald, *Caushmars* (Nightmares), in Yiddish (Buenos Aires, 1929), reprinted in Solominsky, *La semana trágica,* p. 18.
34. Other protests include those in *Di Yidishe Tsaytung,* January 14, 1919; and (by eds. of "Avangard" in) *Di Prese,* February 11, 1919.
35. Solominsky, *La semana trágica,* p. 38.
36. *La Razón,* January 14, 1919.
37. Solominsky, *La semana trágica,* p. 38.
38. Ibid., p. 44. John White, *Argentina: The Life Story of a Nation* (New York: Viking Press, 1942), p. 144, writes that most casualties in the "tragic week" were Jews killed in the last two days while order was being restored.
39. Lázaro Schallman, *Historia de los pampistas* (Buenos Aires: Biblioteca Popular Judía, 1971), p. 40.
40. Information in this section, on José ber Gelbard, is based primarily on the files of the American Jewish Committee, Latin American Division.
41. "Argentina: Summer is a-Coming in," *Latin America,* December 7, 1973, p. 388.
42. "Argentina: Cultural Revolution," *Latin America,* March 1, 1974, p. 68.
43. "Argentina: Exit Gelbard," *Latin America,* October 25, 1974, p. 330.

CHAPTER EIGHT

1. Arturo Jauretsche's comment is from an interview in *Horizonte,* no. 12 (November 25, 1964), cited in Juan José Sebreli, ed. *La cuestión judía en la Argentina* (Buenos Aires: Editorial Tiempo Contemporáneo, 1971), p. 206.
2. *La Prensa,* October 19, 1969, cited by Arnold Forster and Benjamin R. Epstein, *The New Anti-Semitism* (New York: McGraw-Hill Book Co., 1974), p. 277.
3. Máximo Yagupsky to Simon Segal, Memorandum for the American Jewish Committee on "Pro-Nazi Outbreaks in Argentina," January 1960, in the Latin American files of the American Jewish Committee, Blaustein Library, New York.
4. Gino Germani, "Antisemitismo ideológico y antisemitismo tradicional," *Comentario,* 9, no. 34 (December 1962):62 (hereafter cited as "Antisemitismo").
5. Juan José Sebreli, *La cuestión judía en la Argentina* (Buenos Aires:

Editorial Tiempo Contemporaneo, 1971, pp. 239–40; hereafter cited as *La cuestión*).

6. Ibid., pp. 223ff.
7. Ibid., p. 224.
8. Ibid., pp. 225–26.
9. Ibid., p. 226.
10. Germani, "Antisemitismo," p. 59.
11. Interview with Lázaro Rubinson, July 10, 1972.
12. Enrique Pichón Rivière, "Los prejuicios raciales en la Argentina," *Nueva Sión,* January 31, 1964, pt. 3, question 2 of his survey.
13. *Correo de la Tarde,* September 2, 1960.
14. *La Luz,* 41, no. 1,034 (July 16, 1971):6–7.
15. Ibid., p. 7.
16. Ibid.
17. Arnold Forster and Benjamin Epstein, *The New Anti-Semitism* (McGraw-Hill Book Co., 1974) pp. 279–280. Also see *La Razón,* October 2, 1972.
18. *La Luz,* 41, no. 1,034 (July 16, 1971): 8.
19. *Ibid.,* 41, no. 1,035 (July 30, 1971): p. 10.
20. Germani's study ("Antisemitismo") is the pioneering effort on this theme as it applies to conditions in Argentina.
21. Julio Adin, "Nationalism and Neo-Nazism in Argentina," *In the Dispersion,* 5/6 (Spring 1966):151–52.
22. Pinhas Wald, *Avangard,* May 1916, cited in Nahum Solominsky, *La semana trágica* (Buenos Aires: Biblioteca Popular Judía), p. 8.
23. A bulletin by the World Jewish Congress (Argentine Branch), "Conducta nociva de algunos miembros de la colectividad judía," June 7, 1963, details both the crimes of these Jewish bankers and the community's response.
24. Sebreli, *La cuestión,* p. 247.
25. Interview with Marcos Barborosch, July 12, 1972.
26. *Jewish Telegraphic Agency Daily News Bulletin,* March 4, 1974, p. 2. The American Jewish Committee's vertical file on "Latin America, Anti-Semitism, 1970–" contains a transcript of the television broadcast, in Spanish. A similar flare-up over an allegedly anti-Semitic television program is recounted in *CJLA* (1974): 76.
27. Interview with Uruguayan official in that country's Jewish community, July 1972. The official requested anonymity, but was in an excellent position to judge the Argentine situation as a frequent traveler there, representing Uruguay in Latin American Jewish councils.

28. Forster and Epstein, *The New Anti-Semitism,* p. 280, citing *Clarin,* October 14, 1971.
29. *Pregún,* July 8, 1964. Also see *Buenos Aires Herald,* July 7, 1964.
30. Mauricio Dulfano, "Anti-Semitism in Argentina: Patterns of Jewish Adaptation," *Jewish Social Studies,* 31, no. 2 (April 1969):132.

CHAPTER NINE

1. Robert A. Potash, *The Army and Politics in Argentina, 1928–1945, Yrigoyen to Perón* (Stanford: Standford University Press, 1969), p. 211. Many Argentine Army officers since the 1930s admired Mussolini as a Fascist, nationalist hero, most notably, as Potash notes (p. 26), General José Uriburu.
2. Ray Joseph, *Argentine Diary* (New York: Random House, 1944), p. 190.
3. George Blanksten, *Peron's Argentina* (Chicago: University of Chicago Press, 1953), p. 226.
4. Edward Tomlinson, *Battle for the Hemisphere* (New York: Charles Scribner's Sons, 1947), p. 122.
5. *New York Times,* November 28, 1945, p. 8.
6. Associated Press release, December 11, 1945.
7. *Buenos Aires Herald,* November 2, 1945.
8. *Mundo Israelita,* March 19, 1949.
9. Juan Perón, *El pensamiento del presidente Perón sobre el pueblo judío* (Buenos Aires: DAIA, 1954), p. 29.
10. DAIA memorandum, August 28, 1950, to President Perón; Juan Duarte (Perón's private secretary) to DAIA, September 8, 1950.
11. José Ventura (president of the DAIA) to D. Laureano Landaburu (minister of the interior), October 16, 1956.
12. The Organización Sionista Argentina's creation and initial statement of loyalty to Argentina and praise for Perón are recounted in *Mundo Israelita,* May 1, 1947, "Manifesto: Por Que Estamos Con El Gobierno."
13. *Mundo Israelita,* March 19, 1949.
14. Blum and the chocolate factory incident: passages are based on information obtained from interviews with Jewish community officials and editors, all of whom requested anonymity (Perón, at that time, being very much alive and on the verge of returning to Argentina); files of the American Jewish Committee confirming the substance of the affair; and interviews with Rabbi Menachem Blum (1973) and Rabbi Amram Blum's widow (1974), both then living in Cleveland.

15. Blanksten, *Perón's Argentina,* pp. 103 ff., details the abuses of the foundation, including an incident involving the Massone Institute, directed by a noted anti-Perónist, Arnalde Massone. The incident parallels the Groisman affair to a remarkable degree. In brief, Eva Perón responded to Massone's refusal to contribute funds to her foundation by vindictively bringing false charges that he had mislabeled his biochemical products. The directors of the institute were imprisoned; the institute itself was fined and soon forced into bankruptcy.
16. The quotations are based on interviews with Blum's widow and a son, Menachem. In the context of what is known of this affair and its outcome, the conversation appears plausible though it cannot be conclusively confirmed.
17. *La Prensa* editorial September 20, 1945, cited in Blanksten, *Peron's Argentina,* p. 210.
18. Juan José Sebreli, *La cuestión judía en la Argentina* (Buenos Aires: Editorial Tiempo Contemporáneo, 1971), p. 239.

CHAPTER TEN

1. Julio Adin, "Nationalism and Neo-Nazism in Argentina," *In the Dispersion,* 5/6 (Spring 1966):139–40 (hereafter cited as "Nationalism"). Adin also elaborates on the German role in the Argentine economy, in these pages.
2. Simon Wiesenthal, *The Murderers Among Us,* Joseph Wechsberg, ed. and trans. (New York: McGraw-Hill, 1967), p. 318 (hereafter cited as *The Murderers*).
3. Ibid., pp. 154, 156, 157.
4. Mengele even located himself in the best part of the capital, living in a villa and posting his name and title on the door. See Jacob Beller, "Anti-Semitism in Argentina," *Congress Bulletin* (April 1963):3.
5. The account of Mengele's escapes is based on Wiesenthal, *The Murderers,* pp. 154–70.
6. Ibid., p. 99.
7. Secretary to President Aramburu, Colonel Victor J. Arribau, to the DAIA, July 20, 1956. This was a reply to a DAIA directive to the national government dated December 9, 1955.
8. Ibid.
9. Ibid.
10. Ibid.
11. Ibid.

12. *New York Times* (hereafter cited as *NYT*), May 25, 1960, p. 20.
13. For Wiesenthal's role in the capture of Eichmann, see Wiesenthal, *The Murderers,* pp. 125–28.
14. Ben-Gurion later sent to President Frondizi a letter expressing his hope that the Argentine leader, who had himself fought against dictatorship and repression, would realize "the supreme motivations that have guided, the imperative moral force that has pushed and the deepness of the feelings that pressed those who found Eichmann and, with his consent, brought him to trial." The letter is reprinted in English translation from the Spanish version received by Frondizi, in *NYT,* June 11, 1960, p. 4.
15. The Russian dilemma over the issue is described in *NYT,* June 19, 1960, p. 6. Also see *NYT,* June 20, 1960, p. 1, for the Polish dissenting position.
16. The debate at the United Nations Security Council is recorded in *NYT,* June 23, 1960, pp. 1, 4.
17. Ibid.
18. *La Prensa* editorial in May 1960, cited in *NYT*, June 19, 1960, p. 10.
19. *El Mundo* editorial, June 17, 1960, cited in Hausner, *Justice in Jerusalem.*
20. *Jewish Telegraphic Agency Daily News Bulletin,* June 20, 1960, p. 3.
21. Ibid., July 24, 1960, p. 4.
22. Meinvielle gave a revealing interview to Edward Burks, printed in *NYT,* August 21, 1962, p. 13.
23. Simon Segal to Abraham Monk, confidential memorandum for the American Jewish Committee on *"Tacuara's* Doctrines and Instructions to Membership," 1963, p. 10, in American Jewish Committee files on Argentine Anti-Semitism. The source reprints extracts from the *Tacuara* manual on pp. 1–10.
24. *NYT,* January 18, 1962, p. 3.
25. Ibid., September 16, 1962, p. 30.
26. Ibid., August 2, 1962, based on compilation by *El Mundo,* p. 3.
27. Adin, "Nationalism," p. 148.
28. "Argentina: Spreading Anti-Semitism," *Time* (Latin American edition), July 6, 1962, p. 21.
29. *NYT,* September 16, 1962, p. 30.
30. *Time* (Latin American edition), July 6, 1962, p. 21.
31. Julian H. Singman, "Report on Anti-Semitism in Argentina," report for the American Jewish Committee, September, 1962, p. 5.

32. *NYT,* July 3, 1962, p. 4.
33. Ibid., October 19, 1962, p. 4.
34. Ibid., October 30, 1962, p. 14.
35. Jacob Beller, "Anti-Semitism in Argentina *Congress Bulletin* (April 1963):3,"
36. Mauricio Dulfano, "Anti-Semitism in Argentina: Patterns of Jewish Adaptation," *Jewish Social Studies*, 31, no. 2 (April 1969), p. 126. Also see *CJLA* (1966), p. 21.
37. Adin, "Nationalism," pp. 146–47.
38. Ibid., p. 153.
39. Ibid., p. 154.
40. Ibid., p. 155.
41. Juan José Sebreli, *La cuestión judía en la Argentina* (Buenos Aires: Editorial Tiempo Contemporáneo, 1971), p. 245.
42. Adin, "Nationalism," p. 158.
43. Ibid., p. 155.
44. *Di Yidishe Tsaytung,* February 5, 1965.
45. Nissim Elnecavé, "El antisemitismo desparacerá cuando el gobierno lo quiera," *La Luz,* 35, no. 885, (September 3, 1965) :1.
46. *Mundo Israelita,* February 6, 1965.
47. Adin, "Nationalism," p. 152.
48. Ibid., p. 150.
49. American Jewish Committee Foreign Affairs Department, "The Coup in Argentina and its Initial Impact on the Jewish Community," July 22, 1966, p. 3.
50. Arnold Forster to Morton Rosenthal, "The Argentine Situation," memorandum for the Anti-Defamation League of B'nai B'rith, July 21, 1966, p. 2.
51. Ibid. See also *NYT,* July 6, 1966, p. 9.
52. Arnold Forster to Morton Rosenthal, "The Argentine Situation," confidential memorandum for the Anti-Defamation League of B'nai B'rith, August 18, 1966, p. 5.
53. Ibid., p. 2.
54. Ibid.
55. *NYT,* August 1, 1966, editorial, "Terror in Argentina," p. 26.
56. *Crónica,* August 18, 1966.
57. Arnold Forster and Morton Rosenthal, eds., "An Argentine Scholar's View of the Argentine Situation," August 30, 1966.
58. *Buenos Aires Herald,* August 6, 1966.
59. Sebreli, *La cuestión judía en la Argentina* (Buenos Aires: Editorial Tiempo Contemporando, 1971), p. 251.
60. *Encyclopaedia Judaica,* 1:416.

61. Report of the American Jewish Committee by its executive, Dr. Simon Segal, in *NYT,* October 13, 1968, p. 4.
62. *NYT,* September 26, 1968, pp. 2, 30. During this time, a Zionist meeting house in Rosario was also destroyed by bombs.
63. Arnold Forster and Benjamin Epstein, *The New Anti-Semitism* (New York: McGraw-Hill Book Co., 1974), p. 272, citing Orient News International Service, November 12, 1971; and *New York Post,* June 12, 1972.
64. *Jewish Exponent,* April 7, 1972, p. 3.
65. Forster and Epstein, *The New Anti-Semitism,* p. 273, citing *Noticias,* February 3, 1972.
66. *New York Post,* June 12, 1972.
67. *CJLA* (1974):79; DAIA clipping dated April 1972.
68. *New York Post,* June 12, 1972.
69. *Jewish Exponent,* April 7, 1972, p. 3.
70. DAIA clipping for April 1972.
71. Perón's interview with Colonel Cornicelli in Madrid is reprinted in full in *La Nación,* July 14, 1972, pp. 1ff.
72. Interview with Marcos Barborosch, July 12, 1972.
73. *Jerusalem Post,* April 18, 1973.
74. *La Opinión,* June 14, 1973.
75. Merwin K. Sigale, "Argentina: Terror in the Streets," report from Buenos Aires, September 23, 1976.
76. "Argentina: What to Tell the World," *Latin America,* 10, no. 36 (September 17, 1976):284.
77. "Argentina: Obscure and Pogromist Forces," *Latin America Political Report* (formerly *Latin America*), 11, no. 30 (August 5, 1977): 234.
78. "Report by Jacobo Kovadloff to Lay Leaders and Staff of the AJC in the USA and Abroad," July 6, 1977, p.2.
79. Ibid., p. 7.

EPILOGUE

1. Walter Laqueur, *A History of Zionism* (New York: Holt, Rinehart, and Winston, 1973), p. 89.
2. Hannah Desser and Seymour Lachman, "Current Trends in Certain Latin American Countries," report for the American Jewish Committee, April 1973, no. 13, p. 5.
3. Moshe Kitron, "Yahadut America Ha-Dromit Ubayoteha" (Latin American Jewry and Its Problems), in Hebrew, *Bitfutzot Hagola,* 30/31 (Winter 1964):156.

4. Harold Himmelfarb, "Jewish Education for Naught: Educating the Culturally Deprived Jewish Child," *Analysis,* 51 (September 1975):1.
5. Interview with Rabbi David Kahana, July 29, 1972.
6. Eduardo Rogovsky, Elías Widuczynski, and Fanny K. de Winograd, "Estudio de actitudes, intereses y opiniones de asociados a la Sociedad Hebraica Argentina," *CJLA* (1968):235 (hereafter cited as "Estudio de actitude").
7. Interview with Nissim Elnecavé, July 17, 1972.
8. David Nasatir, *Estudio sobre la juventud argentina* (Buenos Aires, 1963) is the basic study from which the American Jewish Committee elaborated the disparate attitudes of Jewish and non-Jewish students, in *Primera conferencia sobre identidad e identificación judía* (Buenos Aires, 1965), pp. 10–11.
9. Nissim Elnecavé, *Jewish Chronicle,* September 7, 1973.
10. David Roizin, "Acercamiento de la juventud a la vida udía," *Annals,* III: 28-29.
11. "Cuatro años de labor del departamento de la kehila," *Annals,* III: 34.
12. *Memoria y Balance General* for 1970 (Buenos Aires: A.M.I.A., 1971), section entitled "Cuenta de gastos y recursos."
13. Interview with Paúl Warszawski, July 13, 1972.
14. Bernardo Kligsberg, "La juventud judía en la Argentina," *Nueva Sion,* informe especial (September 1971):4.
15. Barnard L. Collier, "A New Group of Reform Jews Meets Suspicion in Argentina," *New York Times,* March 19, 1967, p. 25.
16. *Di Yidishe Tsaytung,* 25th anniversary issue, 1940, p. 19.
17. *Anuario,* 1945–46 (Buenos Aires: AMIA, 1945), p. 33.
18. *Di Yidishe Tsaytung,* January 19, 1950.
19. "Algunos indicadores de pertenencia a la comunidad judía en dos comunidades argentinas," *Annals,* IV:195.
20. Zeev Zvi Rosenfeld documents the Spanish volumes during the period 1961 to 1968, in *Annals,* IV:166–80. He cites the Hebrew and Yiddish volumes in this same period in *Annals, IV* (Yiddish section): 276–387. There were 393 Spanish books on Judaism published compared with 224 Yiddish volumes.
21. *Arkhiv Fun Prese Oyshniten 1970* (Archive of Press Clippings) (Buenos Aires, 1971), p. 133.
22. *Di Yidishe Tsaytung,* December 7, 1966.
23. Interview with Rachel Hendler, August 14, 1972.
24. *Di Yidishe Tsaytung,* September 4, 1969.
25. *Di Prese,* September 7, 1969.

26. Interview with Yitzhak Zudiker, July 13, 1972.
27. "Comunidad judía: 'el establishment' y los rebeldes," *Raíces,* 11, no. 20 (July 1970), p. 62.
28. "Estudio de Actitudes," p. 235.
29. Interview with Paúl Warszawski, July 13, 1972.
30. Bernardo Vertibsky, "La visita," *Tesoros del judaísmo,* Eduardo Weinfeld, ed. (Mexico City: Editorial Judaica Castellana, 1959), 10:201–10. Excerpted passages, pp. 208–9.
31. *Raíces,* 11, no. 20 (July 1970): p. 4.
32. M. Glicko, "Al margen del problema juvenil en Latino América," World Jewish Congress Bulletin, in Spanish, New York Office, undated. The heart of Glicko's essay is a commentary on the dissolution of Argentine Jewry by the Yiddish writer Shmuel Rollansky.

INDEX

Abruzzi (Italy), 7
La Acción Sionista Sefaradí, 166
Acculturation, 175, 208; economic activity, 175–84; literature and other cultural media, 184–97; politics, 197–208
Acevedo, Alvaro Rodríguez de, 21
Acosta, Diego Pérez de, 22
Adat Yeshurun, 164
Adin, Julio, 242, 252, 257
Agrarian National Council, 51–52
Agriculture, Jewish, 49–56, 70, 102, 106, 175–76, 188. See also Colonies and colonization, Jewish
Agudat Israel, 93–94, 143
Aisenstein, Jacobo, 102
Akerman, Salvador, 271
Albandek, Yusaf, 265
Alberdi, Juan Bautista, 29
Albertal, Estela, 191
Alem, Leandro, 30
Aleppo (Syria), 157–59, 161, 164–65
Alexander II, of Russia, 39
Alexenicer, José, 237
Aliyah (settlement in Israel), 95–101, 114, 128, 153, 162, 167, 172
Allende, Walter Beveraggi, 264–65, 269
Alliance Israélite Universelle, 137, 165
Alperson, Marcos, 107
Alsogaray, Julio, 65–66
Alterman, Raoul, 254–55
Aluar, 273–74
Amadeo, Mario, 247–49, 259
Amanecer (daily), 111–12
Ambrose, Warren, 261
América (literary review), 186
America. See United States
American Jewish Committee, 10, 95, 113, 263, 274

American Jewish Year Book. 151–52
American Tool and Die Company, 177
Americas, 37. See also South America; Spanish America
AMIA. See Asociación Mutual Israelita Agentina
Anarchism, 67, 199–200
Andinia conspiracy allegations, 265, 269
Androgué, César, 253
Angel, Aaron, 161
Angelini, Raul, 253–54
Anglo-Argentine community, 28
Ansel, Bernard, 48
Anti-Americanism, 8
Anti-Defamation League, 265
Anti-Semitism, 7, 66–69; complacence toward, 111; forces of, 9–11, 57, 94; groups, 182; Perón and, 227–40; Perónist exile and, 241–75; polemics, 15; roots of, 209–225; Russian, 39; toward immigrants, 43–44, 51, 66–69; violence and terrorism, 4, 11, 92, 96, 100, 188, 193
Arab, culture, 156, 172; lands and politics, 169–70, 207, 247–48, 266, 269; language, 122, 164; League, 11, 209, 221–23, 254–58, 265, 269, 280, 286
Aramburu, Pedro, 205, 238, 245–46
Arbena, 177
Aretz, Isabel, 192
Argentina, la tierra (textbook), 220
Argentina, acculturation by Jews in, 175–208; agricultural settlements in, 49–56, 70, 102, 106, 175–76, 188, 277–78; anti-Semitism in. See Anti-Semitism; Catholicism in, 7, 15–17, 23, 25, 29–31, 33–34, 36, 48, 91, 117, 124, 126, 128, 168–69, 198, 200, 216–19, 250–51, 259, 267, 269, 271, 279; colonial era, 9, 15, 25;

community, Jewish, 57–83. *See also Kehillah;* Constitution of, 29, 232, 245; economic activity, Jews and, 175–84; economy of, 182–84, 206–8, 269–70, 275; education, Jewish in, 137–54; Jews in. *See* Jews in Argentina; Jews and Jewish community (origins); names of individual Jews; literature and other cultural media, Jews and, 101–14, 184–97; New Christians in, 15–25; as a new nation, 26–38; politics and, 29, 31, 197–208, 237–254; religion, Jewish, 115–35. *See also* Religion, Jewish; Russian Jewish settlement in, 42–49; Sephardic Jews and, 155–72. *See also* Sephardim; Zionism and, 87–101. *See also* Zionism
Argentine Agrarian Institute, 204
Argentine Council, 217
Argentine Jewish Institute of Culture and Information, 74, 120, 198
Argentine Press Association, 251
Argentine Radical People's Party, 249
Argentine Writers' Association, 185–86
Argentine Zionist Federation, 120
Argentine Zionist Organization, 216
Arroyo Beta, Battle of, 90
Art, Jews in, 189–92. *See also* Culture
Arturo (art journal), 190
Asa, Haim, 133
Ashkenazim, 48, 76–77, 81, 111, 118, 122–23, 128, 146, 155–57, 160–61, 163–72
Asia, 205
Asociación Filantrópica Israelite, 81
Asociación Mutual Israelita Argentina (AMIA), 92–93, 100, 118–19; 125–26, 129, 131, 179, 196, 285–86; age distribution of AMIA affiliates, 77; education and, 141, 143–44, 149, 151, 153; origin and character of, 75–81; youth groups and, 114, 282–83
Assimilationism, 38–42, 54
Association of Jewish Secular Schools in Argentina, 142
Asunción (Paraguay), 243
Auerbach, Segismundo, 35, 43
Auschwitz, 243
Austria-Hungary, 90, 121
Der Avangard (Bundist monthly), 106, 201
Avelleneda (Argentina), 63
Avni, Haim, 69, 148–50, 160
Ayerza (Buenos Aires), 91
Azpiazu (Catholic priest), 219

Babel (literary review), 186
Bahía Blanca (Argentina), 265
El Bajur de Yeshiva (painting), 192

Balbín, Ricardo, 205
Balfour Declaration, 95, 116
Banco Cooperativo, 171
Banco Hipotecario Nacional, 182
Bandurek, Wolf, 192
Bank Le'umi, 153
Barborosch, Marcos, 222, 268
Barenboim, Daniel, 192
Bar mitzvah, 119, 161–62
Barón Hirsch (colony), 55, 105, 274
Barracas (Buenos Aires), 58, 158
Basavilbaso (Argentina), 52
Bavaria, 44
Bécher, Emilio, 185
Beef supply, 183
Beersheba, 99
Beilis, Menahem Mendel, 195
Belgrano (Buenos Aires), 78, 172
Bellamy, Edward, 187
Beller, Jacob, 115
Bendarsky, Benito, 102
Ben-Gurion, David, 114, 247
Benzakan, Benjamin, 162
Benzakan, Saadia, 162
Berlin, 255, 267
Bernadotte, Folke, 256
Bernheim, Joseph Alexander, 31, 35
Bessarabia (Russia), 193
Bet din (rabbinical tribunal), 129–30
Bialik, Haim Nachman, 141–42, 163
Bialik primary school, 171
Bible, 20, 116, 137–38, 195
Biltmore Program, 95
Blazko, Martín, 190
Blejer, David, 204, 237
Di Blum (humor magazine), 105
Blum, Amram, 121–28, 234–36
Blum, Menachem, 125, 127
B'nai B'rith, 4, 74, 120, 219, 254, 265
Bocado de pan (verses), 187
Bolsheviks, 200–1
Borges, Jorge Luis, 113, 155, 184, 187
Bormann, Martin, 242–43
Borochov, Ber, 41, 141
Botoschanski, Jacobo, 104
Botvinnik, Mikhail, 195
Braque, Georges, 192
Bratislava (formerly Pressburg), 121
Brazil, 18, 22, 28, 30–31, 184, 194
Brie, Louis Hartwig, 30, 48–49
Britain. *See* England
British Merchants' Society, 28
Brodsky, Aarón, 106
Brussels, 190–91
Buber, Martin, 113
Bucharest, 89

INDEX

"Una buena cosecha" (short story), 189
Buenos Aires, acculturation, Jewish, 175, 181, 188–91, 194, 196; Catholicism, 217–19. *See also* Catholicism, Roman, Constitution, 33–34; education and, 112, 124, 131, 141–51; factory workers in, 102; farm colonies and, 50; government and politics, 20, 23–24, 26, 32, 35, 197, 200–2, 204–5, 230, 255, 257, 259–60, 263, 265, 271; newspapers, 31; political evolution, of Jewish community, 57–69; population and local concerns, Jewish, 3–8, 10, 19, 29, 35, 38, 71, 88, 107, 116, 277, 279, 281–82, 285; province, 28, 34, 53, 272; religion and congregations, 30–31, 91, 119–20, 129, 132–33, 139, 143, 224; Russian Jewry of, 42–43, 45–46; Sephardim and, 156–59, 161, 163–64, 167–69; social organization, Jewish, 69–80; theater in, 103–4; University of, 6, 11, 250–52, 261–62, 264, 268, 280–81; war criminals in, 243, 247, 249
Building industry, 177
Bulgaria, 110
Bund (Socialist Jewish workers' organization), 40–42, 102, 106, 142
Burial, rites and traditions, 117–18, 159–60; societies, 37, 58, 61–62, 79–80. *See also* Hevra Kaddisha Ashkenzai
Businessmen, 176–79, 183, 206, 233, 239, 260, 268; community life and, 74–75; German Jewish, 81–82
Bustos (bishop), 200
Bustos, José María, 43
Byelorussia, 187

Caggiano, Antonio, 217–18
Callao (Peru), 15
Calle Larea (Buenos Aires), 74
Calle Libertad, 260
Cámara de gas (industrial exhibit), 191
Cámpora, Héctor, 268–69
Camp Ramah, 132
Cansinos-Assens, Rafael, 184
Cantors, 130, 193–95
Carlos Casares (province), 53, 205
Cartagena, 19
Casa de la Educación Judía, 149
Casa Rosada, 272
Caseros, Battle of, 28, 30, 32
Castellano (Spanish dialect), 7
Castilian, 159
Catamarca Province, 31, 205
Catholicism, Roman, anti-Semitism and, 216–19, 269; Argentine, 91, 117, 198; church of, 34; conversion to, 17; Fascism

and, 250–51, 259; marriage with Jews, 30–31, 48, 168–69; parishes, 36; power of, 25, 200; priests of, 7, 33, 271; religion, 15, 29, 33–34, 126, 128, 250, 267, 279; rituals of, 16; theology and education in, 23, 34, 124
Caudillos (military leaders), 28, 31
Cemetery, Jewish, 61, 75, 158–59, 168
Central Conference of American Rabbis, 95
Central Education Office, 141–42, 149. *See also* Education
Central Organization of Jewish Secular Schools, 141
Central Unión Israelita Polaca, 108–9
Centro Cultural Israelita, 55
Centro Obrero Israelita, 199
Cervantes, Miguel, 159
Chaco Province, 55, 188
Chagall, Marc, 192
Chess, Jews in, 195–96
El Chico Entreriano (sculpture), 191
Chile, 16, 90, 186, 243, 265, 278
China, 206, 214
Christianity, 219–20; families and, 55; graves, 46; Jews and, 187, 250; leaders of, 120; mysticism in, 185; New Christians in Spanish America, 15–25; ritual and dogma, 33, 37. *See also* Catholicism
Circulo Militar, 259
Circumcision, 16, 117, 131
Civita, César, 178
Clara (Argentina), 50–52, 73, 106, 187
Clarin (journal), 224
Class groups in Argentine society, 178–79
Cleveland (Ohio), 127
Club for Foreign Residents, 28
Club Oriente, 171–72
Cohen, J. X., 80
Colegiale (Buenos Aires), 158
Colonial Argentina, 18. *See also* Argentina; Spanish America
Colonies and colonization, Jewish, 42–49, 98, 184; progress of, 49–56; social organization, 69–80;
Comentario (magazine), 113
Comité Nacional Partidario, 204
Comité Sefaradí, 160, 166
Committee Against Anti-Semitism and Racism, 67
Committee Against the Persecution of the Jews in Germany, 67
Communications, Jews and, 177–78
Communism, 72, 141, 149, 200, 202, 220, 250, 253, 255, 261–62, 267, 272; Jewish, 67, 142, 199
Community of Israel Temple, 254

Community, Jewish, 37–38, 57–83, 117; early history, 52, 56; German Jewish, 81–83; Old World legacy of, 3–4; Perón and, 227; political evolution, 57–69; social organization, 69–80. *See also Kehillah,* Sephardim

Confederation of Argentine Jewish Youth, 283

Confraternidad Judío Cristiano, 217

Congregación Israelita, 132

Congregación Israelita Latina, 157

Congregations, in Buenos Aires, 91; early, 47–48; synagogues and, 119

Congregation of the Argentine Republic, Jewish, 35

Conservative Judaism, 11, 82, 115, 120, 129, 130–35, 145, 161, 284

Conservatism in Argentine Society, 66, 82, 152, 198, 200, 202

Conservative Party, 198

Constantinople, 110

Contra el odio de las razas (writings in defense of human rights), 203

Cooperatives, Jewish, 52, 80, 92, 106, 149, 183, 187–88, 197, 260

Córdoba (Argentina), 18–19, 21–23, 55, 71, 74, 118, 147, 150, 168, 200, 223–24, 237, 271

Córdoba, Diego Padilla de, 18

Corrientes (Argentina), 168–69

Corrientes (street), 3, 8

La Courrier de la Plata (French daily), 31

Credit unions, Jewish, 260

Criollos, 8, 43, 48, 54, 66

Criterio (Catholic journal), 216

Crítica (journal), 200

Crónica Sefaradí (journal), 167

Cuentos de Kleinville (book by Pecar), 110

Cuestionario (magazine), 207

Culture, Jewish, 85–172; education, 137–54; religion, 115–35; secular, 87–114; Sephardic, 155–72

Cuzari (treatise), 190

Czechoslovakia, 68, 121, 190, 249

DAIA. See Delegación de Asociaciones Israelitas Argentinas

Dali, Salvador, 192

Damascus, 157–59, 164–65

Danzig, 192

Darom (periodical), 113

Daughters of Israel, 120

Davar (journal), 113

Davidowich, Noé, 266–67

Davis, Moshe, 92

Davke (scholarly journal), 107

Delegación de Asociaciones Israelitas Argentinas (DAIA), 67–69, 82, 100, 125–26, 209, 212; anti-Semitism and, 67–69, 217, 220, 222, 230–31, 234, 245–46, 253–55, 257–58, 268, 274

Delegaciones de Entidades Sefardís Argentinas, 160, 166

Demographic strength, 4

Denominational trends, 134–35

The Depression, 140–41

Diaspora, 5, 7, 57, 88, 94, 99, 101, 111, 128–29, 153, 225, 255

Dickmann, Enrique, 116–17, 125, 202–3

Es difícil empezar a vivir (book), 188

Dinamix, 178

Di Tella, Torcuato, 7, 74–75

Doble escolaridad (school program), 150

Don Jacobo (television program), 197

Don Quixote, 159, 185

Dora (colony), 55

Dreyfus, Alfred, 195

Dujovne, Leon, 112–13

Duker, Abraham, 57

Dulfano, Mauricio, 254

Durcansky, Jan, 249

East European. *See* Jews and Jewish community (origins)

Economic activity, 175–84

Edery, Marcos, 132

Editorial Abril, 178

Education, Jewish (in Argentina), 137–54; ideological upheaval, 140–42; interior communities, 146–48; Jewish, 6, 10–11, 41, 78, 124–25, 129–32, 158, 164–65, 168, 171, 179, 278; levels of instruction, 143–46; roots, 137–40; the worsening condition, 148–54

Egypt, 97, 185, 218, 231

Eichelbaum, Samuel, 189

Eichmann, Adolf, 244–45, 258, 271

Eilat (Israel), 99

Einstein, Albert, 113

Elman, Mischa, 113

El-Masry, Esam Helmy, 257

Elnecavé, David, 110–11, 165

Elnecavé, Nissim, 110–11, 165, 168, 218, 257

Emanuel Congregation, 284

Emporio de la Loza, 82

England, 215, empire of, 23–24; mass action in, 64; Palestine and, 95, 122

Enlightenment, 4, 37, 39, 115, 137, 163

Entre diós y satán (poetry), 187

Entrepreneurs' Central Federation, 205

Entre Ríos (Argentina), 28–29, 31–32, 52–

INDEX

53, 55, 73–74, 89, 146, 155, 184, 186, 189, 191, 228, 274, 285
Ephraim, Menashe Ben, 78–79
Eretz Israel (illustrated magazine), 111
Eretz Israel, La patria de los hebreos (book by D. Elencavé), 110–11
Espinoza, Enrique (Glusberg pseudonym), 186
Esta tierra es mía (novel), 188
Estero, Santiago del, 20
Europe, 8, 24, 26, 37, 60. *See also* Jews and Jewish community (origins)
European Common Market, 206
Ezra (hospital), 37, 58, 78

Faierman, Arón, 102
Faigenblum, Moses, 190
Falcón, Ramón, 200
Far di kinders vegn (children's story), 102
Fascism, 66–67, 121, 188, 223, 241, 246, 248, 251, 258–59, 270, 274; Arab League and, 256–57; Catholicism and, 250; Perón and, 227–29, 231, 266
Federación Israelita Argentina, 58–59
Federación Sionista Argentina, 106
Federal Coordination (Argentine), 253–54
Finance, Jews in, 176, 183, 206, 221
Finances, Jewish institutions, 80
Fink, Jacob, 128
Fischer, Robert J. ("Bobby"), 195–96
Fischer, Jacobo, 193
Fischerman, Joaquin, 212–13
Fitterman, Menachem, 128
Flores (Buenos Aires), 58, 158
Fonseca, Mario, 260–61
Ford, Henry, 230
Fortune (magazine), 177
Foucauld, Charles de, 156
Fragmentation of Jewish community, 57
Framine, Andres, 266
France, 3, 36, 41, 194, 247–48; culture of, 162, 190–91; education and, 165; journalism and, 31, 178; language of, 34, 43, 107, 122, 286; prostitution and, 59
Frankel, Zacharias, 82
Frank, Waldo, 113
Franseschi, Gustavo, 218–19
Fraternidad Agraria, 53
Freemasonry, 220, 228, 267, 279
Fresco, Manuel, 257
Friedman, Tuvia, 246
Friends of Israel, 217
Frondizi, Arturo, 204–5, 238, 246–47, 251, 263
Fun mayn gemit (tales), 102

Galilee, 99
Gallo, Exequiel Avilla, 265
Gálvez, Manuel, 185
García, Rolando V., 261
Gaucho, 32, 50–51, 250
Los gauchos judíos (novel), 5, 184–85
Geiger, Abraham, 82
Gelbard, José Ber, 205–8, 273–74
Gelman, Juan, 271
Gemeinschaften (communal centers), 81
La generación olvidada (book by Pecar), 110
Geniza (funeral chamber), 118
Gentiles, 6, 27, 49
Gerchunoff, Alberto, 5, 51, 74, 109, 111, 184–86
Gerchunoff Prize, Alberto, 189
German, 108, 252; armies, 228–29; community in Argentina, 67, 241–44, 259; language, 34, 101, 104, 122. *See also* Jews and Jewish community (origins)
Germani, Gino, 212–13, 215
Gesang, Nahman, 142
Get (divorce), 130
Gezelshaft far Yidishe Veltlekhe Shuln in Argentine, 142
Ghettos, 37
Glusberg, Samuel, 109, 186
Goebbels, Joseph, 216, 256
Goldenberg, Isaac, 220
Goldman, Moisés, 74, 137
Goldstein Breads, 177
Goldstreich, Zenan, 254
Goren, Shlomo, 128
Granada, 22
Granitstein, Moisés, 102
Graiver, David, 272–73
Great Britain, 27, 242, 248. *See also* England
Greece, 34, 194
Green, Enrique Horacio, 252–53, 259–61
Greenberg, Louis, 39
Groisman family, 233–36, 238, 267
Grünberg, Carlos, 109, 186–87
Guerrilla, bands, 6–7; violence, 10, 271–72, 275
Guggenheim Foundation, 191
The Guide of the Perplexed (Maimonides), 169
Guido, José María, 251, 253–54
Güiraldes Prize, Ricardo, 188
Gutierrez, José, 35–36

Ha-Bima Ha-Ivrit (Hebrew periodical), 113
Hafetz Haim, 143–44
Haggadah, 134, 190
Haifa (Israel), 99
Halakhah (Jewish law), 123, 126, 128, 130, 134

339

Halevi, Judah, 190, 193
Halevi, Solomon, 15
Halphon, Samuel, 62, 120
Ha-Melitz (journal), 114
Hanneman, Pablo, 190–91
Hapoel Hatza'ir, 41
Hart, Henry Naftali, 28, 34–35
Hashomer Hatza'ir, 93
Hasidim, 3
Haskery (Turkey), 110
Ha-Tzefirah (journal), 114
Havana, 89
Hayesod, Keren, 100
Hebrew, beliefs, 92, 138; education, 78, 119, 146–47, 149, 164, 171, 193; knowledge, 47; language, 3, 41–42, 101, 105, 111, 113–14, 122, 127–29, 141–42, 144, 155, 159, 166, 168, 172, 184, 190, 193, 285–87; people, 230–31; poetry, 167
Hebrew Association, 113–14
Hebrew Immigrant Aid Society, 108
Hebrew Midrasha, 114
Hebrew University (Jerusalem), 74, 110, 145
Hebrew Yiddish Teachers Seminary, 107
Heder (East European Jewish school), 129, 137–39, 143
Heine, Heinrich, 186
Helfman, Israel, 102, 106
Heller, Abraham, 182
Hendler, Rachel, 286
Heredía (literary journal), 186
Herzl, Theodore, 88, 105, 141, 193, 277
Herzlia (Israel), 142
Hess, Moses, 201
Hevra Kaddisha Ashkenazi, 48, 58, 61, 75, 80
Higher Council of Synagogues, 120
Hilfsverein Deutschsprechnender Juden, 82
Hirsch, Maurice de, 44–45, 51, 53, 89, 91, 221, 277
Hispanic, -American influence and society, 3, 25, 37, 38
Hitler, Adolf, 185, 218, 238, 242–43, 249, 251, 256–58, 262, 270
Hoffman, Israel, 191
Hogar Huérfanas Israelitas, 78
Holocaust, 7, 70, 94, 101, 108, 122, 133, 187, 191, 287
Holy Days, Jewish, 78, 193, 197, 237, 263. *See also* names of specific days
Honori Patria Club, 257
Horim (Hebrew parents' federation), 149
Horowitz, Irving Louis, 38
Hospitals, Jewish, 37, 58, 78
Hovevei Zion, 40, 88, 105

Ibergus (play), 103–4
Iberia, 22
Ibsen, Henrik, 103
ICA. *See* Jewish Colonization Association
Illia, Arturo, 204–5, 220, 238, 254–55, 257–58, 263
Immigration and immigrants, Jewish, to Argentina, 5, 9, 90, 214, 245–46, 285, 288; categories of Argentine immigrants to Israel, 99; colonies, progress of, 49–56; communal solidarity, 57–69; economic activity and, 175–77, 179; experience of, 109; groups, prejudice toward, 215–16; to Israel, 96, 98; literature and culture of, 184, 187, 189–90, 195–96; national period, 26–38; Perón and, 231–32; politics and, 197–200, 202; quotas, 115; social organization, 69–80. *See also* Jews and Jewish community (origins)
Immigration (non-Jewish), 4, 7–8; New Christian, 15–25
Imperialism, Yankee, 8
Indian tribes, 26, 43
Industrialism, in Argentina, 7–9; Jews and, 5, 175–84
Inflation, 152–53, 183, 275
Ingenieros, José, 185
Inquisition, 9, 26, 184; Spanish American, 15–25, 33
Institute for Colonization of the Provinces, 51–52
Institute for Jewish Studies, 143–44, 152–53
Instituto Geográfico Argentina, 90
Instituto Judío de Cultura y Informacíon, 113
Intermarriage, 10, 37, 131, 162, 168–69, 172, 197, 278
"The International Jew," (pamphlet), 230
Invention (art journal), 190
Isaacson, José, 111
Isidor, Lazare, 36
Islam, 169, 172
Israel (magazine), 166
Israel, 127–29, 164, 219, 237, 239; Air Force, 128; Daughters of, 120; education, 145, 153; Friends of, 217; opposition to, 220; political activities, 198, 205, 218, 244, 246–51, 256, 263, 265, 271, 280–82; population, 3, 218; pro-, 178; rhetoric against, 11; settlers to, 4, 108, 121, 167, 209, 277; as a state, 92–101, 108–11, 114, 133, 162, 186, 222–23, 229, 258, 279, 286–88; war of October 1973, 269
Issaev, Behor, 161, 163
Italy, 29, 122, 227, 286

INDEX

Jaime Liebling Company, 177
Jaroslavsky, Bernardo, 259
Jauretsche, Arturo, 209
Javits, Jacob, 263
Jerusalem, 34, 99, 110, 122, 145, 246, 248–49, 280, 287; ancient, 156
Jesus, 21, 216, 219, 251
Jewish Agency, 121, 153
Jewish Association for the Protection of Girls and Women (JAPGW), 62–65
Jewish Colonization Association (ICA), 44–45, 49–53, 70, 91, 120, 137, 139–42, 144, 165
Jewish Congregation of Buenos Aires, 59, 139, 143
Jewish Defense League, 67
Jewish Hospital, 37, 58, 78, 181
Jewish immigration. *See* Immigration, Jewish
Jewish Institute for Advanced Studies, 114
Jewish Institute of Culture and Information, Argentine, 74
Jewish Mutual Aid and Burial Society. *See* Asociación Mutual Israelita Argentina.
Jewish Orphanage for Girls, 78–79
Jewish Social Democratic Group, 40
Jewish Telegraphic Agency, 222, 249
Jewish Theological Seminary of America, 132, 145
Jewish Youth Association, 59
The Jew in the Mysteries of History (anti-Semitic book), 250
Jews and Jewish community (origins), Alsatian, 31; Austrian, 81, 193; Balkan, 59, 156, 158–59; Belgian, 35; Bulgarian, 159, 165; Caucasian, 159; Central European, 48, 76, 87, 120, 155; Czechoslovakian, 68, 190; Dutch, 35, 78, 156, 169; East European, 3–5, 10, 38–42, 47–49, 61–62, 70, 72, 75–79, 83, 88, 101, 105, 108, 115, 119, 123, 127–29, 131, 135, 137–40, 143, 165, 179, 192, 199, 286, 289; English, 27–28, 34–35, 37, 49, 156; European, 4, 27, 58, 62, 64, 66, 70, 81–82, 88, 90, 94, 96, 101–2, 112, 114, 122, 128–29, 131, 142, 184, 187–88, 190–95, 200, 205, 220–21, 229–31, 242, 244–45, 286; French, 3, 33, 35–37, 50, 215; German, 30, 35, 37, 49, 67, 70, 76, 81–83, 87, 105, 149, 161, 190, 210, 215, 223, 225, 231, 238; Greek, 165, 194; Hungarian, 116, 121; Italian, 7–9, 29, 35, 159, 178, 199, 214–15, 223; Lebanese, 218, 222; Lithuanian, 58, 106; Middle Eastern, 59, 158; Moroccan, 61, 156, 158, 162, 165, 170; North African, 59, 162; North European, 155; Old World,
3, 11, 43, 106, 115, 117, 142; Oriental, 76, 156; Polish, 3–4, 6, 39, 49, 58, 60–61, 64, 70, 81–82, 106, 108, 112, 128–29, 138, 190–92, 196, 205, 215, 221, 248; Portuguese, 172; Romanian, 58, 60, 89, 111, 215; Russian, 3–4, 6, 38–50, 58, 60–61, 70, 73, 81–83, 89–90, 102–3, 105–6, 128, 156, 161, 165, 169, 176, 184–86, 193, 197, 199–200, 203, 209, 220–21, 238, 277. *See also* Russia; Slavic, 38, 70, 75; Spanish. *See* Sephardim; Swiss, 120; Syrian, 122, 157–59, 161, 164, 166, 170–71, 210, 218, 222; Turkish, 110, 156, 158–59, 170; West European, 34, 37, 45–48, 61, 77, 87, 105
Jews in Argentina, acculturation, 175–208; agricultural settlements, 49–56, 70, 102, 106, 175–76, 188, 277–78; anti-Semitism and. *See* Anti-Semitism; communal organization, 57–80. *See also Kehillah;* early national period, 26–38; East European legacy, 38–42. *See also* Jews and Jewish community (origins); economic activity, 5, 9, 49–55, 70–71, 77, 81–82, 156–57, 171, 175–84, 221; education, 4, 6, 10–11, 41, 78, 124–25, 129–32, 137–54, 158, 164–65, 168, 171, 179, 278; German Jewish community, 81–83. *See also* Jews and Jewish community (origins); interior communities, 10, 69–71, 130–31, 146–48, 168–69; New Christians in colonial Argentina, 15–25; Perón, Juan and, 54, 68, 124–27, 199, 203–7, 227–40, 266–70, 279; political activity, 197–208; population figures, 3, 49–50, 70–71, 75–76, 81, 155; religion, 115–35. *See also* Religion, Jewish; secular Jewish culture, 4, 5, 87–114; Sephardic Jewish community, 155–72. *See also* Sephardim; and Jews and Jewish community (origins) for specific national groups; Socialism and, 4, 56, 72, 82, 87, 88, 91–93, 104, 106, 115, 140–42, 166, 197–202, 285; Yiddish, 3, 10–11, 34, 41, 45, 61, 64, 72, 76–77, 87, 92, 101–15, 119, 122–23, 127–28, 131, 140–42, 163, 166, 171, 194, 197, 199, 228, 245, 283–89; youth and change, 10–11, 279–89; Zionism, 11, 58, 72, 87–101, 104–6, 110–11, 114–15, 122, 128, 140–42, 160, 165–67, 178, 186, 193, 197, 199, 220, 222, 224, 255–56, 258, 265, 271, 273, 279–83, 287–89
La jofaina maravillosa (essays), 185–86
Johnson, Lyndon B., 263
Joint Distribution Committee of the United States, 153

Jordan, 97
Joselevich, Jacob, 105–6
Joseph, Henry, 36–38, 42, 45–59, 62, 75, 119–21, 127
Journalism, Yiddish, 104–14
Judaic literature, 101–14
Judaica (journal), 210
Judaism, 3–5, 10–11, 27, 41, 47–49, 54, 56, 82–83, 94–95, 100, 107, 111, 115–35, 161, 187, 214, 219, 278, 280–85, 287, 289; attacks on, 222, 267; *bet din,* 129–30; Conservative. *See* Conservative Judaism; conversion to, 37, 163; and education, 4, 6, 10–11, 41, 78, 124–25, 129–32, 137–54, 158, 164–65, 168, 171, 179, 278; in the interior, 130–31; Judaizing in the colonial era, 15–21, 25; Orthodox. *See* Orthodox Judaism; rabbinate, 119–29. *See also* names of individual rabbis; Reconstructionist, 115; Reform. *See* Reform Judaism; Sephardic Jews and, 157–69, 171; synagogues, 4, 42, 46, 57–58, 62, 119, 125, 132, 144, 158–60, 224, 228, 241, 284; youth and, 10–11, 278, 284, 287, 289; Zionism and, 4, 93–95, 99, 101, 128, 287, 289
"Judaizers," 15, 17–21, 25
Judeophiles, 209, 239
Judeophobia, 20
El Judío Aarón (play), 189
Juedische Kulturgemeinschaft, 81
Juedisches Wochenblatt (weekly), 82
Juedische Wochenschau (weekly), 82
Junta, military, 270–75
Justicialista coalition, 206, 237, 267–68
Justinian, 23
Justo, Juan B., 202, 214
Juventud (journal), 110, 112

El Kahal (anti-Semitic novel), 227
Kahana, David, 128–29, 278
Kahana, Joseph Elimelech, 121
Kaplan, Isaac, 73, 106, 187–88, 199
Kaplansky, Solomon, 106
Karlsbad, 110
Kashrut. See Kosher dietary patterns
Katz, Label A., 254
Kehillah (organized Jewish community), acculturation and, 189, 198; anti-Semitism and, 209, 218, 245, 274–75; Argentine, 108, 115, 131–35, 278; character of, 4, 10–11, 58; education and, 137, 140, 142–43, 145–54; elements of, 284; history and traditions, 110, 112–114, 116, 131; leadership, 71–75; parochialism, 111; Perón and, 227, 229–35, 237, 239, 267, 277;

politics and, 69, 203; religious activities, 79–80, 118, 122, 124, 126–27, 129; Sephardim and, 159–60; social and philanthropic activities, 120; white slavery and, 59–62; Yiddish and, 107; Zionism and, 87, 92–95, 99–101. *See also* Community, Jewish
Kennedy, John F., 256
Kennedy, Robert F., 263
Keren Hayesod, 100
Keren Kayemet, 166
Kiriat Shmona (Israel), 99
Kishinev (Russia), 41, 193
Kitron, Moshe, 96, 98, 278
Klausenburg (Czechoslovakia), 121
Klenicki, Leon, 133–34
Kliguer, Abraham, 106
Klingenfus (Dr.), 242
Knesset (Israeli parliament), 281
Kolonist Kooperator (journal), 106, 187
Kook, Rav (Rabbi Abraham Isaac), 163
Koremblit, Bernardo Ezequiel, 189
Korn, Solomón José, 64–65
Kosher dietary patterns, 7, 10, 37, 44, 78, 115–16, 119, 130, 161–62, 196, 223, 228
Kosice, Gyula, 190
Kovadloff, Jacobo, 274
Krislavin, Abraham, 237
Kubovy, Arie L., 218–19
Kuhn, Augusto, 199
Ku Klux Klan, 260

Ladino, 159–61, 164–65, 170–71, 192
Landsmanshaften (immigrant societies), 157
Lang, Deborah Manassen de, 78–79, 169
Lanusse, Alejandro, 264, 266, 273, 275
La Plata. *See* Plata, Río de la
Lasansky, Mauricio, 191
Lasker, Emanuel, 195
Latin America (journal), 206
Latin America, 108, 112, 261; history of, 217, 227; Jews of, 98, 122, 133–34, 181–83, 186, 189–90, 277; languages of, 7, 159; nations of, 8, 110, 241, 243–44;
Latin American Rabbinical Seminary, 132, 145
League of Nations, 59
Legally Recognized Societies, 63
Lehman family, 27
León, Diego López de, 22–23
Lerner, Falik, 100
Lerner, Natan, 100
Levene, Ricardo, 23
Levingston, Roberto, 264
Levin, Shmarya, 138

INDEX

Levinson, Pablo, 188
La levita gris (collection of stories), 186
Levy, Solomon, 33–35, 49
Lewin, Boleslao, 46, 112
Liacho, Lázaro, 50, 109, 187
Liachovitzky, Jacob Simon, 88, 105–7, 109–10
Liberal religious movements, 131–34
Liebermann, José, 109
Lieberman, Rachel, 64–65
Liebeschutz, Solomon, 47
Liga Theodore Herzl, 105
Lima, 15, 17–23, 25
Linares, Juan Carlos Cornejo, 224
Liniers (Argentina), 158
Lisbon, 18, 22
Literature and other cultural media, 184–97
Literature, Judaic, 101–14
Litoral (region in Argentina), 112
Lodz, 3, 112
London, 100, 190, 200
Looking Backward (novel), 187
López, Lucio, 91
Los Angeles (Calif.), 127, 176
Lucienville (Argentina), 52
Luco, Juan, 257
Lugones, Leopoldo, 185
La Luz (magazine), 110–11, 166, 168, 218, 257

Madi group, 190
Madrid, 265, 267, 279
Maghreb, 255
Maimonides (Moses ben Maimon), 107, 158, 169
Maimonides Day School, 161, 164
Maimonides Secondary Day School, 149
Maimon, Solomon, 138
Makhon Lelimudei Hayahadut, 144
Malick, Leib, 64, 103–4
Manguel, Pablo, 232, 237
Mann, Thomas, 113
Mapai, 92–93
Mapam, 93
Maria Eva Duarte de Perón Social Aid Foundation, 233
María, Pablo de Santa, 15
Marranos, 18–19, 23, 288
Marseilles, 194
Martínez Zuviría, Gustavo, 227–28
Marxism, 4, 41, 92, 141, 187, 200–2, 218, 279
Mataderos (Buenos Aires), 58
Mathov, Arthur, 249
Matragt, Sujer, 232
Mauricio (Argentina), 53, 107

Mauricio Silbert company, 177
Médanos (Argentina), 53
Medicine, Jewish, 179–81
Mediterranean, 156
Mein Kampf, 256, 270
Meinvielle, Julio, 216–17, 250, 264
Meir, Golda, 248
Mejía, Ramos, 27
Memoirs of a Militant Socialist (book by Dickmann), 117
Mendele Mocher Sforim, 142, 286
Mendelson, José, 107, 111
Mendoza (Argentina), 18, 116, 118, 125–26, 150, 168, 267
Menendez, Armando Braun, 90
Mengele, Josef, 243–44, 247
Merchants in Spanish America, 20–22
Mester de judería (book by Grünberg), 186–87
Mexico, 19, 22, 89, 204, 278
Meyer, Marshall Theodore, 132, 145, 284
Mezuzot, 131
Mibashan, Abraham, 111
Middle East, 266, 269, 281
Midrasha Ha-Ivrit (secondary school), 149
Midrasha Teacher's Seminary, 143, 149
Mikvah (ritual bath), 46
Military, Argentine, anti-Semitism and, 210–11, 251; *junta,* 270–75; regime, 10; repression, 258–64
Minhag (Ashkenazic custom), 123
Minkowsky, Moritz, 191–92
Minsk (Russia), 4, 51, 103
Minyan (Jewish religious quorum), 34, 46, 119, 168
"The Miraculous Doctor" (short story), 74
Mirelman family, 74, 78
Mitre, Bartolemé, 31, 43–44
Mizrachi party, 93
Modigliani, Amedeo, 192
Mohalim (ritual circumcisers), 117
Moisésville (Argentina), 45, 52–53, 55, 74, 130–31, 147, 195, 285
Moment (Yiddish daily), 108
Mondarin, Frederick Fernández de, 254
Le Monde (French daily), 178
Monin, José, 19
Montevideo, 26, 194
Montoneros, 271
Moscovich, Abraham, 102
Moscow, 201
Mosaic Law, 115, 133, 162, 169, 221
Muchnik, Carolina, 191
Mujica, Carlos, 224
El Mundo (journal), 249

INDEX

Mundo Israelita (Spanish-language Jewish weekly), 111, 113, 284, 288
Munich Olympic massacre, 218
Mussolini, Benito, 227, 251
Myriam la Conspiradora (anti-Semitic novel), 227

La Nacion (newspaper), 44, 185–86, 210
Nadie la conoció nunca (play), 189
Nagykároly (Austria-Hungary), 121
Najdorf, Moshe [Miguel], 195–96
National Federation of Temple Youth, 133
Nationalism, Argentine, 6, 214–16
Nationalist Restoration Guard, 254–56, 259
National origins, Jewish, 75–76. *See also* Jews and Jewish community (origins)
National Socialist Front, Argentine, 270
National Socialist Party of Argentina, 255
Navarro, Angel Aurelio, 31
Navarro, Mordecai, 31–32
Navarro, Octaviano, 31
Navarro, Ramón Gil, 31
Navarro-Viola, Miguel, 33–34
Navon, Itzhak, 281
Nazis and Nazism, catastrophe, 82; criminals, 3, 246–54; movement, 10, 67, 112, 190, 192, 209, 216, 221–23, 228, 255–59, 270, 274; threat, 241–46
La necesidad es ingeniosa (play), 187
Negev desert, 99
New Christians, 15–25
New Testament, 20
New World, 16, 18–19, 23–24, 38, 60, 109, 117. *See also* Spanish America
New York (city), 72, 112, 145, 176, 197, 263, 274
New York Times, 261–62
Nogas, Isaias Juan, 257
Noroña, Juan Acuña de, 20–21
North America, 104, 193, 205, 215

Ocampo, Manuel Rodríguez, 65
Occupational distribution, Jewish, 179–81
Odessa, 41
Old Testament, 15, 20, 162
Olivia, Gilberto Hidalgo, 220, 258
Once (Buenos Aires), 3, 5, 158, 161, 176; Plaza, 72, 254, 260
Onganía, Juan Carlos, 258–64, 270
La Opinión (weekly), 178, 273
Organización Israelita Argentina (OIA), 68, 232
Organización Sionista Argentina (OSA), 99–100
Organización Sionista Sefaradí, 167

Origins, Jewish, 15–56; Jewish national, 75–76. *See also* Jews and Jewish community (origins)
Oro (anti-Semitic novel), 227
Orphanage for Girls, Jewish, 78–79
Orthodox Judaism, 46, 93–95, 112, 115, 119–20, 123, 125–26, 128, 130–35, 145, 163, 196, 278, 284
Ostwald, Simon, 87–88

Pact of Friendship, Trade, and Navigation, 27
Padilla de Córdoba, Diego, 18
Palacios, Alfredo, 198, 201–2
Palacios, Pedro, 45
Pale of Settlement, 39
Palestine (Israel), 70, 88, 91, 94–96, 103, 121–22, 159, 163, 189, 218, 221, 281
Pan de Buenos Aires (tales), 187
Paraná (Argentina), 147, 191
Para la pausa del sabado (poetry), 186
Paraguay, 30, 192, 243–44
Paris, 104, 165, 190–92, 255
Paso Street (Buenos Aires), 161
Passover, 121, 134, 185, 190, 287
Patagonia (Argentina), 91, 224, 265
Pavlotzky, José, 188
Payró, Robert, 185
Paz, Enrique Martínez, 260
Pecar, Samuel, 109–10, 114
Pedro, Dom, 31
Peña, Roqua Saenz, 185
Pentateuch, 131
People's Organization Against Anti-Semitism, 67
Peretz, Isaac Leib, 102, 142, 163, 286
Perón, Juan, anti-Semitism during and after exile, 241–75, 279; election 1946, 8; fall from power, 126–27; friendships, 124–25; immigrants and, 199; Jews and, 227–40; political decisions of, 54, 182–183, 186; presidency, 68, 203–8; purges, 112; return of, 264–70; successors, 96; support of, 212, 224
Perón, María Estela Martínez de ("Isabel"), 10, 207–8, 268, 273
Perón, María Eva Duarte de ("Evita"), 124, 126–27, 232–35, 265, 268
Peru, 18, 22
El Pescador (sculpture), 191
Philanthropy, Jewish, 74–75, 77–79
Philo, 107
Phylacteries, 115, 131
Picasso, Pablo, 192
Pichón-Rivière, Enrique, 210–11, 215–16
Pilpul (dialectical analysis), 139

344

Pinchevsky, Moshe, 106
Pinelo, Antonio de Léon, 23–24
Pinelo, Diego de Léon, 23
Pinsker, Leon, 40
La Plata (Argentina), 71, 112, 168
Plata, Río de la, 18–24, 30
Pluralism, Argentine, 7
Po'alei Zion, 41, 141–42, 201
Pogrom, 200, 239, 274. See also Anti-Semitism
Politeama (theater), 104
Political evolution of Jewish community, 58–69
Politics, Jews in, 197–208
Popper, Julius, 89–91
Popper, Máximo, 90–91
Porteños (townsmen), 32, 175
Portnoy, Antonio, 109, 111
Portugal, 18–21
Los postreros de una magna generación (book by Turkow), 109
Potosí, 19–20
Der Poyk (humor magazine), 105
Prague trials, 68
La Prensa (daily), 186, 210, 237–38, 248–49
Di Prese (journal), 107, 201, 286
Pressburg (Hungary), 121
Primera Plana (weekly newsmagazine) 178
Professionals, distribution of, 179–82
El Progresso (periodical), 31
Progressive Democratic Party, 257
Prostitution, Jews in, 59–66, 104, 163. See also Zevi Migdal
La Protesta (periodical), 199
Protestantism, 27, 33, 36, 284
"Protocols of the Elders of Zion," 224, 230, 256–57
Public Works and Urban Development, Department of, 260
Publishing industry, 178
Pueyrredón, Patricio Errecalte, 260
Puig, Augustín Luchía, 217–18
Purim, 166

Rabbis, 34–37, 46, 49, 131; Grand, 47, 119, 125–28; Grand, of Palestine, 122, 163; ordainment of, 11, 144; the rabbinate, 119–29
Rabinovich, José, 109
Rabovitsch, Liberto, 237
Racism, 8, 213–16, 237
Radical Party, 204–5
Radowitzky, Simon, 200
Raíces (magazine), 100, 288
Raichemberg, Hayim, 149–50

"Rapprochement of the Arab States Toward Latin America" (television program), 222
Rauch, Enrique (Heinrich), 256, 259
La Razón (journal), 202, 210
Los rebeldes y los perplejos (book by Pecar), 110
Red Sea, 99
Reform Judaism, 11, 82, 95, 115, 130–31, 133–34, 284
Rega, José López, 207–8, 269
Religious freedom, Jewish, 34–35
Repression, military, 258–64. See also Military, Argentine
Reshevsky, Samuel, 196
Resistencia (Argentina), 146, 265
Resnick, Solomon, 111
Resnizky, Nehemias, 274
Reyes, Alfonso, 189
Reyes, Cipriano, 233
Rhodes, 158–59
Rio de Janeiro, 26, 194
Río Negro (Argentina), 53
Rivera (Argentina), 51
Rivadavia, Bernadino, 27
Roca, Julio, 43
Roizin, David, 282
Rojas, Ricardo, 185
Romania, 89
Rome, 192
Roosevelt, Franklin Delano, 228
Roosevelt, Theodore, 89
Rosario (Argentina), 71, 112, 129, 147, 150, 168, 224, 279, 288
Rosas, Juan Manuel de, 28–29, 31
Rosenthal, Morton, 265
Rosh Ha-Shanah, 3, 235, 237, 251
Rosh Pinah (Palestine), 189
Rot, Dina, 5, 192–93
Rothschild family, 44
Royal Spanish Academy, 111
Rubel, Iaacov, 90
Rubinson, Lázaro, 99, 216
Rubinstein, Arthur, 113
Rubinstein, Daniel, 223–24
Rubinstein (rabbi), 120
Rucci, José, 264
Russia, 51, 106–7, 115–16, 196, 206, 247–48. See also Jews and Jewish community (origins), Russian

Sabadomingo (poetry), 186
Sabatión Argentino (poetry), 186
Sabbath, Jewish, 5, 37, 115–117, 119, 144, 161–62, 168, 192, 287
Sainetes (popular forces), 8
Sajaroff family, 73, 187

INDEX

Salonica, 165
Salta (Argentina), 168
Salvador (Argentina), 124
Samuel Gutnisky Corporation, 177
San Antonio (Argentina), 194–95
San Juan (Argentina), 27
Santa Fe (Argentina), 6, 27, 29, 45, 71, 168
Santa Isabel (colony), 55
Santander, Silvano, 185
Santiago, 16, 186
Sarmiento, Domingo Faustino, 31, 44, 191, 214
Saslavsky, Colman, 103, 193–95
Satanowski, Marcos, 112–13
Schallman, Lázaro, 106, 111–12
Schapira, David, 205
Schehebar, Isaac, 166
Schlesinger, Guillermo, 80, 120, 132, 235
Schmilkel the Gaucho, 51
Schvartzman, Pablo, 32
Schwartz, J. J., 115
Scobie, James, 26
Scrutinium Scripturarum (anti-Jewish polemic), 15
Sebreli, Juan José, 213–15, 221, 238
Secret Service (Argentine), 260
Secular Jewish culture, 87–114
Security Council (UN), 247–48
Segura, Luis Gabriel, 31
Semana Trágica (Tragic Week), 200–1
Semikhah (rabbinical ordination), 121, 145
Semitic language, 127
Señorans, Eduardo Argentino, 260
Señorita (play), 189
Sephardic Jewish Association, 159
Sephardic Jewish Association of Culture and Welfare, 158
Sephardic Jewish Association of the Sons of Truth, 158
Sephardic Jewish Community Association, 159, 170
Sephardim, 59, 76–77, 110, 118, 122–24, 127, 149, 155–72, 199, 215; change in, 169–72; communities, 155–61; culture, 161–67; dialect, 193; interior communities, 168–69
Settlers, Jewish, 13–83; community, 57–83; origins, 15–56. *See also* Jews and Jewish community (origins)
SHA. *See* Sociedad Hebraica Argentina
Shalom school, 171
Shamash (synagogue attendant), 130
Shatzky, Jacob, 58, 118, 130
Shohetim (ritual slaughterers), 116, 118, 125–26, 130
Sholem Aleichem, 141–42, 163, 195, 286

Shriften (Yiddish publication), 107
Shtetl (small East European community), 3, 44, 138, 278
Siddur (prayer book), 129
Silva, Diego Núñez de, 15–19
Silva, Francisco Maldonado de, 15–19
Simselovich Drug Firm, 177
Sinai, Reuben Hacohen, 62
Singerman, Berta, 103
El Sionista (newspaper), 110
Sirota, Graciela Narcisa, 252–53
Sisters of the Sacred Heart, 265
Sithon, Shaul David, 162–63
Six-Day War, 4, 94, 95, 167
Social Democratic Party, 106
Socialism, 4, 40–41, 56, 72, 82, 87, 104, 106, 115, 285; education and, 140–42; political party, 198–202; Zionism and, 88, 91–93, 106, 166, 197
Social organization, Jewish, 69–80. *See also* Community, Jewish
Social roles, Argentine acceptance of Jews in, 211
Social sectors, Anti-Semitism among, 212–15
Sociedad Hebraica Argentina (SHA), 6, 112–17, 149, 189, 193, 278
Sociedad Industrial Americana de Maquinarias, 75
Society of Argentine Jewish Women, 79, 169
Society for the Dissemination of Enlightenment Among Jews, 40
Soiffer (rabbi), 121
Songs and melodies, Jewish, 5, 193–95. *See also* Culture
Sonsino, Rifat, 133, 284
Sánchez Sorondo, Matías, 224
South America, 187; congregations in, 132; rabbis in, 34; settlers in, 30. *See also* Latin America
Soviet Union. *See* Russia
Spain, 103, 268; Argentina's independence from, 9; baptism in, 17; empire of, 24; Sephardim and, 155–56, 158–59, 167, 169, 172
Spanish, America, New Christians in, 15–25; Civil War, 203; colonies, 9; inhabitants, 26; language, 3, 7, 11, 101, 103–4, 107–14, 119, 122, 129, 132, 159, 165, 172, 193, 197, 228, 245, 257, 285–86, 288; literary tradition and press, 87, 166, 284; rule, 199, 216
Spassky, Boris, 195–96
Spinoza, Baruch, 107, 113, 186
Spivak, Aarón, 109, 111

346

Spivak, Raúl, 192
Sports, Jews in, 160–61
Stalin, Joseph, 68
Steingart, Mario, 74
Steinitz, Wilhelm, 195
Stereotypes, Jewish, 212, 216, 219
Stern Gang, 122
Stray, Adolfo, 197
Streicher, Jacobo, 102
Suárez, Jorge, 155
Sucat David, 171
Sulamit (symphonic composition), 193
Sunflower seeds, cultivation of, 53, 175
Sur (literary magazine), 113
Swarensky, Hardi, 82
Synagogues, 58, 62, 119, 125, 144, 158–60, 168, 228, 241, 284
Syndicalists, 199
Syria, 97

Tacuara, 244–54, 256, 260, 262–63, 281
Talmud, 47, 121–22, 125, 129, 137, 139, 143, 163, 169, 193, 195, 223
Talmud Torah (school), 58, 151, 164–65
Tangiers, 158
Taylor, Marsha, 193, 197
Teacher's Institute for Community Day Schools, 151
Teacher's Seminary, 143, 149
Technology, Jews in, 178, 180–81
Tel Aviv, 99, 142
Television industry, 178
Temple Bet-El, 132, 284
Temple Emanu-El, 133–34
Temple Paso, 125, 127
Temple Shalom, 161
Tenembaum, Jaun, 55
Tercera Sinfonia (symphonic composition), 193
Terrorism, political, 7, 178, 207, 218
Textile industry, 156, 176
Theater, Yiddish, 61, 103–4, 108. See also Yiddish
Theodore Herzl school, 171, 286
Theresiendstadt, 244
Third World, 8, 11, 22, 280
Tiempo, César (Zeitlin pseudonym), 186, 193, 238
"La Tierra" (short story by Liacho), 109
Tierra del Fuego (Argentina), 89–91
Time (magazine), 57
Timerman, Jacobo, 178, 273
Der Tog (journal), 106
Topolevsky, Gregorio, 203, 205
Torah, 129, 168
Tormenta de dios (play), 189

La Torre de marfil y la política (social critique), 189
Tragic Week. See Semana Trágica
Tres piezas sinfónicos según el Talmud (poetry), 193
Triki, Hussein, 255–57
Tsentraler Veltlekh Yidishe Shul Organizatsie (ZVISHO-Central Organization of Jewish Secular Schools), 141
Der Tsionist (journal), 105–6, 110
Tucumán (street), 3; (town), 15, 18–19, 22, 31, 168, 265
Tunisia, 255
Turkow, Itzhak, 108
Turkow, Jonas, 108
Turkow, Marc, 108–9
Turkow, Zygmunt, 108
Twelfth Zionist Congress, 110
The 29 Oathtakers, 258
Tzedakah (charity), 79

Uganda, 88
Ugarte, Fernando Arias de, 23
Ukraine, 73, 107
Unión Cívica Radical Intransigente, 204
Unión Cívica Radical del Pueblo, 205
L'Union Française (journal), 43
United Nations, 229, 247, 249, 256, 262, 267
United Provinces of the Río de La Plata, 18
United States, 89, 113, 172, 222; Constitution, 29; culture, Jewish, 191, 195–96; economic activity, Jewish, 176–77, 183; immigration quotas, 115; influence in Argentina, 8–9, 242; Jewry, 57, 94–95; mass action in, 64; politics, 247–49, 252–53, 260, 262–63, 265; population, Jewish, 3–4, 10, 72, 100, 127, 197–98, 273–74, 278, 287; religion, Jewish, 6, 83, 119, 129, 132, 134, 145, 161, 284; trade relations, 66; travel to, 26; west of, 51; Zionism in, 4, 94–95, 100
United Workers Party, 93
Unzer Vort (journal), 106
Urbanization, Jewish, 54–56, 70–72, 188
Urdapileta, Felipe, 229
Uriburu, Alberto Ezcurra, 217, 251
Uriburu, José Felix, 66–67, 182, 258
Urquiza, Justo José de, 28–33, 42, 155
Uruguay, 28, 30, 112, 194, 222

Va'ad Hahinukh Hamerkazi Be-Argentina (Central Argentine Education Office), 149
Va'ad Hahinukh Haroshi (Head Education Office), 139–40, 149–51, 153

INDEX

Vadamecum del cooperativistas (book by Kaplan), 187–88
La Vanguardia (newspaper), 199, 202
Vasena (Argentina), 201
Vega, Perla de la, 222
Veniste, Eli Ben, 172
Vermont, Abraham, 47, 105, 110
Vertibsky, Bernardo, 188–89, 288
Vertibsky, Gregorio, 50
Vida Nuestra (journal), 110
Videla, Jorge Rafael, 272–73
Der Viderkol (journal), 104–5
El Viejo (sculpture), 191
Vienna, 192–93
Villa Crespo (Buenos Aires), 58, 158
Villa De Voto (Argentina), 191
Villa miseria también es América (book by Vertibsky), 188–89
Vilna, 3–4, 40, 118
"The Visit" (short story), 288
Vital, Noé, 102, 106
Vitoria, Francisco de, 22, 24, 31
Volunteer Movement of the Jewish Legion, 96

Waisman, Bernard, 103
Wald, Pinhas, 102, 106, 201, 285
Warsaw, 59, 61, 108, 190
Warsaw Society for Mutual Assistance and Burial Rights, 62–63
Warszawski, Paúl, 264, 283, 287
Wassertzug, Zalman, 102, 131, 286
Wast, Hugo (Zuviría pseudonym), 227, 250
Weinfeld, Mariano, 204–5
Weinstein, Marcos, 111
Welfare, Jewish, 77–79
Welfare Society for German-Speaking Jews, 82
Werthein brothers, 178
SS *Weser,* 42, 45, 104, 156
West Germany, 242, 244, 247
White Slavery. *See* Prostitution, Jews in
Wini, Daniel, 262
Winsberg, Morton, 51, 55
Wiesenthal, Simon, 243, 246–47
Wolf, Jaime, 102
Women's International Zionist Organization (WIZO), 100
World Jewish Congress, 82, 108, 283, 288
World War I, 96, 200
World War II, 51, 94, 122, 128, 159, 177, 182, 231, 241–42, 244, 255

Xenophobia, Argentine, 9, 25, 44, 213, 219, 274

Yagupsky, Máximo, 210
"Yankee imperialism," 8
Yankelevich, Jaime, 178
Yarcho, Noé, 73–74, 179–80, 187
Yeshiva Gevoha, 145
Yeshivah, 39, 41, 115, 121–23, 128, 137, 139, 143–45, 193
Yesod Ha-Dat, 164
Yiddish, 101–14; anti-, 140; beliefs, 92; education and, 141–42; language, 3, 11, 34, 41, 45, 72, 76–77, 119, 122–23, 127–28, 163, 171, 197, 199, 228, 245, 283–89; literature, 87; theater and press, 10, 61, 166, 194; writers, 64, 115, 131
Di Yidishe Folkshtime (daily), 105, 110
Di Yidishe Hofnung (daily), 106
Dos Yidishe Lebn (newspaper), 106
Der Yidisher Fonograf (newspaper), 105
Yidisher Kolonist in Argentine (journal), 106
Yidisher Visenshaftlikher Institut (YIVO), 107, 112
Di Yidishe Tsaytung (daily), 107, 113, 257, 285–87
Di Yidishe Velt (journal), 106
YIVO *Bleter* (journal), 112
Yom Kippur, 117, 127, 236–37, 264
Young Workers organization, 41
Youth, Jewish, 10–11, 96, 98, 132, 279–89; education and, 137–54
Youth Counsellor Corps, 282
Youth groups, Jewish, 282–83
Yoyvel Bukh (commemorative), 107
Yrigoyen, Hipólito, 66, 182, 200, 202
Yugoslavia, 121

Zaslavsky, Rudolf, 104
Zeitlin, Israel, 109, 186
Zevi Migdal, 59–60, 63–65, 104
Zion, 49, 167
Zionism, 87–101; *aliyah* (settlement in Israel), 95–101, 114, 128, 153, 162, 167, 172; American, 4, 94–95, 100; attacks on, 11, 220, 222, 224, 255, 256, 265, 271, 279–81, 283; beliefs, 58, 115, 122, 128; education and, 140–42; European, 40–42; literature, journalism and, 104–6, 110–11, 178, 186, 193; politics and, 72, 197, 199, 255–56, 258, 265, 271, 273, 279–83, 285, 287–88; Sephardim and, 160, 165–67; youth and, 11, 96, 98, 279–83, 287–89
Zionist Federation, 59
Zohar, 131
Zudiker, Itzhak, 287